D1598840

A Sailor's Odyssey

At Peace and
at War 1935-1945

Alvin P. Chester
Captain, USNR(Ret)
Master Steam or Motor Vessels
of Any Gross Tons Upon Oceans

Special Edition for the
Destroyer Escort Sailor's Association

Odysseus Books
Miami

© Alvin P. Chester, 1991
First Published 1991

"LIBRARY OF CONGRESS CATALOGUE
CARD NUMBER 91—172665"

ISBN 0—9631239—0—4

This publication is protected by International Copyright Law. All rights reserved. No part of this publication may be reproduced, stored in a retrieval system, or transmitted in any form or by any means, electronic, mechanical, photocopying, recording or otherwise, without the prior permission of the copyright holder and the publisher.

Printed and bound in the United States of America

Contents

Dedication

In memory of my mother and father who motivated me to seek a life of adventure and excitement, and to those who shared it with me during the turbulent times I relate. And to my wife, Virginia Moore Chester, who left the peace and tranquility of California for a marriage and a world that offered insecurity, separation, uncertainty, and little hope of a future.

To the sailors who shared this adventure with me: those who taught me, those I taught, and particularly those poor souls who sailed under my command during World War II. Fortunately down through the ages are born great men, unheralded and mostly unremembered, who are responsible for what is good in the world. I had the honor of being a shipmate of such men. I am thankful; God bless them all.

Foreword

Webster's defines "odyssey" as an extended wandering or journey. Homer in his Greek epic poem follows the adventures of Odysseus during the ten years after the fall of Troy. *A Sailor's Odyssey* is aptly titled for it traces the voyaging of the author across the oceans and into the ports of the world during the ten-year period from 1935 to 1945. We travel with the author as he advances from mate of ocean liners to command of men-o-war in combat. The saga that unfolds is a contemporary observation of ships, their crews, and the maritime events of the intense period preceeding and during World War II.

This book has the imprint of the professional mariner. Although it brackets a decade, the author's life has been ships and the sea from 1933 to the present. Al Chester has attained the rank of Captain in dual categories: Merchant Marine Master (Steam and Motor Vessels of any Gross Tons/Oceans) and Captain in the United States Navy. Fortunately for we who read this book, he has the gift of bringing to life from the printed page the ships in which he served and the men with whom he shared these adventures.

It was my privilege to be his shipmate in 1942. From then to the end of the war our paths leading to command, and in command, ran parallel. We have since retained that special bond of friendship unique to those in every branch of the military who serve together during war.

This odyssey views the times through the eyes of a merchant marine cadet then mate serving in a variety of merchant ships calling on a wide variety of ports. We travel with the author during the transatlantic liner runs of *S.S. Washington* and *S.S. Manhattan* in the fascinating days of "The Only Way to Cross." We share the excitement of wandering the African coasts and rivers and the littoral of the Mediterranean Sea in merchant ships. When war is imminent we follow the author's call to active duty in the Navy aboard a ship in the Pacific, command of an armed guard crew, a submarine chaser, and ultimately two destroyer escorts. We feel the personal pride and commitment to his ship and crew as the author refuses an order from General McArthur's staff (to the apparent delight of Admiral Nimitz). Then we confront Hitler's U-boats in the Battle of the Atlantic. Finally the author takes us through traumatic battles against Japanese kamikazes during amphibious operations in the South Pacific.

This book will have particular appeal to Merchant Marine buffs of the '30s. Those who served in the subchasers and the "Trim But Deadly" destroyer escorts also will find special significance in this story. And for those who enjoy looking over the shoulder of the seafarer, these pages will provide rewarding hours of reading.

There are many books of personal experiences during this period, informative, dramatic, inspiring. This account is all of these, but with the added dimension of a special insight into the human equation whether it be personal relationships during long weeks at sea or reactions of men in combat to stress.

Sheldon H. Kinney
Rear Admiral, Retired
United States Navy

Preface

A Sailor's Odyssey is not an autobiography in the strict sense of the word, nor is it an accurate history of the time, or for that matter an accurate portrayal of many of the people mentioned. This book was written over 45 years after the events occurred. I never kept a diary or any other recording. Written in the twilight of my life, the objective was to portray the atmosphere or flavor, if you will, of the times as influenced by the people who lived them with me. Although I had limited resources and not time for as much research as I would have liked, I have attempted to be accurate and honest in my story—it was all so long ago.

Acknowledgments

If not for the encouragement of the Officers of the Destroyer-Escort Sailor's Association, including Sam Saylor, President; Don Glaser, Executive Administrator; and John Cosgrove whose professional guidance and wisdom helped me through some difficult times, I would have dropped the project. I am equally appreciative of the support of my fellow skippers of the Destroyer Escort Commanding Officer's Association and their Wardroom Officers.

The original editing and encouragement of Barbara Feinberg guided me through the early stages. The final editing by Tom Cameron and Bob Linder is greatly appreciated. Preparation for publishing, including typesetting and printing, was accomplished with Tom Cameron's professional assistance.

I shall be ever grateful to Louis Broderick Fichtmann who was part of my early and post war years and who in retirement in our twilight years encouraged and assisted me in this effort until he died in 1990. Frank O. Braynard, Curator of the American Merchant Marine Museum Foundation at Kings Point, gave freely of his time and knowledge and provided rare photographs of merchant ships. Tom Freeman, the foremost marine artist in the portrayal of our beloved DEs also cooperated. Pat Sutherland and

Forest Cotton, both survivors of *U.S.S. Kanawha* provided information and pictures. Harris Emmerson of *U.S.S. Edward C. Daly (DE-17)*, who served in the ship from the beginning to the end, provided most of the interesting information about the memorable rescue of downed pilots as well as miscellaneous information and pictures.

Had it not been for the tremendous assistance of Bob Linder, I doubt whether I could have found the courage to dig into my memory, the log books, the war diaries, and bring it to life with the culmination of it all in *U.S.S. Cofer*. Bob was a teenage radar operator in *Cofer* whose memory, astuteness, and brilliance enabled me to write the most difficult part of the book. Correspondence between us is longer than the whole book. Bob went back to college after the war and among other things became a journalist. With the exception of two meetings at reunions, our communication was by mail and telephone between Miami, Florida, and Medford, Oregon. In many ways relating to *Cofer*, this is Linder's book and those of the crew who cooperated with him.

Many others too numerous to mention assisted together with the many ghosts that inhabit my mind, and whose presence in my life I can never forget. They are with me all the time, and I trust I did not fail them in portraying "our time."

Prologue

May 22, 1935, would have been just another day in my life as a Cadet at the New York State Merchant Marine Academy, but I unexpectedly became involved in our country's first National Maritime Day celebration. President Franklin D. Roosevelt proclaimed this date to commemorate the first successful transatlantic voyage under steam propulsion by *S.S. Savannah,* which had sailed from Savannah, Georgia, for Europe on May 22, 1819. Little publicity surrounded this proclamation, and the cadets themselves were unaware of it.

During the afternoon of the 21st, the Cadet Corps were busily preparing for their annual three-month training cruise to Europe. At the time all cadets lived aboard the training ship *Empire State,* which was moored in the Brooklyn Navy Yard. I was a First Classman (senior); and if I survived the cruise, passed the final exams and the license examination, I would graduate with my class in September.

On the evening of the 21st, the duty Officer summoned me to his stateroom. He informed me I was being placed in charge of a squad of lower classmen for a special assignment in Battery Park at noon the next day. I was to assemble the squad, he said, to participate in the National Maritime Day ceremony. We were to be in dress uniform, he added, before handing me the list of the lower classmen assigned. He then gave me the name of the woman in charge who would meet me at the park.

On May 22nd, a beautiful, sunny day in New York, my squad and I made the long walk to the Sands Street gate of the Brooklyn Navy Yard. After taking the trolley to a subway station in Brooklyn, we boarded a train to Bowling Green Station, which exited into a small park. The U.S. Custom's House stood south of Bowling Green Park. To the southwest of the Custom's House was Battery Park, which extended to the sea wall on Upper New York Bay. Both the East River and the Hudson River flow into the bay at this juncture.

In 1935 a mixture of high rise and small office buildings, some dating back many years, surrounded Battery Park. Slips for ferries to Staten

Island, Governor's Island, and New Jersey were located on the bay and the rivers flowing into the bay. Literally hundreds of ships berthed at the finger piers extending northward on both rivers, as well as in Brooklyn, Staten Island, and New Jersey.

From the piers surrounding the park, a steady line of ships could be seen arriving to and departing from the Port of New York. Passengers and cargo from ports around the world created much of the business activity in the vicinity of the piers. This center of shipping was logistically supported and administered from the commercial district adjacent to Battery Park. Yet only a small percentage of ships engaged in international trade flew the U.S. Flag.

During this Depression year I would be graduating into an industry that offered little opportunity. Jobs were scarce in U.S. Flag ships, and compensation barely met subsistence levels. Aside from trades protected by the government, most U.S. Flag ships required a building and operating subsidy to compete for a small share of international trade. This then was the world of trade and commerce I was staking my future on, and would soon have to learn how to survive in.

Just before noon my squad entered the park. At the same time hordes of office workers descended into the park to eat their box lunches, hot dogs, and other fast foods purchased from push carts. Masses of unemployed milled with the usual park population—a symbolic gathering depicting the times and the industry. I searched for the chairlady or any sign of a ceremony, but found neither. If there was to be a ceremony, no one seemed to be interested or appeared to know about it. We stood amidst a sea of people, few of whom, I am sure, knew what our uniforms represented, or cared. It became obvious the chairlady would have to find us. At least she knew what to look for.

The lady finally found us, and soon we were joined by others. A Seaman's Church minister appeared, as did a man carrying a medium-sized wreath, which he handed to me. Shortly thereafter two reporters and two cameramen from New York newspapers arrived. We waited several minutes expecting others, but no one came.

There was no band, no big name, and I felt sorry for this person who had been given a job with no support. She seemed discouraged but carried on as we looked for an appropriate place for the ceremony. My squad lined up near the sea wall, the minister said a prayer for those who had died at sea, the chairlady said a few words, the cameramen were alerted, she gave me a signal, and I threw the wreath into the bay as the cameramen took pictures. No more than ten people paused to note what was going on. Not one asked a question.

As the wreath floated away and sank, thousands walked by, uninterested and unconcerned.

The lady thanked us; and after a few parting words with the minister, we dissolved into the crowd. I still remember the crowd's apathy—indicative of the times, I now realize, and unfortunately setting a trend for the years to follow. We still observe National Maritime Day, and we do so with much more pomp and ceremony, but the apathy still exists.

As we returned to the Brooklyn Navy Yard that afternoon, none of us realized the ceremony had been one of the maritime industry's historic moments. Great changes were coming, changes that would radically alter this essential but neglected industry. But a cadet's life was one of total involvement, and I, soon busy preparing for the cruise, rapidly forgot the incident.

Although activities involving Mussolini and Hitler were being mentioned, they caused little concern. World War I was becoming a memory, and the Depression absorbed most people's attention. As I write this book some 55 years later, I remember at age 19 I had chosen a career that would transport me from the trade winds to the winds of war and back again into a disturbed era of war and peace. Problems were rarely solved. Interminable delays or the "quick fix" sufficed—as a result of an ever present "political expediency." In the final analysis greater problems, even crises, result from this inertia. The plight of the maritime industry, for example, is only one of these problems. But as these problems multiply, our future becomes less secure.

As we enter the 1990s communist countries are trying to solve their problems by attempting to become democracies, while democracies are choking on their failures. We enter this decade still struggling with "political expediency," along with the awesome influence of an elite of lawyers, accountants, merchant bankers, promoters, and wheelers and dealers—many seemingly still awash in the financial greed of the 1980s.

During the years I earned my living from the seas, I pursued as my "quest" the elusive goal of accomplishment in life. I tried desperately to find solutions to the difficulties existing in my industry, only to realize that one industry's solution depends on an overall solution. As the results of international events have often illustrated, the United States, to remain a sovereign nation, must be able to defend, support, and intelligently administer its affairs.

We cannot defend ourselves unless we recognize the importance of maintaining essential industries. We cannot defend ourselves with service-oriented businesses substituting for the critical manufacturing base necessary to safeguard our present and future sovereignty. But our industrial productivity continues to decline as promoters speculate rather than create. Our system, unfortunately, has developed a self-destructive nature that, in rushing to meet the expediencies of the present, is eroding future stability. Although we should cooperate in world affairs, we must first be sure our sovereignty is secure. We cannot permit essential industries to be subordinated by foreign interests to the point of extinction.

This, the beginning of my story, is in the context of my time, my successes, and my failures. I, like the wreath, cast my destiny into the eternal sea. Now I wish to relate the flavor of those days, the good and the bad, to show where I succeeded and where I failed and seem to have run ashore.

One

Preparation

The Early Years

I was born on January 25, 1916, in an apartment in upper Manhattan, the only child of J. Nicholas Chester and Dorothy Sophrin Chester. My mother was in her early 20s, my father in his 40s, and too old to be eligible for war service. Although a war baby, I have no specific recollection of the time. I was informed I was a healthy and smiling baby.

My entire youth before entering the New York State Merchant Marine Academy was spent in an area of New York known as the Fort George section of Washington Heights. The city's population thinned out before this northerly point. The West Side Subway line emerged from its tunnel here, became an elevated train, and completed its run less than three miles further north at Van Cortlandt Park. My maternal grandparents lived in Riverdale, an area northwest of Old Albany Post Road. My early world was mostly confined to these two areas.

Many of our outings included trips to New Jersey's shores and lakes, boat excursions up the Hudson River, and walks with my parents and friends on Riverside Drive. We also took trips to my father's office in an old red brick building on Broad Street. He was in the import and export business. When we visited his office, my father would show us around the waterfront of lower Manhattan, explaining the lore of ships and foreign lands.

Because he made annual business trips to Europe, my father's world extended far beyond mine. My mother and I would go to see him sail. Transatlantic sailings in those days were festive occasions with more

1

visitors than passengers, bands playing, parties in staterooms, confetti, whistle-blowing—all of which culminated with a ding-dong bell and the announcement "all ashore who are going ashore." Finally a prolonged blast of the ship's whistle sounded as the huge liner slowly backed from the dock into the North River to begin the long voyage to Europe. As the passengers gradually left the decks and the visitors left the dock, a strange quiet would descend over the ship. I, a little boy mostly confined to a small area only slightly expanded by bus, trolley, and subway, was greatly impressed by these momentous occasions.

Although between New York and the European destinations lay a mean, miserable sea, it was the only way to travel. At times the Atlantic would become enraged. Even large liners such as *Aquitania* and *Mauritania* were buffeted around, making life difficult for passengers attempting to adjust to the traditional liner atmosphere. Still my father coveted this experience, and looked forward to each crossing. When I was a child we lived in a lovely middle-class area surrounded by woods where I played and dreamed. My father had many friends from around the world, including ship captains who visited for dinners and parties. I also enjoyed visiting my maternal grandparents at their home in what was then the secluded woods of Riverdale.

My maternal grandfather, a tall, large-framed, rugged man, had lost one eye in an explosion at his carbonated beverage factory. After the explosion, he sold the company to the General Carbonic Company and then went to work for them as a sales manager. Later the company merged with the Liquid Carbonic Company, where my grandfather continued to work until he died of a heart attack in his late 60s.

He made an excellent living, shared his income with family and friends, and was always there when his children needed him. Strong yet gentle, he would give a home to a stray dog and nurse it back to health. My grandmother, also pleasant and strong, lived mostly within his shadow. Essentially they were both simple people who adjusted well to their life and times. I felt surrounded by a loving family, even though my father was a disciplinarian of the "old school," but fair. It was "yes sir" and "no sir." I was trained from an early age not to expect to have everything I wanted. I recall him always meticulously dressed in striped dark suits, stiff collars, a homburg hat, and a cane. Table manners were strictly enforced because all meals with my father were formally served.

My father was not unkind, and during the few years I was able to share with him I enjoyed his company. I respected him enough to follow his

2

bidding although I did not always understand. When I requested an explanation, he was patient, thoroughly providing his reasoning. I now realize the patience and the restraint he had to exercise, resulting from the persistent questions asked by a little boy. After he would thoroughly answer a question, he would usually be confronted with a "why," and again and again another "why."

My mother was a very pretty woman, also meticulous in dress. Until my parents separated, my mother was the one to accede to my requests while my father usually was the one to deny them. With my father's absence and later his death, my mother was just as strict as my father had been. And so I spent my preschool years in the basically happy but lonely existence of an only child. These were peaceful years. It was safe to travel in most areas of the city. I cannot recall worrying about crime. Certainly it was a different world in the early 1920s.

At this time horses and wagons were still used for transportation. The smell of manure from the stables was often in the air, later to be replaced by the smell of gas fumes. Radio and television did not exist—only silent pictures augmented by vaudeville in larger theaters. Prior to beginning school, a child depended entirely upon parents for preschool preparation for learning and life. I was fortunate, for my mother and father were people of culture, and they tried to pass as much as possible on to me.

Both were excellent pianists, and when their efforts to interest and teach me failed, they hired a piano teacher. I reluctantly relented in my defiance, but progress was poor and the lessons soon stopped. I liked to draw and paint, and was well into this art form by the time I entered grammar school. My mother had a high school and business school education, which was above par for a woman at the time. Careers for women were limited, and traditionally they became housewives and mothers. I don't know the details of my father's formal education other than he spoke several languages and was familiar with the arts, literature, and sciences. Although interested in sports, he seldom participated, except to practice ice skating once in awhile. I think in his early years he may have skied. For reasons of their own, my family did not attend church.

My father, enamored of ships and the seas, was a frustrated sailor who worked at his roll-top desk most of the year, living for his annual trip to Europe. Somehow he passed this love for the sea and adventure on to me. I started to read before attending school; and together with the tales my father told me, I was soon dreaming of ships and far away places. Today it seems inconceivable that in my preschool days my character and love for adventure were already being molded. At times I question whether it was possible for my father to have instilled within me the desire to strive for a destiny he coveted, but failed to achieve. I often wonder how much more I could have learned and attained later had I known him for a longer time.

In 1922 I entered P.S. 189, a new grammar school at the time that no longer exists. I vaguely recall my first two years there. But I vividly remember the trip to Europe with my parents during the last semester of 1924. My father had to have planned this trip long in advance because travel abroad in those days was complicated. Visas, rarely required for Americans traveling in Europe today, were a common requirement then. My father secured one passport that covered my mother and me. The passport picture was the same size, but we both appeared in it. Visas were either stamped or pasted to the passport for most of the countries to be visited. We would leave shortly before the school year ended and return in time for the beginning of the next semester.

Except for business, which required passage on a fast luxury liner, rarely were trips to Europe limited to one month. Most people sailing on the average transatlantic liner of the times had to allow as much as a month for the two transatlantic voyages. Without aircraft, travel between cities and countries in Europe also required much more time.

The trip would take us to Denmark—to what are believed to have been the free states of Memel and Danzig—and also the countries of Latvia, Germany, France, and England. We would take a train through other countries while en route from one destination to another. Although a trip of this nature was routine to my father, both my mother and I were excited as we purchased new clothes and a steamer trunk.

My father rarely spoke about his family or his childhood. He came to the United States from Europe on business in the early part of the century and became a naturalized citizen. Until World War I he kept in close contact, both personally and in business affairs, with his family in Europe. The war changed that relationship. I gather few of his family survived. His true business is difficult for me to identify, but his European trips always were centered around London.

This trip, however, was different. I soon learned its main purpose was for me to meet his older, wealthy widowed sister, Helena Pines, who lived in Libau, Latvia. She and my father, remnants of a large family, were very close. And so in 1924, for the first time, I would emerge from the confines of my small, comfortable world to experience an urge to travel overseas

4

that was already nagging at me at the tender age of eight. My father, probably by plan, had set my future course.

On this voyage my father broke with his tradition of sailing to England on the Cunard Line. Instead he booked first-class passage on the Danish Flag *S.S. Estonia* owned by the Baltic American Line. A 14,000-ton coal burning passenger ship, she cruised at 14 knots. The first-class section on this three-class liner had room for few passengers. Although not a luxury liner, the upper deck had a charming, small dining room with an excellent view of the sea. My father, I now believe, must have had some interest in the company.

Estonia, although a relatively small ship, looked large to me. Two huge, yellow smoke stacks on the boat deck, which I could stand near and look up to, added to the illusion of great size from the perspective of a little boy.

We boarded at a remote Brooklyn pier rather than the main transatlantic-liner piers on the North River. Still the visitors came, a band played, and the confetti flew when we backed away from the pier. As we moved down the bay and out to sea, I had no idea this would be the first of many sea and air crossings of the Atlantic and other oceans I would make in the years ahead. Although there were few passengers in first class, the ship was booked to capacity in second and third class. My mother and father shared a double room. I had a stateroom to myself.

The only child in first class, I was catered to by the captain, officers, crew, and passengers—which included a Danish prince. My father knew the prince, and the Captain had dined at our apartment on one or more occasions. Even though the ship took the northern route, and I don't recall very bad weather, the seasickness I feared did not occur. Neither my mother nor father suffered from this malady. I enjoyed the voyage immensely.

We arrived in Copenhagen after 12 days at sea. With a member of the royal family on board, we were escorted to our berth by a fleet of sailing yachts. We did not disembark there, but my father did go ashore to take care of some business.

We sailed on to Memel and Danzig with their cobble-stone streets and cold beaches, and finally to Libau on a small Baltic steamer. It was a very rough trip, and I did get seasick. Although embarrassed it did not cool my enthusiasm for the sea.

As we approached Libau my father pointed out the rusting hulk of an Imperial Russian cruiser that had run aground on the breakwater prior to World War I. He described the catastrophe to me in great detail. I have often wondered if this incident, together with others, was a way of preparing me for something he sensed about my future, which I had no way of foreseeing.

My aunt, who had traveled by horse and carriage, met us at the dock in Libau. At that time in Latvia automobiles were rare. Libau was a beautiful city of parks and wide tree-lined avenues. The ride to my aunt's home, located on a tranquil residential street close to the main avenue, was a new and pleasant experience.

My aunt spoke perfect English and used this language with my mother and me. She was obviously a grande dame but appeared happy to have us visit and seemed particularly delighted to see me. When we arrived at the house, her staff, dressed in uniform, was lined up to greet us. They smiled and were friendly, but none could speak English. My mother and father were given a large bedroom, and I was given a small room of my own.

The house was large, yellow in color, with big windows on the ground floor; the rooms, also large, had very high ceilings. The furniture was strange to me and probably consisted of antiques and heirlooms. The grounds were beautifully landscaped, although only about an acre in size. Little, colorful, dwarf-like figures were placed around the well-maintained garden.

During our visit Helena was correct but not affectionate to my mother. But my aunt's charm, the servant's friendliness, and the general atmosphere in this house made me feel at home. Aunt Helena, over 60 at the time, projected a strong but friendly image. I believe our visit, in fact, was centered around her meeting me.

My aunt owned a sailing yacht and took us all sailing. None of the women made any concessions in their dress to the sail—all were formally dressed. My father broke with his tradition and wore a tweed suit with a vest and tie. A professional captain manned the helm.

We stayed in Libau for several weeks—riding to the beaches and other places of interest by horse and carriage. The weather at the beach was usually cold, and the Baltic rough and gray. The shoreline was lined with dark brown seaweed. Amid the seaweed was amber, and I searched for it but never found any piece of value.

While we were in Libau a U.S. Navy four-stack destroyer paid a courtesy call. After calling on the officials of the town, the captain and two other officers called on my aunt and my father for either drinks or tea. Arriving by horse and carriage, they were resplendent in their full-dress uniforms, consisting of a frock coat with epaulets, fore and aft hats, and gold-striped pants with dress swords. They made a powerful impression on me.

The occasion for the call might have been that we were the only U.S. citizens in Libau at the time. Another reason may have been some connection between my father and Philander Knox, Secretary of State in 1909 under President Taft, who died in 1921. On numerous occasions I asked my mother why I was given the horrible middle name of "Philander." My father, she told me, had insisted on it. My middle name became a constant source of ridicule by my friends. I knew of no other person bearing that name, and asked her if she did not realize the embarrassment it would cause me over the years. She said she understood; it had been the cause of strong arguments, but my father had been adamant. She could no longer recall the connection between the two, but my father greatly respected Knox. If he knew Knox he probably knew and was known by others in high office, and possibly he had some connections with the Administration that resulted in the courtesy call.

As the time approached for our departure, a pervasive depression overtook the house. In what was an unemotional family, I sensed our departure was dreaded. The day we left my aunt and father had tears in their eyes. Behind disciplined demeanors were two highly sensitive people whose love for each other was strong. I believe as they said "good bye" they realized it meant forever. Aunt Helena had children, but they were never mentioned and probably were dead. I sense there was much more to this trip that I was too young to understand at the time. I also believe my father was ill and knew he did not have long to live. Helena also could have been near death. With this prevailing atmosphere, we boarded the train to Riga and other stops on our way to Paris.

In the late 1930s, when events in the Baltic became critical, I regretted I had not tried to locate and assist Helena. I now realize, however, the chances of her being alive in 1939 were poor. She must have been nearly 65 in 1924, which would have made her over 80 by 1939. Having not heard from Helena, nor being able to locate any but a distant cousin, I suspect there were no other close relatives.

If this is correct it would lend a certain credence to the trip to Libau. I think my father and Aunt Helena were the last of an old international family line, and I was the only future it had. Under such conditions my father must have felt compelled to take me to meet his sister. As time went by this family mystery became more confusing. My mother made sure that references to my father and his family were kept from me as much as possible. I now understand the later part of the trip was secondary to the visit with my Aunt Helena in Libau.

Our hotel in Paris was off the Champs Elysees and close to the Arc de Triomphe. But even now this strained May to September marriage of my parents was coming to an end. We had expected to go with my father from Paris to London where he conducted most of his business, then return from England to the U.S. on the Cunard Line. Instead of taking us to London, my father left us in Paris and went on to London alone. Prior to departing he took us to the Louvre, Versailles, Notre Dame, the Eiffel Tower, and many other places of interest—to be sure I saw as much of Paris and the surrounding area as possible. He spoke French perfectly and was able to explain these historic sites to my mother and me.

My mother and I remained in Paris for about two weeks awaiting his return. We then took the boat train to Le Havre to embark in *S.S. De Grasse* of the French Line. A new vessel on its first or second voyage, it was larger and faster and much more luxurious than *Estonia,* but still took eight days to make the crossing. Unlike *Estonia, De Grasse* had the traditional promenade deck with its rows of deck chairs. It also had a full complement of passengers returning from Europe as the season ended. This was my first exposure to the French way to travel, with formal and excellent dinners, morning bouillon, afternoon tea, music for dining and dancing, and people watching. My father had some problems getting me permission to eat with the family in the main dining room rather than the children's room. He prevailed.

The tranquillity and the security of my life ended after our arrival in New York. My parents separated soon after our return. My mother and I moved into a smaller apartment. Europe, the sea voyage, and the time spent alone with my mother in Paris, in the parks, and with other children were now only a memory. Most of all I missed my father. It was a bitter separation; and because I loved them both, I was caught in between. For awhile I could visit my father at his office and at arranged meetings. But these encounters became less frequent as my mother gradually shut him out of her life. She went back to work as a legal secretary in a large law firm; and during the years that followed, my contacts with my father were cut off.

I looked to both for some explanation. Neither would say a bad word against the other. My mother simply said that she could no longer live with my father. My father told me I was too young to understand, but when I grew up I would. Since growing up I have learned that it is impossible to define the differences that arise between a man and wife. In this case an age difference and my father's deteriorating health and financial position contributed. Other problems also had to exist. Meanwhile my mother kept me busy and my mind off the tragedy in our lives.

My infatuation with ships increased as my interest in school decreased. My mother worked all day and could not adequately watch over my studies. Even though I made good grades and even skipped a grade, a serious problem surfaced: I was able to get high marks without doing homework or studying. I was playing ball when I should have been studying. I had become an under-achiever. This failure to develop a study ethic would haunt me later.

In 1929 I graduated from P.S. 189 and entered George Washington High School. The school's stadium was located across the street from where I lived, and the school itself was one block south. George Washington High School was an excellent school in those days; a high percentage of its graduates went on to college and graduate school. I received reasonably good marks in all but French, for there was no way one could pass without studying very hard. Even my French-born friend, Andrew Hirth, who flunked English because he spoke it with a French accent, barely passed. Another friend born in Spain, fluent in Spanish, and an excellent student, Hugo Castello, flunked. In 1933 before I entered the New York State Merchant Marine Academy, I had to attend an expensive summer session at the Dwight School on Park Avenue to make up for my French lapse and to get my diploma.

When my father died before I graduated from grammar school, my mother created a cover story and made sure I was away at summer camp at the time. She explained later she did not want to upset me and he had been sick for many years. I had suspected as much, but the subject of my parent's relationship was very sensitive. When my father's financial condition deteriorated, he was unable to assist my mother with child support.

Although my mother's salary was $35 a week, an excellent wage for the time, her brother and her father contributed to our support. I worked during the summers and sometimes after school. In 1931, when my mother leased a summer cottage in Rye, I caddied. In 1932 she got me a summer job with the Pioneer Instrument Company, which was a client of her firm. The company was a division of Bendix Aviation. Although the work was interesting, I had a long subway ride to and from Brooklyn five days a week. They were pleased with my work and offered me a job when I graduated from high school.

Friends from grammar and high school were friends for life. The late Louis Broderick Fichtmann worked with me after the war. He retired at the same time I did. John William Wheeler has been a close friend for life. For many years he was the senior partner of Thacher, Profit & Wood. Andrew Paul Hirth, who followed me to NYSMMA, became the Chief Engineer of the battleship *U.S.S. Maryland* during World War II. I was the best man at his wedding. I attended his funeral with another mutual and lifetime friend, Dr. Hugo Castello. Hugo, now retired, served in the Navy, became a lawyer, and succeeded his father as the fencing coach of the NYU fencing team. I had many other friends from that early period, but these have been with me through it all.

I often spent the weekends in Riverdale. At times my cousin Irene would visit with her parents from their home in Kansas City. Irene, who was ten years younger than I, was an unusual child, beautiful, always cheerful, and brilliant. She became a talented artist who gained wide recognition, but died much too young. My uncle's family from Ohio only visited once that I can recall. His son, Allan David, was five years younger than I. He flew for the Army Air Corps in the ETO in World War II. After the war he gave up a law practice to settle in the woods of Vermont. Other than a doting and loving younger sister of my mother, her husband, and my grandparents, I played alone in the woods and streams surrounding the house.

I was small for my age. When I entered high school, I was about five feet two inches. As a junior I was still only five feet four inches, but had grown close to five feet ten inches at 17 when entering the Academy. I was six-feet tall when I graduated at the age of 19. I would have tried out for varsity sports, but I was very thin and in a school where varsity sports were at the highest level, I was simply too small and light even though a good athlete.

Although my marks were adequate for me to qualify for all but a few colleges, costs were high. I had no interest in attending the City College of New York, which at that time was harder to gain entry to than Ivy League schools. Nor could I qualify for a scholarship as John Wheeler had done for Columbia; the tuition was simply not available to me. An Annapolis appointment was highly political, and even though I stood much higher in the class than the young man who got it, I never really considered it once I discovered the New York State Merchant Marine Academy (NYSMMA).

Founded in 1874 NYSMMA had a low visibility. It offered a two- year course leading to a diploma and a license, but no degree. Fees to New York State residents were a very affordable alternative that fitted into my dreams. A license could be obtained as either a deck or engineering officer. Since my original objective was to become a shipmaster, I applied for entry to NYSMMA as a deck cadet in the middle of my senior year of high school. I was discouraged to find out that although I met the height requirements, I was under the standards for weight.

Physicals were given by the Academy doctor, who was an active Naval Lieutenant in the Medical Corps. The same strict standards applied to Naval Academy applicants were required by the State school. But there was one important difference. Rarely was a physical waiver granted to a midshipman in the 1930s. At NYSMMA, however, waivers were possible, and I received a waiver on my weight.

NYSMMA's school was aboard *T.S. Empire State* based in the Brooklyn Navy Yard. Applications were handled in the Admissions Office in the New York State Building at 80 Center Street in Manhattan. Captain Carl Cetti, an alumnus and Secretary of the School, handled the procedures for admission. I called on him several times, and he was always friendly and cooperative. I was surprised when he told me 139 applicants had applied for the class. Budget and other restrictions, however, limited the number of deck and engineering cadets to 50. This was discouraging because I still had to earn my high school diploma before I could enter with the Academy class in September 1933. Although I was concerned Captain Cetti said I should not be. Many applicants still had to take physicals, educational credentials had to be verified, and some people had applied to several schools. He was impressed with my desire to go to sea, and he implied that I would be given points for motivation.

The odds, nevertheless, appeared to be against me. Some candidates were college graduates; about 20 percent had been to college for a year or more. While still at Dwight School, I was notified I had been chosen as an alternate. Subsequently, after passing the school and State Regent's examinations, I was accepted to the Academy. I had made it. I had received my Regents and George Washington High School diploma, and was on my way.

I felt a sense of finality about all of this. My mother, who ordinarily would have been expected to oppose my choice of a profession, did not. I believe she accepted it as something my father had long ordained and no one could ever change. She never doubted I would be accepted at the Academy, nor that I would graduate and go to sea. She helped rather than hindered a decision that would take me away from her for long periods of time. And she was well aware of the dangers I might encounter. Yet when I left she gave me her blessings. To this day I do not believe I had a choice.

The New York State Merchant Marine Academy

Having experienced neither romance nor adventure, I could not fulfill my dreams without experiencing them both. Just how, where, and when was something else again. I was just a skinny, tall boy, naive in the ways of the world, whose favorite authors were Saavedra Cervantes and Joseph Conrad.

My mother, an avid reader, playgoer, and a repressed romantic, took me to many Broadway shows and movies. She introduced me to the books that flavored my life but were so greatly removed from its reality. It all added up to the "impossible dream" I hoped to find—at the end of a rainbow or perhaps at the Merchant Marine Academy.

With some 43 others who made up the second-half of the Class of '35, and in the midst of the Depression, I entered into an expanding scholastic and living experience. The class was about evenly split between deck and engineering categories. We were assigned to divisions led by first classmen. We fourth classmen were commonly referred to as "mugs." NYSMMA's home was aboard *T.S. Empire State*, a schooner berthed alongside was used to berth the fourth classmen. It was outfitted with classrooms to augment the overall facilities during the academic semesters. The Academy Superintendent, Captain James Harvey Tomb, USN (Ret.), had graduated from the U.S. Naval Academy in 1899. Captain Tomb, only 57 in 1933, appeared older to the cadets. He was a disciplinarian, but basically he was a warm-hearted human being who made it his business to get to know each student. He was a man of average height, chubby, meticulously uniformed, who looked at the cadets and the world through his pince-nez glasses, which he toyed with when he spoke. He was a kindly but intrepid old gentleman of the old school. To the Cadet Corps, he was known affectionately as "Blubby."

Captain Tomb dedicated the remainder of his life to the school, working to expand it into a four-year accredited college similar to the U.S. Naval Academy.

In 1933 he became involved in a political battle with State Commissioner Robert Moses, who was trying to circumvent the school's acquisition of Fort Schuyler. Captain Tomb wanted the U.S. Government to cede Fort Schuyler and the property leading to it to the State for a permanent home for the Academy. Moses wanted it for a state park. To those "in the know,"

Captain Tomb appeared to be conducting a fruitless crusade. After all he was just a retired naval officer up against one of the strongest and most clever politicians in the state. But for all his political naivete, Captain Tomb still won the battle.

The U.S. Government ceded the largest and best part of Fort Schuyler to the State for its use by NYSMMA. None of the property was used for a park. Captain Tomb got his campus, and before I graduated work began to convert Fort Schuyler and a large area adjacent to it into a college. Dormitories, laboratories, athletic fields, classrooms, parade grounds, a campus, messroom, and a dock for the schoolship were built. Over the years the facilities were improved and expanded as the student body increased in size. Although Captain Tomb did not live long enough to see it all come to fruition, his dream came true. Now a part of the State University of New York, with a graduate school, NYSMMA justifies everything the venerable Captain envisioned.

All the great things that were to happen to the school over the many years were in the future. In 1933 the situation was much different. The campus was limited to the little leisure space aboard *Empire State* and specific areas in an industrial navy yard located in a depressing area of Brooklyn. And so one dreary day in September 1933, I reported on board *T.S. Empire State* with other members of my class.

The reality of my course to adventure hit quickly. Upperclassmen started shouting at us as we meekly stepped off the gangplank. We were taken to our quarters on the schooner tied up alongside, which consisted of one large bunkroom and two tiers of metal berths. We were each assigned a berth and an adjacent locker.

From uniforms to socks, skivvies, shoes and shirts, we were completely re-outfitted. We now wore sailor-style undress blues, undress whites, and sailor white hats with a black cadet stripe around them. These were similar to the blue-striped white hats worn by midshipmen. Added to this were neckerchiefs, leggings, and duty belts. We were also given stenciling equipment and instructed how to stencil all of the clothing and the gear distributed to us.

We had been measured for our dress uniforms by a landmark uniform tailor named "Battleship Max Cohen" whose business was located on Sands Street. The ranking officer of this battleship was Max's widow, who was experienced in dealing with both enlisted and officer personnel of the U.S. Navy. The company had the contracts for the Merchant Marine Academy. Cadets had to pay in advance to the school's supply Department for all their uniforms. Dress uniforms would not be needed until our first liberty, two to three weeks later.

While all of this was going on, the shouting continued, and so did our transformation from civilians to mugs. Over the next two years, they hit us hard and fast with rules and regulations. For two weeks before the start of classes, they thoroughly indoctrinated us on how to "act" as part of the Cadet Corps. We rarely saw an officer other than the Bos'n and the Master at Arms. Neither would interfere in the procedures unless they saw an upper classman abusing authority or being remiss in exercising proper authority. We were taught how to stand, sit, walk, and drilled in the manual of arms with rifles. We were instructed in how to care for our uniforms and where and how to wash our clothes. With only three pieces of dirty laundry allowed, washing clothes while on our knees on a cold deck became an everyday chore. Within this short indoctrination, total strangers adopted a shipmate relationship as they fought to survive together.

For the first time in my life, I was in a new and strictly controlled environment with a group of other young men. Most of the class came from the cities, towns, and farms in the State of New York, with one graduate of the University of Puerto Rico, and a few out-of-staters. As we each struggled to cope with what appeared to be impossible demands, we looked to each other for assistance and solace. At the time we did not always understand the objectives of the unrelenting pressure. But as we moved on in our careers and faced the stresses of working at sea and sometimes the loneliness of command, we began to understand. We grew to realize that what might not be possible acting alone might well be possible acting as a group, suffering and working together. In two years of training classmates became shipmates who, with few exceptions, would persevere.

For generations military schools have operated with this highly directive, highly disciplined teaching technique. To those who found it too overbearing, the door was always open to leave. But from those who stayed the course, new leaders emerged. It is a time-honored way to discover the leadership qualities of each man. In our society such men, whether they stay in the military or move into the private sector, carry with them a desire to protect the dignity and rights of free men. Moreover they understand that to do so, they must act in cooperation and coordination with others. Over the years, as I watched the degradation of a country or ethnic class unable to defend itself as a group, I looked back at my NYSMMA training with more understanding than I had at the time.

We received our dress uniforms just in time for our first weekend liberty.

All hands, except those on weekend watch, proudly departed the ship to go home or to follow other pursuits, depending on the individual cadet's desire and finances. Those short of money could live and eat aboard ship and use the recreational facilities in the Brooklyn Navy Yard. I was one of the youngest cadets in the class. But I felt a great sense of accomplishment for having survived the first of many hurdles. Several cadets had given up or were dropped from the program for one reason or another.

With the start of the academic semester, our class settled into a spartan routine wherein every minute of our time was accounted for. The atmosphere became gloomy, particularly as fall passed into winter. This transformation from a leisurely existence of a high school or college student into the restricted and disciplined life of a cadet was traumatic. But A.C. Ingersoll, Jr., with two years of experience as a midshipman at the U.S. Naval Academy, took it all in stride. Observing what to him must have been a sea of comedy, he watched, with a snide grin, as new classmates struggled through their dilemma.

T.S. Empire State, built under emergency conditions during World War I, was just about as unimpressive as a ship could be. She was one of many "three-island type" ships designated as the "Hog Island A-Class." Many of these dry cargo ships were still in use in the essential trade routes of the United States. Hog was an appropriate name for these ugly ships. The lines were all straight, with no design consideration made for appearance. The emphasis was on economy and speed of building.

The only difference between *Empire State* and its many sisterships was the additional Liberty boats, cutters for sailing, and the Captain's Gig carried on deck and the configuration changes below decks. Cargo holds and other spaces were converted to messing, living, berthing, and class-rooms to accommodate 150 cadets plus the teaching, administrative, and small support staff. Little areas of luxury were on the deck above. Here the Captain and officers lived in virtual seclusion from the Cadet Corps.

The mess deck, a large area midships, served as the center of most below-deck activities, inclusive of office space. It included the cafeteria, scullery, and dining facilities, where the entire Cadet Corps could be fed in one sitting. This area also was used as a study hall—cadets had no rooms or special places for studying . Lower classmen alternated in duty-sections to provide the services in the cafeteria as well as the scullery. Professional cooks and bakers were employed.

A recreation and leisure area for the cadets, the mess deck contained a store, a barbershop, and a small section of lounge chairs where cadets could mingle, relax, and meet visitors. Aside from the deck space, which was even more limited, the mess deck comprised the "campus" of the school. Dances and receptions were held there. And most important it housed the pay telephone from which cadets could make and receive calls.

This was the small campus I found myself restricted to, but which would carry me to many foreign shores and lands before I graduated. Limited in its formal studies but unlimited in so many other ways, this campus, in terms of learning, had few peers. For the unknown period of history for which I was preparing, I was in the right place at the right time.

Painted gray in U.S. Navy fashion, *Empire State* was hard to distinguish from standard U.S. Navy auxiliary ships. On cruises she often received honors customarily reserved for a commissioned naval vessel. *Empire State* routinely dipped her ensign in response to the dipping of a passing merchant ship's flag.

Time passed quickly. With classes, watches, ship's maintenance, and other activities, little leisure time existed other than for study and sleep. Reveille varied between 0545 and 0615 hours, depending on the schedule for the day. Aside from watch assignments and special extra study periods, all cadets had to be in their berths by 2200 hours for "lights out." In the short time between reveille and the start of classes, we would run a mile course in the navy yard, make our bunks, clean our quarters together with deck areas, shower before breakfast, take less than 30 minutes to eat, and then be in our classrooms between 0800 and 0900 hours.

For work we wore dungarees. We attended classes, however, in undress blue or white sailor-style uniforms, the color depending on the temperature, season, and the weather. The Cadet Officer-of-the-Day wore his dress uniform with leggings and gun belt. Other members of the watch section wore undress uniforms, leggings, and a gun belt. Those working in food service wore undress white uniforms. Uniform changes were a constant problem. Dungarees could only be worn during work periods. But we could leave the Brooklyn Navy Yard only in dress uniforms. They were similar to Navy and Merchant Marine officer uniforms except we had the half and slanting stripes on our sleeves, rather than the full gold stripes of an officer. Our cap badges and lapels had the New York State Shield. Our whites had the shields on the shoulder boards.

Cadets led a complicated life. Their bunks, uniforms, lockers, and personal belongings had to be neatly organized and stowed at all times. Space was limited. Textbooks and other study materials added to the problem. Since no washing machines were available, we spent many hours on our knees washing clothes. Dress uniforms, dress shirts, detachable stiff collars, and dress coats had to be sent out for cleaning and pressing. Cadets paid for this, as they did for uniforms, personal effects, haircuts, textbooks, and tuition.

Tuition for New York State residents was only about $250 per year. Out-of-staters paid all or part of the difference in the total cost to the state less the Navy subsidy. The school's overall budget could not have been very large; much of the work was done by the cadets, and the small staff was paid very poorly. Food for a cadet cost about 34 cents a day. Aside from the teaching and administrative staff, only a small number of employees supplemented the work of the cadets, who basically maintained the ship and themselves. After the Navy subsidy the cost to the State could hardly have been more than $2,000 a year per cadet. I personally paid this back to the State of New York many times over, and this does not count the taxes of my company and the employees domiciled in the State. Many graduates, I am sure, not only paid back the State through taxes, but also with their lives during World War II.

My payback situation was not unlike many other students of my time and those who followed in later years. Still the school has had to fight continually for its budget. The Federal Government and the State of New York have been paid in full many times over for the funds advanced for the education of the Cadets at the Academy. Few if any other taxpayer-financed schools are in this category. As far as I know, no effort ever has been made to track the payback record tax by individual school graduates.

As a taxpayer in the State of New York for many years, I was aware the educational budgeting system paid little if any attention to the payback situation, and basically used other standards in the budgetary process. Yet this is one of the fairest manners in assessing the effectiveness of a school and comparing one against another. I believed at the time I received a valuable education and much more. Then as well as now, one could hardly expect to receive so much education for so little cost.

The hazing was rough, and by tradition officers did not interfere. Most upperclassmen limited the torment, which was more instructive than mean. But like other military schools, a small percentage of people exceeded normal boundaries. This part of the learning process served to toughen us. To be effective leaders we had to experience abuse of power to understand its unfairness. And as leaders we would have to call on our total experience to inspire others to follow our lead. Restraint of power is most difficult when under pressure. But a well-trained leader will understand this, and know just how much pressure his men can handle. Soon we would graduate into a cruel world, even then experiencing the abuse of power by tyrants. We needed to prepare for it.

Academic subjects taught in this stressful environment created an atmosphere that, in reality, broadened our knowledge and honed our talents. Although fundamentally geared towards a life at sea, the training was much broader. Nothing, I now know, could have prepared me better for the tumultuous period to follow.

Although I had had a love affair with ships most of my life, I knew nothing about them. But I was about to learn. My world changed quickly. A floor was now a deck, the ceiling an overhead. The front was the bow, the other end the stern. Right was starboard, left was port. A toilet was a head. We were taught marlin spike seamanship by Bos'n "Ducky" Holmes. Close to 80, Bos'n Holmes had spent much of his life at sea under sail and steam in the Navy and in merchant ships. He was a legend in his time and greatly respected.

Practical seamanship was only a small part of the subject matter. Whereas Knight's Seamanship was the Navy text, Riesenberg's was the Merchant Marine text. Captain Riesenberg was a graduate of NYSMMA. Classroom seamanship studies varied greatly from the practical seamanship taught by Bos'n Holmes. Humanities were excluded from the curriculum because cadets were expected to be well versed in these subjects prior to entering the school. NYSMMA emphasized practical and technical subjects. Instructors made it clear that graduation would only be the beginning of a lifetime of learning. They would teach us the basics on which to build, and the world would be our post-graduate school. The Third Mate's or Third Engineer's License would be our starting credential. Except for the time requirement, we also would be capable of passing the Master's or Chief Engineer's License examination on graduation.

For the deck classes, courses in seamanship and navigation were comprehensive and theoretical as well as practical. Nearly all other courses addressed our profession, although many were given only one semester. These included electrical engineering, steam engineering, maritime law, naval architecture (ship's stability), meteorology, and communications.

During the harsh winter of 1933, we still had to wash down the decks and bulwarks. We had to stand watches on the cruelest nights, yet be fresh for the next school day. Duty sections rotated every fourth night and every fourth weekend. If a cadet drew a night watch of four hours, he might end up with only four hours of sleep.

None of our instructors were professional teachers. One thing they had in common was a commitment to pass on their knowledge of the sea and ships to us. In this teaching environment, it was not simply a job any more than the cadet's role was simply that of a student. Our instructors had been cadets too. They accepted the responsibility of preparing us both academically and for the hardships of life they had already experienced.

Starting school in September gave my class about eight months to become acclimated to the ship and the routine before sailing in May. On the cruise we would be third classmen rather than fourth classmen. Although still lower classmen, we would have more privileges and better assignments for the ship's operation. On the second cruise we would be first classmen. Although second classmen were also upper classmen, again we would get the preference in assignments, responsibility, and shore leave. I was not aware of all of this prior to entry, but soon realized I had been lucky.

Because I was basically naive in many ways of the world, upper classmen hazed me a good deal of the time. My mother did not help my desired anonymity, which was the greatest state a mug could aspire to, by telephoning me religiously during the noon meal. The telephone booth was in the mess hall, and the calls were a source of embarrassment. She called during her free time, and in spite of my pleas she never desisted. Ultimately the Cadet Corps understood my plight and stopped riding me about it.

My first year, however, was miserable. I was disenchanted by the overall environment. The academic courses were not difficult, but one did have to concentrate in class. I managed to pass without studying very much. Study Hall was supervised in the mess deck from 1900 to 2145 hours every night, but I managed to read or draw and study very little. Cleaning heads, working in the cold on deck, drilling and marching, together with the hazing was not all that bad, nor was the extra duty accumulated by demerits I received. Basically dreams and reality are quite different, and although I was making excellent friends, I still felt homesick.

In one of our phone conversations, I told my mother I wanted to quit. But she told me I had better finish what I started or not come home. Dorothy Chester was a strong character. Although some people believed I would never make it at sea, I was not one of the many who dropped out before the first cruise. Many cadets bitched and talked of resigning. But those who were dropped became very depressed; they really wanted to remain.

Actually I was becoming more and more used to the routine and life of a cadet. I did spend most weekends at home with my mother and friends.

Faced with a dreary and cold winter, I found no more pleasure at home than I did at school. Although I knew little about it, I often joined in the discussions about girls and sex with other cadets. They seemed more knowledgeable about it than my old high school friends. Few if any cadets, however, had the money or the time to do much more than talk.

In early May the whole Cadet Corps moved aboard *T.S. Empire State* for the cruise. A few days were spent in drydock, and we returned to our regular berth in the Brooklyn Navy Yard before we sailed. The itinerary included Bermuda; therefore, we would get close to ten days of sailing experience before the long leg to Europe. We were too small a school to engage in intercollegiate sports, so we competed with the various units of the U.S. Navy on ships or ashore in the navy yard. We formed a tennis team for the cruise. Although the administration was not sports-inclined, they went along with the idea, as long as it was at no cost to the State of New York.

In the middle of May we departed from the navy yard with much fanfare. My mother and many of the parents and friends of the cadets were there to see us off. The New York newspapers also covered the sailing. A sense of excitement rippled through the crew as the tugs broke the umbilical cord to the dock and we proceeded under our own power towards the Atlantic Ocean. We were finally under way, first to Bermuda and then to Europe. Sea watches were set and would not be broken until we arrived in Bermuda. The routine and life of a cadet was altered completely on the cruise. We concentrated on operating the ship and on-the-job training. Instructors conducted practical seamanship classes between watches.

The moment of truth hit soon after we dropped the pilot and the ship started to roll as she proceeded eastward. We faced rough seas, common in that area at that time of the year. I was seasick the entire time. The ship had no cargo, was light in the water, and had the most sickening roll I ever experienced. I had to hide my malady from the officers, or I would be sent home from Bermuda. This was all aggravated by the smell of fuel oil fumes that penetrated the deck and below area of the ship from the overflow outlets.

I was not alone in my misery. Some cadets gave up and were sent home from Bermuda. Others, like me, suffered but did not turn themselves in. As I would dash for a porthole to "unload," I often would bump heads with another cadet in the same predicament. By the time we reached Bermuda, I had my sea legs. Nevertheless I called my mother and told her that I had gotten seasick and probably it would be better if I resigned and came home.

This remarkable woman would have none of it, and I would not dare to risk her wrath. It was the last time I would think of resigning.

Bermuda was delightful. We had several hours of shore leave every other day. Our tennis team, however, ventured forth to do battle nearly every day. We always lost, and our hosts, delighted that they had beaten the Yanks, entertained us royally. Every day we took turns sailing and racing our cutters.

Port watches were not as frequent as sea watches, and classes were suspended while we were in port. We anchored about one-half mile from the main Hamilton dock, which meant we had to run our U.S. Navy-type liberty boats between the ship and the dock. We also swam from the ship. Bermuda treated us well, and the annual calls were mutually enjoyed.

Most of us, not used to alcohol, drank for the first time in Bermuda. I did not get drunk but felt tipsy. The "in" bar in Hamilton was the Quarry, and many cadets spent too much of their limited funds drinking there. They also acquired the demerits that went along with intoxication. My mother had given me a $150 allowance, which had to suffice for the entire three-month cruise. This limitation, together with the little time allowed ashore, curtailed any chance of my successfully pursuing women. Needless to say some of my shipmates told tales of intriguing adventures, most of which were figments of their imaginations.

After ten delightful days in Bermuda, we continued to Gibraltar and Northern Europe. I no longer had problems with seasickness and enjoyed the cruise more as time passed. In Gibraltar we met the Pennsylvania schoolship, *Annapolis*. She was a sailing ship with a coal-burning auxiliary engine. The cadets were busily engaged in the filthy job of taking on coal. She sailed before we had a chance to go ashore and meet their cadets. In 1934 *Empire State* was the only oil-burning state schoolship, and coal was already as outmoded as the sails carried on older schoolships.

Our tennis team went ashore to do battle with British Army Teams from the "Rock," and we continued our losing record. The more we lost, it seemed, the more friends we made. Gibraltar offered little entertainment for cadets. After a frightening lecture about the dangers of venereal disease, given by the doctor, we left to visit LaLinea, Spain. Officially this was to see the bull fights, but some cadets found their way to more interesting but more perilous activities.

The cruises were the highlight of the school year. On the first cruise as lower classmen, we did the work of seamen. On the second cruise as upper classmen, we did the work of ship's officers. We learned to function in both calm and rough seas. We were taught and practiced launching boats and handling the ship in rough weather. The cadets, depending on their class, worked in every function concerned with the operation of the ship, from the most low level to the most difficult jobs. Living aboard ship enhanced our ability to adjust to the working conditions while under way. But the final test was the rating of our performance on the cruise. Deck cadets were required to take frequent sexton sights of the sun and stars and to maintain their own position plots. The cruise served as a laboratory in which we were tested on whether we could project our training to the bridge of a ship at sea.

As a lower classman I worked in the scullery. We collected the dishes, placed them in racks, and passed them through a dish washing machine. This presented no problem in port or in calm seas; but in rough seas, the racks would come flying out as the ship rolled. We could not contain the racks without risking serious injury to those who tried to hold the rack back. Racks full of dishes hit the deck with a loud crash. Every member of the scullery team would be given a demerit for each dish broken, so we devised a system.

If more than one dish were broken, we rushed to throw all but one dish over the side through the nearest porthole before Master-at-Arms Reiser arrived. With a downcast look in our eyes, we held the one broken dish up to show him. Reiser would look at the dish and then at us with no expression. We knew he was near sighted, and we could see him blinking through his eye glasses. I was never certain whether he went along with the charade or whether he actually was unable to see clearly enough to assess the situation. I am inclined to believe we were not fooling him, but we still received only one demerit for each incident.

The problem did not end there. Inevitably, as time went by and more and more dishes were broken, we would not have enough remaining to feed the Cadet Corps. We, therefore, prevailed on the lower classmen at the head of the line to rush through their meal so we could get the dishes back before the end of the line reached the cafeteria. Lcdr. Gandleman, the Supply Officer, not fooled by this situation, sympathized with the cadets. He issued replacement dishes until they ran out—which ultimately happened. Towards the end of the cruise, it became a foot race, but a solution nevertheless.

From Gibraltar we sailed to Northern Europe, stopping in Antwerp, Belgium, Plymouth, England, and Cork, Ireland, before setting sail for the long return voyage. In those days we cruised slowly for long stretches at sea, interrupted by ten-day visits in each port.

In Antwerp we tied up alongside an elevated promenade where people out for a stroll looked down on us as we looked up at them. I visited Paris with a tour group. One of my best friends, now a retired professor of engineering from King's Point, met his future wife during the tour. I saw the Sandberg family often in the years to come. Meanwhile girl watching and flirting between shipmates and women strolling along the promenade became an interesting pastime. In later years I spent a great deal of time in Antwerp, but specifics of the 1934 port-call are only a blur.

The Royal Navy gave us an excellent reception in Plymouth, England. Gieves, the venerable British tailor to the Royal Navy, delivered the topcoats we had ordered some months earlier in New York. Most naval and the few merchant marine officers who had access to these excellent coats cherished them. We could wear them with either uniforms or civilian clothes.

As I neared completion of my first year, I was making friendships that would last for a lifetime. Even our mortal enemies in the upper classes stopped their harassment and accepted us as friends and shipmates. Captain Tomb and the officers, who rarely paid attention to us, now took a personal interest in helping us make the grade. As the cruise progressed much of the tension eased and the overall atmosphere improved.

We sailed from Plymouth to Cork, where the Royal Cork Yacht Club held a reception for us. Later we played a British Officer's tennis team in the rain on a grass court. The Major explained that if they waited for a clear day, rarely would they get a chance to play. Needless to say we lost, thus continuing our perfect record. I joined the Major and his wife for dinner that evening. After Cork we began the long voyage to New York. By now we knew the ropes—we knew what it took to man the ship. A calm, professional attitude replaced earlier chaos.

We were welcomed home by a large crowd of visitors, including my mother and the press. No longer was I the insecure young man who had sailed away. My mother and I embraced. She smiled, and I smiled back. No words were necessary. She knew immediately I had matured from a boy into a self-assured young man.

The cruise lasted three months. On our return we were granted 30 days leave. How or where I spent the time is no longer a memory. Once back at the Academy, however, I worked hard to be sure I graduated. Classes continued very much as in the prior year, except I no longer was a mug, free of harassment, and knew the routine. I was at ease in the environment, and although still restricted in my social life due the lack of funds, I was surviving.

I do not regret the formal, advanced education I sacrificed by selecting this unique school. Something about it could not be equaled. Where else would classmates endure such hardships together, live in close quarters, and literally become a family? The two NYSMMA Classes of '35 graduated fewer than 60. In comparison the U.S. Naval Academy Class of '35 graduated 442. When the Naval Academy made its summer cruise, the midshipmen were aboard battleships. Together with the total complement of officers and crew, they overwhelmed the ports they visited. We just sort of touched the ports lightly.

In the winter of '35 the usual routine was broken by a short cruise to Savannah, Georgia. We sailed into a rough winter sea. Not far out of port we responded to a distress call from a coastal schooner. Soon we sighted her listing heavily in rough seas. After we established she was not sinking, we shot a Lyle Gun line over. They attached a tow line. We winched it in, secured it to a bit on the stern, and then towed the schooner to a safe anchorage. Commander Charles Schutz, our Executive Officer, who ran the day-to-day routine of the Academy and the ship, was an excellent seaman. We jumped to his orders; and with the successful completion of this rescue, we arrived in Savannah on a high note. It was a happy ship.

In Savannah cadets, each in their own way, were trying to come to grips with the repressive times that, together with the general lack of cash, impeded their practical sexual education. One of my classmates, who looked younger than I but was actually older, tried desperately to give the impression of maturity. Although he had pink cheeks and hardly shaved, he smoked big cigars and spoke in a gruff voice. In short he had adopted the attitude of a hardened sailor man.

Houses of prostitution, alive and well in Savannah, operated close to where the ship docked. One night as several classmates and I returned to the ship, we passed an unimpressive old house on a quite street. Suddenly the quiet of the night was shattered. Tumbling out the door came one of our classmates. As our hero stumbled and fell to the ground, a huge bouncer threw a black bowler hat after him. At the same time a window was opened on the second story. An equally huge woman, her breasts falling over the sill, shouted out, "Yo skinny ass, get outta heah fast or I'll thro a pot o piss in yo face."

We watched in amazement as our classmate picked up his hat, gave the woman and us a dirty look, and moved off in haste. Our boy simply was trying to grow up too fast. We never learned about what happened in the house.

Cadets had to leave and return to the ship in dress uniforms. By adding a black bowler hat, this cadet was attempting to disguise his cadet identity and beat the system. Basically he was comical, but he took himself seriously. He never bothered anyone, got along, was a good student, but had few close friends among the Cadet Corps. Our hero was not known to be a cadet of means. He graduated, but after graduation he just disappeared. I never saw him again nor in later years did I meet other classmates who saw or heard of him. He could have died at sea during the war, or have been killed in a bar-room or whore-house brawl.

The ship returned from Savannah without incident. In May we sailed as first classmen to Bermuda and Europe on our last cruise as cadets. Again we were given receptions at the ports of call. The U.S. Minister to Denmark, the first woman believed appointed to so high a diplomatic post, held an unusual reception when we reached Copenhagen. The coordination and a large percentage of the cost of the event was paid for by Captain William Rague. A graduate of the Class of '14, Captain Rague was the General Manager of the Moore-McCormack Lines for Scandinavia.

Nearly 100 sailing yachts escorted us to our berth. The party, which continued during our entire visit, began with a beach party given by the Madam Minister. Each cadet paired off with a lovely young Danish girl. I don't recall one escort who was not comely or who could not speak English. A number of cocktail and dinner parties followed. As a first classman I was able to attend many of them.

Some of us, having spent too much money in Bermuda before reaching Copenhagen, were already short of cash. Although we experienced another tennis team loss in Bermuda, we had no time for tennis in Copenhagen. We were sad to leave. The party was fantastic beyond our wildest dreams. Unfortunately I was running short of cash, and there were two or three more ports of call prior to our departure for home.

I was to be the recipient of money from Heaven; however, I had no indication that it was on its way. Sometime before National Maritime Day, the Propeller Club offered $50 to the cadet who wrote the best essay on the American Merchant Marine. I snooped around and was unable to find any other cadet interested in the contest. It took me about one hour to write the essay, have it typed in the ship's office, and send it in. Then I forgot about it. While still in Europe, not knowing how and if to approach my mother for more funds, I received a letter from Arthur M. Tode, President of the

Propeller Club, with a check for $50. I don't recall what I wrote about.

Our next stop was Leith, the port of Edinburgh, Scotland. Here I saw a parade in which King George V and Queen Mary passed by in an open, horse-drawn carriage. The pomp and splendor of the parade impressed me, but the Scots standing nearby were quite disrespectful.

As our voyage progressed my time at NYSMMA was coming to an end. I had passed the cruise requirements and was prepared to sit for my Third Mate's License on arrival in New York. Shortly after we arrived I sat for my license before the Steamboat Inspection Service, which was the government agency in charge. I passed. In September I graduated with my class in a ceremony held on the floor of the Maritime Exchange at 80 Broad Street. My mother attended.

Although the class had grown close over the two years, we would soon disperse to the far corners of the world. Future meetings would be rare. Steamship companies had very little in common, and thus no common denominator to draw us together, such as in the Navy or the Coast Guard.

In 1935 licensed officer jobs were rare and wages quite low. I started looking for employment before graduation. At that time the list of the major steamship lines serving New York was impressive, yet only one unimportant line still exists today. The number of ships providing scheduled liner services carrying passengers, mail, and freight must have numbered in the hundreds. Other than U.S. Flag ships engaged in domestic trades, most were subsidized if they operated in the essential trade routes of the U.S.

I felt I had little or no chance of getting a job based on my license, but I was determined not to take any more money from my mother. I would take the first job offered. On graduation day I heard that Grace Line was hiring. If interested I was to be in the front of their main pier in Brooklyn early the next morning. This type of hiring was not unique on the piers of New York. Longshoremen were hired daily in the same manner, except they referred to it as a "shape up." In this case at least it would not be a daily event. And if there was mutual satisfaction, the job would last.

It was a demeaning situation, one that exists today only in the theater. Those not hired simply walked away discouraged and went on to the next event. In this instance an official from the Grace Line personnel office stood on a platform. Below him a clerk sat at a desk. Using a megaphone he shouted out a job description. Qualified seamen presented their credentials to the clerk. Those that passed the initial screening, which was quick, were then selected or dismissed as the case might be. Those selected received a slip with the name of the ship, the pier, and when and to whom to report.

When they called for a Cadet Officer, I went to the desk. With a license I was promptly hired to sign on *S.S. Santa Clara*. She was berthed alongside the adjacent dock loading for her southbound voyage to about 15 ports including Havana, Kingston, Panama, and the west coast of South America as far south as Southern Chile. Within an hour I signed the ship's articles and reported to my assigned cabin. I found A.C. Ingersoll, Jr., standing there. We would be sharing the cabin.

Ingersoll stood number one in the class. He was 22 or 23 at the time, while I was still only 19. His father owned the Ingersoll McNally Towing Company, which operated on the Ohio River. Ingersoll was brilliant but somewhat eccentric. In spite of the differences in our ages, we had gotten along at the Academy, and we were to get along well together aboard *Santa Clara*.

Looking Back

The cruises were the most important part of my education at the New York State Merchant Marine Academy, and the military training gave the whole experience something extra. Academic hazing was somewhat inconsistent with the boiler plate studies required for a degree in those days. But in two years, and counting the cruises as a lab experience, we put in more hours than those required for a degree in many colleges. The courses were not easy, and the graduates as a whole compared favorably with those of many of the accredited colleges of the time.

Moreover it was an experience difficult to equal today. Our instructors, all amateurs, instilled in us a desire to learn and the wherewithal to survive not only at sea but in the world that awaited us. It was a school afloat in a world that held the key to adventure for those who desired it, but would never have found it without NYSMMA.

Superintendent Tomb was an exceptional leader. Commander Schutz, who ran the Deck Course, was an excellent instructor, administrator, and seaman. The Chief Engineer, Commander Gronbeck, and Carl Maas, the Assistant Chief Engineer, were talented instructors, as was our electrical engineering instructor, Lt. Perkins, affectionately known as "Juice." The bane of my existence was Master-at-Arms Reiser. I disliked him at the time, but in retrospect I appreciate him. He never got off my back when I was a lower classman. But I now realize he had not signaled me out for his ire. He was consistent in his harassment, and it was all part of my education. Hiram Gandleman, a respected Supply Officer, spent a lifetime at the school, always helpful, and liked and trusted by the cadets. Lucien Pineda, a Filipino, ran the barbershop and the cadet store. These were our leaders.

All those I mention here are long gone from this earth but are among the many "ghosts" in my memory. In my days at the Academy they were important. They did the job extremely well.

Dorothy Chester, mother of Alvin Chester, About 1920.

Alvin Chester,
about age 3,
in his first sailor suit. Father,
J. Nicholas Chester,
in background.
Photo taken in the area
of Fort George, Washington
Heights, upper Manhattan.

My first sail,
Libau, Latvia, 1924. J. Nicholas
Chester, foreground,
informal for this event in a
tweed suit, vest, and tie, with
his sister and friends in
in her yacht.

NYSMMA Tennis Team in Hamilton, Bermuda, spring 1935. L-R: Cadets Nissen, Barnard, Keats, Warrant Officer Penn, Cadets Chester (Captain), Finnan, and Ebbets.

T.S. Empire State, *Antwerp, Belgium, July 1934, during Cadet 3rd Class Al Chester's lower-class cruise to Europe.*

*3rd Class Cadet
Al Chester in undress whites
on the forward well deck of
T.S. Empire State,
1934.*

*NYSMMA
graduating class,
September 1935.
L-R:Cadets Ivanyshyn,
Barrett, Hoskins, Sierra (Cadet
Officer of Day), Sefton, N.N.
Robinson, Beale, Longhurst,
MacKenzie, Chester, Van
Hoesen, Kunz, Ingersoll, Flint,
W.F. Robinson.*

Two

Adventure

S.S. *Santa Clara*

Although a Cadet or Apprentice rating had been common in the merchant marine for years, "Cadet Officer" was peculiar to U.S. Flag ships and an expediency of Yankee economy that evolved following World War I. Faced with a shortage of licensed officers at the start of the war, the Steamboat Inspection Service had relaxed its requirements in order to generate officers for a rapidly expanding fleet. By the end of the war, surplus ships were laid up or sold to foreign carriers. But the surplus of licensed officers created economical options for the lines.

In most maritime nations you had to serve three years of sea time in an unlicensed capacity before becoming eligible to sit for a Third Mate's License. Some companies, to ensure a supply of officers with a basic education, set up their own cadet system. A young man's parents would pay the line to teach their son a trade. Permanent employment would be offered when the young man completed his apprenticeship and passed his license examination.

It was a kind of indenture. In Britain this system was common in the Navy and the Merchant Marine. The Royal Navy school at Dartmouth accepted young men in their early teens and, after two-years training, assigned them as a Midshipmen in the Fleet. The Merchant Marine conducted two shore-based pre-cadet preparatory schools aboard the sailing ships *Conway* and *Worcester*. Needless to say better lines selected cadets from the schoolships. Still once at sea as either a Midshipman or a Cadet, the only stipend a Cadet might receive was a bit of spending money. But he did live and eat with the ship's officers.

The Apprentice-Cadet System was rarely formalized in U.S. Flag ships. You went to sea either as a Cadet at a very low salary or as an ordinary seaman. Once Cadets put their time in, they attended a cram school before taking the examination. Life in the focs'l was rough, and many intelligent young men were discouraged. Aside from marlin spike seamanship, their formal education came to an abrupt halt. One reason the state merchant marine academies and the state nautical schools were formed was to ensure a regular supply of qualified licensed officers.

With an oversupply of licensed officers in 1935, several passenger-line companies replaced the two-officer watch system ordinarily used with one licensed officer and one licensed Cadet. When they could hire one, Grace Line paid a Cadet $30 a month. Licensed Cadets received $50 a month. Not only did these Cadets perform duties ordinarily performed by officers, they also did the work of unlicensed seamen, whom the companies had to pay much more. The Cadet Officer gave up a great deal to eat and live better, and hope for a faster promotion. On boarding *Santa Clara* as a Cadet Officer, I fell into this category.

The U.S. government at the time recognized the need to maintain a U.S. flag Merchant Marine as an essential industry of the United States. This was and would still be a good policy if it were not abused and distorted. Grace Line, for example, had a subsidy for the area it serviced. The direct benefit to the U.S. economy was evident—U.S. exports successfully penetrated the markets they served, and imports entered the country at a fair rate.

Grace Line's virtual monopoly in the trade was at its peak in 1935. *S.S. Santa Clara,* one of three similar fast passenger and freighters, operated a biweekly service to Havana, Kingston, Panama, and the west coast of South America. This service was supplemented by small ships that sailed intermittently between the three principal ships scheduled in that service. Two newer and slightly larger ships, *Santa Paula* and *Rosa,* serviced the Caribbean , Venezuela, and Columbia.

Santa Clara, nearly 8,500 gross tons, carried over 200 passengers and about 6,000 tons of freight and mail. She was a modern turboelectric, twin screw propelled ship that cruised at about 20 knots. Her Captain was of Norwegian origin, taciturn, and an excellent seaman. Although I was often in his presence, he rarely spoke to me and even kept his conversations with senior officers to a minimum. The Chief Officer, an ex-Imperial Russian Naval Officer, was a screamer and an over-reactor. He was intelligent, nevertheless, and not really a bad guy, even though Cadet Officers working

30

under him never had a free moment. Often he came by Ingersoll's and my room to pass on some words of wisdom or an order.

This ship had an unusual atmosphere I never again experienced. No one was deliberately unfriendly, but each officer rarely referred to matters unrelated to the job. Ingersoll and I spent eight hours on different watches, which left only eight hours off watch together to perform other jobs yet still find time to sleep. Sea watch schedules of four hours on and eight hours off were maintained throughout the voyage. At sea we stood watches on the bridge. In port we worked in the hatches discharging and loading cargo. Although a less demanding routine than we were accustomed to at school, something about the atmosphere repelled me. I never felt comfortable on this ship.

Though the routine itself was not difficult, the work schedule was inhuman, and the restrictions placed on us archaic. Fraternizing with passengers was not allowed. Associating with the waitresses, many of whom were quite pretty, was taboo. One of my off-time assignments was to help the Sea Post clerks in the mailroom, and I had to pass through the female quarters to get there. I was supposed to ring a bell and count to 30 before starting my "eyes-forward" passage. Instead I rang the bell, shouted, "coming through," and slowly walked through the quarters. The women threw brassieres, panties, and stockings at me, but they went along with the game and never made a complaint. On the few occasions when Ingersoll and I could talk, we joked about this little "to do" in what was mostly a monotonous voyage.

What could have been a good job was offset by a fear of losing the job for any number of reasons unrelated to reality. Seniors among the deck officers seemed to be the most affected. With more than ten ports on the itinerary, they were either tired or completely exhausted. Loading and discharging cargo for a large number of ports creates tremendous problems. At each port we had to separate the cargo. We had even greater problems sorting it under the time pressures of the southbound voyage. Inevitably some cargo was carried to the next port or even to a subsequent one. The officer responsible could be discharged for this oversight, and those senior and junior to him reprimanded. In the short time I served on *Santa Clara,* I knew the officers to be sober and competent.

Many ports were open roadstead ports where we had to anchor off the port and discharge cargo into small lighters. Passengers disembarked onto a launch through a sea gangway rigged from a sideport. In some cases they stepped directly off the sideport exit to the launch. Occasionally a swell

31

would cause the ship to roll heavily, creating a potentially dangerous problem with the discharge operation. Things were easier in port. We docked in Havana and Kingston, and I spent a few hours ashore in each city. Havana was an exciting port for sailors. If you had the money nearly anything you desired was available. I had just enough money to look, but neither the time nor the money to enjoy the better offerings. Kingston was just hot. We docked in Buenaventura, Columbia, during a rain storm, which made the town appear to be a mud hole. Since I had to work I went ashore for only a short time. We also stopped in Guayaquil, Ecuador, where the thing to do was buy a Panama hat. I did.

The ports we docked at prior to passing through the Panama Canal offered little to visiting sailors, except the usual tropical fleshpots that were interesting to observe but dangerous to touch. On the Pacific side we stopped at Valporaiso and Callao. Callao served Lima, the capital city of Peru. Somehow I found time to spend an evening in Lima with a ship's officer who knew his way around. The city itself was beautiful, steeped in history, the food good and cheap, and the diversions exciting and safe.

I visited Valporaiso, another beautiful city, where again I was in the company of a seasoned ship's officer. The problem in these shore escapades was always time, money, and being tired from an exhausting schedule. Rarely did I ever sleep more than four hours a day. I coped, but the senior officers did not fare as well, if at all. Being unable to keep up the pace did not bode well for a future in the Grace Line. I did not covet these officers' position.

Although no one complained openly on the ship, the unhappiness of many was obvious and surfaced in different ways. Grace Line demanded 100 percent loyalty, promised security and advancement in return, but expected personnel to work much harder for less than available elsewhere. In my experience Grace Line was the greatest proponent of lifetime security during a depression, while still being very inconsiderate of the basic needs of their people. It was an outstanding example of a type of management that gave the union movement, only simmering at the time, the opportunity to exploit an adversarial position towards the shipping industry.

When we returned to New York, I was undecided about making another voyage. At the time sailors contracted for employment aboard ships by signing articles of employment for a single voyage. These articles were witnessed by the Master with whom you agreed to sail, and also by a Shipping Commissioner ostensibly there to ensure your rights as a seamen were protected.

This procedure was a carry-over from làws originally enacted to protect illiterate and ignorant seamen from being exploited by ship owners and ship masters. Seamen, in a sense, were considered wards of the court. The contract articles they signed stipulated not only wages but the conditions on board as well. In 1935 continued employment was ordinarily accepted.

It had been a long, hard voyage, and I worked many hours in the cargo holds, on the bridge, and on menial jobs. But it was an invaluable learning experience. This was the first time I got my feet wet in the mean, old, hard world of the sea. I discovered going to sea was more than a job; it was a way of life. I did not care, however, for the way of life on *Santa Clara.*

For the first time I did not make a close friend, nor did I look up to or respect anyone enough to care to emulate him. When the Chief Officer gave me an argument because I asked for a few hours off to go to the dentist, I used it as an excuse to resign. He was not out of character in his denial, and would have granted the time after an argument. I surprised him when I quit.

Owen Murphy of the alumni employment office knew every graduate; only 13 had completed the deck course in my class. So after leaving the dentist's office, I gave him a call. He asked me why I left the Grace Line, and when I told him, he understood. He did not know of any Third Mate jobs available at the time. Murphy, however, thought I should ship out as a Cadet Officer for a few months to gain more experience. He knew of several Cadet Officer jobs and recommended one in *S.S. Excalibur,* the flagship of the American Export Line. I'd make only $50 a month, but the job would be much more interesting. Since they carried only one Cadet Officer, I would have a room to myself in the Officer's Quarters. In reality I would be a Junior Officer.

The Mediterranean itinerary intrigued me, and I told Murphy I would take the job if he could arrange it. He telephoned the Port Captain and confirmed it. Owen Murphy ran his office well. When I left, I knew I not only had a friend, but also was a part of a family that followed the sea. I reported aboard *S.S. Excalibur* at the Harborside Terminal in Jersey City the next day.

S.S. Excalibur

Somewhat ahead of its time, Harborside Terminal housed stores, restaurants, office space, warehouse space, and a whole range of interrelated businesses connected with shipping into one center. Aside from the tenancy of the American Export Line, however, it failed either to generate much business for other lines or exploit the peripheral businesses contemplated.

To get there I took the Hudson Tubes commuter line from its downtown terminal and stopped at Jersey City, a ten-minute ride. *S.S. Excalibur,* docked at Pier D, was one of four post World War I built passenger and cargo ships designed and constructed for the American Export Line. The others, *Exeter, Excambion,* and *Exchorda,* were popular though small. Called the Four Aces, they sailed on alternate weeks from New York to the Mediterranean. Basically a new vessel *Excalibur* and her sisterships, although much slower, smaller, and less luxurious than their foreign competitors, were the only U.S. passenger ships built for this trade.

At least a dozen Hog Island A Class vessels similar to *T.S. Empire State,* all built during World War I, supplemented the work of the Four Aces. They carried freight, mail, and a few passengers. Enemy action sank *Excalibur* and *Exeter* during World War II.

Compared to the luxurious 50,000-gross ton Italian liners *Rex* and *Conti DI Savoia,* the Four Aces were of little consequence in size and speed. Under 10,000 gross tons, they had a hard time making 16 knots against the 20 knots or more of their competitors. Biweekly sailings against the weekly sailings of the Italian Line didn't offer much competition either.

But the Four Aces traveled the whole of the Mediterranean as far east as Beirut. Transatlantic Italian Line ship routes terminated in Italy. Each U.S. ship carried about 250 passengers and 7,000 tons of freight, which was heavily counted on for income. They also benefited from the differential operating subsidy paid by the U.S. Government. Although I was too young to realize it, the USA had forfeited its rightful position in the trade to the Italians, whose subsidy, indirect and direct, to their ships was much greater than ours.

As soon as I stepped aboard *Excalibur,* I felt more at home than in *Santa Clara.* I reported to the Chief Officer, an alumnus of the Massachusetts Nautical School, who was unpretentious and friendly. He questioned me about my experience and schooling , and seemed pleased to hear I was an Academy graduate. Before his steward showed me to my cabin, the Chief Officer told me he would introduce me to the other officers at lunch, but the Captain was usually unavailable. My cabin was smaller but nicer than the room in *Santa Clara,* and it was all mine. Privacy at last. No one rushed me as I stowed my gear, and when I finished it was lunchtime.

Unlike the quiet, dreary mess of *Santa Clara,* the crew here was friendly and talkative. I met the First Officer, also a graduate of the Massachusetts school. As the Senior Watch Stander he told me I would stand the four to eight watch with him at sea. I would have nights off in ports when sea watches were broken, as they were in New York. He also said that if I had business to finish before we sailed to just notify him when I left and when I would return. Even though the officers and unlicensed personnel were friendly, no one would give me a direct answer when I asked about the Captain. They knew I would find out in time. I easily fitted into the routine as the ship finished unloading cargo and then loaded for the outbound voyage. The constant tension in *Santa Clara* did not exist in *Excalibur*. Together with fellow crewmen, I oversaw the cargo operations and the various preparations for the voyage. Unlicensed personnel kept tally of the unloading and loading. Our schedule called for an eight-week turnaround with one week in New York. Within a few days we sailed, and I began my fourth eastbound voyage of the Atlantic Ocean. Although we were taking the southern route, all indications were that it would be a rough crossing— and it was.

When I was introduced to the Captain, he paid no more attention to me than he seemed to pay to anyone else. A tall, bandy-legged, heavy man, he seemed oblivious to all that went on around him. Rarely did anyone have a conversation with him. The officers and crew referred to him as "Poppsy." On his ship, however, we could mingle with passengers.

Once we were under way my on-the-job training began in earnest. The First Officer meticulously taught me the routine by making me do everything he did. We took sights together, worked out star positions, compared our celestial positions with our dead reckoning, and charted the course. Every watch I stood with him was a post-graduate course. He made it almost a crusade to pass as much of his knowledge as possible on to me. In reality I had a private tutor in this brilliant man. But he had a problem.

He was separated or divorced from his wife, and he had a son. Apparently he missed them both. But torn between his love for his family and his love for the sea, he could do little about it unless he left the sea. He did not want to work ashore, however. This infatuation with the sea was not uncommon, even though the job typically required you to spend all but two weeks of the year at sea. You might catch a few days shore leave when the ship docked at a port close to your home. More often than not a seaman had no choice—his education was too limited. The First Officer had a choice; he could have hacked it ashore, and he knew it. He just could not bring himself to leave the sea.

I learned this from the many conversations I had with the First Officer during our hours on watch, and from things the Chief Officer said to me. The Chief Officer had managed to keep his family intact during his long periods at sea. Still family life seemed to me a hopeless situation for anyone who followed my chosen profession.

We crossed the Atlantic in about eight or nine days and made a short stop in the Azores. I went ashore with the Captain to clear the ship in Palma, Majorca. I doubt if he even knew I was along. Poppsy was in a world unto himself. He didn't say much, and when he did talk his comments were irrelevant. Occasionally he sat in his high chair on the bridge chewing on a cigar. Whenever we went over the waves, he would exclaim, "Whee!" One time as *S.S. Rex* passed us in the Straits of Gibraltar, he became annoyed. He lumbered out of his high chair, wallowed to the end of the bridge, and screamed at this beautiful, huge, luxury liner, "You think you're good, but one of these days we'll open this ship up and pass you." Then, disgruntled, he worked his way to his cabin mumbling to himself. The officers and crew were accustomed his behavior. And since he rarely bothered them or interfered in the routine of the ship, they tolerated him. Although he looked like a typical old sea dog, he most often acted confused.

We sailed to Marseilles without incident. The First Officer did most of the navigating, and I worked along with him. Because it was a rough trip and they rarely came on deck, I saw little of the passengers. Mostly I studied the work laid out for me: the cargo plan and the procedure for unloading and loading in Marseilles. Our schedule of port calls was not as tight as in *Santa Clara,* and communications between the officers were better. When arrangements for the cargo operations were in place and under way, I want ashore with the Second and Third Officers while the Chief Officer and the First Officer supervised the cargo operations. The First Officer had arranged this shore excursion for me as a "learning experience."

Old timers in the trade, the two Mates knew all the colorful joints. In turn they were known by the owners and others who frequented them. The clubs had unusual names, and we visited a few before arriving at the most infamous: the "Bucket of Blood." Here the music was French, with singers and sad love songs. The dancing was sexual. The customers were mostly seamen, and the women were all professionals of varying ages, types, and dress. Owners and the girls welcomed back old customers, giving them confidential advice about a new girl, or an old one who had a new trick.

This sailor's home away from home became an outlet for sentiments that had built up over long periods at sea. Some seamen, after a few drinks, became melancholy and within this atmosphere found their "Dulcinea." In turn some of these hardened prostitutes, heavily under the influence of liquor, and looking for their "Man of La Mancha," would find him. Each saw in the other what they dreamed of rather than what was there. A mutual illusion might give a short time of pleasure and satisfaction, provided one did not sober up before the other. It was a play between people with toughened emotions. A sudden personality change could and did occasionally end in violence.

Seamen in those days of low wages, hard work, poor food, and impossible living conditions hoarded their meager pay over long periods for a few hours ashore in places that catered to them. They were like latent time bombs. Club owners were obviously in it for the money. They dealt with a new cast of characters every night as the ships rotated in their calls at port. Still they too became attached to some of their customers over time. In some cases the affection shown to a sailor "home" from the seas was not altogether put on; the girls became as much a part of the atmosphere as those who patronized them. This exception and not the rule ordinarily resulted in a change of attitude once the sailor's money ran out. Clever club owners and the girls who worked for them became masters at keeping customers satisfied and peaceful in this game played on both sides of the bar. Every man was "Cheri" to the girls, and when insulted reacted in different ways. The women could be as violent as the men, being more easily hurt by words.

The night at the Bucket of Blood started well, and I could not imagine a Broadway show more interesting: melancholy music, the sexy singer, smoke filling the air, international characters, spontaneous reaction to the liquor, and constant games played between each other and the girls. While taking this all in with my two shipmates, suddenly I heard someone shout: "So it's chairs you want," and chairs and bottles began flying through the air. I recall nothing more. The next morning I woke up aboard ship in the sick bay with the doctor and the First Officer at my side.

The doctor told me I would be okay and teased me about busting up the Bucket of Blood. I was now initiated into the brotherhood, having contributed my blood to the nightclub. My shipmates had brought me back, and this episode became a subject of kidding for many days at sea. In keeping with tradition a few moments of excitement, love, or whatever ashore have to entertain your shipmates for many dull days at sea.

The Mediterranean was filled with gathering places for sailors in port for a few hours or a few days. All were much more interesting to me than the fleshpots of Latin America. More ships under many different flags called at these ports, whereas few had docked in the Latin American ports I visited. Seamen had friends and enemies on other ships and would meet in the ports with sentimental results on one hand and sometimes murder on the other. Now I was experiencing romance and adventure, and it was a far cry from the peacefulness and tranquillity I grew up in. I definitely preferred these exciting scenes, so soon to pass, to listening to some dull professor talk about something he had read but never experienced.

The nightclubs and brothels covered a wide range of class and style. Some overlapped into more respectable areas and customers, but most were exciting. Although seamen were economically restricted to water-front dives, the officers could wander farther afield into the more affluent places. My fellow officers guided me well, introducing me to all levels of the society of the times. Some of the nightclubs and brothels in Naples, Genoa, Leghorn, and Malaga were almost beyond my imagination. Not all of the women were pretty, but some were not only lovelier than the movie stars of the day but were charming. Spain and Italy were not very expensive; and here in addition to the brothels and nightclubs, I found delightful places to dine, dance, and listen to music now no longer played. The cities were beautiful and bathed in history. Because we stayed in most ports a few days, we had a chance to discover interesting areas and on some occasions get to know the people.

My tutors took it all in with a sense of humor. They guided me carefully and went to extremes to keep me out of trouble, which was often around me. Alexandria, Egypt, featured some of the best and the worst places. My friends only showed me the door to the worst. I remember the address but not the name of one place, No. 9 Sister Street. It was so bad that my companions would not even enter. Another club not far from Mohammed Alley Square, near the center of the city, had a name more colorful than the establishment—"Big Tit Marie's." Again, a French tone played to the nightlife of Alexandria. In contrast to the normal sailor's night club, the Trianon was very expensive. While Big Tits would be friendly to a lowly seaman until his money ran out, prices at the Trianon were high enough to embarrass the rich.

We called at Jaffa and Haifa in Palestine, but could not go ashore in Jaffa. Our stays in small, serene Haifa were short. Beirut was something else again. It was very expensive. At each check point in going ashore, I had to pay baksheesh. We visited a lush place called the Kit Cat Club, and also a lovely beach and an exclusive beach club. Beirut was a little Paris and way beyond my means.

Times have changed. Seamen now get half their time off, and the ships are bigger and manned by fewer crewmen. Container ships are in and out of ports in hours rather than days. Officers often take their wives or girlfriends with them, and seamen are so well paid that most are homebodies. After my first indoctrination, I soon found my own way into the less colorful but more respectable areas of the ports we visited. But I will never forget the fleshpots my shipmates introduce me to. It was something to have seen what no longer exists—the places and the types of people who inhabited them. Ships are made of cold steel, but those that sail them are human. For many of these men, the hardships endured during those days created a psyche within a psyche, which bordered on insanity. Some survived and prospered in spite of it all.

Underlying all this was always the sea, sometimes predictable and sometimes chaotic. The voyage to the Mediterranean and back was very rough that winter. The ship had to be carefully handled in heavy seas, and we were under strong pressure to maintain schedule. We had to get the last knot out of the ship without sinking it, heavily damaging it, or injuring passengers and crew. The First Officer showed me different tactics in different seas, and how to weather them best.

We faced fog and rain, and at times approaching or leaving New York, ice and snow. Rough seas can buffet the largest of ships like a cork. Everything in and on the ship must be secured to withstand these movements. A feeling of depression pervades the atmosphere when barometric pressures fall. The overall job of sailing the ship, loading and discharging it, and constantly being ready for the unexpected might be called a "major" in both seamanship and life. Here the lives of many depended on a few experienced men. The essence of my training was to realize a ship at sea was always in danger and to know how to respond to it.

As *S.S. Excalibur* plied back and forth across the Atlantic and Mediterranean, war clouds were gathering. Subsequent events would not only affect my life but extend all the way back to my friends, safe at home in Manhattan, absorbing words of wisdom from their professors. I was in a different type of school, even though my leading professor was an alcoholic losing his fight with the bottle.

History was in the making at the time. One day I went ashore in Naples, expecting a pleasant visit to a picturesque city. Suddenly everything seemed to erupt. That very day Mussolini had declared Italy an Empire.

Bands came marching down the street. Various uniformed and ununiformed groups emerged as crowds gathered. As night fell fireworks lit up the sky. The enthusiasm of the Black-Shirted Fascists expanded to the ecstasy of the masses shouting "Viva Il Duce." I was pushed and shoved by the crowd, but in no danger—it was a festive occasion. Italians have their own ways of expressing things. Although the fascist salute was giving the crowd sore right arms, here and there I saw a more common Italian expression of "giving the finger." The mass hysteria resulted from the people's reaction to hearing what they wanted to hear and not considering the consequences. If the majority were as happy as they appeared or even if there was no organized opposition, it still was an ill wind.

My window on the world faced in all directions. When *Excalibur* berthed in Naples or Genoa, I saw troopships leaving for Ethiopia, usually during daylight hours, with bands playing and thousands on the dock to see them off to victory and "Empire." Often when working late at night or before dawn, I saw an entirely different scene. In the dark hours a hospital ship would quietly slip into a pier adjacent to us, and ambulances would draw up in lines to the gangway. Without bands or enthusiastic crowds, other than an itinerant seaman on a nearby ship, the wounded—some walking and some on stretchers—would be disembarked. At the same time corpses were quietly removed from the ship into waiting vans. By daylight the ship, the ambulances, and the vans would be gone. Soon another troopship would berth to embark another contingent of soldiers, with the bands playing and the crowds cheering them on. Italy was beginning to pay the price of being an empire and would do so for many years to come.

As I watched the scene from the deck of *Excalibur* and ashore, however, I was impressed by what I saw. Even at a young age my intuition led me to understand that peace and tranquillity, even though accompanied by a depression, were coming to an end.

Mussolini's colleague in Germany was growing stronger, and the Spanish ports at which we called were soon to be involved in an expanding insurrection. General Franco, supported by both Germany and Italy, was on his way to taking over power in 1939. I noticed other signs of war, but I could not as yet place them in the context of the whole.

At the eastern end of the Mediterranean, we anchored off the Palestine port of Jaffa to disembark passengers. Overnight in Haifa we discharged and loaded cargo and embarked passengers. Once in Jaffa I noticed a ship anchored close by what looked like *Estonia*. I asked the agent if it was. It was the sistership *Polonia,* he said, transporting Jewish immigrants to

40

Palestine from northern Europe. By 1936 anti-Semitic undertones growing in force in that area had already created enough fear for many Jews to risk an exodus to an unknown destiny in a land to be embroiled in years of war.

I enjoyed all my five trips in *Excalibur*. We got the trade to non-Italian ports east and west of Italy, while the Italian ships concentrated and terminated in Italy. We were about 60 to 70 percent full in the winter and probably close to capacity in the summer. We were generally full of cargo. And we carried everything. One time we even transported a circus— elephants and all.

One day I was called down from the bridge to intercede in a fracas between a man and his wife who were fighting outside the Purser's office. I arrived on the scene to find the Purser, several members of his staff, and some passengers watching the scene. The wife lay on the deck and the husband was kicking her in the body and the face. With as much authority in my voice as I could muster, I ordered him to stop. He ignored me. No one did anything, and blood appeared on the woman's face. The husband must have been about 45 and not too big, so I grabbed him and started to pull him away. By that time his wife was screaming and yelling curse words that even made this sailor blush.

He resisted my efforts to pull him off, and we scuffled and fell to the deck. As I tried to subdue him, his wife got up, took off a shoe, and started to hit me with it on my head and face. The Purser pulled her away. The husband got up, gave me a nasty look, took his wife by the hand, and the two marched off as if nothing had happened. I didn't know what the argument was all about, nor did any of the others. But I never again would interfere in an argument between husband and wife. They could be killing each other, and I wouldn't intervene!

I had to withstand snide remarks by my shipmates, who considered the incident one big joke on me. But the real joke was to be on them. A very pretty young woman came aboard in Beirut. Her husband worked in the Middle East oil industry. She was unaccompanied and traveling to New York. She flirted and the officers responded. It was a long trip, and I estimate she had three or four affairs. Each lover acted like the cat who swallowed the canary. I was not one of the fortunate; but as the trip wore on, her lovers, one by one, called on the doctor. Word got around fast. The Casanovas were the butt of jokes all the way home, and their little princess was avoided like a leper. I happily missed out on this one, as I did on most, due to my young age.

The Chief Officer quietly kept control of the ship. Poppsy drank, and occasionally would make a foray against some unwilling female passenger. To the best of my knowledge, he failed in his attempts to entice members of the opposite sex into his lair. A ship is a small town, and whatever the Master does gets around quickly.

The infrequent times he came to the bridge he was mostly incoherent and ignored, and he caused no harm. One instance, however, was different. His drinking had been increasing, and his actions became even more odd. In Livorno (Leghorn) we would tie up stern to the dock with anchors dropped ahead of the bow. It was known as a Mediterranean mooring, and in fairly common use in the area. On this particular day we were completing discharge, the Pilot was aboard, and I was on the bridge making the required pre-sailing tests as cargo operations finished. The longshoremen were battening down the hatches, and the officers and crew were taking stations for getting under way. Several Italian destroyers were anchored or moored nearby, and it was obvious the Pilot would have to snake the ship through the channel with great care. I was still alone on the bridge with the quartermaster waiting for the longshoremen to finish their job and disembark before I called the Master and the Pilot.

The Pilot, as was customary, had come aboard in advance to take advantage of the ample food available at all times on a passenger liner. As the cargo work was completed and the holds battened down, the longshoremen started to leave the ship. Officers at departure station with the crew began singling up all lines. Suddenly Poppsy appeared on the bridge without the Pilot and shouted to the First Officer on the bow something like: "Haul in all anchors, let go all lines, and let's get this ship under way." I tried to tell him we had longshoremen aboard. He roared at me, "You heard me, mister. Carry out the orders." He yelled so loud that the First Officer heard him, and followed the orders, but not before he threw his hat on the deck and stomped on it.

Once we started to heave in the anchors, the windlass made a lot of noise, and the ship moved enough to start breaking its mooring lines. Poppsy grabbed the engine room telegraph as the anchors came away, and rang up, "slow ahead." By this time the Pilot noticed the commotion, and he quickly came to the bridge. The ship was slowly moving out of the harbor. The few remaining longshoremen got off, but they either had to make long jumps or swim for it.

It took the Italian Pilot a few moments to realize what was going on. By that time we had grazed or bumped off the sides of one or two destroyers and were headed for another. The Pilot took over in time to avert a collision, and luckily the damage to the two destroyers was superficial. This incident, I believe, finally resulted in Poppsy's relief on arrival in New York. He was not fired but was given a shore job on the dock.

Another incident best describes this strange man. It happened on an early winter trip in which we first called at Boston before proceeding to New York. We plowed through a heavy head sea all the way. The ship plunged into one big wave after another, shaking off tons of the Atlantic Ocean from her foredeck as she shuddered and struggled to stay afloat.

She had to be carefully handled every bit of the way, and that demanded brilliant seamanship. Safety lines were rigged on deck, and in some of the open spaces below deck. Few passengers came to the dining room, and when they did it was a struggle to hold onto the fixed table and keep the chairs from sliding around. The barometer was low, and almost everyone was depressed. Navigation was difficult under an overcast sky. I stood for hours with the First Mate trying to get an occasional celestial sight on a known star or the sun.

Several days late and with all the officers, crew, and passengers exhausted, we arrived in Boston harbor to be met by the ship reporters, who covered most passenger ship arrivals in those days. The Chief Officer, in his quiet and efficient manner, had run the ship with the First Officer. They stood four hours on and four hours off, with one or the other always on the bridge. I rotated with the Second and Third Officers in standing four hours on and eight off. Poppsy stayed snug in his bunk being served drinks and meals.

Poppsy, however, emerged from his cabin in time to meet the press. He had a stubble beard, his uniform was slovenly, and his appearance indescribable. We could not take our eyes off him. He didn't wait for the reporter to ask questions, but came right out with a statement: "Welcome aboard, lads. Have a drink. Roughest trip I ever made, up night and day. Have to get some sleep so kindly excuse me." He then went back to his room. We stood there our jaws agape. The Chief Officer, who seemed reconciled to Poppsy and took him in stride, picked up his cat, a constant companion, and went to his room. But Poppsy was not relieved after that trip. It happened after the Livorno incident.

As time passed I realized what I should have known at the start. My mentor was an alcoholic. The First Officer was a handsome man, but his misery together with his drinking had created dark circles under his eyes. He still continued to teach me, but as I learned, he left more of his job to me. The man was disintegrating slowly before my eyes. Sometimes he just simply fell apart, unable to function; others times he got hold of himself. As time went on his periods of severe depression became more evident. I covered for him; and the Chief Officer, although having given up on his friend, felt confident I could capably pick up the slack. Although it was excellent experience for me, it was very unpleasant. I respected this man, and it pained me to see him lose his fight for control.

On the trip prior to my leaving the ship (Poppsy had left the ship), the Third Mate's job opened up. The Chief Officer and the First Officer highly recommended me for the job. I had turned 20 in *Excalibur*. Already I was handling a watch officer's job and more. I had stood many a watch alone, and the First Officer taught me enough to pass my Master's License. But just as Owen Murphy predicted, the Port Captain, irregardless of the strong recommendation, refused to give the Third Officer job of the Flagship to "a 20-year-boy," as he phrased it.

The job went to a quartermaster on my watch who held a Third Mate's License for many years but had not sailed on it since World War I. He was 60 or more years old, a pleasant and sober man whom I liked. Since it would be many months before I turned 21, I decided to ask for a leave of absence before we departed, to take effect on my return. I called Owen Murphy and asked him to try and find me a Third Mate's job on my return so I could get the full-time credit to upgrade my license. He said he would.

Samuel Groves became the ship's new Master. A former Master of *Exeter he* was a small man in his late 40s or early 50s, whose only vice was to blow three blasts of the whistle as he passed his home in Brooklyn.

The essential trade route to the Mediterranean served by the American Export Line paid for itself in many ways. It was a balanced trade. The ships were basically full of cargo both ways. Still they were greatly out carried by the Italian and other National Lines. The American Export Line could not have carried more than five percent of the passenger trade, most of whom were Americans.

Subsidized ships were in place when the war started and fitted right into their military requirements. *Excalibur* and *Exeter,* together with other ships of the line, served the defensive needs of the U.S. They were there when needed, even though the freight ships were surplus from World War I. The small Merchant Marine served, as did their crews, either as Naval vessels or as merchant ships under the direction of the military. These ships were extremely critical in the early days of World War II as we struggled to build new ships.

As I write this American Export and Grace Line and their ships are no more. Our trading partners have built their own merchant ships and in many cases reserve their cargo for their national flags. Our trade routes are now dominated by third flag vessels. U.S. Flag ships are limited in their versatility. With the lack of equal sharing in our trade routes, we are, in many instances, on the short end of an unbalanced trade. What should have been improved in 1936 has since become much worse.

S.S. Padnsay

I had now spent nearly 46 weeks at sea since graduation less than a year earlier. Although I liked *Excalibur,* the line, the itinerary, and my ship-mates, I was still sailing as a Cadet Officer and making only $50 a month. If I could sail as a Third Mate, I' d make $125. Since I was eager to take my Second Mate's License exam, I wanted to accelerate the sea time requirement for eligibility. This meant I had to sail as a Third Mate—on a ship over 1,000 gross tons and certified for "oceans." Such jobs were rare in 1936, especially for youngsters of 20. Undaunted I called Murphy again, asking for his help in finding a Third Mate's job on any ship that fit the category. He came through with a relief assignment in *S.S. Wind Ru*sh of the Shepherd Line, which had just arrived from the West Coast. She was a typical 10,000 ton World War I built freighter, and I would be employed for one month while she discharged her cargo of lumber in New England. Meanwhile Murphy searched for a permanent Third Mate position for me.

The Master and the deck officers in *Wind Rush* were Norwegian natu-ralized citizens and considerably older than I. On board for the summer as well were the Master's wife and daughter, a pretty woman of 18. I was welcomed into the family and enjoyed easy work with plenty of time off, for we discharged our cargo slowly during weekdays only in areas near seaside resorts. As pleasant as the time was, though, and as attractive as I found the daughter, I grew restless. The tedium made each day feel like a week. When we returned to New York, I—hopefully and immediately—called Owen Murphy.

He had great news. *S.S. Padnsay* of the Barber Line would be ready to sail in four hours, but the Third Mate hadn't shown up. If I could get to Brooklyn in time, the Third Mate's job was mine. In spite of having a miserable case of the flu, I sprang into action. I seemed to be saying hello and good-bye to my mother at once, repacking gear just unpacked, lugging it to the subway, galloping off the train in Brooklyn, and dashing in a cab to the pier. I was under the impression the new assignment would be similar to the previous one. I thought Owen had said something about "coastwise."

The cab driver left me off at the pier, which was nearly deserted and shrouded by the quiet of a Brooklyn waterfront night. I ran up *Padnsay's* gangway, and at just about 2200 hours entered the salon to face an impatient Captain and a Shipping Commissioner seated at a table. I produced my license for the Commissioner, answered a few questions, then signed the articles. I was told to put my gear in the Third Mate's room and go to the bridge to get under way. I took the traditional Third Mate's departure station at the engine room telegraph on the bridge. Within five minutes of my arrival, all lines were cast off, and the Pilot was giving engine and wheel orders as the Captain stood by.

Other than giving orders, no one else talked on that calm night. About one hour after we cast off, the Pilot disembarked, and we took departure from Ambrose Lightship, the Captain setting a course of ESE and ordering full-speed ahead. Still saying nothing to me, he went into the chartroom to write his night orders, then left the bridge. As Third Mate I had the watch until midnight. But the course confused me, so I checked the log in the chartroom to see where we were bound and read "New York to Dakar." Dakar was on the west coast of Africa.

When Owen told me *Padnsay* was a ship of the Barber Line, he was not being totally forthright. The Barber Line, a consortium of Norwegian and other interests under the Norwegian Flag, found it more advantageous to operate in West Africa under the U.S. Flag. In my haste I failed to see the name on the side of the ship: huge white letters on a black hull that announced American West African Line. In fact the offices of the Barber Line and the American West African Line were one and the same. A typical line cargo ship *Padnsay* carried passengers and mail as well, making scheduled trips on a specific itinerary—trips to a "coast" unlike any I had previously encountered.

The Second Mate relieved me of the watch at midnight. With so many unanswered questions, I don't recall whether I slept well or poorly my first night at sea. I do recall being awakened for breakfast in time to dress and eat before relieving the watch at 0800 hours . I dressed in khaki pants and shirt and donned my officer's cap with its American Export Line insignia. I also had words with the steward about getting my filthy room cleaned. He said my predecessor was a slob; but when the Kru Boys came aboard, he would have the room thoroughly cleaned and painted. I did not know what Kru Boys were, or where or when they came aboard, but I figured I would find out in time.

46

The officers' mess for the assistant engineers, the Second and Third Mates, and the radio operator was small, adequate but no more. The only people in the mess at the time were the Third Engineer, a black man, and the radio operator, who was white. The engineers argued constantly, sometimes violently. One of the assistants was Filipino, another was Puerto Rican, and the Chief Engineer was Mexican.

I was on the bridge by 0750 hours and met the Chief Mate for the first time. It was hard to tell his age for he was small, thin, stooped, had dark rings under his eyes, and generally looked unhealthy. He introduced himself politely, and after asking me a few questions, mentioned that sometime later in the voyage he would go over the plans for discharging and loading cargo. It was a beautiful calm day, and he turned over the watch to me, passing the usual information about courses and speed. The ship had no automatic steering, no gyro compass, and the bridge was primitive even for those days. I had my sextant with me, as all licensed officers were required to provide their own.

After checking the course and the wheelhouse compass with the standard compass on the flying bridge, I took sun sights, calculated them, and drew the lines of position on the chart while I carried forward the dead reckoning position. No other ships were around. The Captain came on the bridge about 1000 hours, said good morning but not much else. He checked the chart, noted I was carrying out the routine, and then went below. But I had gotten my first good look at the man.

About 50, of average height, with a ruddy complexion and thinning hair, the Captain's large belly protruded over his belt. Unlike the Mates, who dressed in khakis, he wore white pants and shirt, but no marking of his rank on anything but his cap, which bore the scrambled eggs of a captain on the forepeak. After he left and as time passed, I noticed people moving about the forward deck and aft on the boat deck. I checked the papers in the chartroom and discovered we had twelve passengers, all bound for different ports on the West African Coast.

They were young missionary couples probably on their first assignments. From the way they were walking, this obviously was their first time aboard a ship. They had not as yet found the bridge, so my first full watch in *Padnsay* was spent in peaceful quiet, with only a few words with the wheelman and the lookout breaking the tranquillity. Before noon I prepared to take a meridian altitude sight. The sun is at its highest point at that time, and you get an excellent latitude position. Together with the lines of position taken earlier, and by advancing them to the latitude line, the ship's position can be accurately established.

More than one Mate usually comes to the bridge for this occasion; ordinarily the Captain comes as well, if only to check on the position. Only the Second Mate appeared. I offered some pleasantries, but his opening comment to me was a warning to watch out for the Captain, who he clearly did not like. This man had little education, was careless in his dress, and in need of a haircut and shave. He had a wild-eyed look about him. He had served under Captain for a long time. This, he claimed, was the trip on which he would steal the Captain's false teeth and throw them overboard. It was a bewildering introduction to a shipmate.

We soon settled into a period of beautiful weather and calm seas. I performed my traditional Third Mate tasks, but had little to do off watch. I drew books from the ship's library to read about the ports we were heading for. I also became friendlier with the Chief Mate. He stood the four-to-eight watch, and I would go to the bridge at twilight to practice taking star sights. He seemed to appreciate my interest, and we would work together taking sights. On this long ocean leg we depended entirely on celestial navigation. Rarely did we see another ship as we sailed alone on the wide expanse of the ocean, our ship visible all around the horizon in good weather.

Occasionally I would chat with the missionaries. Mainly from the Midwest, they were pleasant and undemanding. They tried to connect what they were experiencing at sea with the Bible and the Lord. But, in all, not much happened aboard a cargo ship on a long voyage in those days—no movies or music, no entertainment of any kind. Operational and maintenance work would go on as we listened to the subdued whine of the turbine engine and felt the slow roll and motion of the ship. For those two and a half weeks between New York and Dakar, I found a kind of peace I had never known before.

From time to time when I was on watch, I saw the Second Mate snooping around the Captain's quarters. When he noticed I was watching him, he would grin weirdly. My few conversations with him always led to his hatred of the Captain and warnings for me to be careful. Conversations with the Purser, an all-American boy, also were single-minded—the beautiful girl in Lagos he planned to marry. In general none of my mess mates had much education and most of them had been in the West African trade so long their lives were wrapped up in problems like malaria. They accepted this infectious disease and quinine as facts of life. The weather remained excellent throughout the trip. Although I appreciated the peaceful routine, I gradually became eager for what lay ahead. One intriguing thing I learned

48

was the Captain had an excellent business importing wild animals from West Africa. He seemed preoccupied most of the time, and I think he was more concerned with his private business than with the affairs of the ship.

We were heading towards what was then called the Gold, Ivory, and Slave coasts, all of which had a history of violence. In 1936, however, the area was enjoying a period of peace if not prosperity under European management. Our first port of call would be Dakar, Senegal, then part of French West Africa, followed by Sierra Leone, then British. Then we would call at Liberia, a sovereign state, before heading to the British Gold Coast and to Nigeria, also British. Stops at French Equatorial Africa and the Belgian Congo were last. To my young ears the very names of the ports were exotic: Bathurst, Conakry, Freetown, Monrovia, Cape Palmas, Abidjan, Takoradi, Cape Coast Castle, Accra, Lome, Lagos, Port Harcourt, Libreville, Matadi, Sapele, Burutu, and Warri.

As we neared Dakar the Second Mate with his wheelman and lookout relieved me at midnight. It was another beautiful, star-filled night on the high seas, which required no piloting. All the Second Mate had to do was keep clear of other shipping and maintain course. Not another ship was in sight when I turned the watch over.

At 0400 hours, when the Chief Mate and his two men arrived for their watch, they discovered the Second Mate had not been seen since 0200 hours. The Chief Mate called the Captain and me. The man was so odd we generally assumed he was just up to one of his tricks. I felt the guy was playing a game, and left the Captain and the Chief Mate to figure out what to do. But soon the whole crew was called to make a complete search of the ship. No Second Mate. By this time, 0530 hours, the ship had steamed about 40 miles since he had been last seen. Although the chances were slim of finding him afloat if he had jumped or been thrown over the side, the Captain reversed course to a position estimated as the last possible point he could have fallen into the sea. Because this search was carried out in daylight, if he kept afloat we would have seen him. We did not.

We now had two problems. We had to find someone among the unlicensed personnel qualified to stand watch, which essentially meant qualifying a seaman reliable enough to call the Captain, the Chief Mate, or me if anything important occurred. And we had to investigate the Second Mate's death to see if foul play were involved. This job, given to the Chief Mate, was a hopeless assignment. If a crew man had thrown the man overboard, he would hardly volunteer the information. The Second Mate had been on the ship a long time and with many of the same crew. They were a hard bunch, and he had mixed with them a great deal. He was not liked, and I estimated the odds at 50/50 between murder and suicide. No evidence surfaced to incriminate anyone, and the Captain left it at that. Personally I thought he committed suicide by jumping overboard. From time to time on long night watches, I would stare at the wake of the ship as it moved through the water. Often I felt beckoned to dive in to solve some mystery of eternity. Many seamen have fallen under this spell and departed for places unknown.

Thus with the Second Mate's work now divided between the Chief Mate and myself, and with little assistance from the Captain, we arrived in Dakar, the "Paris" of West Africa. In 1936 the city had European-style buildings, streets, restaurants, cafes, and nightclubs. Nonetheless it was West Africa, alive with mosquitoes and a kind of cricket that descended in the millions. The heat was unbearable, and air conditioning of course did not exist. Although a nightclub provided familiar music, food, and girls— French and a mixed bag of other races—the heat and insects told you another story. Dakar looked better from the sea.

After the long voyage the crew now had their first and only chance for time ashore in a port with any so-called European atmosphere. Not surprisingly a quarter of the crew failed to return when we were ready to leave. I went ashore with a clerk from the agent's office, who then got the police to help us round up our missing troops. They knew exactly where to look. Some were at the police station itself, detained on various charges; others were visiting the usual fleshpots. We did not find them all, however, and those we corralled were drunk (at this point I heard the first reference to the Second Mate's ghost). With some baksheesh for the police and officials, we finally gathered the stragglers, who stumbled or were carried aboard, and sailed southward. By this time I had learned we would take aboard the "famous" Kru Boys in Freetown, Sierra Leone.

As we approached Freetown the Chief Mate patiently explained the procedure to me. We would embark the Kru Boys along with their paraphernalia—absolutely everything they needed to live and work entirely on deck and in the holds. Aside from their Headman and the few assigned to assist in maintenance and upkeep, rarely would a Kru Boy enter the officer's or crew's quarters. They would bring their own cook and food. Instead of local stevedores, and with few exceptions as we sailed south, the Kru Boys would handle all the loading and unloading operations under the Chief Mate's and my supervision.

The Kru Boys were from the same tribe that had worked the ship since

50

its first voyage in this trade. Members of a West Coast African tribe skilled as seamen, their tradition of augmenting ships' crews went back to the time of sail. They rarely worked ships between regular contracts and could live quite well in the interim on wages of no more than $5 a month per man. Seamen on some foreign ships did not make much more. This was all very new to me, and I anticipated our arrival in Freetown with interest, if not with concern.

Some 50 Kru Boys swarmed aboard, all smiles and greeting crew members as old friends whether they knew them or not. Their skin was intensely black, unlike the varying shades of brown and tan I was familiar with in the States. The Headman wore pants, a shirt, and a sun hat, as did three or four of his underbosses. The other Kru Boys covered themselves with either loin cloths or skirt-like garments. All were professed Christians, and the Headman, in addition to being the boss, was the Deacon of their church. At this point in my travels I began observing the concessions missionaries made to tribal traditions, so their converts could be baptized and retained in the fold!

First they loaded a "West African Ensign," a wooden head built to serve one at a time and mounted overlapping the stern. Next came the "Mammy Chair," also of wood, but supported by steel straps. They used it to transfer people to and from surfboats while the ship was at anchor. We attached it to the same hook at the end of the boom that handled cargo in the open roadsteads. After that appeared Wula, the toothless cook, and the tools of his trade: a large metal cooking vat which attached to a steam line.

The Kru Boys an end to the peace and tranquillity. They kept up a constant chatter that only ceased when they were asleep and when cargo and maintenance work stopped. Although they spoke English I had difficulty understanding them at first. It took several weeks of hearing the pronunciation before I could communicate easily with them. Pidgin English was the international language on foreign docks in those days. Although the words were the same in various places, the inflections differed greatly.

Sailing from Freetown with the Kru Boys settling into their routine was an unusual experience. The West African Ensign was in constant use. Wula set up on the forward deck under the break of the forecastle, practicing his culinary arts, which revolved around the vat. He would prepare his special of the day on the greasy deck by chopping and readying the meat or fowl for the meal. He would then sweep it with a cut-down broom into a scoop and dump it into the vat, which was filled with water, rice, and other strange concoctions. This he stirred with the broom handle. When I passed by he would ladle some of the "ingredients" and, flashing his toothless smile, offer it to me saying "good, good." As I declined, with thanks, he would then slurp it down his throat with an expression of great satisfaction.

The Kru Boys' professionalism in handling cargo under almost impossible conditions put the International Longshoremen's Association to shame. Most ports were open roadsteads. We always anchored at least a mile offshore, usually in a moderate groundswell with the ship rolling. The cargo was discharged or loaded from large wooden lighters shaped like huge whale boats. Local natives would paddle these to and from the ship through the surf, or from a small shallow-water pier. Because of the size and weight of the cargo, many oarsmen manned these surfboats. This practice of handling cargo also went back to the days of the sailing vessels, and probably to "blackbirding," as the slave trade was called.

In 1936 the colonial economic system was still solidly in place. We carried a cargo of manufactured goods to the coast, returning with agricultural products such as cocoa, latex, and palm oil, but little or no coffee. We also loaded mahogany, mostly rough logs, with the remainder cut for better stowage. In some ports we loaded and discharged at the same time; at some we only discharged; and a few, like Freetown, we loaded and unloaded on both legs of the voyage. Added to the cargo were the Captain's animals. The gorilla and crown birds were destined for zoos; the snakes and monkeys were destined for research laboratories.

Work at open roadstead ports proceeded slowly under difficult, often dangerous, conditions. Our principal and really only competition, other than an occasional tramp ship, was the ships of the Elder Dempster Company. This large British firm serviced the West African Coast from Great Britain, the European continent, and the United States. It had newer post-World War I ships, but they were of the same configuration and speed as ours. French, Portuguese, and Belgians were also in the trade. We would anchor and berth near these vessels, but overall we were a small presence in the area. The American West African Line had only four or five ships similar to *Padnsay.*

Once we left Freetown and headed south, we fell into what was called the West African syndrome. I entered fully into this strange world, so remote from civilization and its benefits. The ship was an oven and remained so both night and day; the steel decks intensified the heat, and in the cargo holds it was unbearable. Shade offered little protection, and both the shower and cold water taps delivered near boiling liquid. Only during the evenings when we sailed between ports and created our own breeze was the heat tolerable.

Aside from the Captain, Chief Mate, and me, the officers and crew did not even try to maintain civilized standards of cleanliness and dress. We were a slovenly lot. I worked hard at it, but the battle was all uphill. The cockroaches were huge, the flies and mosquitoes a constant nuisance, and though I slept under a mosquito net, the mesh kept out what little air there was, and I simply lay in my own sweat. But I had dreamed of adventure, so I couldn't complain when it arrived.

After Freetown came Monrovia, Liberia, which an American rubber company administered. We discharged a great deal of cargo in the port and loaded raw rubber (latex) for the States. Open roadstead ports followed. Then we docked at Takoradi, which is now part of Ghana. Because we were to stay overnight, I planned to go ashore with the Chief Mate to visit a British club on a hill overlooking the dock.

The Chief Mate had been to Takoradi many times, but he had never been further inland than this dock. The agent told me about the club and said we would be welcome to dine there. We left the ship on a dark, moonless night, and "dark" in this part of Africa meant black—only the weak lights of the club were barely visible. We had dressed for the occasion and carried flashlights.

The road close to the dock went around a hill. But the hill was not steep and the club no more than an eighth of a mile away, so we decided to climb. We soon came on a drainage ditch; and when we shone our flashlight in, we discovered it was alive with snakes. Panicking we rushed down the hill. Now we understood why the road went around the hill. We picked our way carefully to the club.

At the club several servants in white jackets stood around with little to do. Only one couple was dining, a man and his wife being fanned by a young boy also in a white jacket. A ceiling fan rotated slowly because the power supply was weak. The head waiter, the agent having informed him of our arrival, personally welcomed us. After seating us, he handed us a surprisingly large handwritten menu and wine and liquor lists.

The man and wife were British. Middle aged and formally dressed, the man wore a white mess jacket, black bow tie, and black pants; the woman wore a long silk gown. Neither spoke. With their forks in their left hands and their knives in their right, they ate slowly and with excellent manners. One could imagine a summer evening in an exclusive London club, were it not for the lack of other diners, the insects, an the oppressive heat, which caused the woman's make-up to run down her face. Sweat seeped through their clothes. When they finished eating, they left, still not saying a word to anyone but nodding to us. Perhaps they had come in from the bush for a night on the town.

I was amazed by their equanimity and dignity; to me they represented an ethereal part of the British Empire. When I returned to the ship, I was even more determined to maintain my standards despite the environment. I noticed that foreign ships anchored close to us made a much greater effort to remain civilized, particularly the British. Work would stop around 1700 hours, and whereas our engineering officers would sit around drinking beer in the dirty clothes they had worn all day, British officers would appear on deck in white uniforms with short pants, and have cocktails before a formal dinner. If I dressed in white clothes, however, I would upset the others, who wore either dungarees or dirty khakis. There was no reason for this, since with the Kru Boys aboard we could have all our laundry done for a few cents. But I had long discovered that the way to survive in a strange environment was not to try to change it or go against it. Others had been on the ship before me, and I was not about to antagonize them, particularly at age 20. All I could do without being conspicuous was wear clean khakis.

At Cape Coast Castle the ruins of an old fortress were still visible. The agent told me it had been a major embarkation point for slaves. In the fortress captains of the slave ships would bid or barter for their human cargo. The process began, he explained, with rival black chieftains warring against each other. The winning tribe enslaved the losers, who were then sold to Arab slave merchants. These merchants then brought their human merchandise to the seaports on the Slave Coast. The fortress served a purpose, according to the agent. Because the traders sometimes fought each other, the fortress "discouraged" warships sent to disrupt the trade, which was illegal in Europe by the late 18th century. The agent claimed the Arab slave traders were still active in a small way but no longer brought slaves to the Coast. They ended up in Arab countries instead. I listened to all this in astonishment.

In Accra I met the line's cocoa representative, who was pleased to find someone interested in his activities. He felt isolated in West Africa and would have left long ago if the money hadn't been so good and his expenses nil. I learned from him how important the cocoa cargo was to the line. Cocoa was one of the largest income producers of the area. He tried to interest me in being assigned to his office, but I had no intention of leaving my world to live in West Africa. The area satisfied my craving for adventure but was hardly my ideal future home.

And so we moved southward to Lome and Continue on the way to Lagos. Distances between ports were short, and we primarily occupied our time discharging and loading in open roadstead ports. All the while the Purser was "propagandizing" me about his beautiful girl in Lagos. Because he was a good looking man, I imagined he had found an enchanting, lovely creature, although so far I had not seen a women who fit the description.

The Kru Boys' life was in the holds of the ship and on deck. Even in torrential rains they were relegated to the decks. Sex was also. On regular occasions a "mammy" would come out to the ship in a surfboat, to be hoisted aboard in the Mammy Chair in the same way agents, passengers, and others boarded and left. It was an important event, and the Kru Boys became even more vocal than usual. The large size of these women fascinated me. They were evaluated by their weight. I don't know how the Kru Boys reconciled these organized "events" with their religion, but I gathered the ritual with the "mammy" predated the missionaries. It had to be one of those concessions missionaries made. Thus I was interested in the Purser's intended.

Lagos, a major port in West Africa, was filled with ships. We docked there for a number of days. It still looked like a shantytown to me, and like elsewhere, the weather steamed. But added to the insect population and the heat was a distinct odor. Sanitation systems, if in existence at all, obviously had not kept up with the population. At my first free moment the Purser took me to meet his sweetheart. It must have rained shortly before our arrival, for the streets were deep in mud. The town was spread out, and we had to walk some distance to the house of the Purser's future wife.

We came to a shack with no "amenities." As we entered this hovel the Purser's eyes shone wide with adoration, and he leaped into his loved one's arms. This was no Heddy Lamarr but an immense woman not dissimilar to the "mammies" who visited the Kru Boys. Once we were introduced and he was convinced I saw the beauty in the woman he did, he was anxious for me to leave so he could get on with the business at hand.

I returned to the ship. Although I could have taken more time off in Lagos, I stayed aboard and worked. The Purser returned shortly before we sailed, still proclaiming the beauty of his fiancee to anyone who would listen. I was learning that life was not all it appeared to be; more important I was appreciating the meaning of tolerance. My environment was completely at odds with many of my ideas about human behavior. To survive within the narrow society of the ship and the people touched by it, I had to steel myself to accept things for what they were and try not to change them. Had I adopted any other stance, I doubt I would have lasted the voyage. Work and conditions aboard ship were miserable; and if I had not been pushed to the limit of endurance by my training at the Merchant Marine Academy, I never could have made it.

This was a dangerous business. Loading huge five- to ten-ton mahogany logs in an open roadstead as the ship rolled had killed many a Kru Boy and Mate over the years. We had many close calls and some minor injuries, but so far no deaths. After the logs were placed into the holds, they were positioned so they would not shift at sea. We had eye pads strongly secured to the fixed frames of the ship. Thus fairleads could be placed so that the "bull ropes" (actually wires) could be set at a number of angles leading to the large steel claw that bit into the log. At times a claw at the end of a free wire would break loose under the strain and move like a cannonball through the hold. Danger and death ran hand-in-hand on this mean coast. Because much of our work was carried out in open seas, the stress on the masts, booms, winches, and running rigging made log handling even more treacherous. The Kru Boys pulled constantly on guidelines attached to prevent large heavy loads from thrashing about before finally settling into position in the hold or on deck. They were adept, but the equipment and the people were strained to the breaking point. One day the Kru Boys' screams suddenly intensified. Work stopped, and my group ran forward. One Kru Boy rushed to me repeating the name of the Chief Mate. When I got to the foredeck, I was shocked to see a boom had come loose from the gooseneck attaching it to the mast. I pushed my way through the crowd to find the Chief Mate, surrounded by blood, lying on the deck and being ministered to by the Headman. He was dead.

The Chief Mate was no Admiral Nelson, and he did not die in combat in an historic battle capped by victory; he had merely been the victim of an accident caused by the working conditions. He was a quiet man who kept to himself. I knew nothing about his family or even if he had one. He engendered respect by his competence, his reliability, his consistency, and his decency in dealing with the Captain, officers, crew, and the Kru Boys. I don't believe any man was more respected on that violent coast. His death was traumatic for me, for I worked more with him than with anyone else on board.

Sometime after I arrived on the scene of the accident the Captain appeared. Although I am certain he was affected by the loss of his shipmate, he did not show it. We soon cleaned up and re-rigged so work could continue. Miraculously no one else had been killed or seriously injured. The Kru Boys could react quickly to accidents of this nature, but the Mate had not been well and probably could not move fast enough to save himself. Soon he too became another ghost in an area already overflowing with remembrances of its horrible past.

The Captain and I agreed on an able seaman whom we would upgrade to unlicensed Mate. The seaman appointed earlier was working out well, but we now had only two licensed deck officers on the ship. As we continued on the Captain's bouts with malaria worsened, and the navigation of the ship increasingly became my sole responsibility.

The Captain's frequently suffered periods of delirium, yet refused to go ashore. He kept raving about a gorilla. I could not leave the ship (and would not have gone inland for anyone), but he convinced the Headman to take a party to buy a gorilla from his contact. The Headman was to buy the animal as long as it could stand. I don't know how much it cost, but the gorilla arrived in a cage. His appearance, oddly enough, created no unusual curiosity in the crew.

The Purser and I continued to treat the Captain's malaria with ample supplies of quinine. The fever raged, and we even had the Kru Boys' medicine man attend to the Captain. The Purser told me this was the worst series of attacks he'd ever seen. Sometimes the Captain vomited, so we kept his false teeth in a jar of water by his bed. Every time I looked at those choppers, I thought of the Second Mate and what he would have given to get his hands on them. Fate played an interesting hand.

After we reached our southernmost point, we headed north again to call at ports on the Warri River mainly for loading out. I, in acting command then, was concerned because we had to go 125 miles upriver into the interior. The chart simply indicated a river with no navigation aids, but it did show where the ports of Warri, Sapele, and Burutu were. As we rolled about five degrees in a groundswell at the mouth of the Warri, several pilots approached us in their boats carrying their own wheelman and cooks.

Because the Captain was delirious, I had to deal with this group alone. Four or five boarded, each shoving letters of recommendation in front of me. Their dress was comical: old captains' hats and coats with skirts and other strange combinations of dress that set them apart from their fellows. The Purser knew what to pay them but was unable to recognize any who had piloted the ship before.

Pushing the letters towards me, they said things like, "Me best pilot on

Warri River, Mr. Mate," pleading with me to read the documents. They themselves obviously could not read English, and the letters were mostly derogatory, indicating that the Captains who wrote them probably were drunk at the time. None of the latter came from Captains on our line. All were from British ships whose names were unfamiliar to me. The letters contained remarks like "this bastard is incompetent and ran me aground." Still I had to pick someone and I did. He seemed capable, and we started up the river under his direction and with his wheelman at the helm. We were heavily loaded, and as we proceeded over the bar between the river and the sea we touched bottom several times. I complained to the Pilot, but he cheerfully said "no problem," and we continued to stagger and bounce our way up the river. The Warri, like other rivers, was a muddy light brown, narrow from the onset, with many snake-like turns. The stern just about cleared the jungle that surrounded us. Occasionally we passed primitive native settlements and at various points saw objects hanging from trees. The Pilot told me these were "jujus," placed there to keep evil spirits away.

I spent all my time on the bridge as we navigated the river, even though I soon realized the Pilot knew what he was doing. He would occasionally relieve his wheelman and was served food by his cook. The river ports were very small, each with a dock that could only be worked by one or two hatches at a time. There were also moorings of a sort, up and down the river from the dock, to which our bow and stern lines were fastened. Each town had an agent and a few buildings. Most of the river was too narrow for ships to pass one another, but our Pilot skillfully guided us, and we were able to proceed north to Freetown.

By the time we returned to Freetown to discharge the Kru Boys, the ship looked like Noah's Ark. She was down to her Plimsoll mark and full of cargo below and on deck: large amounts of cocoa in bags, palm oil, lumber, and of course, our zoo, but only the crown birds and some monkeys were on exhibit. The Captain, who was still ill, personally tended the gorilla. We had hundreds of snakes in boxes and hundreds of monkeys in cages. The noise was incredible, with the monkeys' constant chirping, the birds' squawking.

The Captain had cabled for replacement Mates but none were available in Freetown. A seaman's and officer's strike, which probably accounted for the lack of relief personnel, was going on in the U.S. at the time. There was as much ado at the Kru Boys' departure as when they arrived. They had been an excellent crew; and in addition to having done all the cargo work, painted the whole ship (and my room). Towards the end only a small portion of the deck was left for them to live on, and they clustered on the bow and stern. But they had become the soul of the ship for two months; when they left, the ship experienced an utter silence, punctuated only by the cry of an animal.

We prepared to sail to Havana, but these orders were changed to Boston shortly after we left Freetown. The weather soon deteriorated and we pitched and struggled through head seas, although we had to expect this when heading WNW in the late fall. The lumber was securely fastened on deck by wires and chains that could be tightened by turnbuckles. But as the bad weather continued it started to work its way loose, and we had to chock it in with small pieces of wood—a tricky job, for as the lumber shifted, we could get our legs caught or even fall in between the logs. Somehow we all survived.

Africa and its particular charms began to fade, and the only reminder for me was a small elephant table I had bought carved out of a single piece of mahogany; this was my only souvenir. Even the ghost of the Second Mate had evaporated. The sailor who tended the animals reported that some snakes had gotten loose and everyone became more preoccupied by snakes than by ghosts. The Captain spent most of his time with the gorilla, who was not holding up well in the colder climate we had entered. And we were all aware of the union strike, a subject the crew continually discussed.

Bad luck now stalked the ship. Before arriving in Boston the gorilla died. The Captain, aware of this possibility, had arranged to sell the carcass for stuffing. I heard he still made money on the deal. We finally arrived in Boston on a cold December day in a driving wind and were told to anchor out overnight. As a sympathy gesture for the strikers one seaman uncaged some monkeys. The crew scurried around the deck trying to catch them, but rather than be captured again, most jumped into the bay. They were able to swim and seemed to be doing fine for awhile, but the cold water triumphed and they drowned. It was a pitiful ending to our trip.

Ironically we never did dock in Boston. Most of the cargo was bound for New York, and the ship owners were afraid we might get stranded in Boston because of the strike. The next day we sailed to New York where both the ship's crew and I were paid off. I expected to get a taxi to the ferry but was unable to do so and began walking instead. It was dark and I noticed some men coming out of the shadows—hungry strikers. They chased me all the way to the ferry where I jumped the gate just as the ship was leaving. It was a close call.

I returned to the ship the next day, riding in taxis each way, to pick up my elephant table and to meet with operational executives. The Port Captain congratulated me on my performance and invited me to stay with the line, offering waivers so I could sail as Second Mate until I accumulated enough time for my Second's License. Meanwhile the Port Engineer, Mr. Topping, was listening and called me over. He told me his brother was the Port Captain for the U.S. Line, and the future was there, not where I was. I should register with the Union, picket one or two days, and then get a job ashore until the strike was over.

Suddenly all the commotion and adventure stopped. I found myself in my mother's apartment learning that both my maternal grandparents had died. Their house had been sold, and with her small inheritance, my mother was buying a house on Long Island. So much had happened so quickly I decided to slow down for awhile. I reported to the Union and did one day of picket duty—unfortunately in front of the U.S. Line pier. The next day, walking up Fifth Avenue after lunching with my mother, I passed the Thos. Cook & Son building and impulsively walked in to apply for a job. After an interview I was offered a position with the party line: "We pay low, but we've been here for years, and once employed, you'll always have a job." I would get $20 a week, to start the following Monday. I thought I would now be staying ashore for some time, sorting out a life that had been going along too rapidly. Little did I know.

(In 1961 my business took me again to Dakar, only this time I arrived by air accompanied by my 15-year-old son. Outwardly the city appeared changed, but in reality it still belonged to the bugs and the heat.)

Three

Countdown:
War in Europe

S.S. Washington

Although I had no intention of remaining with the American West African Line, I might have made a few more trips at full time to accelerate my eligibility for a Second Mate's License. But Mr. Toppings' offer to assist me in finding work with the United States Line was not to be taken lightly. The United States Line was the equivalent of Great Britain's Cunard Line and the French Line. If I stayed out on strike and continued to picket the U.S. Lines piers, my chances of employment with them would be poor at best. A job ashore eliminated me as a picket carrier and gave me time. The Depression was still on, and companies such as Thos. Cook & Son could pick and choose. "Walk-ins" were unheard of.

My job was about one or two steps above office boy. Because Thos. Cook & Sons was a British-based firm, many British customs were followed and a caste system was in place. Every minor manager coveted his position, his title, and his authority, even though he had no more than four people and a few file cabinets in his domain.

The job attracted applicants from the best schools who, like me, were intrigued by travel and far away places. But the desks on Fifth Avenue never moved, even though employees issued tickets to tourists and business travelers bound for distant shores. The atmosphere was pleasant but the work unstimulating. It is difficult to categorize studying schedules and rates as anything but boring. Itineraries were created for ships, trains, hotels, and individuals, but often they were boiler plate lists. I placated clients whose arrangements were fouled up, and those whose were not, but thought so. I did have more time to spend with my mother and friends, but my wanderlust was not curtailed. Sooner or later I was bound to go back to sea. The strike had ended.

Fate again intervened. I boarded *S.S. Manhattan* to be sure an escorted tour we had booked was properly looked after. *Manhattan,* the flagship of the United States Lines and her sistership, *Washington,* were the newest, largest, and fastest ships in the U.S. Merchant Marine.

I arrived at the pier at about 10:00 a.m. My group was scheduled to board at 10:30, and the ship was to sail at noon. When I boarded I met a tall, good looking, perfectly uniformed Junior Officer. I did not know him, but in our conversation he told me he was a '33 graduate of NYSMMA. His name was Rogers Emmons. I told him I was a '35 graduate of the Academy, currently working for Thos. Cook & Sons. He mentioned how much he liked his job. I checked the tour group and then left the ship. Something drew me in the direction of the personnel office on the dock. I filled out a job application and used Mr. Topping as a reference. When I returned the application to the clerk, I pointed to Topping's name and requested the clerk to take the application into Captain Topping. I am certain that if I had not done this, the application would have ended up in the waste basket. For a moment the clerk demurred, and then took the application into the office. When he came out he told me to go in.

Captain Topping looked me over. I was dressed in the uniform of the day for Thos. Cook & Son, which was a Brooks Brothers-type suit with a white shirt, striped tie, and polished black shoes. This Ivy League style was common among both white collar workers and students. Civilian life in offices in the '30s had an unwritten conformity to it, and the disciplines, although geared to petty standards, were more strictly observed than in the military. Thos. Cook & Sons was no exception.

As an ex-West African Coast mate, very young, and looking even more so, I was not what Captain Topping expected to see when I entered his office. He said nothing for a few minutes as he studied the application form. Noting I had a job he asked me if I could be ready to report for work a few days prior to sailing two weeks from that day. I said I would be ready.

He gave me a slip to take to the medical department on the dock and a list of uniforms required for the Junior Third Officer of the ship. He then commented about my being a legend on the West African Coast, welcomed me to the U.S. Lines, and shook my hand. Just like that. I could hardly believe my good fortune. I passed my physical exam the same day. Three days prior to sailing I reported to the Executive Officer of *S.S. Washington.*

All the Senior Officers in *Manhattan* and *Washington* had Master's

Licenses. As I discovered on boarding, even the Senior Junior Officer in *Washington* had a Master's License. The others had at least a Second Mate's License. I would be the only officer on the ship with a Third Mate's License.

As a Junior Officer I would still only get half-time credit on my sea time, but the job paid $160 a month—more than a Second Mate was making on most ships, and much more than the $20 a week I was making at Thos. Cook. I had been happy, even if frustrated, at Thos. Cook, but in spite of everything I enjoyed it. Until the last day I worked there, I literally walked on air. My mother was somewhat confused because she wanted me to return to college, make up the necessary courses for a degree, and then go on to law school. It made for good talk, but I never had any intention of becoming a lawyer.

Manhattan and *Washington* beat the system. Their main competition on the run to Hamburg, Germany, was the Hamburg American Line Cabin Class ships: *Hamburg, Deutschland, New York,* and *Albert Balen.* (When the Nazis came to power, *Albert Balen's* name was changed to *Hansa.* Balen had been Managing director of the Hamburg American Line. But there was a slight problem: he was Jewish.) At 18,000 gross tons, they cruised at 18-plus knots. But with a cruising speed of 22-plus knots, the 24,600-ton *Manhattan* and *Washington* could beat them to Hamburg and still call at Ireland, England, and France en route both ways. Unfortunately we only had two fast ships. The alternate weeks were serviced by slower and smaller 16-plus knot ships—World War I built *President Harding* and *President Roosevelt.*

Manhattan and *Washington* could anchor off Cobh, Ireland, on the sixth morning, England on the sixth afternoon, and dock at Le Havre, France, on the sixth evening. This equaled the time of all first-class ships other than *Queen Mary, Normandie, Bremen,* and *Europa.* By being able to maintain their speed better in heavy weather and by "cutting the corner," *Manhattan* and *Washington* could meet these demanding schedules.

By law ships had to follow specific shipping lanes. All lanes followed a Mercator course to the corner, which was about 800 miles from New York, and then a great circle course from there to Fastnet or Bishops Rock. Taking into consideration weather, ice, and schedule pressure, ships would cut the corner by sailing one great circle course from Nantucket to Fastnet or Bishops Rock, and vice versa. Because the arc of a great circle is the shortest distance between two points on the earth, hours could be saved. But this procedure had its risks. If the Coast Guard should catch you, the

Master would be subject to a $1,000 fine; however, Coast Guard cutters could only make 16 knots, and we kept a good lookout for them. Fog was another risk. The route was in a heavily used fishing area, and the chances of hitting a fishing vessel or its dory were high. If a Master risked sailing in an iceberg area, the vessel could be lost. The precaution against running into icebergs was to monitor water temperatures constantly. If temperatures went down, the Master had no alternative but to gradually proceed at slow speeds, using the water temperatures as a guide.

Competition for business on the North Atlantic put a lot of pressure on ship owners and Masters. Operating under such conditions without radar was not for the faint-hearted. As soon as I stepped aboard *Washington,* I was in a different world. Nothing was taken for granted, and nothing was casual. The Captain, Giles Chester Stedman, was a perfectionist. He served his original unlicensed time in the Navy as an enlisted man, then passing and raising his licenses over the years to that of Master. At age 40 he was the youngest Captain of a major transatlantic liner at the time. He personally controlled the operations of the ship and dealt directly with the Senior and Junior Watch Officers.

The first Executive Officer did not stand watch. John Hart, the First Officer, was senior watch stander. The Senior Second Officer was Henry Bradford; Hugh Andrews was the Junior Second Officer. The senior of the Junior Officers, James Knowlton, was the only other deck officer from the NYSMMA on board. Lee Argall was the other Junior Officer.

When I came aboard I reported to the Executive Officer. He told me to report to Mr. Bradford, with whom I would stand watch. The Senior Officers kept an overall watch, and the Junior Officers navigated and worked the watch. Unlike the Grace Line, where you wasted time washing down decks, we were a part of a team that had to navigate and pilot with great skill. I learned systems and methods unknown on the other ships I had sailed on or even at the Academy. This was the big league of shipping.

We had no radar in those days, but we made use of every aid to navigation then known, even unknown. Some systems had been developed aboard the ship, and all were dedicated to reducing the great risks often taken at sea. Each trip was a race against time. The rare times we were late were the result of conditions that made other ships much later. In a sense we were in a war against the North Atlantic we could not win. If we wanted to survive we had to accommodate its nature. My shipmates and I battled the elements, which as time passed, included war clouds gathering over Europe.

Washington, although half the size of its major competitors, was still a very big ship. It transported 1,300 passengers in three classes and had a crew of about 550. The deck officers' quarters were directly below the bridge and at the forward part of what was called the boat deck. Although two of the Junior Officers shared a room, the senior Junior Officer and the other watch standing officers had rooms of their own. The Captain and the Executive Officer had suites, and the double room I shared with Lee Argall was spacious. We had room stewards, and service was on a first-class basis. The downside was we had to tip both the room steward and the waiter when we ate in the first-class dining room $10 each, about one-third of what a first-class passenger tipped. Still the pay was the highest I had ever received.

Washington remained in New York about five days. Although the ship carried about 5,000 tons of cargo, one of the Second Officers was designated the Cargo Officer and stood no port watches; we only assisted on special occasions such as in connection with specie (gold and silver) and special cargo. There was a Sea Post Office aboard attended by the Railroad Postal Service, but unlicensed personnel assisted them. Our main job was standing bridge watches at sea and gangway watches prior to sailing, as well as being duty officers in port.

We had collateral jobs such as supervising the lifeboats and firefighting equipment, but crew members did the physical work. We had the responsibility for surveillance of passengers and crew regarding safety and adherence to the laws and orders applicable aboard ship. We had personnel to assist the Masters at Arms, which equated to sea-going policemen. They were under the Executive Officer, but reported to and were supervised by the Junior Officers. All of this and many other responsibilities were secondary to the navigation and our watch standing. Every knot of speed had to be forced out of the ship, as we raced to maintain schedule under the constantly changing conditions in the North Atlantic. I had to learn systems and procedures unique to the two sisterships.

I boarded *Washington* several days before sailing. Recently turned 21 I was several years younger than Lee Argall, then the youngest deck officer. Lee was a friendly and cooperative roommate, who was also neat and clean. Henry Bradford, my new mentor and boss, was in his 30s and married to Margaret Reynolds Bradford. Her family was well known and her brother, Lincoln Reynolds, was a diplomat who eventually retired to become a vice president of Pan American Airways. Margaret, older than Henry and childless, adopted me in a way. Henry Bradford was a patient and excellent teacher. Without his close monitoring of my work and looking after me at the beginning, I don't know whether I would have ever made it.

Captain Stedman was aloof and formal. He addressed us as "Mister," treated us as officers, but expected that we perform our duties accordingly. He protected the privileges of the Deck Junior Officers as he protected his own. In return we had to, and did, live up to what was expected of us. We could talk with the passengers, but were to keep our distance, especially with the ladies. Many engineering junior officers, electrical engineers, reefer engineers, and others all lived aft of us on the boat deck. There was little intermingling. They had their world in the engine rooms, their elevators to and from their jobs, and although allowed to eat in first class, they found the dress restrictions onerous and rarely did. Further the same restrictions of dress applied to them on deck, and out of uniform they were restricted to a small area. When I had the gangway watch in first class in port, girl-watching and celebrity-watching added to the interest.

Our uniforms were similar to those worn by U.S. Naval Officers, except for the cap insignia. We wore them with care, and Captain Stedman's disciplines were as tight or tighter than what I later experienced in the Navy. This U.S. Flag ship presented a proud face to the world. Dinner in the main dining room was formal and black tie. The orchestra played in a pit above the deck; like the rest of the ship, the decor was delightful.

The transatlantic liners had interesting, frequent travelers who became friends with the officers. On each trip the officers were given a "Who's Who," and I noted many of the most important people of our time on the list: ambassadors, generals, admirals, business leaders, screen stars, debutantes, Olympic teams (in third class), and society leaders. Even foreigners enjoyed the atmosphere and cuisine of this American ship.

In first class you could get almost anything you wanted to eat or drink any time of the day or night. Walking the promenade deck was a social event, as the two or three tiers of deck chair occupants observed their fellow passengers with a critical eye. Bouillon was served on deck in the morning and tea in the afternoons. There were the tea dances and after-dinner dancing. The pace was leisurely.

Passengers got to know the ship's personnel and felt both at home and safe on board. The Captain had a tremendous following, as did other officers and direct service personnel. It was an age and an atmosphere that no longer exists. As the signs of war increased, the situation on board took on a more serious aspect, due to the various nationalistic beliefs of the passengers and crew. With the advent of Hitler the large number of German "nats" in the crew found themselves in a quandary. Over the years these men of German birth but naturalized as U.S. citizens gradually worked themselves in to more and more jobs in ships that called at ports in Germany. None of the deck officers were in this category, nor were the senior engineering officers or pursers, but many steward officers, whose department was the largest on the ship, and chefs were German nats. With Hitler's ascendancy they were torn between their loyalty to their native land and that of their adopted country. Many had wives and children in Germany. Some probably had wives in both countries.

The Nazi party clandestinely established its turf on these ships. An Arbeitch Front was established; and although I recall no confrontations, I was aware of "another world" on board. The ships were Naval Reserve vessels; and even though the rolls were closed for a Reserve Commission when I graduated, they did open up a few years later. I could not be commissioned until I was 21 at any rate, and actually did not receive a commission until February 1938. Captain Stedman held a commission as a Lcdr., which before the war was raised to Commander. Bradford, Knowlton, and Argall all had commissions.

In Hamburg at night, as in other foreign ports, a bugler sounded colors as we lowered the flag. U.S. born members of the crew saluted, and the German nats as a rule ensured that they were not on deck at the time. Thus, this fracture in our country, which was evident in those times, was more so aboard the ship. Actually German nats were careful not to disturb the U.S. officers, or for that matter anyone other than their own group. At the same time they had to protect themselves and their families from their leaders .

This spreading sickness also resulted in a strained atmosphere among the passengers. Spain was in a civil war, and the feelings among Spaniards ran high. With our international mix of passengers, the events transpiring in Europe took their toll, yet we rarely had to break up fights. I recall only one stabbing. Our job was busy and difficult. The North Atlantic was mostly rough, and going east was a prevailing following sea which created a heavy roll. Going west we mostly had head seas, and at times carried the ocean on our forward deck. When it was not rough it was foggy, and at times we would stand for hours with sextant in hand attempting to get a sun or star sight and thus confirm or correct our dead-reckoning position. We had to be sure we sailed the shortest route while still checking sea temperatures to get the advantage of the Gulf Stream going east and to avoid its full impact going west. All of this had to be correlated with the expected weather. Argall and I started to make weather maps from radio position reports of ships received by the Weather Bureau and retransmitted to ships wanting them. Argall also took the upper air ballistics for both the Weather Bureau and Pan Am, a job which he was happy to pass to me. We then transmitted information to the Pan American clippers and the Zeppelins, which would pass over us frequently.

Captain Stedman was no "Poppsy" nor was he similar to the Captains of *Santa Clara, Padnsay,* or *Wind Rush.* He was no old sea dog. In fact he had the reputation of being the Clark Gable of the western ocean. He was a fine looking man, sober, and with good manners. He never yelled and kept his cool at all times. In rough seas he was generally on the bridge putting on and taking off propeller revolutions, thus adjusting speed, and also changing courses so that we were not inundated by the mountains of water coming at us. Even in lesser seas when the Captain was not on the bridge, the officers on watch were careful to ensure that one of the waves coming at us was not much bigger than the ones we were riding out. When going east, as we used up fuel, stores, and water, we had to watch our roll most carefully, while still not capsizing the vessel. In fog the Captain was always on the bridge regardless of the time span.

In the English Channel and the North Sea where we had to cope with strong currents, a system had been developed over the years so we could proceed in poor visibility, allowing for the currents as shown in the current charts, which were timed to High Water Dover. Records had been kept from the maiden voyage, and we had worked out ready reference to a voyage at the same time of the year and period related to HW Dover, as well as similar conditions of wind and seas. Even with soundings and radio bearings, position-keeping was difficult because there was heavy traffic in the area, mostly crossing, and requiring changes in courses and speeds. With no computers, no radar, and tremendous pressure to maintain schedule, we did so and even to this day I marvel at the accuracy of that system and our ability to stay out of trouble. Then there was the passage up the Elbe River, which was often foggy and very cold in winter. We had to alternate at-anchor watches in the event of steering casualty. We were the longest and I believe deepest draft vessel to safely navigate the Elbe and to be able to turn around in the Port of Hamburg turning basin.

We had a distinguished retired German Navy and Merchant Captain as the company pilot, Captain Neb. When I first joined the company, he was sociable. But as time went by and his Germany changed, he became reticent and distant. He had a large family. One could see the hurt in his eyes. He was one of the first to realize the seriousness of the situation. Other Germans, together with some of our Foreign Service officers, believed until much too late that Hitler would go away like a bad cold.

Hamburg, a city of contrasts, was the other end of my window on the world. On the one hand there was the beautiful side around the Alster Lake, a city of parks and lakes that once led the Hanseatic League. Its citizens were more worldly than the average German and proud of their city. On the other hand there was St. Pauli or the Reeper Bahn as it is known, where practically every type of debauchery and fornication was practiced and available at a price and a risk. We remained four- to six-days in Hamburg.

As a major seaport Hamburg's St. Pauli made sense. The crews of merchant vessels were much bigger then, and many more ships called for longer stays at Hamburg than do today. Seamen were rough and tough, and if you did not give them their playground they would drift into the main city and disrupt its tranquillity. So St. Pauli, in effect, was a safety valve for the thousands of sailors and others who needed to let off steam.

Actually most of the Reeper Bahn was one big trap to separate the seamen and others who cared to be tempted by the human merchandise from their cash. Friendly when the sailor's' money held out, it was rough and offensive when it did not. Fights were commonplace. One cabaret had a telephone where dancing partners unknown but seen by each could contact the other. Among the fleshpots were a few decent places; but overall it was a dangerous part of town to be in, particularly late at night and into the early morning hours. Still going strong it is no longer mainly a sailors' area but an attraction for those of all pursuits looking for what they never really find and can only imagine. In one of the Reeper Bahn cafes, the Beatles made their mark.

On our arrival in Hamburg and while going through the long process of mooring, the dock would be crowded with women and children. Only a few passengers remained for the full trip to Hamburg. Most debarked in Ireland, England, and France. The welcome-home committee was made up of the wives and regular girlfriends of the German nats, and others in the crew who had made permanent or semi-permanent connections there. Most of the married stewards who were unmarried in the States would take all their time off in Hamburg. It was a town with many more women than men, thus a man's market at almost any level of its society.

To watch the reunions was heart-rending. The lovers met on the dock sometimes with their kids standing by. But all is not gold that glistens, and this part of the society had a good shaking out. A percentage of the women had a boyfriend or husband on each U.S. Line ship that called at Hamburg. They loved them each dearly, and adherence to schedule and no vacations fitted in with the regularity that some Germans appreciated. Then tragedy struck. *President Harding* had a steering malfunction and hit the breakwater in Le Havre. It was towed to Hamburg for a month of repairs. Many happy romances must have come to an end, for even the most stupid of lovers had to know if his girl was not available when *President Harding* was in port, he was only one of two, three, or four. Still German girls can be resourceful. Tranquillity shortly returned, but whether the same participants were playing the same game one never knew.

The Reeper Bahn was too expensive for me and, although I observed it mostly in the company of either Bradford or Argall, I rarely visited that part of town. The Alster Pavilion, the Four Seasons Hotel, and the Atlantic Hotel were most frequented by the officers from the ship. Nice girls were plentiful, and the goodies we could bring from the ship were most welcome during this spartan period. I spent Christmas of 1937 there. I played tennis at the club on the Alster, and enjoyed my time in Hamburg more than in New York.

At the beginning the political situation was not so obvious and disgusting as it became later. The people from the ship and the natives I congregated with were all privately anti-Nazi. Foreign Service friends and others discussed events, and I now began to understand the importance of being able to defend oneself individually and as a nation. By 1937 I had no doubt in my mind there was going to be a war. I was revolted by the Jewish situation but did not have the least idea how serious it was. Hamburg was not one of Hitler's strongholds, and there was opposition to him. Still we lived in a sterilized world with a safe ticket out.

During the time in port all facilities aboard ship were open to the crew. Movies were shown in the Grand Salon most nights; the swimming pool and gymnasium were open to the officers. The crew would bring girlfriends and wives aboard for the movies, and officers on rare occasions brought friends aboard for meals. Those who lived ashore managed to smuggle food off the ship. Food and other commodities were still in short supply in Germany; and by sharing some with the customs officers, they seemed to be able to manage.

An atmosphere of fun and games permeated life aboard and ashore, mixed in with a grueling amount of work. Still young and naive I managed to start learning a little about women, and enjoying it. This was simple under the circumstances—we had things they wanted, available aboard ship but not in town. Although the lowest ranked and youngest of the deck officers, I was a member of the elite in this strange world of ours. I also began to make friends at the U.S. Consulate in Germany.

Next to Hamburg the most important port of call was Le Havre, the home port of the French Line. We would berth twice at Le Havre, going east and west, discharging and loading cargo and mail both ways. We would debark passengers in Le Havre but rarely would embark passengers from there to Hamburg. On the eastbound leg of the voyage we would ordinarily arrive in Le Havre at about 4:00 p.m. The French Line fleet was so large that a few ships were always at the dock. The ones in the U.S. service at the time were *Normandie, Ile De France, Paris, Champlain, LaFayette,* and the good old *De Grasse.* The British, together with the North German Lloyd Line's *Bremen* and *Europa* , called at Cherbourgh. In Hamburg our only competition was from the Hapag ships. The large North German Lloyd ships were too long to navigate the Elbe River to Hamburg.

Le Havre was an impressive port but a so-so city. In those years it was more famous for its Rue des Galleons, which was a minuscule Reeper Bahn, but the distractions were simply the bordellos and not the shows. It was all business and no nonsense other than sex. And again a contrast. In the middle of this infamous section was La Grosse Tonne, which many believed to be the best restaurant in the world. People came from far and wide particularly to enjoy the sole. They had to navigate a colorful area in which the women sold their wares from windows and on the street. The music and atmosphere were French, as well as the disorganization.

I never heard of anything in Le Havre as rough as the Bucket of Blood in Marseilles, but the town was tough. It was hard to make friends with the respectable French residents. Traditionally the French were cool to strangers, and we never had time to cultivate their friendship. There was one high-class bordello in the better part of town and one of the Pursers married the most beautiful and charming girl in it and brought her back to the States. Many hearts were broken by this unfriendly act, but the last I heard they had raised a family and lived happily ever after.

My few trips to Paris, of short duration, were in company with another officer. Still I had time to try to get into trouble. I was maturing and gaining confidence, perhaps too much. On one trip I was in the exclusive Harry's Bar. One of the ugliest and most vulgar men I ever saw was with one of the most beautiful young woman I ever saw. They were both American, and I could not imagine this being a twosome, for he looked very old. I went over to talk to the woman, and she just froze. From out of nowhere came two tough guys who literally picked me up and dumped me on the sidewalk. Later I learned it was a top Hollywood producer and his "wife."

I was told that in addition to the many legitimate attractions in Paris, I had to see the Sphinx. This was a bordello of so luxurious nature and so distinguished looking a clientele that it is nearly impossible to describe today. Men wearing black tie, white tie, and tails were drinking champagne in an opulent setting, with a variety of women dressed discreetly in ways that still exposed their charms. It was something I never saw again, because after the war it was closed in a rare reaction to what was the best of the worst of this unique French industry.

The situation I observed was an impoverished France with people eating out of our garbage cans, while in Hamburg everyone seemed to have at least enough to eat and were well dressed and housed. There were shortages of luxuries, but the Germany I saw had it very good, even when compared with the Depression in the United States. Le Havre was plainly in bad shape.

Whereas the Germans we met in connection with our work in Hamburg were already afraid to communicate, the French were the opposite. The vocal part of its citizenry was made up of the Front Populaire. They leaned heavily towards the communists, and those I talked with seemed interested mainly in a renaissance of the French Revolution. It was not hard to imagine that they would drag out the old guillotines. Counter to them were the rightists who felt secure in their positions and broke down into two groups. One group were Reserve Officers with mobilization orders to the impregnable Maginot Line. They were confident they could give "les boches" the boot if they ever tried to overrun France. Then, as in the U.S., there were many anti-Semites who sympathized with Hitler. I could find little sign of their pulling together in a war.

I could not figure the future too accurately from the contacts and information I was gathering. But even in my youth, which in experience but not in years was coming to an end, the world seemed heading towards disaster. The officers on *Washington* rarely talked politics, just taking it all in stride.

Yet life aboard *Washington* was everything I had hoped for and more. Captain Stedman demanded a great deal from us, but in turn ensured that we were treated in a more respectful manner than Merchant or Navy officers. I did a great deal of navigation and chart work. When I stepped out of line, or Captain Stedman believed I had, he would leave a little note on his memo paper for me in the chart drawer in the chartroom, which was aft of the bridge. In one instance he had seen me fairly close to a female passenger I was talking to. The next time I went to the chart table, I found a note on one of the memo pads: "Mr. Chester, I trust you will be more discreet in the future," "signed G.C. Stedman. No more, no less, but he could not have made his point more clearly. On rare occasions when he would talk to me on the bridge, he would advise me not to marry foolishly, and to find a wife with ample financial means. He in fact followed his own advice. He married the widow of Col. Schick, the founder of the Schick Razor Company. She was rich and changed the name of the #1 razor from the "Colonel" to the "Captain." Rumor was that when they married she gave him a million dollars.

From that point on the Captain would arrive at the gangway in New York in a chauffeur-driven car. He would be met by the staff purser and the Duty Officer and escorted to his cabin. Captains of transatlantic ocean liners were lords in their domain. Royalty fought for seats at the Captain's table, which was a matter of distinction for any passenger so honored. Captain Stedman was attractive to women, and they chased after him unmercifully. The more distant he was, the more aggressive they became. I would see beautiful women outside his stateroom, which was close to mine, crying. *Washington* at sea was a sovereign state and the Master was the king.

Aside from the passengers who lived apart in various classes of luxury was a vibrant city of some 500 crewmen living below decks. The deck crew lived in an area called the focs'l, the stewards and cooks in the "glory hole"; those that worked in the engine room (called the "black gang") had their own section as did the concessionaires and musicians. Some holding jobs for which tips were prevalent were the big financial hitters of the ship.

It was understood the Chief Deck Steward made the most money, but then he had to divide it among his assistants, the deck gang that washed down the decks, and some of this bosses in the steward's department. A waiter in the dining room had to share his tips with the busboys, the maitre d', and those who served him in the galley. All who lived in the "glory hole" had to pay the steward. Every tip passed through many hands. Unlike the cargo ships and smaller passenger ships in which I had previously sailed, there was a great deal of money around in the larger transatlantic liners.

Needless to say where there is money there are rackets. There was a 24-hour crap game and a 24-hour poker game. These were organized, and I was advised early on not to interfere. Since I did not desire to disappear on a dark night at sea, and realized this activity was sanctioned ashore at a level far above the ship's officers, I did not interrupt tradition. In ports such as

73

Le Havre if the crew were required to be aboard one hour prior to sailing, none of the Junior Officers would place them on the report unless they missed the gangway. In short we did not make waves unless the safety of the ship, the passengers, the crew, or the cargo was endangered. This was a requirement for acceptance, and in return there was little they would not do in return for us. The musicians would play "Happy Birthday" outside our portholes for us, the best Scotch was 90 cents a fifth, cigarettes were six cents a pack. We lived like royalty.

By January 1938 I had sufficient time to qualify to sit for my Second Mate's License. Further I did not have to request a commission in the U.S. Naval Reserve. In December a Lcdr. from the Third Naval District in New York came aboard *Washington* to give me an application to fill out. I was content in the U.S. Lines and no longer interested in active duty in the Navy. There was no better seagoing berth in either the Navy or the Merchant Marine than the one I held. We ran a 28-day schedule from New York to Ireland, England, France, and Germany. We had five days in port in New York and six days in Hamburg, plus time in France and England.

Sensing my lack of interest at the time, the Lcdr. produced a document I had signed while at the Merchant Marine Academy, indicating I would accept a commission if offered. He tendered it to me, and ordered me to report for a physical the next day. I failed the physical on weight, but it was wavered and I was informed I would receive the commission shortly.

By the time I was ready to leave in January 1938, I had become a full-fledged member of the ship's family and knew almost everyone on board. I also had many friends in the ports we visited. Still I requested reassignment to a ship on which I could raise my license after I passed for my Second Mate's License. Although the Junior Third's pay was excellent, and the responsibility much greater than that of a Third or even a Second Mate on other vessels, once I had my Second Mate's License the situation for advancement changed again. I had to sail as a Third Mate to get half time and Second Mate to get full time.

S.S. *American Shipper*

A few days after leaving *Washington,* I took the examination for Second Mate. I passed easily, and on my request was assigned to *S.S. American Shipper* as Fourth Mate with the same pay and the chance of moving up quickly to Third Mate. *American Shipper* carried 100 passengers plus cargo on a run to Liverpool, Manchester, and Belfast. It was winter, and this class of ship did not carry passengers during this season. It was a World War I built Hog Island Class B ship that made 16 knots, and whose Captain was named Sullivan. He was competent, gruff, but not unpleasant. The ocean passages were miserable. We took the northern route, and rolled all the way east and pitched through mountainous seas returning. It was not the type of voyage a passenger would care for.

In February I received my commission as an Ensign, USNR. At the end of the fourth trip, April 19, 1938, I was preparing to go ashore in New York, and was due to sail out as Third Mate on the next trip, when I looked across the dock and saw the gangway of *Manhattan*. I noticed a schoolmate who had been a year ahead of me come running off dragging his gear behind him. His nickname was "Stinky." I walked over to him and asked what was going on. He said the Commodore had fired him. I knew than that I was not going to have my few days off and the Third Mate's job. Only a few officers in the whole of the U.S. Line fleet were qualified for either *Manhattan* or *Washington*. I wished him luck, returned to *American Shipper* and started to pack my gear. Within a half hour I received orders transferring me to *Manhattan,* the Flagship of the fleet, commanded by Commodore A.B. "Rescue" Randall.

Within an hour I was aboard, and Emmons was my roommate. He laughed and thought it was a big joke. Bill Blackburn was Senior Third. We sailed the next day. All three of us were from NYSMMA.

S.S. Manhattan

Manhattan, the first to be delivered from the shipyard around 1932, was followed by its sistership, *Washington*. The similarity stopped there, which was evident from the moment I stepped on board. The atmosphere was completely different, reflecting the policies of the Masters, both competent but in completely different ways.

The Commodore, in his 60s, had previously commanded the largest passenger ship to fly the U.S. flag, *Leviathan,* a 50,000 gross ton pre-World War I German Flag transatlantic liner. The U.S. government had received the ship in war reparations from Germany. The British government was given the sistership.

The U.S. government sold or chartered *Leviathan* to the U.S. Lines, and the British White Star Line received the sistership and named it *Majestic.* They were the most luxurious ships to enter the transatlantic trades after World War I, and they aggressively competed for the post-war luxury business. *Leviathan* was a dismal failure in the service because Prohibition was enforced aboard all U.S. Flag ships. Still, for many years, the U.S. Line tried to compete, unsuccessfully, using *Leviathan* and other reparation ships such as the old *Amerika, George Washington,* U.S. war-built *President Roosevelt,* and *President Harding.* Meanwhile it attempted but failed to get an exemption from Prohibition for U.S. Flag ships. When Prohibition was expected to end, *Manhattan* and *Washington* were planned and built to arrive without this competitive handicap.

Over many years Commodore A.B. " Rescue" Randall had been at sea and involved in several tough weather rescues in the North Atlantic, thus his nickname. He was so small we had little stands for him on the bridge so he could see over the railing. He also had a little pot belly but a roaring big voice. Because he had served as a Master in the Navy collier (coal carrying) service in the early days, he was about the only Merchant Marine Master to have the rank of Captain, USNR; just before retirement he was promoted to the unprecedented rank of Rear Admiral USNR. Randall was a living legend. One of the great mysteries of the sea is the disappearance of *U.S.N.C. Cyclops,* a collier. She was lost with all hands and the wreck never located. Randall had been her Master before she had been lost.

You never knew where you stood with Stedman, who was quiet and would suddenly appear on the bridge without warning. Turn around and there he was. Never with Randall. He would slam the door to the stairway leading to the chartroom and the bridge very hard, a warning of his coming. He was not the least shy about blasting away when dissatisfied. At first I did not know what to make of the man, and my first vision of my old schoolmate "Stinky's" disorganized retreat from the ship did not render any solace about what might lie ahead. Unlike *Washington,* where there were few changes among the officers, there were to be many on *Manhattan* during my time aboard. The Executive Officer, Edward Richmond, re-lieved the Commodore for one trip while the Commodore was on vacation.

Richmond was there for the trip when we brought back "Wrong Way Corrigan" the adventurous aviator who cleared for the West and took off for Europe instead, making a bigger splash with his publicity than with his plane. The Commodore retired before the last trip after the war started in Europe and was relieved by Captain Richardson.

John "Bevo" Bevelander relieved Archie Horka as First Officer when Horka was promoted to Executive Officer. Horka remained until the transatlantic service ceased after the start of the war in Europe. Archie Horka had been turned down for admission to NYSMMA but gained his license the hard way: by shipping out on sailing vessels. Aside from being a sailor's sailor, he was one of the most brilliant men and finest human beings I ever met. The situation with the Senior and Junior Second Officers changed frequently. When I first arrived on board, the Senior Second was a naturalized citizen who had served his apprenticeship in the Furness Bermuda Line, and earned his British Master's License and later a U.S. Master's License. His name was Francis "Limey" Harris. The Junior Second, I will call "Smith," had advanced in rating in the Dollar Line and had a Master's license. Where Harris was capable but sometimes cranky, Smith was cranky, insecure, and really not capable. Otherwise he was a sober and nice person when not under the stress of the job and his inherent fear of the Commodore.

Limey Harris was relieved later by LeRoy Alexanderson, a graduate of NYSMMA Class of '30. He was a big, handsome man with a booming voice who took his job very seriously. Smith had two reliefs over the period of time: one an elderly man named Pearson who was competent, the other an elderly officer I will call "McNutt."

These officers were as different from those of *Washington* as night and day. I was the only officer on board who had sailed in both *Washington* and *Manhattan*. Occasionally I would be queried, "How would you do this or that on *Washington* The routine and the methods were roughly identical, and I had no trouble fitting in.

Emmons was basically a good guy, but one could never tell whether his interest was the job or a girl. He knew his work, but was occasionally late in relieving the watch, yet this was Emmons. Bill Blackburn, the Third Officer, was used to him, and I just accepted this in the overall man who was a pleasant and decent roommate. Smith, however, was very difficult to stand watch with, and as the junior of the three Juniors, I caught him. Blackburn stood watch with the First Officer and Emmons with the Senior Second, usually Limey Harris. Blackburn had been on the ship since the maiden voyage, and although he only had a Second Mate's License, knew the job better than any of the senior watch officers, other than Horka before he was promoted to Executive Officer. But Blackburn did not seem to give a damn. Emmons had been aboard for years, and he knew the job but could be distracted.

The back-up for the Second Officers could not have been stronger. Any one of the three Juniors could have run the watch as well as the Seniors. Smith, a meticulously groomed man in his 30s, concentrated on looking like an officer rather than doing the work. Celestial navigation was jointly done by the Senior and the Junior in good weather, and by the Junior alone in periods of bad visibility and rough seas, when the Senior had to concentrate on keeping watch. Celestial navigation was beyond Smith's capabilities. When he attempted to calculate a position, he looked like a man in complete agony. He also was insecure in most of the other jobs and particularly in responding to any questions the Commodore might ask. If I had to leave the bridge to tend to some matter, he would try to talk me out of it. He depended entirely on me, and when the door slammed, signaling the approach of the Commodore to the bridge, fear struck in his heart. He depended on me so much that any talk of a change in watch partners panicked him.

Navigating and piloting in the English Channel and the North Sea ordinarily was very difficult. Scientifically working with the reference voyage system was something Smith and McNutt could not understand, but fortunately the system saved them, as lookout was very important. This they did, but what they saw and how they would react when they saw it constantly concerned me. At times the Commodore was aware of this, or the Executive Officer would come to the bridge. I would be running around taking radio bearings, visual bearings, soundings, calculating the corrections from the reference voyage calculation, checking the engine revolutions to see that the Chief Engineer was giving us the turns required, and plotting the positions. From all this information I would advise the Second Officer when to change course and what course to change to.

I also had a problem with Mr. McNutt, a large man in his 50s who imbibed. He didn't seem to be with it. He would stand around muttering some gibberish, ignoring me. One night we were proceeding at close to 25 knots with the current, and it was time to change course. I came out of the chartroom and said, "Mr. McNutt, it is time to come left to course so and so." At this point the procedure was for him to see whether the new course was clear of ships, and give the course change to the helmsman. Nothing. He just kept mumbling. At the speed we were going we had about four minutes before we ran aground if we did not alter our course. He ignored me.

At the last minute I ordered the wheelman to come left to the new course. Having observed what was going on, he carried out my order even though Mr. McNutt tried to countermand it. This giant with large fists came at me cursing and swinging wildly. It was dark on the bridge, and I could dodge his alcoholic swings. At the same time, with an emergency turn, the ship leaned over, and brought the Commodore to the bridge in his pajamas. It was about 0330 hours. He could see what was going on—after so many years at sea, good captains can sense things. Mr. McNutt was obviously drunk. The Commodore relieved him of his watch. McNutt docilely left the bridge, and the Commodore, obviously shook up, spent the remainder of the watch with me. He said nothing to me.

On another occasion on the 2000- to 2400-hour watch bound west standing watch with Mr. Smith at about 2030 hours, I noticed the horizon seemed to be false. We were cutting the corner in the northern latitudes. I suggested that we notify the Commodore. He was afraid to annoy the man at dinner. He thought if he did and there was no fog, the Commodore would be upset. Finally about 15 minutes later, I convinced him. We called the dining room and started the automatic fog horn. I stood on the port wing of the bridge, the Second Officer was on the starboard. A few minutes later before the Commodore could get to the bridge, I heard another fog horn ahead and saw a huge liner coming straight at us. I jumped into the wheelhouse and ordered full right rudder. Fortunately the other ship did the same. We both listed heavily but passed clear of each other by only several hundred feet. I saw the other ship clearly: it was *Ile De France*.

When we heeled over you could hear things crashing, and many a new Paris gown must have been ruined in the first-class dining room. The Commodore reached the bridge several minutes later, having been caught in the elevator. I was shook up some, but the Second Officer was a basket case. The Commodore said nothing and reduced the speed. The correct procedure in a fog is to proceed at a speed that you can stop the ship in half the seeing distance. This was followed in congested waters, but rarely on the high seas. If in those days before radar the Masters had done so, the ships could hardly have kept a schedule. The percentage of fog was too high. Thus there was no fear in *Manhattan* that *Ile De France* would report the incident any more than they feared we would do so.

The incident with *Ile De France* occurred on the high seas. Our most dangerous passages, from a collision viewpoint, were in the English Channel and North Sea. The traffic there was tremendous, the percentage of fog very high, and currents deceptive. Yet year in and year out, transatlantic liners crisscrossed with cross-channel steamers, reverse traffic, fishing boats, and utility vessels, including tugs and barges, with few accidents. With many high-speed ships crowding the sea lanes, it was amazing there were not more collisions. More seemed to occur after the introduction of radar. Most collisions I recall were in daylight when ships were in sight of each other. Apparently God looks out for us more efficiently than we do.

Manhattan's Chief Engineer, Patty Brennan, was another legend in his time. He was about 6'4" and big all around. He was tough, with one of the biggest jaws and the biggest fists I ever saw. Although I never saw him in a fight, rumor was he had beaten many a man to within an inch of his life. He was getting older at this time and had become somewhat mellower. Fortunately his backup was Bill Kaiser, and few if any problems were experienced in the engine room.

Manhattan was not a coal burner but one of the most sophisticated ships of its time. Seniority played a big part in appointments, and Patty was the Chief. He also was the first Chief of *United States,* but was soon relieved by Bill Kaiser, who remained to the end.

The cooks and stewards made up most of the ship's complement. The chef was believed to be the highest salaried person on board. The key personnel in this department had their own rooms, but the waiters, room stewards, and others lived in the Glory Hole, which had its own laws as did the galley. In addition to the focs'l and the unlicensed engineer quarters, this was the real inner city of the ship. Just as in *Washington,* there were 24-hour crap and poker games. If the officers or their Master at Arms ever tried to break it up, they would disappear at sea one dark night.

Then there was "the little Fuhrer" who was in the Stewards department. The German nats had to do as he desired or else. Rumor had it that when going ashore in Germany, they had to have a pass from him as well as the Line Pass signed by the ship's officers. The passengers saw little of this, but there was communications between the stewards on the liners of all flags. The names of non - or poor-tippers were passed from one ship to another, for example. We could tell when a passenger complained to the doctor of stomach trouble. The doctor knew it, they did not, but they were getting Mickeyed as non-tippers. Fortunately most passengers got the word. A rumor the stewards passed around was that Rudolph Valentino was killed by Mickey Finns he had received aboard the ships, including *Leviathan,* and I gather some restaurants. He did not like waiters (he had been a busboy) and they apparently reciprocated.

The deck of the first-class veranda cafe was the source of much unhappiness. Long before Hitler it had been designed in blocks of swastikas. This, together with the shock of boarding a U.S. Flag ship and finding that most of the crew were German nats, had a debilitating effect on our Jewish passengers, who were ready to kiss the deck of their deliverance, only to see its pattern. The German crew members, however, were careful to treat all passengers with respect.

There were few German Jewish passengers boarding in Hamburg, and this percentage was reduced as time went by. The State Department would not grant visas to them unless they had a police certificate. They had to get this from the SS, and few were able to do so. On several trips we embarked a large number of unescorted Jewish children bound for Southampton, England. The Nazis, while embarking them, hardly restrained their meanness. It was disgusting, but we could do nothing at that time. But once they were aboard Archie Horka, the Executive Officer, took over. He spent his time and money attempting to ease their fear and pain. In a sense he adopted each one of them. There was no exodus to the USA for the Jewish people from Hamburg. They just could not get the visas, and the State Department never bent in this policy while I was in that liner service. But if they could get to France or England, they could then get to the USA, and many felt secure on an American ship.

As the war drew closer, and as I became more aware of it while in *Manhattan,* I found my time in this ship much more interesting than in *Washington.* I was maturing and learning. I had a particular "window" on Germany from being able to drive around the country in a 1938 Buick convertible with Richard Hallock Davis, a junior foreign Service officer at the U.S. consulate in Hamburg. The car was made available to him after the Ambassador's secretary, Peter Belin, left. I believe Peter was a Dupont, and when he was ordered home from Berlin it was thought Richard Davis could put the car to better use. Information was difficult to get in Nazi Germany, and from later 1938 until the war started in Europe, it became even harder.

The Germans were in the process of constructing a huge network of roads, even though there were few cars in the country. These Reich Autobahns were supposedly being built for the use of the German citizens, all of whom were being taxed for a new car known as the Volkswagen and due to be delivered soon. It was a big joke among those of us who were suspicious of Hitler's motives. Blackburn in particular, with his wry humor, would often come up with comments on the Autobahn and the Volkswagen. The car did not make its civilian debut until after World War II, long after Hitler went into the history books. But the Reich Autobahns were an ominous indication of preparation for war.

Blackburn did not assist our intelligence operation, even though he probably would have been the number one choice of those domiciled in

Germany. He disqualified himself by taking a strong stand against accepting a commission. I had two useful qualifications: I could play an adequate game of tennis and I could sketch well. Davis, who had unusual charm, also was a good tennis player. Bill Blackburn, although uncommunicative on the matter, apparently was having an affair with the wife of a senior foreign service officer. Her name was Suzie. The situation created serious problems for her and did not enhance Bill's position with the Diplomatic Corps in Germany.

The intelligence gathering operation was somewhat makeshift, brought on by the need to work outside regular intelligence and diplomatic channels. Hitler had more friends in high places internationally than enemies. President Roosevelt obviously did not trust them any more than Churchill, out of office at the time, trusted the Chamberlain government. A strong rumor held that our embassy in London was compromised and Joseph Kennedy's loyalty to President Roosevelt questionable. I did not know it then, but President Roosevelt was working closely with Captain Allen Kirk, USN, a mystery man to me.

The 1938 Buick convertible gave us mobility. With practically no traffic on the autobahns, we could speed all over Germany following up leads, having meetings, and talking with German Naval Officers—at times becoming close to them. In most cases they talked freely. Because we paid the bills and had little goodies for them, they often were eager to please. Most were not Nazis at the time. They were ecstatic about the buildup, but tailored their conversation to make it appear as though it was within treaty terms. When they could not, for example, with the accelerated submarine production, they downplayed the situation. They claimed there was never going to be a war against England, France, or the United States.

Strangely the Germans I met seemed to worship everything British, liked the Americans, and tolerated the French. They continually claimed Germany was the bulwark against the Soviet Union, and we should cooperate with them rather than fight them. In my opinion they were totally confused. History has established they were receiving advice from what ordinarily would be highly reliable political, official, and non-official sources, ensuring them the three nations would never go to war against them. Looking back I gather they were playing the same game with us that we played with them. They sounded us out and tried to convince us that they were our friends. We played along with them on the tennis courts, the restaurants, and the nightclubs.

We did not confine our mixing to military personnel but also conversed with government officials and private citizens. Meanwhile Tommy Thayer, Vice Consul, was rarely in Hamburg, and moving around. I believe he crossed from China on the trans-Siberian railroad. Dawson, the senior member of the group, stayed put, mostly in Hamburg with infrequent trips to other parts of Germany. Thayer held a diplomatic passport.

Captain Kirk was moving in the highest levels of the German government, probably meeting with Hitler. It was no secret he was more important than he appeared. Slightly under-average height, he was a good looking man, and unassuming. Yet 50 year-old-Navy Captains were not about to communicate with 22-year-old Ensigns. In fact he was only interested in receiving information and not dispensing it. I would like to have been a close confidant of this man, but I was not.

Neither Davis or Thayer seemed to have any close German government contacts. Allan Dawson, a senior diplomat who appeared too important for the position he officially held in Germnay, did. I took my cues from Davis. We played out our little charade. We were not, however, above playing a few pranks. Davis lived in an apartment on the Alster owned by the widow of a doctor. "Frau Doctor" was a kindly, elderly woman, quite incapable of understanding what was going on around her. One evening Bill Blackburn brought Davis a recording of Ella Fitzgerald singing "Martha" in her inimitable manner. Without telling Davis, Blackburn put the recording on the player and turned the volume all the way up. "Martha" was practically the German national anthem. Windows slammed down, neighbors complained, Frau Doctor caught hell—but Davis had diplomatic immunity, and even the Nazis were somewhat in awe of U.S. diplomats then.

Although the brutality of Hitler's regime accelerated, it was difficult to realize how bad it was unless you were a victim. Meanwhile problems in our little community, in and out of Germany, were increasing. In the personal area Blackburn's affair with Suzie became complicated. Her husband divorced her. No longer on his diplomatic passport, she had to apply for another one. Whether it was pressure from her husband's friends, I don't know, but somehow Suzie ended up stateless. Apparently she was born in the Far East and her parents emigrated to the U.S. Some detail at the time her parents became citizens was used to deny her a U.S. passport.

Strange times and strange characters. An American living in Hamburg who called himself "Baron" spoke good English but poor German. I never knew or cared whether his claim to the title was correct, but he played the part. To me he was a phoney. He worked hard at getting friendly with officers on the U.S. Line ships, and was ready to pick up a check or produce a cooperative young lady. He made little progress that I know of in *Washington,* and I rarely recall seeing him on board or ashore for that matter during that period. It could be he had not set up his act yet.

When I arrived in Hamburg on the first voyage in *Manhattan,* and by the time I finished my work with securing the ship, I found this odd character in my room. In his 40s he was short with blond hair standing straight up in the Prussian manner, and a military German mustache. He was waiting for Emmons. I soon found out that although he was friendly with several officers in the ship, including the Commodore, Emmons was his close buddy.

Emmons liked the girls, was lazy looking for them, tight with a dollar, and the Baron was quick to oblige. He would brag of the great time he had with the beautiful girl he had met. The Baron's Germany soon became that of Emmons. Off they went on many tours of the town. I did not have a suspicious mind in those days, and I did not think much of it. The Baron tried to pass himself off as just a lonely American in a foreign land seeking American friendship.

Blackburn warned me about this guy, and said he was not liked by the American Consulate group. I gather he got what he was after by using Emmons. He made no overtures and showed no interest in me. John Bevelander also went out with him, and I would not be surprised if the Baron bought the Commodore a drink or a dinner. I had things to do, and I did not want to draw attention to myself. The "girl situation" in Hamburg was no problem, and I did not need anyone to find female companionship for me. The Baron was a nuisance—his waiting or being with Emmons in my room was an intrusion on my privacy. I asked Emmons to keep him out, which he did if he could. The Baron was around until we last sailed from Hamburg as the war started.

After the war began I forgot all about the Baron. Several years after the war, the FBI visited me in my office. They asked me how well I knew the Baron. I said not well. Did I know anything about the transportation of Jewish assets from Hamburg to the United States on *Manhattan* I said no. What did I know about the Baron? I told them the little I knew.

They said he had made deals with German Jewish people to transport their assets out of Germany for them. He had introduced these people to some of the officers, and indicated that many on the ship were working for him. There had been complaints that their assets were turned over to an officer and never seen again. It all added up. From what the FBI told me, it seems that the Baron had a mean little racket going for himself.

By appearing in public with officers on numerous occasions, he built up an illusion of a well-organized operation to get articles of value out of Germany. None of the officers showed any evidence of affluence. I am certain Emmons would not become engaged in anything of that sort.

At the end of May 1939 the U.S. Navy ordered me to temporary active duty for two weeks. I joined *U.S.S. Texas,* a battleship based in Norfolk, VA. The only necessary change in uniform was the hat device on the uniform cap. I had to leave *Manhattan* to complete the Navy duty. Again I used this as an excuse to be ordered to a ship of the U.S. Line where I could get time credit towards a Chief Mate's License. Captain Topping as usual was cooperative, and said that when I returned I would be assigned to *American Trader,* a sistership of *American Shipper. Trader* was on the New York to London run.

An Ensign aboard a battleship is one of a mob, and there must have been at least 25 Ensigns on the *Texas.* Shortly after I arrived we left for a ten-day cruise. It was for battle practice, but ammunition was not authorized for firing. All we did was go through the motions. I was assigned to No. 2 turret, and there I spent most of my time as we simulated loading, firing, and training the guns on various targets.

I stood Junior Officer of the Deck watches. Aside from the peculiarities of formation steaming, keeping a prescribed distance from other ships in the formation by stadimeter, and executing turns in formation, my job was elementary in comparison to what I had been doing. The regular Navy Ensigns, all from Annapolis, were there to be seen and not heard. Still I was learning although I was bored to death by the time the cruise ended. The officers and crew were as friendly as possible under the circumstances. I had a short meeting in Washington, D.C., about the situation in Germany. They were surprised to learn I was not returning to *Manhattan.*

S.S. American Trader

Kenneth Sutherland, a NYSMMA graduate of the Class of 1918, Captained *S.S. American Trader.* A gentleman and as good a shipmaster as any I had sailed with, Sutherland above all was a very modest man who could accomplish a great deal with a quiet word. Captain Topping had come through: for the first time, I finally got half time towards a Chief Mate's License.

I was certain I would be assigned to *Manhattan* after returning to New

York. In fact I had packed my bags prior to arrival. When the ship docked I received orders to report to Captain Topping. He said he was sorry, but I would have to return to *Manhattan,* and intimated he could do nothing about it. I returned to *Trader* to tell Captain Sutherland, who was surprised and sorry to see me leave. We had become friendly, and I would also miss my other shipmates. *Trader* was not only a well-run ship, but the friendliest I ever sailed in.

When *Manhattan* arrived I reported to the Executive Officer, Archie Horka. With a sly grin on his face, he welcomed me home. The Commodore passed me in the corridor, sort of looked at me as though I had never left, and went on his way. When I dumped my gear into my old room, both Emmons and Blackburn were there. Emmons went about his business as if nothing had changed. Blackburn, however, had a silly smirk on his face, which indicated my return was no surprise to him.

On or about August 12, 1939, *Manhattan* departed on her 91st eastbound voyage to call at Cobh, Plymouth, Le Havre, and Hamburg and to return via Le Havre, Southampton, and Cobh. The same day *Washington* left Hamburg for New York. Rumors of war were everywhere, and some crew members found excuses for missing the voyage. Blackburn, who followed current events carefully, was certain war was a foregone conclusion.

Little had changed aboard the ship among the deck officers. Although due to retire shortly, Commodore Randall was still in command. Archie Horka was the Executive Officer, John Bevelander was the First Officer, Francis Harris was the Senior Second Officer, and LeRoy Alexanderson was the Junior Second Officer. The three third officers—Blackburn, Emmons, and I—were the same, but the two problem second officers were gone. Patty Brennan was still the Chief Engineer, and Bill Kaiser was the Senior Assistant Engineer. But many things within the ship and in the world were rapidly changing around us.

Ordinarily on a summer trip we carried a cheerful, vacationing group of passengers. But this was not the case now. The routine went on as before, but the passengers were more serious. Many were returning to enlist in the British and French armed forces, some as reservists. Some had been called home for their national service commitment. Our crewmen, German naturalized U.S. citizens who had families in Germany, were concerned. The "Little Fuhrer," as we called the member of the Steward's Department, was particularly nervous. We believed he headed the Arbeitch Front on board.

As the voyage progressed the radio news, reprinted in the ship's newspaper, grew more ominous. By the time we approached Cobh, with arrival scheduled for early morning the 23rd, rumors about schedule changes and canceling the stop in Hamburg were flying among both passengers and crew. Crewmen with families and close friends in Hamburg pressed for more information, but we had none to give them. The Commodore received coded information and orders, which, aside from the Executive Officer, were not circulated.

The news said that American expatriates, tourists, and students were all clamoring for tickets on U.S. Flag and other neutral passenger vessels, as well as cargo ships. Although war had been rumored for over a year, this was the first time it had taken on sufficient meaning for U.S. citizens in Europe to make definite plans to leave for home.

While en route to Plymouth later that day, we were informed we would proceed from Plymouth to Le Havre as soon as we had discharged our passengers and mail. All cargo and eastbound passengers, except what little cargo there was for Southampton, would be discharged in Le Havre. Westbound passengers would be embarked in Le Havre, Southampton, and Cobh. We then would return to New York. This schedule change confirmed there was more to the situation than rumors of war.

Complications arose over space for the increasing number of U.S. citizens fleeing Europe. We filled every spare berth in the passenger section and every spare berth in the officers' and crews' quarters as well. We took aboard cots and sleeping bags. Furniture also served as beds. We rationed food. No room existed for additional lifeboats, but we added as many rafts as we could carry, plus additional lifebelts.

In addition to our original 1,300 passenger capacity, we carried some 500 more souls. This created problems for the deck officers, who hastily prepared new abandon ship and fire precautions. The stewards and cooks planed more austere meals, arranging to feed the additional passengers in an organized manner. The Plymouth call eastbound was routine, but on our arrival in Le Havre increased activity was evident in many ways.

By the morning of the 25th, we knew we were not going to accomplish our usual quick dispatch in the port. Some of the stevedore and shore staff had already been mobilized and assigned elsewhere. Drinking and internal disputes became more of a problem. The local manager worked nearly round the clock. Le Havre was blacked out at night, and the cargo work went very slowly. None of the officers got any sleep. With passengers struggling to get aboard, some ticketed and some not, prewar hysteria built up. For many months now *Manhattan's* and *Washington's* specie rooms had been filled with gold, jewels, and other valuable items. Silver and silver coins in boxes were carried in the open holds. Officers had to supervise these areas because the value was extremely high.

Much of the wealth of the European areas became vulnerable to attack. On an earlier trip, after having discharged all the cargo from one of the cargo holds that also included a fortune in silver bars, we inspected the holds after discharge. We found about ten silver bars hidden behind the battens. At that time they were only worth about $600 apiece, but that still was a great deal of money. Longshoremen had hidden the silver bars during the discharge or even during loading and probably planned to smuggle them from the ship later.

In checking the receipts we were surprised to discover the U.S. Treasury had signed for them in full. We tried to get a recount, but treasury officials said they were certain of their tally. But ten bars were sitting in the square of the hatch, with Archie Horka, Blackburn, and me sitting on the deck looking at them. It was a hell of a temptation to cut them up and just keep them, but that was not our nature. We listed the numbers and marks, removed them to the specie room, which was empty by then, and locked them up. We gave the U.S. Treasury the numbers and marks. They had over-counted and came to pick up the bars. I was amazed they were actually antagonistic towards us for creating a problem, which probably would not have surfaced until they all retired. Were we fools?

The amount of specie, gold and silver, jewels, and other valuable items carried during this period must have been tremendous. The longshoremen would occasionally drop cases of coins, which would splatter all over the hold. We would lose some but not much. Duty in those days was taken seriously.

And so as the passengers boarded in Le Havre, together with valuables and cargo, I was witnessing the end of an era and the beginning of many years of war. Although still not involved, as a neutral vessel we could be in the thick of it all. We painted a large U.S. Flag on each side of the vessel and one on the boat deck visible to aircraft. We departed from Le Havre for Southampton, arriving around the 26th or 27th of August. It was more of the same in Southampton, except the British were better organized.

Southampton was already on war status, and liners of both British and other expected belligerents were taking on extra passengers. Our stay, lengthened by many details and problems, delayed our departure for Cobh until the 29th or 30th. We began our transatlantic westbound crossing several hours after arrival at Cobh. On departure we had the largest number of passengers ever carried on board.

Celebrities were underfoot—Arturo Toscanini, Grace Moore, and Marlene Dietrich had managed to arrange berths in the officers' section. Those of us with heavy duties and who stood watches could not sell our rooms and still do our jobs, even though the prices offered were fantastic. I was caught up in a series of events that placed me in the center of the beginning of upheaval.

Hostilities did not start until September 1 when Hitler ordered the invasion of Poland. Assured by his many friends in Britain that they would only make noise and never go to war over Poland, Hitler miscalculated the British resolve as a whole while depending on information received from a few. The pressure built up so much that Chamberlain, faced with a rebellious House of Commons and a threatened split in his own Cabinet, called for an emergency Cabinet meeting. Shortly before midnight they decided to issue a final ultimatum to Germany the next morning.

The British telegram, delivered about 9:00 a.m., demanded cessation of the German invasion by 11:00 p.m. Hitler was flabbergasted and implied to his foreign minister that he had been misled. Still the die was cast, the war was on, and France soon followed the British lead.

By this time we were halfway to New York. As we received the news this fateful Sunday morning of September 3rd, we also learned that *Athenia,* a passenger ship of the Anchor Donaldson Line, had been sunk. We did not circulate the news, for we did not want to create even more fear among the passengers on our overcrowded ship. The weather was good, and the morale under the conditions excellent. Many passengers, although U.S. citizens, had left assets as well as numerous friends behind in Europe. Some had been abroad for years and were returning home to a country now more foreign to them than Europe.

The sinking of *Athenia* and many of the events going on at this time only added to the uncertainty of safety at sea. Although Hitler had issued orders for German warships not to sink passenger ships, 26-year-old Lieutenant Lemp in command of *U-30* mistook *Athenia* for an auxiliary cruiser. Lemp had surfaced to shoot away *Athenia's* wireless aerials, thus preventing her from transmitting warning signals. Once he surfaced, he realized the ship was a passenger liner, and he quickly submerged. He must have realized he had violated both international law and Hitler's strict instructions, but Lemp departed without offering assistance. Of the 1,300 survivors and 118 casualties, 22 were U.S. citizens.

This was the opening gun in what was to expand into the greatest sea battle of all times, the Battle of the Atlantic. Hitler tried to cover the sinking by blaming it on Winston Churchill. Although proof was not established until after the war, few believed the propaganda. Shortly thereafter Hitler authorized unrestricted submarine warfare, and the war in the Atlantic erupted into a raging inferno.

While we were leaving Cobh, ships of nations that expected to become involved in the war started to scurry for safety all over the world. *Bremen* of the North German Lloyd Line had been scheduled to depart from New York for Bremen on August 28. An executive order to the Steamboat Inspection Service delayed the departure, by a prolonged inspection period, until August 30th. This could only have been ordered by President Roosevelt in an effort to cooperate with the British. *Bremen* was only one of a large number of German merchant ships preparing to depart from neutral ports throughout the world. Those caught at sea would become fair game for the Royal Navy once hostilities commenced. The German-Russian peace pact announced on August 24th left little or no doubt that war would begin within days.

Europa, a sistership of *Bremen,* already bound east, received information about the peace pact. She promptly canceled port calls at England and France and proceeded at maximum speed to Bremen, arriving prior to actual hostilities. *Bremen* and *Europa* were the two largest and fastest vessels in the German merchant fleet and prime objectives for capture afloat by the Royal Navy. Both efforts were thwarted.

The Steamboat Inspection Service ran out of excuses to delay *Bremen's* departure. Meanwhile the Royal Navy, which predominated in the Atlantic, deployed its fleet to interdict as many German ships as possible, concentrating on those in order of importance. Nearly a hundred German ships plied the seas, but none more important than *Bremen* and *Europa.*

During all of this by-play *Manhattan* steamed towards New York. Captain Ahrens of *Bremen* was one of the best of the brilliant transatlantic shipmasters of the era. One of the biggest ships in the world, *Bremen* was difficult to hide even in so large an ocean. The Royal Navy had deployed in a scouting line covering most conceivable escape routes.

Ordinarily *Bremen* would pass close to *Manhattan* if both ships were on their regular courses. Little if any of this exciting news in the making appeared in *Manhattan's* newspaper. The other officers and I were preoccupied with numerous problems of our own. With overcrowded conditions aboard and a war imminent, we followed strict routing orders—a great circle from Fastnet to the corner, and a straight mercator course from the corner to Nantucket, and then home.

But neither the Royal Navy nor we passed anywhere near *Bremen*. Once Captain Ahrens dropped his pilot, and after taking a few short misleading courses, he set a great circle course taking him between Iceland and Greenland. Painting the ship gray en route to reduce visibility in this generally overcast area, he safely arrived in Murmansk eight days later with only a few hours of fuel remaining. It was a legendary voyage, although later *Bremen* was destroyed by fire and never sailed again.

German ships were being scuttled, some remained in neutral ports, some were sunk, and others also made it home. The orderly commerce of the world, which had gained momentum since the end of World War I, had come to an end. These were only the opening moves in a war at sea. After we arrived in New York around the 6th of September, a quick turnaround was arranged. Many Americans in Europe, desperate for passage home, were reluctant to book on vessels flying the flag of a belligerent nation. *Athenia's* sinking underscored the fact that even though the war on land, at the time, was restricted to the east, the Battle of the Atlantic had started. We soon departed from New York to Cobh on Voyage 92 on about the 8th of September. We were full eastbound but not overcrowded. Around this time Commodore Randall retired to take up shore duty as a Rear Admiral in the Navy. He was old and tired.

I was at work on the charts in the chartroom when Randall turned over command to Captain Richardson. I was surprised to hear him say in his assessment of the officers that he considered me one of the best. On leaving the ship for the last time and passing my room on the way to the gangway, he stopped to say good-bye, and gave me one of his black ties. He said something complimentary to me for the first time, and I found his unceremonial passing into retirement dismaying.

There was no change of command ceremony as in the Navy, no dinner, no presentation of even a traditional watch, and the first and last of the great American Commodores of the U.S. Flag Merchant Marine's transatlantic fleet during its prime simply passed from the scene. Although a monarch aboard his flagship, I don't believe he ever earned over $600 a month. Giles Stedman was next in line to be Commodore.

Voyages 92 and 93 to Europe would be the last. Voyage 92 proceeded to Cobh then to Southampton. On September 17th en route from Southampton to Le Verdon, which had been substituted for Le Havre, we passed *HMS Courageous,* a large British aircraft carrier. We passed each other close aboard in an area the Royal Navy called the western approaches. Destroyers escorted her. The activity of the thousands of men on board, together with the noise from the warship, gripped me as I watched her. We followed custom and "dipped" our ensign in salute, and *Courageous* dipped hers in return.

Before we reached Le Verdon, and in daylight hours, *Courageous* was torpedoed and sunk with the loss of 518 officers and men.

When the two ships had passed an hour before, we were both making over 20 knots. The German sub had to have been waiting in a good firing position to fire torpedoes. At the start of the war American and German subs had a top submerged speed of 8 to 10 knots for a limited time. Normal submerged cruising speed was 2 to 5 knots. On the surface German subs made approximately 16 to 18 knots. U-29 had to be very lucky to be in a firing position on a fast-moving escorted carrier. Anti-submarine attacks were made on *U-29*, but she survived.

Le Verdon-sur-Mer, at the mouth of the Gironde River, had an adequate dock, but we were the only ship in the berth. We had already embarked our westbound passengers in Southampton, and the westbound trip to New York was a repeat of Voyage 91 in that we carried returning citizens in every possible area of the ship. Voyage 93 to Cobh, Southampton, and Le Verdon followed in October, but fortunately we had no repeat of the heart-rending experience with *Courageous*. Captain Richardson was a quiet, polite old gentleman, and little changed in the operation of *Manhattan*.

In late October we tied up at Pier 59 in New York, but no further transatlantic voyages were scheduled. Some months later, with *Washington* and the new *America, Manhattan* would be placed into the intercostal service between the east and west coasts of the U.S. An era was over and a war was on. I had been a spectator for the past months, but now the world that I had become accustomed to no longer existed. I was kept employed by the U.S. Lines for several weeks; but as expected, I received orders to report for extended active duty with the first group of 100 Naval Reserve Officers.

I never found out if I had a choice. Jobs in the Merchant Marine were now plentiful, and I could have shipped out as a Second Mate with no trouble. As soon as qualifying to sit for a Chief Mate's License, I could have gotten a Chief Mate's job. This meant that I could have received my Master's License in 1941. Blackburn, who was not in the Naval Reserve, quickly found employment as a Second Mate in the Moore-McCormack Lines. For some reason I did not give the matter much thought. Fate seemed to be changing my course, and I decided to go along even though it would mean a large reduction in pay. War was inevitable. I decided I would rather be in the Navy in wartime than in the Merchant Marine. Still we were at peace, and I was ordered to report to *U.S.S. Kanawha (AO-1)* in San Diego, as an Ensign.

I spent the few remaining weeks of leisure with my mother in her new home in Baldwin, Long Island. I drove around in her car, purchased uniforms and a sword from Battleship Max Cohen, and looked to the future in anticipation, leaving behind the problems in the Atlantic for what appeared to be a peaceful Pacific.

S.S. Santa Clara, *first ship Chester sailed in after graduation. (courtesy of Frank O. Braynard.)*

S.S. Excalibur, 1936. (courtesy of Frank O. Braynard.)

Al Chester, Third Mate, S.S. Padnsay with Kru Boys and port official, West Africa, 1936.

Open Roadsteads - Surf boats, West Coast of Africa, approaching S.S. Padnsay, 1936.

Al Chester on the bridge of **S.S. Washington**, *North Atlantic, 1937. Sighting with sextant was the basis for celestial navigation.*

S.S. Washington, *North Atlantic, summer 1937. First row, L-R: Henry Bradford, Ralph Dooley, Captain Giles C. Stedman, John Hart. Back row, L-R: Al Chester, James Knowlton, Hugh Andrews, Lee Argall.*

S. S. Washington, *sistership to* **S.S. Manhattan**.
*These luxury liners were the largest and fastest ships built
in the United States.* **S.S. Manhattan** *began continuous
transatlantic service in 1932 and made two voyages to
Europe after the war started in 1939.*

Lifeboat drill in **S.S. Manhattan**, *New York, 1939.*

S.S. Manhattan *baseball team, 1939. Al Chester, Coach.*

S.S. American Shipper, *sistership to* **S.S. American Trader.**

Dorothy Chester
aboard **S.S. Virginia**
on stop over in Havana en route
to Los Angeles, 1938.

Hamburg, 1939.
Bill Blackburn and Al
Chester kidding around
in 1938 Buick
owned by Peter Belin
and on loan to
Dick Davis.

Hamburg, 1939.
Al Chester at the tennis club on
the Alster with Richard Hallock
Davis, a U.S. Foreign
ServiceOfficer.
Davis,
now deceased, had an
outstanding career in diplomacy.
He was the American Minister in
Moscow and Charge d'Affairs.
He also served
as the U.S. Ambassador to
Rumania.

Four

Countdown:
War in the Pacific

U.S.S. Kanawha (AO-1)

The close relationship between the Merchant Marine and the Navy predates the American Revolution. John Paul Jones and many of his contemporaries were Merchant Mariners first. Some but not many Merchant Marine officers were commissioned during World War I. The Navy's part in that war at sea was infinitesimal next to what it would be in World War II. Because the Navy was reduced in size after World War I, the Admirals realized if there should be a war at sea in the future, there would be a shortage of officers.

Over 90 percent of the post-World War I Naval officers were graduates of the Naval Academy. A small number rose from the ranks, and some Reserves from World War I received commissions in the regular Navy. Other Reserve Officers from World War I remained in the small organized reserve, which was maintained on a limited budget, but they were not an important factor. Some Merchant Marine officers, who had served as Naval officers during World War I, also were maintained on an inactive status. Most Merchant Marine officers commissioned in World War I served in auxiliary vessels, which in some case were the same ships they had served in prior to the ship being requisitioned by the Navy. Some years after World War I, NROTC was established at eight selected universities. It was a small operation and did not lead to permanent commissions. But it produced a group of high-quality reserve officers who played a role in World War II out of all proportion to their small numbers, particularly in destroyer escorts.

Because of the need for a reserve pool of officers, the Navy supported, in part, state nautical schools. It thus depended on their graduates along with other licensed officers for a nucleus of Reserve Officers, mainly to serve on auxiliary commissioned vessels. Reserve Deck Officers were classified as D-M, reserve Engineering Officers as E-M. When funds were available Merchant Officers were actively recruited. When funds were not available they were ignored. Thus, as war clouds gathered in the Pacific and Atlantic, all indications were we would face a desperate shortage of experienced officers to man our ships.

At first Germany was not feared as a sea power. But in the Pacific the Naval War College was engaged in war games with a Japanese Fleet of sufficient consequence to cause serious concern. We were not ready for a major war at sea against as strong a sea power. In a mostly administrative, becalmed, and low-budgeted post-World War I Navy, some brilliant officers still remained intrepid in their planning. What they could not secure in ships and manpower, they at least had on the drawing board. After many years of disappointment, President Roosevelt was successful in getting the Naval Expansion Act passed in May 1938, followed by a request for a Defense Budget hike in January 1939.

Outwardly little changed at the time. But it was a signal that those struggling within the Navy had gained ground against an establishment reconciled to Congressional indifference to national defense, which also reflected the will of the people. As a consequence of the uphill fight of a determined President, and the clandestine preparations of some dedicated officers who placed the defense of the nation ahead of their personal careers, I, together with 100 other Merchant Marine and other Reserve Officers, was called to active duty in November 1939. This followed the Proclamation of Neutrality on September 5, 1939, and the Proclamation of a Limited National Emergency on September 8. I had no way of knowing the intricacies of affairs of state that were grinding away all around me. I had observed Europe in turmoil and the frantic wave of American citizens fleeing in disarray to save their skins. At the same time I had become aware Hitler was a powerful man, charismatic, and obsessed in his objective to create a new world order no matter what the expense in human misery, death, and destruction.

Back in New York, however, one would not know a war was going on, and it would soon blow into a monumental conflict beyond anyone's imagination. With an expanding defense budget resulting in new jobs, the Depression waned and New York, with its World's Fair, remained remote from it all; going about its everyday business as if nothing would change. I, nevertheless, packed my bags, grabbed my sword, and boarded a train to Chicago where I changed to a train to Los Angeles, with another transfer for San Diego. We were allowed eight cents a mile and as I recall $8 a day for expenses. I had the option of the money or a ticket and chose the money. The salary of an Ensign was only $125 a month plus $18 for a food allowance. Thus I took the money and traveled coach, not wearing my uniform. But I had to carry my hat and the sword, so it was obvious I was a Naval Officer.

Many young people were in the coach compartments, and in 1939 most people did not hold any animosity to the military. In fact most of my generation did not even know what the Navy was. I enjoyed my first trip to the West Coast with people my own age. We had nothing to do for four or five days, so we improvised. From the train window I saw the vastness of our country, which was an interesting to me as were the distant lands I had visited.

I was to make several transcontinental trips during my Navy career, but this was the first. I was not yet carrying the burdens of responsibility I was to carry as the years went by. The Navy, the Pacific Fleet, and *Kanawha* were all new to me. Soon the El Capitan pulled into the San Diego station, where I hailed a taxi to take me to the Broadway Pier. I had chosen travel and adventure, and I was on my way again.

The keel of *Kanawha,* one of the oldest ships in the Navy, was laid in 1913. Commissioned in 1915 she was the first of a class of three 14,500-ton vessels. She measured 427 feet long by 56 feet wide and had a mean draft of 26 feet. Her triple-expansion steam engine was rated at 5,200 horsepower with a speed of 14 knots.

Her armament consisted of four, 4-inch-50-Caliber deck guns, which used fixed ammunition; that is, the projectile and the propellant (smokeless power) were all in one shell casing. When I reported on board the guns were not in operation. She had no antiaircraft guns. Her 136-man crew was attached to what was then known as the Train, Base Force, with the Flag in *U.S.S. Argonne,* Rear Admiral Calhoun commanding.

Kanawha had been in commission for about 25 years and looked like the relic she was. My heart sank as the officers gig carried me towards this very old ship painted black below the water line and battleship gray above. Riding light in the water, she looked more like a balloon. She was not *Manhattan* or *Washington* or for that matter any other ship I had sailed. But I was to be aboard her for nearly two years.

No officer met me at the gangway when I reported on board. The petty officer of the watch saluted me, and I turned over my orders to him. He ordered other seamen of the watch to take my gear to my room and to notify the mess steward assigned to me to report there.

I was escorted aft and shown into a well-decorated wardroom painted green. It contained one large dining table that seated about 16 people and a lounge area. Officers' staterooms were situated around it, as well as in adjacent alleyways. When I entered the Executive Officer, a Lcdr., was reading a magazine with his feet up on a table. He looked up. I gave him a copy of my orders, and he started to question me or, to be more specific, make comments.

His first remark was this was not the Merchant Marine, implying the Merchant Marine was some sort of tramp ship operation. Actually, remembering *Padnsay,* it was a crude standard of living. But compared to *Manhattan* and *Washington,* the *Kanawha* officer's demeanor and way of life was not in a league with it. He made his point and I said nothing.

He then asked if I knew anything about navigation and seamanship. I said yes. He asked me if I knew anything about engineering, and I said very little. He asked me if I knew anything about gunnery, and I said no. He then said I was the new Gunnery Officer in addition to being a Senior Watch Stander and Ship Service Officer. The guns were about to be placed back in commission, and I would be in charge of the operation. I was startled but said nothing. He then asked me if I knew Rogers Emmons. I said I did, that we had been shipmates in *Manhattan.* This was the first I heard we would be shipmates again.

We relieved two regular Navy Lt(jgs) who had been relegated to this Siberia after graduation from the Naval Academy. I relieved Sullivan, who was going to flight school. Emmons relieved Tom McGrath, who was going to the Cruiser *U.S.S. Brooklyn.*

Kanawha was the oldest of 20 oilers in a 500-ship fleet. Of the 415 combat ships in the fleet, about 350 were destroyers and submarines. This included 16 active battleships, 36 cruisers, and seven aircraft carriers. By in large these were old ships. Since the Naval Expansion Act passed Congress, many new ships were being constructed or on the drawing boards. Only some 8,000-plus commissioned officers manned the fleet. Due to budget restrictions the ships spent a high percentage of time at their moorings.

Kanawha's C.O. was a Commander, the Executive Officer a Lcdr., as were the Navigator, Chief Engineer, First Lieutenant, and Supply Officer.

There was a Line Lieutenant and a Lt. Doctor, plus a warrant officer in engineering and supply. With the two junior officer billets that Emmons and I filled, the officer complement stood at 11. Extra rooms in the wardroom accommodated passenger officers. I soon discovered the assignments varied. The main mission was to refuel and provide logistical support for the fleet whether at sea or in port. When the vessel was not engaged in fleet fueling-at-sea exercise, it transported petroleum products, cargo, automobiles, and passengers between the West Coast, Hawaii, Alaska, and the Aleutians, as well as Midway and Wake Island.

She could carry close to 100 enlisted passengers and about five officer passengers. Although the officer's quarters were excellent, the passenger officers and men had to stand watches. Because most of the passenger runs were made to Hawaii, the alternative to *Kanawha* and other Navy vessels for transportation was the Matson Line, which was a luxury passage.

What first appeared to be a hopeless assignment turned out to be excellent for a non-career officer, so long as we were still at peace. The time could be fully counted towards raising my license to Master. *Kanawha* carried cargo, heavy oil, diesel fuel, aviation gas, and regular gas; she was in every respect a cargo ship. I had a fine room to myself. The food was good and the wardroom atmosphere similar to an exclusive private club. I had a steward, called "boys" in those days, who took care of all my personal needs—a valet in every respect.

We spent a great deal of time in the ports of San Diego and Pearl Harbor. Since none of the other officers knew anything about gunnery, I would have to learn for myself. A first-class gunners mate and several others assigned to the ship assisted me in placing the guns back into commission. The magazines had recently been supplied with ammunition, but the guns had not been fired for years.

Pryzbilski, the First Class and Leading Gunner's Mate, had just returned from China Station. Although reluctant to leave that sailors' paradise, he still maintained good spirits. What I could not learn from the other officers and manuals I learned from him. He had about 20 years of service and understood practical gunnery well. With plenty of shore liberty and an interesting job, I soon settled into my new life. No one bothered me about the gunnery situation. I worked away with Pryzbilski and my gunnery division, and slowly *Kanawha* began its transition into a heavily armed Naval Auxiliary. At the same time, even though on a warship, I had left the war many miles to the east.

I encountered problems with the Ship's Service Store and the monthly accounting. You could buy a lollipop or a new automobile through the store. With a complement of 150 officers and men, together with the passengers, we did a tremendous business. Having a ship's service under a line officer, however, made little sense. Ordinarily the store should have been under a Supply Officer, but the policy in those days was that a line officer could do anything. Still the Supply Officer was on the auditing board. There were the usual rules, regulations, and idiot sheets, but since we sold items that cost only five cents as well as items for people's houses, such as washing machines and refrigerators, monthly accounting and inventory was a big job.

I had no skilled personnel in the store operation, and just as in gunnery, I had to learn the system. Fortunately, and unlike in gunnery, I did get assistance and guidance from the Supply Officer. The Executive Officer rarely bothered me about gunnery; but if there was a delay in completing the books and the balance on the store, he would restrict me to the ship until I balanced out. Overall it was still a pleasant environment. Disciplinary problems were rare because there were ten men looking to swap aboard for each one who wanted a transfer. A large percentage of the officers and crew were "brown-baggers," solidly settled in with their families in San Diego.

The ship's schedule was made up months in advance. The time spent in our home port of San Diego was listed as maintenance, leave, and recreational time. If the Broadway Pier was occupied or we had to fuel some ships, we would anchor in the stream about one mile out. Boats were run at regular intervals for the crew, but officers rated, and they could call away a boat when needed. Thus we had what amounted to taxi service to town.

In port, after working hours and on weekends, only one line officer was required on board. Because all the line officers other than the Captain and Executive Officer stood watch, we rarely stood more than one in seven. Gangway watches were stood by Petty Officers with seamen messengers from the watch section. The enlisted men were on a four-section watch basis, but the Chief Petty Officers had about the same privileges as the officers. Aside from Emmons and myself all other officers were married and could not wait to get home to their families. Quite often they would pressure us to stand watch for them. Emmons had a car and as a Lt(jg) made enough money that he rarely cooperated. I did not have the money to go ashore every day, so I did cooperate.

Standing watch in port on *Kanawha* was nothing like it was in the Merchant Marine. In 1940 life was leisurely. A cook and a steward were on duty to serve me meals at any time, and I could have female guests, though they were not allowed to stay overnight. Movies were shown on deck every night, and there was a special area for officers and their guests on a higher deck. In many cases it beat going ashore. Although I would have to pay for my guest's meal, it was a cheap and pleasant date—much better than having a private yacht. At times on weekends we would be tied up at the Broadway Pier, and I would sit in a chair on the after deck to watch the girls walk by. It was a favorite promenade at the time. The singles situation in San Diego, particularly for the Navy, was unique. Although a large percentage of the enlisted men on *Kanawha* were married, there were young singles, though not as many as on larger combat ships. A whole class of girls followed the fleet and loved their "white hats" dearly. This was true love and, with all the hardship that went with it, part of the scene on the West Coast. There seemed to be many more single girls on the West Coast than on the East Coast.

The dock was jammed with mostly young, beautiful girls awaiting the arrival of their "white hat" young boyfriends arriving in the liberty boats from the ships anshored in the stream.. They would never even talk with an officer. That just was not done. Still some of the enlisted men hit the bars and the "clip joints," and San Diego had a small district that catered to them. Needless to say some would end up in jail. The next morning an officer together with the Shore Patrol would attend the hearing and get them off.

Most officers lived in Coronado where house prices as well as rentals were quite affordable. The married senior officers lived well—driving Buicks or Cadillacs. Some of the officers employed live-in maids or houseboys. Tradition dictated that new officers call on senior officers at specific hours; if the officer was not at home, a calling card was left. The senior officer was required to return the call unless the junior officer lived aboard ship. It was a fine custom.

My limited funds made it difficult to exploit this excellent situation. If we were in port over a weekend, I might take the train to L.A. and go to the Biltmore Hotel bar, where sometimes I was successful in meeting a girl for dinner and dancing. One would never know a war was going on in Europe in the Pacific Fleet in 1940, and even less in the cities and towns. This was the good life, although one day in 1940 while I was walking in a crowd outside the Biltmore, a Japanese man jumped in front of me and took my picture. I was in civilian clothes; we never wore uniforms ashore. I would gather they attempted to get pictures and information on all U.S. Naval officers. I had never known a Japanese person.

Our schedule took us to San Pedro to load a cargo of petroleum products. Then we would sail to Pearl Harbor to discharge cargo either to ships directly or into tanks.

Captain Reuse, a Mustang Commander in his 50s, lived in sumptuous quarters and had his own mess. He was a quiet, pleasant man expecting soon to be transferred to shore duty before retiring. I rarely saw him. In port he was mostly ashore; at sea, he rarely visited the bridge, taking his station only during exercises with other ships, battle practice, and entering and leaving port. When I did come in contact with him, he had a way of putting me at ease. He was a good Captain.

Aside from the Junior Officers Emmons and I relieved, the Captain and Executive Officer were the only two line officers who as yet had not been passed over. The Executive Officer had family problems, which had interrupted the fast track he was waiting to regain. He realized he could not do anything outstanding in *Kanawha,* and beyond a bit of pomposity given his exalted position, he wisely did not try to make any waves. He and the other three Annapolis graduates were from the Class of 1920 or 1921. Two of the other Annapolis grads, after having been passed over, were selected for Lcdr. (not to be promoted). The other one was only a Lt., and it was "20 and out" for him. The Chief Engineer, like the Captain, was a Mustang, but also due to retire shortly. (The war canceled the restrictions.)

In *Kanawha* the heavy pressure of promotion competition so evident in combat ships did not exist. So long as I did not rock any boats and did most of the work, the officers were happy to have me aboard. They jealously coveted officer privileges, and also toed the line on demeanor. We dressed for dinner, had our Captain's Inspections on Saturday mornings, swords and all, and I cannot see how anyone could have lived better than we did. After a few weeks of watching me, they accepted me. I was invited to their homes and became part of the family.

Officers had their own mess in those days. Although we did not have the sumptuous menu available in *Manhattan* and *Washington,* it was very good. The Navy supplied the personnel to prepare the meals and serve them, but we bought our own food, partly from the general mess supplies but mainly from commercial vendors. We elected a Mess Treasurer, and if anyone complained about the food or its cost, the usual routine was to elect that officer as the next Mess Treasurer. Because our complement of mess attendants was based on our ship's officers plus passenger officers, we had almost one mess attendant for each officer.

The mess attendants doubled as room stewards, and most of the time it was almost one-on-one. Meals were served in the fashion of the old British Raj Indian Army. The mess attendants, resplendent in their clean white jackets, each carrying a tray, would pass from one officer to the other. Some traditions dated back many years. We had special dinners and lunches about once a week. Some of the cuisines and the manner in which they were served had roots in faraway places. Rice and curry Bombay Style with Bombay Duck was one carried in with a special ceremony. They had more condiments than I ever saw in any of the Indian restaurants I visited throughout the world. And there was the manpower to serve it correctly.

Conversation at meals was interesting, even though people did not often tarry at the table given their work routine. Most of my messmates had been in the Navy close to 20 years and had served all over the world. As a whole they were intelligent men and good conversationalists—gentlemen of the old school. Even in *Manhattan* and *Washington,* the nature of the watches and the work left us little time for mingling. The main difference with the Merchant Marine was that it was never more than a job; the Navy was a way of life, and I liked it. As time went on they catered to me. Emmons was off and running as a bachelor, and on a Lt(jg)'s salary he had plenty of money. I could not afford it, and consequently lived entirely within the Navy community.

When I brought aboard a new girlfriend, my companions took immediate interest. They were mostly family men faithful to their wives yet interested in whoever I would turn up with. I was the only one from the ship to attend the Navy Ball at the Royal Hawaiian Hotel at Waikiki. I had never worn Navy tropical full dress, and my officer friends all worked together to see that I was properly attired. I invited a very pretty young woman, and the Navy Ball was one of the most colorful and beautiful events I ever attended. It was held outside adjacent to the beach. The military officers wore white mess jackets with gold cummerbunds, black tie, and black trousers. The men, of course, were handsome and striking, both young and old. Their beautiful female escorts wore long formal white gowns. The few civilians were similarly dressed. The music was delightful, and the only thing that outdid the decor and the people was the Hawaiian night and sea, background for it all.

We spent a good deal of time in Hawaiian waters, and I made friends on other ships. My high school French-born friend, Andrew Hirth, was an Engineering Ensign on the Battleship *Maryland.* I met Lt(jg) John Besson, Jr. (Mike), the Number 2 Turret Officer in the Cruiser *Pensacola* on the tennis court. Groups of young bachelor officers would meet with their dates for picnics on the beaches. It was not long before I felt more at home in Hawaii than in any other place in the world.

By 1940 the main body of the Pacific Fleet was stationed, if not home-ported, in Hawaii. There were so many ships, all of them could not be berthed in Pearl Harbor. The carriers would anchor off Waikiki, and ships of various types were anchored in a chain leading into the harbor. Hawaii was inundated by the U.S. Navy. Reserves, both officer and enlisted men, were pouring in. The little club of officers was rapidly expanding. The war in Europe was discussed, but practically all the concentration was on the Japanese. Professional officers had been preparing for war with Japan for years; to them it was only a question of time.

In the summer of 1940 I met my future wife. "Nice" girls were hard to find, so I had worked out a system whereby I would watch the ship arrivals in the newspaper. When a Matson liner was due to arrive, I would try to find the time and money to get to Waikiki that day and look around the lobby of the Moana Hotel. There were only two hotels on Waikiki Beach, one movie house, some stores, and little else but private homes and cottages.

It was necessary to work in pairs as usually the girls were in pairs. Boy-meets-girl, a difficult problem in 1940, was almost impossible in Hawaii where young men outnumbered young women by about 100 to 1 when the fleet was in port. It was a girls' paradise. The Royal Hawaiian catered to an older crowd, and the Moana was the best bet to beat the odds. One of the drawbacks was that ordinarily it would be one pretty young woman with one not quite so pretty; the two men would usually zero in on the prettier one. Unless we were on official business, we wore civilian clothes.

A friend and I went to town one day and happened to meet two young women checking into the Moana. I struck up a conversation with the prettier one and found it tough going. She was suspicious, and my line needed improvement, yet we managed to introduce ourselves. The one I zeroed in on was Virginia. I did not get very far that night, but I did manage to move the conversation under the Moana's famous Banyan tree. Virginia relented enough to tell me her name was Virginia Louise Moore and she taught high school in Madeira, California. As expected, she had just arrived in *Matsonia*. She also told me that she was only staying at the hotel one or two nights, then moving to a small cottage near the beach for two months. I got the new address, but follow-up was not easy. It did not take Virginia long to discover it was a girls' paradise and I would have to compete with many other young men. Further, I had to work, and the ship would sortie for gunnery exercises, fueling at sea exercises, and miscellaneous training.

In Honolulu if an eligible young woman was asked for a date, she wanted to know where you were going to take her. If you would not agree to take her to dinner at the Wailei Club or the Royal Hawaiian, you were not even considered. Two dates each semimonthly pay period was the maximum, unless you could get her to relent. The idea was to get her to accept an invitation to dinner aboard ship. When I first got Virginia to accept such an invitation, she changed her mind. She went to the Navy Signal Station at Waikiki Beach and sent a message to me that she could not keep the appointment. I took it for granted she had received a better offer, but Virginia denies this (to this day!). That message made me infamous, however.

The signal station flashed it to an aircraft carrier anchored off the beach, which flashed to 15 or 20 ships in line until it got to the signal bridge of *Kanawha*. All messages were copied and shown to the Watch Communications Officer, most of whom were Ensigns. If they did not know me then, they knew me forever as the Ensign who got stood up. I should have known better but I asked Virginia to dinner aboard a second time, and this time she came. The dinner went fine, and after dinner we watched the "Grapes of Wrath, a very long picture. Most of the crew got bored and turned in; we were due to start fueling a ship early in the morning. The movie did not end until after 11:00 p.m. Because the ship had a full load of fuel and was down on her marks, it was a three-foot step into or out of any of the small liberty boats that came alongside. Meanwhile the gangway had been unshipped and secured. This was a large, cumbersome contraption that took a large number of men about 40 minutes to secure and another 40 minutes to unsecure.

It was a little choppy that night, but not in the least difficult or dangerous for anyone to jump in or out of a boat; and particularly with the boat crew assisting, it was no big deal. Shortly before the movie ended, I had the officers' gig called away, and by the time the movie ended it was alongside ready to receive passengers. I brought Virginia down and she tried a few times but finally froze and refused to take the step down. She could not stay overnight, and I had to get her off the ship. The first ship she ever saw was *Matsonia,* and this all scared her.

I had no alternative but to awaken my division and request them to rig the gangway, which in the deep loaded condition of the ship was even more difficult to climb down. But it was done, and Virginia disembarked. I was embarrassed with my men, and they were not very happy with me. Nonetheless Virginia and I exchanged addresses and kept in touch by letter.

Typically I would awaken about 0700 hours, have breakfast, and muster with my division at 0800 hours. Senior Petty Officer Pryzbilski and I would then assign the men various tasks. I might work with gunnery or my other responsibilities before knocking off for lunch at 1130 hours, having changed into clean khakis. At 1300 hours the division would muster again and go back to work. At 1600 hours we would secure from work details unless we were fueling ships or engaged in other special tasks. Dinner for the crew was at 1700 hours, for the officers a little later. Life was extremely pleasant.

I gave classes in safety precautions for firing the guns and drilled the gun crews at regular intervals. We also mounted two 30 caliber World War I machine guns, the only anti-aircraft defense available to us. I would work in the magazine with Pryzbilski, crimping ammunition so we could test the powder for stability. This was a laborious and dangerous job. We had to detach the projectile from the case by putting the whole shell in a vise, then bang away to separate the two parts. Records were kept by manufacturer's lot number. If the powder in any particular lot was deteriorating, we would either dump it at sea or turn it in at an ammunition depot. The ammunition was obsolete, as were the guns.

The time came for us to test fire them, however. By tradition the Gunnery Officer could assign any officer other than the Captain or Exec to the various safety and observation positions. Being the junior of the officers, no one complied with my request. Pryzbilski and I test fired each of the four 4-inch guns ourselves, while the remainder of the officers and crew stayed as far away as possible. We loaded the shell, locked it in, and then with a long lanyard tied to the firing pin, fired the guns one shot and one gun at a time. After each firing and with the help of the others , we checked the structural areas affected by the recoil. The good old *Kanawha* passed the test. Although aged she had been built well.

Next we fired at a target. The Bible I had to go by was known as OGE 10, which spelled out was "Orders for Gunnery Exercises." By the time we were ready to fire at a target for record, we had already received notice our ordnance was to be replaced and modernized during the overhaul scheduled at the Navy Yard in Bremerton, Washington, on Puget Sound.

OGE 10 was an odd document. As inexperienced as I was and basically self-taught, I studied it with amazement. According to it, long before the shoot, I should know the course and speed of the target. This information was to be combined with the wind, sea direction and force, and temperature into the Ballistic Form. If any of these items to be calculated on the idiot sheet should change, the exercise was to be delayed until the ballistics could be recalculated or canceled. I wrote a letter about this, which Captain Reuse was kind enough to forward. In polite words I questioned the value of a practice predicated on no surprises, delay, or cancellation of the war. They, in turn, reminded me how expensive ammunition was, and it could not be wasted. Our ammunition was all going bad from age, and I could not see the rationale behind the policy.

To make matters worse the Exec had been transferred out of the doghouse to the Battleship *West Virginia* as First Lieutenant. The new Exec had been passed over for Lcdr. (but picked up not to be promoted), thus becoming mad at the world. He would try to belittle me during classes where I was instructing the crew about gunnery duties. While I would be talking this martinet would came by, interrupt, then apologize to the crew for the fact that the expansion in the Navy exposed them to inexperienced reserve officers. I just stood there, and as soon as he left continued with the lecture as if he had never appeared. I never had trouble gaining the respect of the crew.

The day came to fire for record. The tug and target arrived as scheduled and the wind was blowing from the direction I expected. As a result of the constant drilling I had subjected the gun crews to and with my careful studying of the theories of hitting the target, we did very well, even though the methods used were archaic. We got an E (excellent). Most of the credit should have gone to Pryzbilski, who just could not seem to pass the test for Chief, even though I did all possible to help him. He had little formal education, but he had no peer in the area of gunnery we were working in. The E in gunnery should have proved something to the Exec, but it only made him more sarcastic and nasty. I just "Yes Sirred" him and continued to do my job.

We also got an E in engineering. On record our fuel consumption was about half what it was in actuality. Our first Chief Engineer, a Mustang, knew all the tricks. We would heat the oil before delivering it to some unsuspecting Ensign Chief Engineer on a destroyer, and it was a rare one that ever got wise to it. This was standing operating procedure, except during fueling at sea exercises.

Fueling under way was hairy. Our enlisted petty officers were all old hands. Officers stayed in this ship as long as possible. Although some of the officers were very good and contributed to our pioneering performance in this main mission, the continuity and creativity of the Senior Petty Officers made it all work out well.

106

Procedures developed by *Kanawha* and the *Kanawha* "block" were the mainstay of the success our Navy achieved in fueling at sea during World War II. We went alongside and maintained position with aircraft carriers, battleships, and cruisers. All other ships, mainly destroyers, had to come alongside and keep position on us. As time went by I learned how to bring the ship alongside and maintain position in fueling under way, as the Captain at times let me have the conn when I was the Officer of the Deck. We also practiced streaming paravanes, a means of sweeping mines when mine sweepers were not available. This was a difficult and dangerous job of uncertain effectiveness.

While in Hawaii I managed to get assigned to *U.S.S. Phoenix,* a cruiser making a week's gunnery cruise for the advanced training of Gunnery Officers. Whereas no one was qualified to teach me in *Kanawha,* and I could not believe the combat forces were as backwards as we were, I wanted to see for myself how a modern ship practiced the art. I found out, and learned, but I don't think I would have volunteered for this training cruise if I had known how physically damaging it would be.

The training was oriented to anti-aircraft defense. Despite the fact training still pretty much followed the same manual with no surprises, we did accomplish a great deal. *Kanawha* had no automatic gun directors, which were in effect primitive computers. Everything was by hand. Distance triangulation in *Kanawha* was calculated from a range finder only about four feet in width. *Phoenix,* however, had large range finders that had a fair degree of accuracy. We fired for hours every day as well as much of the night . We would rotate in all the jobs, even that of checksight observer, right next to the muzzle of the short barreled 5-inch 25s that made up the secondary battery. The concussions, hour after hour, made our ears bleed.

Then I did a foolish thing. I let the dentist, who sat next to me at the mess, talk me into having an impacted wisdom tooth extracted. For several painful hours he chiseled away through my jaw by hand to "practice." Right after this major operation, I was up in sky aft, which was on the after mast where a gun director was installed. At each firing the mast would vibrate and my head nearly fell off. Fortunately this was towards the end of the torture cruise, but pieces of bone came out of my jaw for months. It was all part of the learning process, and although rarely can you use all the knowledge that you gain, it still serves to sharpen your mind. I wouldn't call it formal education. Even though the math I learned was hard to fit into any category, it still made other things easier for me to absorb.

I also learned a great deal operating the Ship's Service. Salesmen plagued me, offering me all sorts of bribes to buy their wares. I would not even accept a free lunch. Yet I learned to keep and balance books with the aid of another idiot sheet. All departments had budgets in dollars and cents. Whatever we drew from the Supply Department Stores was charged against a department budget. In the Gunnery Department I had to keep a running inventory of ammunition and other items such as small arms, even down to 22-caliber shells. All of this was equated to dollars and cents. The Navy ran on a well-oiled typewriter. The bookkeeping was overwhelming.

I caught various other assignments. At times I would do duty as an officer's secret mail carrier. With a pouch locked on a chain on my arm, I would fly in an amphibian piloted by an enlisted pilot while laying on the mail bags. The Fleet at times would be spread throughout the islands, and Ensigns were assigned to this duty. In one instance I had to stay overnight on one of the out-islands at the best hotel—at the Navy's expense. The hotel was also the rest house for the "working girls" from Hotel Street in Honolulu. On two other occasions I was assigned to the Shore Patrol, together with a squad from my ship, to augment the permanent staff.

Shore Patrol duty on Hotel Street in late '40 and early '41 was an interesting task. A petty officer from the permanent staff was assigned to advise me. The street was the home for the several houses of prostitution that "protected the innocent maidens of Honolulu." Here, for a small sum, the men of the armed forces stationed far from home could find momentary feminine companionship of a sort, and thus look to other leisure pursuits on their shore leave. There were not enough young women to go around on the island. A few enlisted men and some of the officers found local maidens and set up house, but this either fell into the category of "true love" or adequate funds, of which few had.

Local girls, including those from wealthy social families, were sometimes of mixed blood. The Japanese, Chinese, Polynesian, and other races mingled pretty freely with the Caucasians. The results were often beautiful women and handsome men. Yet it was rare that the officers ever made lasting relationships with this group. The group was also so small, their families so protective, that it was dangerous for enlisted men, in particular, to mix.

Thus Hotel Street. Solders, sailors, and marines would line up as they would for chow in front of a particular house. The MPs and SPs security forces would be sure the lines were orderly, and on occasion the local police would be around. This was basically a military operation, however. I had to patrol the street and the houses continually because fights were not infrequent. After standing in line for a long time, sometimes reading comic books, a man would enter the house in turn. He would then pay. I don't recall whether there was any real selectivity, but I would imagine that a regular customer could request a specific girl, if he waited on the availability. Otherwise, a girl having finished her last assignment, would take her boy by the hand, be given a fresh towel, and go to the cubby hole in which she transacted her business. The women were all non-locals; most came from the States to make their fortunes here. That they did, as there was a never-ending line. Customers were primarily sailors. Soldiers were usually permanently stationed in the island and had a better chance of making a private female connection. Most of the sailors were in their teens.

This was a mass production operation, and the women were adept in their performance, sometimes getting their young boys off in a matter of seconds. That was it. That was what they paid for, and usually they were not even permitted to pay for a second chance, which often led to fights. The kids really did not know much about mechanical sex. So the sailor or soldier would start a disturbance. Every once in awhile, of course, the girls ran into a sexual mechanic who could hold out on them. Then the girl would start to scream and complain that her income was being challenged.

All together it was not a nice scene. Navy doctors checked the girls for sexual diseases. Prophylactics were given each man as he went on liberty. If he contracted a sexual disease without the record of having taken a prophylactic, he was penalized. Loss of pay plus lost time had to be made up at the end of his enlistment. Congress changed the policy about 1942.

I and another SP officer had dinner one night with the madam of one of the bordellos. She was very courteous to us for we kept the peace and disruptions cost her money. I questioned her on the economics of the situation. Although it was mind-boggling, she was reluctant to talk about it. I sensed the business was unusually good. The only setback being the payoffs she hinted at. What I got out of all of this was that there had to be a better way.

The hotel on the island where I spent the night with the "working girls" on holiday was a small luxury place on the water. I had drinks with some of the women who were pretty when you saw them out of the environment of Hotel Street. Some could have passed for the average girl back home.

Their earnings were tremendous. It was a volume trade, and the few I talked with said that after a few years they would return to the States and take on a new identity. They gave me the impression the pimps and the racketeers who so often exploited prostitutes were not a problem. These were not stupid women. Most seemed to have a fairly decent education and specific objectives. Whether this rare freedom in a business mostly bordering on white slavery lasted throughout the war, I do not know.

There have been best-selling novels about romances involving some of the girls so engaged, but from my conversations and limited observances this was fiction. From what I could tell most had little respect for men. This was too much of a mass production to leave time for any human feelings. The women probably "serviced" between 30 and 50 men a day.

Hotel Street was no place for any officer to be caught except when on duty. Our lot was essentially limited to the so-called respectable area catering to tourists and some locals. It did not take long for word to get around that this was a great place for a girl to find a husband. Reserve officers were coming into the fleet at an increasing rate. The pickings were good.

The game, however, was not to commit to marriage. The usual line, which only applied to Ensigns with under two years of time, was the Navy would not let you get married. Most of us passed this point, but most of the young women in the crowd were holding out for the "ring." Some junior officers gave up and married their old girlfriends from back home, but some married local girls. Some had, or married, money, and they lived well. Those who had no more than their pay lived in shacks on Waikiki Beach in an area known as "Ensigns' Row." For those enlisted men and officers with no wife or girlfriend in the islands, the situation was grim. Luckily *Kanawha* returned to the west coast at regular intervals, and there the situation was reversed.

The morale in the fleet was not good. Admiral Richardson considered it strategically unwise to keep the Pacific Fleet congested in so small an area. He made many protests to the Navy Department, but President Roosevelt had ordained it was to remain at Pearl. Admiral Richardson did an excellent job of moving the fleet around in the small area, but continued his protest and was eventually relieved by Admiral Kimmel, who was no more enchanted with the situation than Admiral Richardson.

Nothing lasts forever, and the delightful and pleasant atmosphere began to change as the Navy expanded. Lcdr. Burrow was relieved as Executive Officer and transferred. Another Lcdr. replaced him. He was a very bitter man. If I were to grade him as an officer, I would place him in the lower 10 percentile. Captain Rockwell Townsend, who joined the ship in Honolulu on his way home from the Asiatic Station, started to assert himself. He had progressed routinely through the ranks without being passed over, and it was obvious he would not be there long. He was soon relieved by Commander Kendall Reed. The Medical Officer, the Supply Officer, and the Chief Engineer were all to be transferred during or before 1941.

Lt(jg) Charles Starkus from the Class of 1927 relieved Oliver Gaines. Starkus was finished in the Navy unless there was a war and never would have been retained the 20 years required for a pension. He was a passable First Lieutenant, a nice person, and cooperative. But he had problems with a troublesome wife and heavy drinking, and I was the only one who could handle him when he was under the influence. It was very sad. Sometime he would join the picnics and beach parties with my friends. One time at Makupu Beach where the surf was very heavy, and after many beers and with nobody watching, Charley floated out beyond the breakers and the current was taking him out to sea fast. He floated along with his big belly barely visible. Fortunately we had some excellent swimmers in the group, and they were able to push him to shore. Most the time I watched out for him, and in turn he let me use his car and the house he had in San Diego. Still it was impossible to constantly keep him under surveillance, and he could fight well either drunk or sober.

One night in San Pedro after we had taken on a cargo of oil and were ready to leave, several Shore Patrol cars rolled up to the gangway with a handcuffed Charley. Black eyes and bruises were noticeable on several of the SPs including the officer. Charley had been beaten badly and they sort of held him up. The SP Officer shouted up to the Exec, saying that Charley was drunk and disorderly and had been disrespectful to the flag, stamping on it. At the same time the SPs mostly tried to keep the lid on things rather than make a big issue out of it. They had probably been in a number of fights with drunken sailors the same night. Charley was just another one.

The SP asked the Exec what he wanted to do about it. It was obvious he was willing to drop the charges if the Exec was. The Exec roared back to send him aboard and to throw the book at him. This meant a General Court Martial. Immediately on taking him aboard and having the doctor take care of him, the Exec placed him in "Hack," which confined him to quarters, silence, and lonely meals by himself. This poor, sad guy did not even know what happened. I found out later that his wife had given him a hard time.

I antagonized the Exec by assisting Charley in getting a lawyer to defend him. He was not dismissed but was ordered to duty at the Naval Training Station in San Diego from which he retired as a Lt. in 1947. The Navy had more compassion than the Exec.

This was a new *Kanawha*. The new Chief Engineer, a Lt., was professionally competent, but bitter, as were many of the passovers for promotion who were hanging in for retirement. At the same ti me he did not seem to give much of a damn for anything, although he worked hard. He was sarcastic and seemed to take satisfaction in seeing others in trouble. He was the only officer other than the Exec who did not feel compassion for Starkus.

Starkus was relieved as First Lieutenant by a Merchant Mariner. Lt. Hanson was an excellent marlin-spike seaman, a decent enough man, but one who found little in the Navy he believed equal to the professionalism of the Merchant Marine. An assistant was assigned to him, another Merchant Marine Reserve Ensign named Brockway. He, like Hansen, was up from the hawse pipe, and they thought similarly. In their opinion Naval Academies and Merchant Marine Academies were no substitute for the lore one could gain by swabbing decks.

Both were competent, yet neither knew anything about gunnery and were not interested in learning. The new doctor, Lcdr. Patterson, was excellent as was the Reserve Supply Officer, Lt(jg) Borgers. A World War I veteran and a very decent older man, he was good at his work. He had been a city official under the infamous Mayor Hague of Jersey City.

Thus the ship changed. Even as the work went on and the old *Kanawha* kept performing her missions as always, the graciousness and the refinement of the members of the Wardroom Mess had changed. Neither Emmons nor I bucked the system. Once in the Navy we were Navy and not Merchant Marine. I accepted the Navy for what it was and liked the challenges of new assignments unheard of on merchant ships. Now we had a competent but aloof Captain with whom few of us other than the Exec had much personal contact. We had an Exec who was somewhat of a sadist, and the ship was becoming polarized.

I went about my work and when in the States dated Virginia Moore on a few occasions. On a trip from Hawaii in late June 1941, I had written Virginia to meet me at the Biltmore Hotel lobby in L.A. on the first Saturday night after our return. We had already undergone repairs in Bremerton, and *Kanawha* was now armed to the teeth. The ship had new anti-aircraft batteries, and I had a 90 -day Wonder from Oklahoma as an Assistant Gunnery Officer. He was a bright, mannerly man ready to learn. I taught him as much as I could about gunnery. We worked together well. Together we turned the Gunnery Department into one of the best in the fleet. His name was Ralph Muse.

Arriving in San Diego in early July '41, we tied up at the Broadway Pier. I received a letter from Virginia saying she would meet me and then a telegram saying she would not. So I called another girlfriend and made a date to meet her at the Biltmore. I drove to L.A. in Starkus' car. When I entered the lobby of the Biltmore, Virginia was there. I got her out quickly. I was not looking for the war to start just then. Virginia said she changed her mind again and sent another telegram, which I had not received. Having decided we should get married, she had taken some days off. I told her I had no money, no future, and I had to be back on the ship on Monday morning. I did not have the least intention of getting married. Although I expected my commission as Lt(jg), which would be back-dated to February 8, 1941, and the back pay along with it, I had not received it. I was sending a small amount of money home, and besides, I told her, there was going to be a war. Nothing fazed Virginia when she made up her mind. She would lend me the money to buy a car to drive to Yuma or Mexico. I then asked her if she could drive. She said she did not have a license, but she could drive. I asked her how she figured we would get along on my miserable salary, she said she made $150 a month teaching school.

Nothing discouraged this girl. At this time I needed a wife like a hole in the head. Yet I was 25 years old and not what one would call a good bachelor operator. Virginia was pretty, intelligent, and we got along well. She had graduated from San Jose State, cum laude, and it was probably about time I settled down.

Virginia stayed at Charley's house, and he stayed at the BOQ at the training center. I gave her some money to buy a ring while I stayed on ship with the duty. She turned up that night for dinner without the ring, but she bought a hat. I had the next day off, and we bought a second-hand Pontiac for $600. It went from first into third, skipping second, but it was wheels. Virginia then laid out the money for the ring, but, again, this as the car was a loan.

There were problems with the Exec to get a few days off, but he relented—only after taking it upon himself to advise me that marriage was not good for young Naval Officers; that it would not last out the year. Marriage carried a bonus with it in the Navy—$40 per month for Ensigns, $60 for Lt(jg)s.

The Navy did not recognize Mexican marriages, so we drove to Yuma, Arazona. I was tired and asked Virginia to spell me at the wheel. She did and went along fine for awhile, but then going down a hill she seemed to accelerate rather than slow down.

"Ginny, slow it down," I urged.

"How?" she asked.

"Slowly put foot pressure on the foot brake," I instructed.

"Where is the foot brake?"

Somehow I managed to get control of the car and drove for the remainder of the trip. The game-plan was to have a simple marriage; then, with time and planning, have a wedding in San Jose where her folks lived. We found Yuma, we found the license office, and we paid the few dollars for the license. We then went looking for a minister. It was fairly late at night by then. I was getting one of those miserable head colds that have plagued me over the years, and I was exhausted. There was no problem in finding a minister to perform the ceremony. The town was full of neon lights advertising weddings and variations on same, such as Christian Minister Weddings. We stopped in front of one of these houses and rang the bell . A man answered and asked what we wanted. I replied, "We want to get married." His response was to question if we had a license. When I assured him we did. He said he would need to call in two neighbors, and the wedding would be $20 and $5 per witness. I already owed Virginia for the car and the ring, but I came up with the $30.

This guy mumbled a few words and then pronounced us "Man and Wife." Ginny took the Marriage Certificate and has held on to it ever since. I never even got a chance to read it. By the time we got to a motel to celebrate our wedding night, it was very late and my cold and fever had intensified.

And so at the ripe old age of 25, I married a girl with whom I had spent hardly any time and really didn't know. For her part Ginny was married to an itinerant sailor whose future at this time was bleak. The Navy could inactivate me at any time, and the only other employment opportunity was to return to the U.S. Lines.

It was not a memorable or romantic wedding night. I was sick. Ginny's parents had no idea she was getting married, nor did my mother. I was certain my mother would be in shock when I telephoned her. Ginny's parents doted on her. The original plans were for us to drive from Yuma to San Jose in the few days I had before I needed to return to the ship, to give the cheerful news to Ginny's parents. I was terribly sick and would have to do all the driving. I convinced Ginny that, inasmuch as Yuma had little to offer, we should take a detour back to San Diego and spend a day or two at the Roosevelt Hotel in Hollywood.

I had stayed there before and liked it. Neither Ginny nor I could think of any alternative, so we did. I still had my cold while in Hollywood. Probably an allergy from getting married. For my first honeymoon I was deathly sick from Chinese food, and thus the honeymoon continued gloomily. Because the ship was to be in San Diego for about two or three weeks before it sailed, we decided to use the time to get Ginny a driver's license and to rent a small furnished apartment in Coronado.

I started to teach Ginny to drive en route from Hollywood to San Diego. She was okay on the straightway by the time we arrived. Then I tried teaching her driving in traffic in San Diego. That did not work—she tied up traffic. So I hired a professional teacher for her, and in a few day she got her license.

Marriage for the both of us meant learning. We could not have come from more different backgrounds, and there was not much time before I sailed away on a long deployment. It was not difficult in those days to find a reasonable rental apartment, and we set up housekeeping. For a short time I became a brownbagger. Ginny would drive me to the ship in the morning and pick me up at night. For the first time in her life she started to cook, although when I had the duty she would have dinner with me on board. Enlisted men have long memories, and whenever Ginny came aboard they remembered the unfortunate gangway experience in Pearl Harbor.

A change of command was made about that time. Cdr. Kendall Reed relieved his classmate Cdr. Townsend. Ordinarily we would have been given a reception by the C.O. and his family. The Executive Officer was separated from his family, and I did not expect any recognition from him. The other officers made a big thing of the marriage, and made Ginny feel right at home. Lt(jg) Borgers, the Supply Officer, went out of his way to be nice. Emmons thought I was nuts, but he was polite.

We had to reciprocate in some way. I asked Ginny if she could prepare a dinner for as many officers of the mess as we could accommodate and who were free. Considering *Kanawha's* mess served some of the best food in the Navy, this was quite a problem. Ginny did her best, and although over the years she became an excellent cook, she was almost hopeless then. Steak seemed the easiest way out, and she tried. But as our intentions were good, my fellow shipmates never let on, and did their best to make Ginny feel that it was excellent. Our housekeeping period was coming to an end for a long time.

We prepared to depart from San Diego. Ginny had a contract for the 1941 and 1942 semesters at Madeira High School. My future was uncertain. All we could do was have her plan for the formal wedding she always dreamed of. We would try to have it coincide with the leave that ordinarily came with a change of duty assignment, which was itself an uncertainty. I was still on a yearly contract basis the Navy could terminate at any time.

Even with the heavy influx of new Reserve Officers, some Contract Officers as well as some regular officers were still being let go. The ordinary assignment was 18 to 24 months, and I was the officer with the most time in the ship. Thus I worked towards selecting my assignment rather than leaving it up to fate.

I had already tried to get aviation and submarine training and failed. Prior to my marriage I had tried to swap with a married Ensign friend aboard *U.S.S. Houston* shortly before this Flagship of the Asiatic Fleet was scheduled to depart for the Far East.

Having been regaled by Pryzbilski about the life of luxury I could live on the Asiatic Station, I was tempted to get on the cruiser. I had a good chance but there was insufficient time, and my friend sailed in my place. I never heard from him again. Perhaps he sank with the ship when it was sunk by Japanese gunfire and torpedoes February 28, 1942, or he may have died in a Japanese prison camp.

Fate seems to have intervened in my life quite often. Emmons applied for Lighter Than Air Training. This led to duty in "Blimps," known as a safe sinecure. He got it. I applied for Gunnery School and reassignment. But no matter how well I had done in *Kanawha,* there was no way I was going to get an outstanding fitness report. They were made out by the Executive Officer and rarely changed by the Captain.

Later I did see the reports and they were average, which for a senior officer is a kiss of death, but for a junior officer basically affects your next assignment only. I never believed I was an outstanding officer, but everything is relative, and I am certain I performed equally or better than the others. This was not a ship with any real competition. At the same time as I was about to leave *Kanawha,* and being a realist, I understood I was leaving a ship of no particular standing and had the same poor prospects as the other officers.

Being an officer on the fastest and largest passenger ships in the U.S. Merchant Marine meant something from a prestige point of view. I had learned a great deal on the ships, which was even more important. No prestige was to be gained from duty in *Kanawha.* But I doubt if there was any other ship in which I could have learned more in the same amount of time. During my time aboard I held almost every assignment on the ship other than Chief Engineer. Even Brainard Bock, as difficult as he could be, allowed me to work and learn in the engine room and taught me what he could. As we prepared for my last trip in *Kanawha*, Ginny left for San Jose, driving the car on her own. In July *Kanawha* sailed for Pearl Harbor via San Pedro. There was a tremendous amount of work for the gunnery department. We got new armament, and I had to drill the gun crews unmercifully. I sensed we were going to have to use the guns very shortly.

The ominous feeling of war was all around us as we sailed west to Hawaii. Upon arrival we immediately noticed changes. We were ordered to be at General Quarters at daybreak and sundown every day, as were the other ships in port. Live ammunition was kept in the ready boxes adjacent to each gun. I continued to take groups of people to the pistol and rifle ranges for qualification, and we had a fueling at sea exercise and actual anti-aircraft battle practice.

We sailed to Midway in late summer 1941. This was an interesting experience and proved the versatility of *Kanawha*. She had a huge towing engine on the stern plus a reel of strong towing cable. Towing is a tough seamanship job. Senior Watch Standers had to work watches as never before. The OOD constantly had to watch the tow and the wire and at regular times "freshen the nip," which meant paying out or heaving in some of the tow line so not to wear it out in one place.

The Captain had been given instructions about the "Rules of Engagement." For the first time since reporting aboard, I had a one-on-one conference with him. Our orders were to keep all ready boxes on deck full of ammunition and every gun ready to shoot on short notice. This did not entail manning the guns unless we were in sight of unidentified ships or aircraft. We were not to initiate action but be ready to respond instantly.

In short the high command had passed the buck to the Captain, and he in turn passed part of it to me. Giving the other guy the first shot can at times decide the action before one can return fire. Calling the ship to General Quarters every time a ship or aircraft was sighted could tire the crews unnecessarily. At the same time I had to be ready. There was only one way to interpret such orders. As I saw it war was near.

I had worked long and hard to prepare the Gunnery Department to fight realistically. I fashioned my drills to take in the element of surprise, which the OGE-10 did not. I read every and anything I could get my hands on about anti-aircraft combat. Every item of armament was ready to shoot and sustain fire. The old *Kanawha* was more heavily armed than the old four-pipe destroyers. With the built-in compartments of a tanker, we could expect ordinarily to sustain heavy damage without sinking. The Gunnery Department and I were ready to fight.

117

I worked long and hard with Ensign Muse, Pryzbilski, and my division. Whereas up to that time I had expected we would enter the war soon, I had no idea war would start in the Pacific and we might have no warning. With the new guns and ammunition came a feeling that the Gunnery Department, if not of any interest to any of the others, had better get my fullest attention. The serious talk with the Captain about the rules of engagement, although frustrating in their ambiguity, was ominous.

Always a hard worker I became even more intense. Ralph Muse was an easy-going cowboy type, far out of his environment, but he was bright and he began to acclimate himself to our predicament. He too set to work with, if not the same intensity, a much more concerned approach to our problems than ever before. *Kanawha,* although an antiquated auxiliary ship, was no exception in having been poorly armed for a modern war. Our surface guns could not elevate to fire at aircraft. Our range finder with a four-foot triangulation and our old Lewis-type 30-caliber machine guns hardly gave anyone any confidence in the ship's ability to defend itself. Now we had some guns to fight with.

In our private meeting I received the Captain's permission to initiate and implement training programs with our new weapons. Now I had the independence at least to dedicate the Gunnery Department to combat, and at the same time force the other divisions to augment manning and servicing the guns. They were reluctant to cooperate, but I scheduled the drills and increased them in the face of ridicule and criticism. Mostly ignorant of gunnery, they took refuge in treating the armament as decorative. The Navy had long been at peace. The many bright and outstanding officers were often check-mated by the peace-time criteria of following protocol for promotion, not rocking the boat, and adherence to antiquated doctrines. Enough officers, fortunately, were successful in circumventing the martinets who feared change. These officers were very evident by the strategies used in creating aircraft carriers and the tactics and the planes that went with them.

What hurt was not the loyalty to the battleship, but the failure to recognize that aircraft had arrived, of these officers having to fight anyone when they might in any way question battleships' invincibility. Armored decks and sides were considered protection against anything an enemy might throw at them from the skies. Anti-aircraft gunnery was secondary. It was accepted that an anti-aircraft defense was required but hardly given the priority it demanded. Thus the problems I faced in *Kanawha* as we proceeded west of Hawaii in the second half of 1941 were not unique to this antiquated auxiliary ship.

Midway was simply a sand strip in middle of the Pacific mainly inhabited by gooney birds that ignored the intrusion of the Marines on their private preserve. Prior to establishing a fueling station there by Pan American Airways, the island was unpopulated. Yet it was strategically located, and the Navy set up a base there. Little elevation was over sea level.

We berthed at a dock and transferred passengers, mail, petroleum products, and supplies. There was a small Officers Club where we could get a drink, but little else. It was a hardship station, and no dependents of military and civilian personnel were permitted on the island. One thing was self-evident; no one was relaxing, and I could sense they, like me, expected hostilities to break out soon. It was all business and no play on Midway. This small sandpit was to become an historic island with an important role in the War in the Pacific. I continued my job in the old *Kanawha* as if she were a capital ship. We returned to Pearl and then on to Wake Island, which was even further west than Midway. While in Pearl the same procedure of twilight battle stations was in effect. We like other ships were required to be at general quarters during this period, although it was a modified one where the routine of the ship could continue. This procedure is something I have never been able to reconcile with what apparently was a standdown on December 7th.

Wake was not much different from Midway. Desolate and alone it was another extension of our military strategy. The same intensiveness prevailed. I maintained the same level of readiness in *Kanawha* as we steamed out and ultimately back to Pearl and then on to San Pedro. Just before we were ready to return to Pearl, I received my orders to a gunnery school in San Diego.

The timing allowed no time for even good-byes. I had to pack and leave. I turned over to Ralph Muse, called Ginny, telling her I would be ashore in San Diego for awhile. But she was under contract and could not get away until Christmas vacation. Because this was the end of November, it was not far off. I did not even have time for feeling nostalgic as I scurried to report in San Diego. I had not received my Lt(jg)'s commission as yet, even though I had heard it was on the way, and I was not happy about reporting to a new assignment as an Ensign.

Five

War: Pacific

S.S. Matsonia

For the first time in just under two years, *Kanawha* sailed without me while I made my way to San Diego from San Pedro. San Diego had already changed; the Navy was expanding at an accelerating rate, with 90-Day-Wonder Ensigns and Seamen Recruits all over the place. Disorganization was the order of the times. The new Gunnery School was in the Destroyer Base. Its gunnery facilities were more obsolete than the ordnance I had been working with in *Kanawha*. Although we were at peace the atmosphere was of a nation on the brink of war, just as it had been in Pearl and during our voyages west.

The officer in charge of the school, as obsolete as the equipment and either a Mustang or an old-time reservist, was confused. But his orders were even more so. The students were all Ensigns. Some came from line ships of the Fleet and some from the 90-day schools. Most were younger than I, and I felt like an old man among them even though I was only 25.

There was talk that we were going to man merchant vessels with Naval gun crews. This did not appeal very much to me since I was eligible to sit for my Master's License. In the interim officer availability had changed into a seller's rather than a buyer's market. I probably could have gotten at least a Chief Mate's job, and possibly even a Master's job, because the Merchant Marine was expanding like the Navy. The difference in pay was tremendous. Blackburn was after me to get out of the Navy and join him at Pan American Ferries as a navigator. The pay there was even better, and I could have taken flying lessons at the same time. My discreet inquiries indicated, however, although the Navy was not reluctant to drop any officer it did not want to retain, the chances of my getting a release were poor.

120

I liked the Navy and had not given up the idea of working my way out of the "dog house" into combat ships and hopefully the Regular Navy. Although I was about one step above the poverty level, I was reluctant to quit. At the same time I was upset my Lt(jg)'s commission had not been received. I should have had my additional half stripe and the pay that went with it ten months earlier. My only solace was that none of the others in my seniority group, whether line or aviators, had received their promotions either. This influenced some of our best pilots to join the Flying Tigers. Nonetheless ever since I graduated from the Merchant Marine Academy, I had been wearing the one stripe, which to me was the equivalent of a dunce cap.

I stayed at Charlie Starkus's home during this short period. When school started on December 2, 1941, no real organization existed. I recall no curriculum, but I was assigned to conduct some informal classes. The week went by very fast, and we were off for the weekend.

On Sunday morning December 7, 1941, Virginia telephoned me from Maderia. "Turn of the radio," she said. It appeared as though we were at war and California might be attacked. She was requesting emergency leave to come and see me, expecting I would be in combat very shortly. On the radio I heard all Naval personnel should report to their ships or stations.

All I can recall was "this is it," the moment I had really been expecting for a long time. I dressed in my uniform and reported to the school. Everyone seemed to want to do something, but no one knew what. All sorts of rumors were floating around to the effect the Japanese were landing or about to land. We were confined to the base, and the following day another attempt was made to teach gunnery. At times I would instruct. At other times I would be a student in a class being taught by someone who had never fired a gun. I was totally frustrated.

In the interim I had phoned Virginia and told her there was no point in coming to San Diego for I was confined to base. I advised her to wait before she requested leave. Soon after the restriction was lifted, and I moved back to Charley's house.

By the end of the second week in December, I was called into a conference by the officer in charge of the school. He said three of the four large Matson Liners were already in San Francisco or about to arrive. Installing the guns and assigning officers and men to man the Armed Guards aboard the ships were a priority. He then gave me orders to proceed to the Armed Guard Center on Treasure Island in San Francisco for further assignment as the C.O. of the U.S. Naval Armed Guard unit aboard *S.S. Matsonia*.

Like the school the Armed Guard Center was organized confusion. The Merchant Marine was meeting the Navy for the first time since World War I. The C.O. of the Center was a youngish Reserve Lcdr. who had been in the middle management level of a West Coast U.S. Flag steamship company. I could never conceive of him at war in a ship at sea.

This was my first encounter with a new area of the Navy—the Navy that never went to sea—which was personified later by Robert MacNamera and other self-styled geniuses who came into their own after the war. The C.O. had the demeanor of a steamship company executive dealing with the great unwashed that sailed the ships.

On arrival our accommodations were not available, but this problem was solved by the local administrators. It did not take an MBA to offset one problem with another: they would berth us aboard commercial trawlers the Navy had requisitioned but had not manned.

Several difficulties lay with this plan. A storm of considerable violence was expected to hit San Francisco that night, and the trawlers were not moored well enough to withstand a storm. None of the enlisted men and the officers in our group had ever served in a trawler. We did not know the condition of the engines, the fuel aboard, nor had any of us ever handled such a vessel.

Early in the evening two enlisted men and I tried to get the generator started. Somehow we did. We also tried out the engine and found it worked. We were nested among many other trawlers, some manned, some not. It did not make much difference, for the night was black; none of us knew the waters or the currents, and we did not have communications equipment.

Shortly after midnight the storm hit with tremendous velocity. We were in an unprotected area subject to the winds and sea. It rained in buckets, and it was cold. None of us had foul-weather gear. My two enlisted men and I were lucky to be able to break away from the nest, for we soon would have been crushed and sunk. But where to go in the black night with four-foot waves in the harbor? All we did was try to dodge anything and everything whether it moved or not. We bounced around like a cork all night.

As daylight arrived and the wind, seas, and rain subsided, we found ourselves close to a mass of junk, some of it afloat, some swamped. All vessels except for the few that were able to get under way were badly damaged. I tied up to those still afloat and with my crew went ashore. I was never asked to make a report, and I was told to go to *Matsonia* that day.

As C.O. of the U.S. Naval Armed Guard in *Matsonia*, I was assigned an Ensign, Ted Croisette, a survivor from one of the battleships at Pearl, as my

Exec. I also was lucky in getting a Chief Boatswain's Mate from *U.S.S. Maryland* as the Chief of 30 enlisted men. We were to assist the yard and contract workers in installing the guns. We would have one 4-inch-50-caliber on the stern, four 3-inch-50-caliber dual purpose guns, and about 24 water-cooled 50-caliber machine guns. The 4-inch gun was on the lower after deck amidships. Two 3-inch guns were on each side of the fore deck, and two 3-inch guns were on each side of a higher after deck.

It was late in December and *Matsonia* had already been painted gray. This beautiful white ship that had carried Virginia to Hawaii already had the somber look of a troopship. On boarding I paid my respects to the ship's Master, Frank Johnson. A senior Matson Line Captain, he was in his 50s by then. His suite was abaft the bridge. He was shaving, but the door to the head was open and I could see him when I entered. His wife was sitting in one of the lounge chairs, and looked up at me as I quietly said, "Captain Johnson, I am aboard to install the guns and to sail with you. My name is Ensign Chester." I must have stunned him because he cut himself as he turned around.

He finished shaving, and we had a cup of coffee together as I explained what had to be done. His wife joined in the conversation, and our first meeting was leisurely but business-like. It set the tone for a relationship that lasted all the time we served together. I was charged with the defense of the ship, and he and I worked in complete harmony.

We spent the last days of December installing guns, ready ammunition boxes, magazines, storage rooms, repair facilities, and quarters for our personnel. Concurrently we altered the vessel from a luxury liner to a troop transport. She had been designated an Army rather than a Navy Transport; thus, three independent organizations reported to their own chain of command.

As he had done before Captain Johnson worked directly under the Matson Line administration. He was responsible for the navigation and operation of the vessel, the large civilian crew of Merchant Marine Officers, and unlicensed personnel numbering close to 400. The Army Troop Commander was an Army of the United States (AUS Reserve) or a National Guard LtCol. He had a small staff of Army personnel and was directly responsible for the berthing, feeding, and other matters involving military personnel being transported. I had charge of the defense of the ship and the overall security. I also was responsible for communications.

Organizationally there were strict lines of authority. In a practical sense, however, it was essential that the three organizations, together with a fourth—the embarked military personnel being transported—work together as a unit. This was all new ground and required a great deal of give and take, and more important, understanding and cooperation. Ordinarily one might expect trouble between the Merchant Marine and the Navy. All areas of conflict that could be imagined existed. The Master of an ocean liner ordinarily demanded and received the respect that went with so prestigious a job. Suddenly there is a war; he has to surrender much of his authority to a 25-year-old Ensign, completely independent of him and who in a time of combat in many ways superseded his authority. Then there was the difference in pay between the Navy crew and the Merchant crew, each living independently of each other and yet thrown together by necessity and not by choice. In a sense we were interlopers into the orderly life the Merchant Marine had been leading prior to the war.

Although I had a crew of more than 30 men, I depended on others to augment my gun crew. I could use military personnel being transported, but they were not aboard long enough to train. They also had their own problems in training both for the war that awaited their arrival and for orderly abandonment of ship should the war catch up with them en route. Army personnel assigned to the Troop Commander were few in number and were not combat trained or oriented. They had their own preoccupation, and there was little or no mixing.

Fortunately as the Commanding Officer of the Naval Armed Guard Detachment, I had independence and authority far exceeding that of either the Master or the Troop Commander. If abused it could create many problems. But my position was so strong, should anyone try to interfere with my mission, he could be easily checkmated. I had been in the Navy long enough to know the power of a C.O. I was not about to abuse it any more than let anyone interfere in the Navy's business and mission.

As the work proceeded Captain Johnson assigned the First Officer, William Dodge, to act as liaison between his staff and mine. Bill Dodge, an unusual man, was self-educated, very literate, and professionally sound. He had an excellent rapport with the union delegates on board. With the outstanding and unusual cooperation of the Captain and all the officers of the ship, we were able to accomplish a month of work in a matter of days.

One of the most sticky problems was getting the ship's officers and crew to assist in servicing and manning the guns. They had the usual fear and distrust of weapons, yet with Bill Dodge I was able to dispel this. We ended up with more volunteers than we could use. The Merchant crew adopted

124

my people, and a miracle came about. The Merchant Marine could not do enough for the Navy and vice versa! Not so with the LtCol. Troop Commander and his small group, who quickly disenchanted almost everyone by nit-picking. This probably stemmed from the policies of the Troop Commander. Wherein Captain Johnson was a father figure to me, and in most ways more of a help than any of the previous C.O.s either in the Merchant Marine or Navy with whom I had sailed, the Troop Commander was an irritant whose nose seemed out of joint because he had no control over me. I was polite and respectful to him, and I discussed matters with him when there was an overlap. Nevertheless he was annoyed that an Ensign had so much more authority than he.

I very carefully deferred to Captain Johnson on our mutual responsibilities, and in fact looked to him for advice and counsel, which he readily provided. He had adjusted to the fact times had changed, and his life had to change with it. From our many conversations over the months, I got the impression he took comfort in being a man of peace, and was relieved he would never have to give the order, "Commence Firing." He was a patriot and a brave man. Although he would risk his life to save lives, he was not inclined to take one. If I had not seen what was occurring in Germany and had not lost so many friends at Pearl Harbor, I too could have easily reacted to the war as Captain Johnson did. When it was all over he had served at sea for the entire war, safely transporting over 170,000 troops, together with huge amounts of supplies. This is a great accomplishment, and I was privileged to have known this fine man.

Arming the ship was not difficult. *Matsonia* was a well-built vessel, although older, smaller, and slower than *Manhattan* and *Washington*. The problems we encountered in strengthening the support structures for the guns were minor, and within days I had a defense-oriented Gunnery Department with which I was confident.

Originally built as *Malolo* in the late '20s, the ship was given more stability than most ocean liners. She had a strong righting motion in a roll, whereas many liners were at times unstable due to a low GM, which resulted in a slow roll that was less taxing on the passengers. (GM—metacentric height—is a calculation for stability of the vessel. To be stable a positive GM is needed to return the ship to an upright position.) Often there is a large ground swell between San Francisco and Honolulu, and it was not long before *Malolo* passengers called her Rololo. The company added some topside weight to her, cut down the roll a bit, and changed the name to *Matsonia*. Still she had a high GM. This was a plus when we added the topside weight of the guns, and gave us a more stable platform.

I selected a nice stateroom for myself on the forward port side of an upper deck where I could look through the portholes. It was strategically situated, and I had quick access to the bridge from where I had set up communications to the guns. It served as a room and office. My Executive Officer, Ted Croisette, also had his own room as did my Chief, Loiselle. I was also able to get excellent quarters for the enlisted men as a whole, even though they had to double up.

The food for the ship's permanent staff including officers, enlisted, and unlicensed personnel was the same, whether served in the main dining room or elsewhere. The troops other than senior officers did not eat as well and only received two meals a day. We carried over 3,000 troops, so water also had to be rationed. At this time we were full of troops going west, with very few passengers coming back east.

Speed was the main defense of the few fast ships such as *Matsonia*. Proceeding at over 20 knots and zigzagging in suspicious waters, we were almost an impossible target for the submarines of the time. While I was in the ship, we knew the U.S. Fleet was almost nonexistent, and we were subject to attack by Japanese carrier aircraft.

Ginny had come to San Francisco for the holidays, but shortly after the first of the year *Matsonia* sailed for Pago Pago in Samoa. We sailed in company with *Lurline* and *Monterey,* two other Matson Liners, accompanied by the carrier *U.S.S. Enterprise,* cruisers, and destroyers. With the First Marine Division embarked in the three ships, no one was taking any chances with the first high-speed convoy. My Siberia turned out to be an interesting assignment. From a future Naval career point of view, it was at best a lateral move from my assignment in *Kanawha*. The country, however, was at war, and a career had to take a back seat to winning. Even with my Merchant Marine background, there still was no precedent for assignment as anything other than an engineer to a major combat ship.

I soon found out how important my job was. Before sailing and even as the Marines were embarking, I attended a conference of the senior Marine Officer Command of our Marine passengers. Neither the Master nor the Army Troop Commander was invited. The meeting, in the large suite of the Senior Officer, was attended by his staff and battalion commanders. He first appointed a huge Marine Captain, nicknamed Tiny, as my liaison officer. He said he would work with me and cooperate in any way to assist in defending the ship at sea. I was amazed. I was the only junior officer present. I can't conceive of another assignment for which an Ensign would have so much responsibility.

In the first few days of January, no one knew where the Japanese Fleet was or whether they were going to continue the momentum of their first attack on to the Pacific Coast. Although specifics of the disaster at Pearl Harbor were not generally known as yet, it was no secret we had been dealt a severe blow. The three Matson Line's ex-beautiful white luxury liners were now dull gray troopships with men and guns bulkhead to bulkhead. The lovely public rooms had been torn apart, and the ship was one big barracks. All bets of the past were off, and for me there was no going back. Along with so many others I was being swept away by events.

We were supposedly going to slip away quietly from the Matson Line pier on the Embarcadero. I can't recall whether it was by day or night, but there was no way three large liners could sneak out of San Francisco Harbor without being seen. In my meeting with the Marine officers and in the Convoy meeting with the Masters of the three ships, the C.O.s of the Armed Guard and a representative of the Task Group Commander readily acknowledged our departure time, date, and course would be known by the enemy. Perhaps they would not know our destination, but a later event indicated they did.

Once we sailed all the guns had to be test-fired and the safety check carried out. Because we were accompanied by other ships and were immediately joined by our escort, I had to get permission for the firing. This I did at the first opportunity. Unlike *Kanawha's* officers and men being reluctant to participate, between my crew, the Merchant men, and the Marines, there was no lack of volunteers.

With little time for instruction prior to sailing, I had to train my people on the job. Tiny introduced me to Gunnery Sergeant Rogers, who was right out of the book. He knew his job. Together with Ted Croisette and Chief Loiselle, we set to work drilling the makeshift gun crews. Instructions in safety, loading, sighting, firing, and misfiring were carried out with an intensiveness I did not have to force. We got permission to fire at targets thrown over the side that would sink whether hit or not, and thus we practiced with our stern gun. Three-inch 50 bursts would be shot off to be fired at by other guns for anti-aircraft practice.

Merchant, Marine and Navy men who had never been exposed to the noise and concussion of gunfire soon realized this was no Fourth of July. Without OGE 10 I set up my own practices on every possible combat situation I could think of. Those involved with my unit had busy days and nights. I became close to the Marines, and this whole ship within a few days was welded into an excellent fighting unit. We were not well enough armed to take on a major combat ship, but anything short of that and a submarine would find us a potent adversary.

Our escort was unlike any I was to experience again. *Enterprise* and other combat ships would move off in different directions going hull down at times over the horizon before returning. We would zigzag at times and at other times proceed on a straight course. It was obvious the command was improvising as they went along. With a speed in excess of 20 knots, we had little to fear from submarines. The convoy proceeded to Pago Pago.

While en route the Marines kept their men constantly busy, a difficult task in close quarters. You could hardly walk down an alley way without tripping over Marines, who were sleeping, reading, cleaning their weapons, writing home, or playing cards. Rarely did they have a chance to go on deck. They were like sardines in a can. Some were seasick. But the work was challenging and life was pleasant enough. My room was beautiful. The food was good, and I had interesting conversations with Captain Johnson, First Officer Bill Dodge, Marines, and many others. War correspondents took our pictures as we practiced firing the guns.

Several days prior to our ETA in Pago Pago, we received word the island was being bombarded by a Japanese submarine. There was immediate concern. The Marines intended to go ashore in Pago Pago unless we were turned away by our own command. We made plans for a fast discharge of the troops and their equipment using lifeboats and anything that could float coming from the shore. In reality we were planning an amphibious operation that probably would have ended in disaster. Fortunately the submarine quietly slipped away and with it went the threat of an invasion of Samoa. All was peaceful on our arrival in Pago Pago, and with farewells to my friends in the First Marines, we disembarked our first troops without trouble.

At times the Japanese showed genius in carrying out the war at sea, but this instance was not one of them. Submarines are not suitable for shore bombardment, and the shelling of Pago Pago hardly made any sense at all. The sub did little or no damage and then apparently sailed away. But one thing that bothered me, which I mentioned to the Marines while discussing the contingency planning resulting from the attack, was our vulnerability to a torpedo attack from a submerged submarine as we entered the harbor. A submarine commander could easily predict our course, as well as the direction of our approach. Our speed would have to be reduced, but even at high speed we would be a fairly easy target for a submarine.

If the Japanese knew we were on our way to Pago Pago, their orders should have been to keep the submarine in position. The most logical conclusion is that the Japanese knew a convoy was on its way to Pago Pago, but had the wrong date. I am inclined to think the submarine had been waiting for us for over a week. When we did not show up, it received orders to leave for another area and target. Probably frustrated in not being able to wait until we arrived, it surfaced before leaving and fired off a few rounds.

We would have expected CincPac or the escort to have some intelligence, or if not, to establish some precautionary measures to ensure entry and departure from the port. It is possible the destroyers had made a sound sweep of the area. Our speed of advance was so high, however, it's unlikely a destroyer could move out ahead and accomplish this mission without running out of fuel.

I cannot understand why Japanese submarines did not take station off the Australian and New Zealand ports we, and other large transports, including *Queen Mary,* entered and departed from. Although I doubt that during the early days of 1942 we had the ships and facilities to adequately carry out such sweeps, we should have tried to cover our key ports.

One such opportunity occurred on a stormy day, with high seas, high winds, and poor visibility while we were pounding our way to the Port of Wellington, New Zealand. This was about the roughest weather *Matsonia* experienced. We were steaming independently, and radar was not as yet installed. The after-main 4-inch 50-caliber gun was always manned and ready at sea. I was on my way up to the bridge when suddenly the after-battery started firing away. When I arrived on the bridge, I looked aft but saw nothing. Captain Johnson and others on the bridge saw nothing. I immediately contacted the gun captain, who said they saw a submarine on the surface, got their shot off fast, and hit it with the first shot at very short range. They fired away, continuing to hit. He continued to fire where they thought the sub might still be even after it was lost from sight.

We were on one of those vulnerable approach courses at the time, but with poor visibility the submarine did not see us until we had passed it. Under those conditions a stern shot from the surface was a very long shot. I spoke with Capt. Johnson for a minute before leaving to question the gun crew. We both agreed we had no reason to believe the crew was wrong in their assessment in that visibility from the lower decks was better than from higher ones in foggy and hazy weather. I don't think Capt. Johnson was looking for any medals or would get any pleasure out of sinking any ship.

He was a dedicated peaceful Merchant Mariner who would risk neither the lives of his people nor the ship itself for a combat purpose.

I could not justify searching for debris to confirm the kill. Our mission was to avoid action, not to seek it out. I ordered the ship to General Quarters in case there was another sub or subs in the vicinity. It was a long walk aft to the after gun. The ship was laboring so hard it was impossible to run, and I had to hold on even to keep my balance. When I arrived the gun crew were exultant—they had done the impossible and sunk a sub. Some were Merchant Mariners who volunteered on their own time, and they too were ecstatic. Shell casings were rolling around the gun tub, and I had to dodge them or they could hurt. I congratulated the crew on the speed and accuracy of their response, but said that under the circumstances it would be difficult if not impossible to get a confirmation. But I would work on it. Not to dampen their morale, I asked them to write down what they saw and did and make a sketch of what they saw. We arrived in the Port of Wellington without further incident, and within about four hours of the shooting we were secure in our berth.

By that time practically everyone in the vessel was convinced we had sunk a sub. *Matsonia,* a ship of peace, had struck a vital blow for victory. I received the written reports quickly. The art work and literary efforts were crude but consistent. No one other than the gun crew had observed the sub or the hits. We had no debris to collect or even report. It was obvious to me that unless the Japanese admitted to the loss or damage of a sub in that area, there would be no confirmation from the Navy. All I could do was report the expenditure of ammunition in connection with the firing on a Japanese sub that the crew reported was either damaged or sunk. Until I left the ship I was constantly asked if we had received confirmation.

Meanwhile we continued to carry troops around the Pacific. At regular intervals we practiced gunnery, and this was a big thing for the war correspondents. It was as close to actual fighting as many of them got at that time of a few fast naval engagements.

The first voyage west in *Matsonia* was unique. Once the Marines had disembarked we proceeded independently back to San Francisco. Gone were the other two troopships and their escorts. Our decks, public rooms, passageways, and cabins were mostly deserted; we were a moving island unto ourselves. Although I missed the Marines, who were a pleasure to work with, tranquility descended on the ship. The weather was good, and I was able to spend more time with my people and with Capt. Johnson and his people. While we worked to smooth out problems we had encountered, the pace was more leisurely. We got to know and trust each other, and whatever the future held for us, we knew we would be able to cope.

Radio operations received wireless news each day, and a daily newspaper was circulated. But we had no intelligence reports on enemy activity in our area, nor did we see other ships or aircraft. It was obvious that in the Southern Pacific, out of range of Japanese shore-based aircraft, except for an enemy submarine that might luckily be in our path, what we had to prepare for was an enemy carrier air search, a quick raid by enemy surface forces, or a surface raider such as the Germans used on occasion.

On arrival in San Francisco I received the official copies of AlNavs, which confirmed I had been temporarily promoted to Lt(jg) together with all other Ensigns of my date of rank or before. I had heard of this while in Samoa, but I took the physical and signed the necessary papers at the Armed Guard Center. My pay and allowances went up about $100 a month, and my permanent commission was now overdue by one year. My back pay, which I could well use, amounted to about $1800, a fortune in those days. I had begun to feel like Ensign was part of my name.

While we were in San Francisco an experienced Armed Guard officer was needed to sail as C.O. on a ship ready to cast off, and Ensign Croisette was detached and ordered to go. His relief was Ensign Lester Cook, who had never been to sea. Les Cook, an ex-college professor who had been trained in communications, was about my age. He was a quiet, reserved, intelligent man. Although not a mover in the manner of Ted Croisette, he got things done in his own way. The Armed Guard Center was going full blast, and the C.O. was busy shipping crews out.

There had been no shore leave in Pago Pago, but there was plenty in San Francisco. I had no night watches, and so long as I did my work, I could take as much time off as possible. Although I had been to San Francisco in *Kanawha,* and spent several days there before sailing in early January, the transformation of the town was tremendous. Soldiers, Sailors, and Marines were everywhere. The old days of the Fleet Followers ended when the Fleet sailed to Hawaii in 1940-41 and did not come back. In this new atmosphere the military dominated because San Francisco was the main port of embarkation on the West Coast. Ginny joined me for a time, and once I was promoted she gave her notice she would not renew her teaching contract when it ended in June. At this time, however, she could only get a few days off, mostly on weekends. The St. Francis Hotel bar was very popular, and the one Matson Line officers mostly frequented. We stayed at the less expensive Plaza Hotel on the same square. Because I was integrated into

Matson society on board ship, I also spent time with them ashore. What had once been their private preserve was now overwhelmed with officers due to go overseas. In the first half of 1942 war news was all bad. Although there was an atmosphere of bravado, cynicism prevailed as well. Army Air Corps fighter pilots in particular faced a bleak future. Many were bound for Darwin, Australia, with flying machines that were no match for the Zero. This was no secret, and occasionally you would see one of them light his cigarette with a $10 bill.

We sailed independently on our next trip to Australia, transporting Army troops. Army combat people were mostly nonprofessional while the Marines had mostly been regulars. One of the regiments we carried was part of the 32nd National Guard Division from Hartford, Connecticut. From Australia they would soon embark for New Guinea, take heavy casualties, and not be relieved until late 1944. At the time of the crossing, they had no idea about the hardships they would encounter in the jungles of this distant land. Their morale was high, and they too were a pleasure to work with.

Conditions for the troops on board were miserable. Neither a Ship's Service Store nor a Post Exchange were available. The private concessioner who had the contract in peace time just expanded the company's business to service the troops. Prices were greatly inflated, but it was a monopoly. The troops paid prices way out of line with the base pay of a private, which was about $30 a month. My people complained as did passenger officers. They could not understand why they had to pay 10 cents for a Coke when all service stores charged 5 cents, and all other items were marked up at the same ratio. I first spoke with Capt. Johnson about the problem, and he cautioned me to be careful, indicating there could be wheels within wheels. He would support my effort, however, to substitute the concessioner with either a Navy Ship Service or an Army Post Exchange.

The concession was held by an American company, but the manager was Australian. I told him about the complaints and asked him if he could tell his people to get their prices in line with service troopships. He literally screamed they were not exploiting the troops. I used the Cokes as an example. He said he had to throw the bottles away. He could have returned the bottles, but I knew he was selling them in Australia for more than he would get as a rebate in the States. I had seen the bottles being taken off the ship. Bottles were carefully collected, for rules against throwing anything over the side were stringent. It was general knowledge there was a shortage of bottles in Australia, and the empties were being sold there. At this point he threatened me personally, telling me to mind my own business.

This was my business and that of any officer responsible for men in the armed services. By the time I got to the Troop Commander with the problem, the concessioner had been there first. The LtCol. was rude and he also told me to mind my own business. I stood up to him and said that if he did not do something about what I considered his business to protect Army personnel, I would do something to protect my own men by starting a Ship's Service Store myself, which was within the authority of a C.O. in the Navy. He was livid, claiming he took orders only from people at Fort Mason in San Francisco.

On the return trip I wrote a report to be forwarded through Navy channels. The officer in charge of the AG in San Francisco was lukewarm and basically wanted no flaps. I received a call from a Col. at Fort Mason who was furious and also threatened me. I had obviously touched a sensitive nerve because the concessionaire in question operated stores on many Merchant Marine transports. A lot of money was at stake. Just the fact I had written a report describing the situation, with reference to the privately run concession that was exploiting military personnel, created an explosive situation aboard the ship. The concessioner had a large staff, and the opportunities for individual exploitation, with a captive market paying all cash, were innumerable.

As long as the store was open, GIs lined up to purchase cigarettes, cokes, other beverages, candy, souvenirs, and almost everything a PX or Ship Service store carried. I would estimate they did a gross business in excess of $6,000 a day while the troops were on board. The gross profit level had to be at least $3,500 a day. Although the lower ratings received as little as $30 a month, the average pay must have been about $60 a month. Many also received money from home.

Zeroing-in on the cokes, I knew from my experience in *Kanawha* they cost less than two and one-half cents apiece plus a bottle deposit of about two cents. There was at least a three-quarter cent profit per bottle. A 20 percent gross profit at five cents a Coke would be a very conservative estimate if the bottles could not be returned. If the bottle was returned or sold, the gross profit was in excess of 100 percent. Since the concessioner was selling them at ten cents, the profit had to be about 300 percent.

One of the problems I had as a ship's service officer in *Kanawha* was to remain within the profit limitations, even though the profits were transferred to the Welfare Fund. Cokes and other soft drinks in the same category were a constant problem. If I sold them at one cent there was a heavy loss. If I sold them at five cents, there was a tremendous profit; anything between was a bookkeeping nightmare.

Store employees passed the word I would disappear over the side on a dark night either at sea or on the Embarcadero. But that had the opposite effect. The Merchant crews rallied around me, and my own crew was ready to kill. I had a number of discussions with Capt. Johnson about the matter. He was concerned that someone ashore in the Matson office could be involved as well as others at Fort Mason. The Troop Commander was the only supporter of the concessioner, and he seemed confident his boss and he could prevail and establish an authority aboard that had not existed so far.

I could not get across to the Troop Commander that the situation was so rotten, regardless of any actions of mine, it would have to blow up. I also suspected they were exporting goods to Australia through their store. So it was the manager of the store, his personnel, plus the Troop Commander without the support of his own personnel, against the whole ship. If the manager had not reacted and had made some concessions, the situation might have continued longer. There has been tremendous inflation since 1942. In today's dollars the gross receipts of that store would exceed $100,000. I never looked for conflict, but somehow it seemed to find me. The wheels of the Navy ground slowly. Although people reacted to this situation and removed the concessionaires from all ships, it was not until after I had been transferred. I carried a 45 cal. pistol as did all officers during wartime, and Loiselle, an ex-fleet boxing champ, never was far from my side. He told the manager if anything happened to me, he personally would tear him into little pieces and throw him to the sharks.

Incidents like this seem to have plagued combat forces in the U.S. since the Revolutionary War. Politicians exploited them, as did the many bureaucrats and the private sector. Many banded together with those non-combatants in uniform behind the lines to make the prosecution of the war difficult for those who had to fight it. This represented a relatively small percentage of the whole, but it was sufficient for many in combat to realize they fought two enemies. Somehow the support elements in many cases failed to realize they were there to support us, and not for us to support them.

The store problem was more of an undercurrent than an everyday affair. Other than making a report and keeping a weather eye out for some skullduggery, I never allowed this to interfere with the mission of defending the ship. Nonetheless I was not going to stand by and see any military personnel exploited, or more important, be unprepared to defend their ship and themselves. I had a strong enough position with everyone of importance on the ship to checkmate the adversary. I could and did go though the motions of setting up a Ship Service but never intended to do so, nor did I waste any time on it.

The Troop Commander type will always be there, pussy-footing around, mainly protecting his own prerogatives and privileges. Somehow the exploiters always seem to be able to find someone at a Fort Mason in a position to protect them. The officer in charge of the AG in San Francisco forwarded the report, without comment, which was par for the course; such types never take a stand. It was obvious he did not want controversy, and a C.O. like me might in the end draw him into conflict.

The ship and I, however, were touched by the real war in many ways reaching far from our latitude and longitude. We carried the first U.S. combat forces to go overseas in the Pacific. Many of the officers and men I had come to know died or were severely wounded in action. Although at times people recognize the valor of those in the front lines, more often than not the difference between victory and defeat depends on a low rating enlisted man or an officer in the lower ranks. They simply get blown away with no witnesses; or the witnesses take the bows for their valor; or like the large majority of the men, they just did not give a damn about recognition.

Some of these men I met again later in my life or read about. Most simply were a part of something bigger than life, and either lost theirs in pursuit of a noble cause, or simply did what they had to do, mainly to protect one another. Still they performed. The closer one got to where the blood was let, the fewer the heroes.

I spent much time with Captain Battle, a jovial and interesting British Merchant Mariner. He was a Cunard Line Shipmaster who was trying to find *S.S. Aquitania*, which he had just missed in Australia. He was to relieve the present Master, but had to find the ship first. Troopship movements were top secret and subject to change. Next to *Queen Mary, Aquitania* at that time was believed to be the second largest troopship operating. Passage was arranged for him to sail to San Francisco in the belief *Aquitania* was due there shortly.

Aquitania was very similar and of about the same vintage as the ill-fated *Titanic*. She was a four-stacker of close to 50,000 tons. I believe Capt. Battle was the Number Two Master in the Cunard Line, junior only to the Commodore in *Queen Mary*. He was a large man of about 60. We spent many hours talking, and he had a wealth of maritime lore to relate. During one of our numerous conversations, he said my last name was familiar.

Many years ago he had crossed the Atlantic with another Chester who might have been my grandfather. I immediately became very interested. I believed he was referring to my father, of whom I knew so little. He had made several crossing in Cunard Line ships before 1924, and my father would have been in his late 40s or more at the time. From the description Capt. Battle gave, I was certain it was my father. They had crossed more than once in more than one ship. Capt. Battle must have been in his early forties then and either a First or Chief Officer.

From experience I knew that regular passengers from the transatlantic liners looked forward to seeing old friends among the officers, and my father in particular had invited some officers home to dinner. Capt. Battle recalled no more than interesting conversations dealing with ships and the business; however, I gathered he liked and respected the man.

Many war correspondents were with us on the eastbound voyages. They were friendly but frustrated aboard a transport, which although cruising a war zone, could just as well have been on a pleasure outing. One who had become famous during the Spanish Insurrection and worked for the Chicago Tribune tried hard to create news, but there was nothing to base it on. Another traveling with his photographer took many pictures of my crew and me, but he was killed shortly thereafter and never wrote or at least transmitted the article. I did get several of the pictures, however.

We also started taking survivors from the Philippines back to the States. On the westbound leg of the voyage, I spent a great deal of time with our few passengers. The main subject of the conversation, with both men and women, was hate. I talked with a Colonel from the Philippine Scouts and nurses who had managed to get out in some manner or other, including an Army Nurse and an Ensign from the MTB Squadron that took MacArthur out. Because *Matsonia* was a merchant ship, drinking was legal, and the survivors would sit for hours venting their anger about General MacArthur. All I knew of the man was what I had read, and the press was good. What I heard from those who had served in the Philippines, if true, was a horror story.

All of these officers had been highly decorated by MacArthur. They came from different outfits and services, but they hated this man with a venom I never witnessed before or after. One high ranking officer used to sit in his room snapping in on his pistol, pretending that he had MacArthur in his sights. The nurses, well rewarded by MacArthur, had been treating the wounded and the dying and held this same hatred.

People claimed he lived a life of luxury in Corrigedor, while the fighting was in Bataan. They said he had received a priority for planes over that of Pearl Harbor. He had a day's advance notice of the war, and yet his planes were mostly caught on the ground and failed to fight as a whole in the air. What active interest he did take was debilitating, and he was directly responsible for failure to get the planes in the air.

I got the impression from the Colonel the officers and men wanted to fight, and might have even held the Philippines, but MacArthur tied their hands. As time went by they all seemed to hate MacArthur more than the Japanese. The Colonel told me he planned to tell the story on arrival in the States, but as we pulled into San Francisco he had a heart attack. I doubt whether he survived it, but his story was never told. The tales about the General were terrible, and I was shocked. I was aware we went into the war with inferior equipment, that a peacetime high command rarely adapted to war time, but the MacArthur story as told in *Matsonia* raised doubts in my mind about winning the war.

Matsonia sailed back and forth across the Pacific, and we lucked out all the way. Australia and New Zealand were beautiful countries. My time ashore was limited, and the ship stayed in port for only a short time. The Australian men were off fighting and dying far away from their homes. The women, who outnumbered the men even before they went away to war, as a whole were not only beautiful but cheerful and pleasant. The temptation was there, but the opportunity was lacking for those of us just passing through. I have fond memories of the people of this lovely land.

On my last trip in *Matsonia,* I called at Brisbane during a torrential rain. Soon after arrival I received a message from General MacArthur's headquarters that all guns were to be kept uncovered in expectation of imminent action. The Troop Commander made a big thing of asking me why I had not uncovered the guns. I told him that we had some 24, 50-caliber machines guns that, if left uncovered for any length of time in the rain, would be inoperable. I said that we were in a condition of readiness and we could uncover the guns in a matter of seconds.

Further I told him that with the heavy rain we could not see anything to shoot at nor could anyone see us. He said, notwithstanding, I should carry out the General's orders. I told him that I, not the General, was responsible for the defense of the ship, and I was not going to immobilize it, orders or no orders. I explained to him that uncovering the guns was unrelated to readiness and was not the way a war was fought. I said readiness was the ability to shoot and to maintain the fire when required. I also said the 50-caliber guns were very subject to water damage, and if I exposed them unnecessarily this large part of our anti-aircraft defense system would be demobilized for a long time. I also told him we only had four gunner's mates trained to clean and repair all of our guns.

In truth the 50-caliber water-cooled machine gun had to be carefully assembled. A slight error in the headspacing and someone could be killed. Already a merchant seaman who volunteered to man one of the 50s had been injured by a headspacing problem. Fortunately we had an excellent Army surgeon attached to the ship who patched the man up so well he returned to duty in short order and was even back at his gun station.

I could not convince the Troop Commander. He reported me to General MacArthur's staff as failing to carry out the orders. Within a short time two SPs from the Office of the Commander South Pacific came to pick me up in a jeep and took me to Vice Admiral Leary's office, which was adjacent to that of the General. A Lcdr. came in and told me there was a battle going on in the Coral Sea, and the General had ordered all the guns on ships in the harbor uncovered.

I told him what I had told the Troop Commander. He went in to see the Admiral, who came out to see me. He told me to get those guns uncovered, and intimated that they had enough trouble with the General to let a few guns stand in the way. I reiterated that as the C.O. of the unit responsible for the safety of the ship, I would have to be relieved if he wanted me to immobilize my ship. He went in to see the General, and I realized I was in trouble. From what I had heard about the man, he would never back down. This guy's priorities were obviously at odds with those for the successful fighting of the war.

When Admiral Leary returned he seemed completely exasperated: "God damn it, Chester, uncover those guns or I will have you relieved." I said I would like to comply, but it was still raining, and General MacArthur or no General MacArthur, the ship had many miles to sail independently of escort, and required all of its gunnery functional. He became flushed, and it was obvious he could do without this confrontation. I had to be stupid to take on the "Great Man." But that is my nature. When I am convinced I am right in a serious situation where lives are at stake, I am just plain stubborn.

Admiral Leary told me to "sit right there." I would be relieved. He had to go through channels with a radio message to Cincpac and Cincpac had to go to BuPers (Bureau of Naval Personnel) to relieve a C.O. In this instance he probably could have done it himself, but he realized the issue was not the uncovering of the guns, but whether he should support the

General, who was wrong, or throw me to the wolves. He played it carefully. About three hours later he came out of his office and said, "God damn you, Chester, get back to your ship." Not a word was mentioned about uncovering the guns. When I returned to the ship, it was still raining. The Troop Commander was at the gangway. I just passed him and went to my room. The guns stayed covered. I was expecting new orders soon, but I was certain they would now be changed to the Murmansk run.

I was sorry to leave *Matsonia*. I had an excellent unit, and we were at peace with all around us but the Troop Commander and the store manager. The Captain and all the officers were aware of what was going on, and I believe they too were unhappy to see me go. Others were also due to leave. Both the Chief Officer and the First Officer, with whom I had been particularly close, were to get their own commands. So the trip home was rather sad in a way. And it looked as though I was a loser.

Some years after the war Matson Line refurbished only one of the newer ships and named it *Lurline*. One day I was in San Francisco and saw her, completely rebuilt, and scheduled to sail on the first Matson passenger voyage after the war. Captain Johnson was in command, and I decided to call on him on sailing day. I worked my way up to the Captain's quarters. His suite was abaft the bridge. The door was open, and as before, I could see him when I entered, and he was shaving. Mrs. Johnson was sitting in one of the lounge chairs. She looked up at me as I quietly said, "Captain Johnson, I am aboard to install the guns and to sail with you. My name is Ensign Chester." He turned around fast. Mrs. Johnson at first didn't put it all together and was agape, and the Captain did it again—he cut himself. It was quite a scene. Tears were in all our eyes, nostalgia hit fast. We had coffee together and talked over old and new times in the limited period allowed. Then I left, but as I did the few old timers still around searched me out, and the contrast to that dull gray ship and their now beautiful white one soon overwhelmed me.

Six

War: Atlantic and Caribbean

U.S.S. SC 981

The ships and the men who manned them, along with the land and air forces, were simply pawns in a global war game being orchestrated and played out by people not actually engaged in overseas operations. I had gradually eased into the pre-war buildup as a child, a student, and as a Cadet at the Merchant Marine Academy. This had all been on the East Coast and European waters, what was later called the European Theater of Operations.

I was now bound back to the East Coast after two and a half years in the Pacific, two of which were at sea in peacetime, and the last six months during wartime. I had left the East Coast as an Ensign and was now returning as a Senior Lt. and a command of a combat ship if I did not foul up. I was now 26 years old and had matured a great deal. Two years as Gunnery Officer of *Kanawha* had been excellent experience, and six months in command of the U.S. Navy Armed Guard in *Matsonia* at war had been a unique and challenging assignment. Although I did my best to keep in touch with events in the Atlantic, I was almost totally consumed with the problems in the Pacific.

I knew I would soon become involved in the Battle of the Atlantic, which had begun with the sinking of *S.S. Athenia* in 1939, a battle we were losing at this time. I was aware of Hitler's successes on land, but was confident of our ultimate victory in the Atlantic as well as the Pacific. What did concern me was my ability to rise to command of a combat ship, even a small one. I had command of a Navy unit in *Matsonia* but not command of the ship. Although I had operated *Padnsay* for many weeks during the captain's illness, he was still on board. The fact was, all I had ever commanded was the fishing trawler that stormy night in San Francisco Bay.

Everything seemed to have come about suddenly. Expecting nothing but bad news and exile on return to San Francisco, the opposite happened. In addition to my promotion to Lt. senior grade, I received my permanent commission as a Lt(jg) back-dated to February 8, 1941, together with back pay. Most important was the assignment to the Sub-Chaser Training Center (SCTC) in Miami. This was an elite school. I could make the reporting date if I departed immediately for Miami. I telephoned Ginny with the good news, and off we set for Miami in the old Pontiac—command instead of exile.

Command is much sought after but rarely successfully exercised in combat. War is inhuman to begin with, which reflects on the individual in command in different ways, times, and conditions.

In addition to courage, competence, training, and charisma, there is another element difficult or impossible to identify until the individual is put to the test. Some may call it "grit" or determination. Even then performance can vary with the situation. This is what concerned me as I started my drive to Miami and the Atlantic.

Virginia was now able to drive a reasonable share of the time. To reach Miami on schedule we had to make 500 miles a day. Given the roads at the time, the scarcity of gas (even with ration tickets), delays were frequent. There would be no formal wedding for Ginny; this trip had to be our honeymoon.

I didn't know much about the school, but the vibrations were good. A sub-chaser (SC) was still a combat vessel, and anti-submarine warfare (ASW) in the Atlantic was appealing to me. Information about the Battle of the Atlantic that reached us in the Pacific Fleet before we entered the war was very limited. What little news there was clearly indicated we were not doing well in early '42.

Although soon to be into this important phase of the war, as I approached Miami, I had no inkling of what I actually would be doing. I had no idea what an SC or a PC was like; I had never seen one, nor had I had access to any information on anti-submarine warfare. Nonetheless I was on my way to an ASW command.

SCTC was located at Miami's old Pier 2 on Biscayne Boulevard. I soon

141

discovered my classmates to be Annapolis graduates mostly from the class of '32, NROTC Ivy League graduates of the rank of Lt. or above, and a sprinkling of junior officers, most of whom had had some sea time. The group was much too senior for SCs and PCs. I did not realize this class had been selected in preparation for the Destroyer Escorts, a secret new building project.

As Ginny and the other wives searched for more suitable quarters mostly on Miami Beach, I reported to SCTC with the others in Group 16. Lcdr. MacDaniel was commanding officer of SCTC. Much older and senior to our Lcdrs., he let us know that for the next several weeks we should consider ourselves midshipmen. Next we listened to a fiery lecture about the brutality of the enemy, illustrated by a merchant ship lifeboat riddled with bullet holes.

And so we started to punch our ticket for an ASW qualification. Many of our days and nights were spent a sea on SCs and PCs, and the training was rigorous. PCs, 173-feet long, were made of steel. The 110-foot long SCs were made of wood. An early version had Donald Duck's picture on a canvas screen on the flying bridge. It was crowded, rough, and uncomfortable on board SCs. Intermingled with all of this were classes and tests. Even though the methods of running an attack at the time were elementary, we were pressured to compensate for what we lacked in equipment with determination and instinct. The four weeks passed rapidly.

During World War II 300 PCs and 300 SCs were built. They were no-name ships, just numbers; yet they were commissioned vessels of the U.S. Navy capable of sailing to any part of the world. SCs rated three officers, but mostly received only two at the time; PCs rated four or five officers. I received orders to command *SC 981*, being built in the Milford Shipyard in Milford, Delaware. I had hoped for a PC, but only two or three were ready when I graduated, and several regular Lcdrs. and a few reserve officers were senior in rank to me in the group being assigned.

Some in Group 16 have remained in contact for much of their lives. It was a short, rough, close time together. SCTC was the beginning of a period of working in various combat areas, with our paths crossing regularly. Over the years one classmate, Lt. Sheldon Kinney, became my closest friend. He earned the Navy Cross and practically every other decoration other than the Medal of Honor. He also became a Rear Admiral.

Ensign John (Jack) Millar, a graduate of Choate and Princeton, about my age, also a member of Group 16, was assigned as Executive Officer of *SC 981*. Both Millar and I rented rooms in a private home in Milford while surveilling the completion of the ship. Jack was still a bachelor but competing for an ex-debutante. She was an obsession with him, and a Navy flyboy was giving him tough competition.

The Milford Shipyard had built sub-chasers during World War I and was inactive until it started to build the new vintage for World War II. Milford was a one-street town, about as removed from the war as it could be. The yard was at the end of a creek which led into a small river that flowed into Delaware Bay. At night, while Ginny helped Jack compose his love letters and I did my paperwork, the crew slipped into the only bar-and-grill in town. We would hear rumors of fights and goings-on, but somehow our U.S. Sailors never seemed to get caught, and in the afternoon they were back on their rooming house porch, sitting in rocking chairs and nodding to the townspeople who walked by.

SC 981, with a maximum speed of 16 knots, was powered by two General Motors Diesel 500-HP engines. It had a World War I 3-inch 23-caliber gun on the foredeck and two 50-caliber machine guns. We also carried depth charges on the stern, and later a mousetrap—a forward-throwing rocket launcher. A depth charge would explode whether it hit or not, but the mousetrap would not explode unless it hit something solid. Though a part of the so-called Donald Duck Navy, our emblem was Popeye the Sailor Man. I painted it on myself.

The vessel was soon completed and ready for fitting-out in the Philadelphia Navy Yard. We sailed down the creek with little fanfare with a pilot and our skeleton crew. Fitting-out took several days, and we—30 or more of us jammed into this little craft loaded with equipment—were very busy. We finally received orders to sail for Miami and shakedown. Prior to departure we held a short, informal commissioning ceremony. I read my orders to command and hoisted the commission pennant. This was my first ship command, and few of my people had any sea experience at all.

The smaller the ocean-going vessel, the harder the job. The weather as we left for Miami fortunately was not rough, but the rain was constant and visibility poor. We had no radar and no gyrocompass. Practically everything on the ship broke down at one time or another. The senior petty officers, other than the engineering ones, were made watch officers, but Jack and I were almost always on the bridge. Actually there was no where else to go. Movement around the ship was difficult. Steel bulkheads were built between each compartment, so when you went from one compartment to the other you had to climb up and down a vertical ladder hand-over-hand. As we proceeded south the weather worsened and we became more uncomfortable, a sign of things to come. We arrived in Miami just before a hurricane was due. SCTC was being secured, the staff was going home, and no ships were to be at the dock. We were ordered out of port.

I decided to take my time, however. Experienced North Atlantic sailor that I was, I explained to my frightened crew they should imagine the ship upside down and secure everything to withstand this as well as shock, for we would be buffeted. I had them prepare sandwiches, secure the galley, start recording the barometer every half hour, and check and double-check all equipment, particularly the pumps. Someone came down from the SCTC staff to ask why we had not yet departed; most of the other Navy vessels had already left. I had selected an area close to the port to maneuver in during the storm and was in no hurry. So long as we had time to reach the area, I did not want to leave the dock before I was certain our preparations were complete.

My crew were nervous but not as much as I. Having developed a touching faith in my seamanship, they were unaware of my shortcomings or my uncertainty about our ability to survive a hurricane in so small a ship. I thought about the differences between handling a small ship rather than a large one in heavy weather. Although we had rough trips during our training cruises at SCTC and moderately rough seas en route to Miami, I had not been able to experiment with the ship in very bad weather. I was concerned.

We left the pier in time to reach the selected area before the wind and seas were strong enough to deter us. The game plan was to try to ride over the waves rather than have them engulf the ship. At the same time I had made the ship as watertight as possible and rigged life lines on deck so the crew could function during emergencies.

It now was a battle of *SC 981* and her crew against the sea. I can't think of a better shakedown, but the stakes were high. As the wind and seas increased and the barometer dropped, it became more difficult to keep the ship from either being swamped, broached, or pooped. So long as the sea's direction was consistent, I could find a position on either the bow or the quarter to ride over in relative safety. But as the center of the hurricane approached, conditions grew confused, and at times we took a heavy sea on deck. Although the winds were hurricane force, the seas were not as high as I had experienced in the North Atlantic; nevertheless, most of the crew became seasick.

We worked the engines by remote control from the bridge. There I had a seat from which I could reach the controls to alter the engine revolutions while still giving orders to the helmsman. It was almost impossible to sit let alone stand. The ship bobbed around. Rarely would she answer the helm at our slow maneuvering speeds, and I changed course by using the port and starboard engines. At times the sea took over completely, and we were at its mercy.

The night wore on and the storm center came and passed. Wind and seas moderated. Everyone in our little ship was bruised; the crew was physically exhausted, sick, tired, and very much respectful of the power they had combatted. As the seas abated and the barometer climbed, I started working our way back towards port. We reached the sea buoy at the first sign of daylight and sailed up the channel to Pier 2, taking the same berth from which we had departed. But as the first ship back, no one was there to handle our lines; the pier was boarded up and battened down tight. Once we docked I went below to get some sleep. Unfortunately there was not a dry spot on the ship, and my bunk like the others' was wet. Sea water had leaked from the deck, the sides, the hatches, and the bottom. Luckily the pumps had been able to handle the situation.

When a ship is in danger a few people stand out. During the storm some equipment and machinery failed, requiring repairs and replacements. Tom Owens, the oldest man in the ship, an Assistant Postmaster from Baltimore now a Second Class Electrician's Mate, volunteered to take care of the situation. Although seasick daily even in calm weather from the very first, he was clearly a key man on the ship. He suffered so much from seasickness it was pitiful. I offered him a transfer to shore duty, a recommendation for OCS, or even a chance at a direct commission, but he simply said this is where the Navy sent him and this is where he was going to serve. Dedicated men like Tom Owens won the war.

In Philadelphia we installed a new type of sonar gear (RCA WEA-1). Though it sent out a "ping," we got no return signals, bearing, or range. En route to Miami I tried it on deep-laden merchant vessels at anchor in the ports or navigating in the harbors. Nothing. I reported this to the sound personnel at SCTC, who decided to send us to Key West the next day to run tests. So we made a number of runs on a sub in Key West pinging to no avail. The technicians worked on the gear; their best sound operators took turns with it, but nothing. Finally an RCA technician arrived. He pinged on the submerged sub and again nothing. He then lost his composure: " This God damn unit never did pass its test. We told the Navy not to install it because it required more work, but they told us to do so anyway." He left. I told the command the result, and they told me they needed the ship, and I should ping even though I got no echo.

Those who designed the sub-chasers should have had to sail them. It was bad enough when you could proceed on a straight course, but maneuvering around ships being escorted was pure murder. You needed to strap yourself in your bunk. It took tremendous energy to stand or sit. When you moved around, you crawled hand-over-hand. We escorted several short convoys out of Key West, and the shore staff would send us right out again. It seemed to be a conspiracy to break us physically before the ship sunk itself. Our main mission was to protect merchant vessels from submerged submarines; if we could not locate them with the sonar, we would not be able to accomplish our purpose.

I soon realized it was an exercise in frustration, but continued to work on the WEA-1 and to ping, hoping to keep up the morale of the crew and to bluff any submarine in the vicinity. We were constantly at sea, operating independently escorting subs, barges, and nondescript craft. As we patrolled around our area of responsibility, our forward speed was about four knots. At times we would spend an entire day looking at the same lighthouse.

Conditions were terrible. Aside from seasickness, the sheer effort to keep oneself from being pitched around by the ship was tremendous. You had to be an acrobat to eat. The noise of the engines and generators, together with the constant pinging throughout the ship, made life mostly unbearable at sea. Our officers' wardroom was adjacent to the Radio Room and the Sound Room. As we altered courses in an escort pattern, the motion of the ship would change, tossing around those not holding on at the moment. Often we would hear a crash: the sound operator, the radio operator, and the yeoman, also working in the compartment, had ended up on the wardroom deck.

Problems were not confined to the forward area. With about 30 men crammed into so small a space on a gyrating ship, life was sheer misery. Still we plodded along, and the bluff seemed to work. The area we patrolled in 1942 was a submarine's happy hunting ground. They were having a field day sinking ships as the SCs and PCs slowly came on the scene. PCs sunk one or two subs, but they also were mostly bluffing. Yet it worked, and the sinkings declined. I never lost a ship I escorted.

The physical and mental strain on the crew was reaching a climax when one day we received orders to escort a Seatrain ship from Key West to the harbor entrance of Havana, then return to Key West for one day's maintenance. In 1942 Key West was a very bad liberty and recreation port, with no place for the crew to go other than a few bars where they usually

146

got into fights. So I planned to take *SC 981* into Havana for the night.

We approached Morro Castle and the harbor entrance on a calm, sunny day. I called the Chief Engineer on deck. I said, "Chief, I hear a knock on the starboard engine, and the port engine doesn't sound right either." He answered, "No Captain, everything sounds fine." I said, "Chief, take a look ahead, that's Havana, isn't it a pretty sight? Don't you hear that knock?"

By then Millar and Owens caught on, but I had to repeat it a few times for the Chief, who had a one-track mind about his engines.

Finally he came through and agreed we had better get into port as quickly as possible to make emergency repairs. I radioed the command that I had to shut down the engines for emergency repairs and requested permission to do so in Havana. Spares were on board, and I expected we could still be back in Key West to meet our next commitment.

I required some luck and got it. First I needed a Watch Operations Officer who knew little about engines and, as it was after 1700 hours, would not make a big thing out of it. I needed to have a message sent to the Naval Representative in Havana so he too would not create a stir. In addition I had to set the scene aboard the ship so anyone coming aboard would be adequately impressed with our plight. Most important I had to ensure that once ashore the crew would do whatever they did without disturbance. That was the most dangerous part. We proceeded very slowly towards Havana until we got approval. In the interim I had the Chief set up an explainable casualty and start taking heads off some of the cylinders as we got to the dock.

I had been in Cuba a few times before. *Manhattan* had made one or two winter cruises to Havana, and I had also called there in *Santa Clara.* The docks were now mostly empty; and with no specific orders, I proceeded to the San Francisco dock where the liners had tied up before the war. Cruise ships no longer called at Havana, and Navy ships were restricted to Guantanamo. Nonetheless an industry of promoters living off tourists was still around.

As we approached the dock word must have gone out fast, because a whole army of these characters descended on the dock hoping to exploit my hungry but not wealthy crew. Some of these guys even remembered my name. In true fashion of the maritime industry, they greeted me as a long-lost friend. *Manhattan* had been one of the biggest liners to make a rare cruise to Havana, but they were now presented with the smallest ship ever to tie up at the prestigious San Francisco dock.

Cubans are born businessmen, and those engaged in this particular trade faced lean times. They were not allowed aboard ship and had to talk to the crew from the dock. I had cautioned the crew that none were to go on the dock until I had cleared the ship with the Cuban authorities and the Naval Representative, whom I expected shortly. Business, as usual, preceded officialdom. We had no liquor, but we had plenty of cigarettes. This the Cuban officials expected, and I was ready for them.

I told them I had an engine casualty that had precipitated the call at Havana, and I expected to sail at dawn. I told them the Naval Attache would take care of all details. As I passed about ten to fifteen cartons of cigarettes their way, I requested they grant the crew the hospitality of the City of Havana for the night. They were only too pleased to do so, left a policeman and customs guard at the dock, and took off with as many cartons as they could carry. So far so good.

The entrepreneurs, having established contact with the crew, dispersed before a Navy Lcdr. arrived. He was in a white uniform, obviously dressed for a party, and was annoyed by our intrusion in his private preserve, or better described, paradise. He was a Reserve Officer who must have had friends in high places to get such a lush assignment. I was certain he would not go down in his whites to the engine room from which banging sounds were already coming. He didn't. But he said Havana was not a prescribed liberty port for the Navy, and shore leave would not be granted. I told him I had already received permission from the Cuban authorities to come ashore, and I was not about to upset the crew by denying them what they already believed they had received. Further I told him he would have to get a confirmation of this from Key West, and suggested it would be better for all if the matter were left alone. We would be away by daybreak, and I assured him there would be no international incidents. I was polite. He was suspicious. Yet he was impatient to get to wherever he was bound that evening, and I did not expect to see him when we sailed early in the morning.

I then met with the entire crew in the messroom, the biggest compartment on the ship. I cautioned them they must not have more than a few drinks. They could get drinks in other places, but only Havana offered a variety of distractions not available elsewhere. Havana was known as the "Paris of the West Indies," and if they treated the Cubans with respect, they would be treated likewise. Any infraction on the rules would be dealt with harshly. So ashore they went in groups, with about a fourth of the crew on board at all times. They followed the rules to the letter, and there were no incidents.

Most of the crew not only had never been to Havana. In fact they had not visited any foreign port. This became one of the most interesting nights of their lives—whatever one desired Cuba had it. I went to the famous Tropicana that evening, which was operating as if there were no war or even a rumor of it. The show and the girls were beautiful, and it was just what we all needed as a relief from our confinement aboard a seagoing roller coaster. Proper notations were made in the deck and engine logs, and we quietly sailed at daybreak, arriving just a few hours later in Key West with no questions asked, on time and ready for our next assignment. The crew never stopped talking about their experiences in Havana. I had broken the tension.

Our next job was to escort about 20 ships, tugs, and barges—all looking like they had been assembled in a junk yard. They were all bound for Curacao, a trip that required only several days with a fast convoy, but was going to take us much longer because the speed of advance would be gauged by the slowest vessel in the group. We hoped for six knots, but averaged less than four. We would also be going through one of the most dangerous submarine attack areas.

It was a rough, slow trip. Fresh food ran out, and we started to fish for our meals. At slow speeds we could and did do quite well. On some mornings we would find flying fish on deck, and they made an excellent breakfast. By the time we reached Curacao and turned over the convoy to local forces, we were completely out of food, fuel, and other supplies. Ships had been sunk all around us while en route, but our group was not attacked, and none of the escorts had made any contact with a sub.

After we arrived in Curaco a U.S. Naval Officer boarded the ship. He told me it would be a few days before we received orders to escort some ships from Curacao to Trinidad. He gave me carte blanche to buy the supplies I needed from local merchants and to send the approved bills to him for payment. So our crew had another bonus in the two or three days in Curacao after the night in Havana. Yet the trip there had been another exercise in misery. Our new Third Officer was so seasick we thought he would die. Unlike Owens he could not function when he was seasick. The physical hardship on the crew was almost unbearable. Yet even with their weight losses and other ailments, enlisted men have a way of finding entertainment. I don't know how and where, but they had a good time in Curacao.

Under the circumstances I allowed liberty until one hour before sailing, except for the watch. Anyone who broke the rule would be detailed to lookout duty in the crow's nest. This could make the most hardened Sailor seasick. It was so bad up there in even a mildly rough sea that we only used it when sailing was smooth, which was very rare indeed.

Yeoman Frank Balun was late, as well as somewhat drunk, so as we left the dock he did not need to be told. He climbed the ladder to the Crow's Nest, where his cries coincided with our movements. There was a heavy swell and a moderate sea running as we left the protection of the harbor and took station on the convoy. The voyage to Trinidad thus started with Frank wailing to come down, and after about a half-hour of torture, aggravated by the alcohol, he was adequately chastised. No one could criticize me for cruel and inhuman punishment, for the Crow's Nest was supposed to be manned at all times. For the remainder of my command of the ship, Frank behaved himself, and the thought of being assigned to lookout in the Crow's Nest was quite sufficient to ensure no one else misbehaved.

A friendly but suffering crew sailed *SC 981*. We had no place to relax, hide, cool off, or sleep without constantly adjusting to the violent moves of the ship. Working out of Trinidad the routine was usually ten days out and an overnight in. We would get a variety of jobs from convoy escort to meeting and escorting friendly submarines into port. The whole of the Section Base we worked out of seemed to be organized to get us out to sea as fast as possible.

Although enemy activity in and around Trinidad was tremendous at this time, the escorts, although basically ineffective, did discourage attacks. Convoy routes were well established, but we did not have enough escort vessels to service all the routes adequately.

SCs and PCs assigned to rescue duty with an occasional overage destroyer were more active in rescuing merchant seamen than in sinking submarines. The convoys bound east from Trinidad were designated "Trinidad East." With insufficient escorts available, all but the very critical convoys were left by their escorts 600 to 800 miles east of Trinidad. At this point the ships would proceed individually for their specified destinations. They were easy targets for German submarines, and many were torpedoed. Soon after turning back, the escorts would chase after the scattered convoy in an attempt to pick up the survivors. Even though we heard distress signals from numerous sinking ships, *SC 981* was never assigned rescue duty. It was a bad year for the good guys and an excellent one for the submarines.

One day after a very rough period, I brought my crew into Trinidad in a state of complete exhaustion and reported to the Operating Officer in the Section Base, a Lt. He was an obnoxious, pompous ass and always made

150

me feel he considered the forces afloat a nuisance. When I arrived in his office, he was sitting with his feet on his desk. He asked me if the ship was ready to go to sea the next morning. I told him the ship was, but the crew were not—they were near exhaustion. He gave me the usual shore command propaganda: "Don't you guys know there is a war on?" I shoved his feet backwards, he fell all over himself, and I walked out, figuring if he had sailing orders for us he could deliver them himself. None came and the next day I went into Trinidad by bus. Queen's Park, the center of a hotel and recreation area, was full of temporary quarters for survivors of merchant ship sinkings. The town was alive, but there was nothing there for me or any of the crew. It seemed to be wall-to-wall people, with most trying to sell you something.

As I was moving through the crowd, a monkey jumped on my shoulder and cuddled up. He was cute and looked at me with the saddest eyes—he seemed to want me to rescue him. The owner said, "Nice monkey, you buy for five dollars." I don't know what moved me to do so, but I gave the man the money and took the monkey back to the ship. Jack Millar and the crew were astounded. The monkey, scared by the new environment, stayed close to me.

But he adapted. He had his likes and dislikes among the crew, however, seeming to sense who was fond of him and who was not. He also sensed that Jack Millar and I were the bosses. He had his ways of showing his disdain for those he did not like. When they tried to retaliate, he would jump into my arms and "dare" them to touch him. He adjusted to our strenuous voyages better than we did, and fortunately, bananas were plentiful. We dressed him in sailor suits, and for the time he was a distraction and source of amusement. He basically had the freedom of the ship, and was so agile it was unlikely that he would fall overboard in any sea. But one morning after I was transferred, the monkey was missing. Some believed the Bos'n had trapped him and threw him overboard. They argued like two people, and their dislike for each other was intense; there was real bad blood between them. Nothing could ever be proved, and perhaps the monkey misjudged a jump and fell overboard on this own. In the meanwhile there was a war to fight, although as the New Year approached my war was more with the shore establishment than the enemy at sea. I figured I needed another diversion for all of us, but I could not think of a thing.

On New Year's Eve Jack and I tied one on together at the Section Base Officer's Club, which was in the middle of the local jungle. The next day while we were still asleep, we felt a sudden, noisy crunch, and the ship listed sharply to port. Running up on deck I noticed a PC coming in from the sea and attempting to moor astern of us had hit and then sideswiped us. It took me a minute or two to take it all in. Jack started to yell for the crew to start the pumps, but I stopped him. I realized the force of the crash had opened up the seams and we were taking on water, but we would not take on much more.

A quick but thorough inspection indicated the leakage had stopped and other damage was superficial. I had my ticket to some leave and recreation for the crew. The dry-dock in Trinidad was always backlogged, but I knew there was a small dry-dock in Barbados that might be able to handle us. About 180 miles to the North, Barbados had no military station and was considered a Garden of Eden. I told Jack and our key petty officers to keep the list on the ship, and I went up to the repair office.

As I suspected all either had hangovers or were still happy. A Lt. carrying a heavy load from the night before was ordered to return to the ship with me and assess the damage. He was lazy, bent over, and inclined to do what I wanted. He called Barbados and found the dry-dock to be free. I had Jack scurry around and get some bottles of liquor—I planned to keep this easy-going officer content. They made arrangements for us to depart immediately for Barbados and for the Lt. to accompany us.

I had Jack leave the water in the ship, but told the Lt. our pumps were just able to handle it as we sailed to Barbados. Only a few petty officers knew what was going on. The first thing we did on arrival was to tie up at a dock in the old port. I had Jack arrange for a few rooms in a seaside hotel, one of which was for the Lt., and to see that it was well stocked with his favorite drink. I told the Lt. this was a wooden ship, there was no need for him to bother, and I would take care of everything.

After he left I pumped the water out and placed the ship on an even keel so we could enter the dry-dock. The dock was only about 95-feet and the ship was 110-feet. The turning basin was only about 115-feet, and the small harbor was jammed with little schooners coming and going. Somehow I lined the ship up and the yard people took over from there.

The man in charge was about 70 years old. After talking to him for a few minutes, I could tell he knew more about wooden ships than anybody in the Navy. I needed a cover story in that I was fairly sure the seams had resealed themselves. When the ship was pumped dry, there was in fact no real damage; some of the caulking had fallen out and we had some growth. At the same time I was hoping to get three or four days in Barbados. Since the repair officer was happily ensconced in the hotel, I told the manager to give the bottom the works so that we could put off the next scheduled dry-docking. The costs were about 20 percent of what they would be in the States, and further, this yard knew how to repair wooden ships. That was a lost art in the U.S.

So the yard went to work. The repair officer sobered up to find I had handled everything and at very low prices. We stayed at a lovely hotel on the beach. Local newspapers reported our arrival as, unlike Havana, we were the biggest ship ever dry-docked in Barbados. Everything is relative. The island entertained us as if we were visiting royalty. As the only warship in the port, and a rare visitor at that, it was a delightful break in the war— the last I would experience for a very long time.

When we returned to Trinidad, we had orders to return to Miami accompanied by another SC with sound gear similar to ours. They decided to place us in an area where our mission would not depend so greatly on our hopeless equipment. I also received personal orders. On arrival I was to report to Norfolk as the prospective Executive Officer of *U.S.S. Edward C. Daly (DE-17)* being built at Mare Island, CA. I was to be relieved by Jack Millar, whom I had recommended for command and who had been promoted to Lt(jg).

Although *SC 981* presented a difficult, frustrating, and uncomfortable job, I could not have had more independence and better training for future commands. Because *DE-17* was one of the very first of a new class destroyer escort, I was being placed in a highly selected position. I would assemble and train part of the crew in Norfolk and then accompany them to Mare Island. Little *SC 981* was going to the Pacific, and I left my shipmates sadly. It was now mid-February 1943, and I was 27.

Seven

War: Pacific

U.S.S. Edward C. Daly (DE-17)

Not unlike everyone else who survived the first year of World War II and entered the second, I was being carried along by events rather than exercising any control over my life. During the first half of 1942, I sailed around the South Pacific in command of a U.S. Navy Armed Guard unit aboard a large Merchant Marine passenger liner converted to a troopship. It was a strange experience; the ship and those of us in her were at peril every moment. The U.S. Navy did not control the seas we sailed, and, in fact, was in a state of confusion resulting from the devastating blow at Pearl Harbor. Those who sailed in the ship, from Captain Johnson and me down to the lowest ratings, were aware that at any moment we could take a torpedo, and chances were we would sink with very heavy casualties. Yet no major transport was sunk by enemy action in these vulnerable areas while I was operating there.

The tension remained whether one actually experienced combat or not, so long as one was in a combat area. This weighed heavily on those with responsibility. I was there, ready for action, but for some fortunate reason untouched by it.

Moving into the second half of the year, I could not have been in a more exposed position on a more vulnerable vessel. German submarines were sinking a large percentage of Allied ships in our area of operation, mostly with ease, while we had very few successes against them. In *SC 981* I had been continually in a combat area. Ships were being sunk all around us, but we lost none we escorted, nor did we see or make sonar contact on a submarine. Actually, in maneuvers with our own friendly submarines, the sonar equipment installed in our SC could not make contact even at the shortest of ranges.

My time in *SC 981* was isolation from any and everything. Even when we did observe something or receive interesting news, nearly every day was a struggle as the little ship bounced around the seas. This was in many ways a living death, and ships operating under such conditions rarely execute their missions well. British Corvettes were small, but large enough to just about get by. PCs were somewhat better than SCs, but neither were qualified to operate for long periods in rough seas and adequately do the job assigned. The Navy, well aware of these limitations, had long planned to replace SCs and PCs with DEs.

I was still a Lieutenant Sr. Grade in 1943, but at age 27 that was about all anyone could expect. More importantly I had survived. Death at sea was always at hand, and in most cases struck without warning. I had done my job without losing any men in my ship or those in other ships for which I was responsible. The way of life had changed completely in a short time. Those of us assigned to sea duty rather than to safe shore duty had to expect the worst, and there was little reason to plan for the future. The Navy and the war took precedence over all else. Although the "cause" we were fighting for was a noble one, it rarely was part of our thinking as we struggled to survive. We became closer and closer to our shipmates and to our mutual interest than to all the propaganda constantly being shoveled at us.

For over a year I had been the boss, but under my new orders I would drop back to second in command. In *SC 981* I was responsible for the defense of all on board and those we escorted, now someone else would have the destiny of the ship and me under his control. The DE was a newly designed vessel, oriented to do many jobs, but with the primary mission of escort and ASW warfare. I had never seen one, and although there was talk of this new class, they were untested in combat. *Edward C. Daly* was designed to British specifications, but only about 20 were transferred to the Royal Navy. They originally had a BDE designation; and BDE 1 to 50, contracted for on November 1, 1941, were built with lend-lease funds before our entry into the war.

These ships were 289 feet long with a 35-foot beam and a full-load displacement of 1360 tons. The ships were propelled by four General Motors diesel electric engines generating 6,000 H.P. that resulted in a maximum cruising speed of 20 knots. Armament consisted of three 3-inch 50-caliber guns and two 40mm and five 20mm antiaircraft guns; there were no torpedo tubes on the short-hull DEs. Two radars were in the combat Information Center (CIC): an SL for surface search and an SA for air search. The best sound gear available was also installed.

My orders were to entrain for Norfolk where a training center for those being assigned to DEs was being set up at the Naval Operating Base. I was to take charge of more than half the officers and crew assigned, while the Captain and a few of the officers and key ratings supervised the ship's building at Mare Island. This class of DEs was only built in Navy Yards. My group would report when the ship was ready to receive the entire crew prior to trial runs, final outfitting, and commissioning. I left warm Miami in the winter for cold Norfolk, where I checked into the Bachelors Officers Quarters (BOQ) and something new.

We were one of the first DE crews to arrive, and getting us organized was difficult. As the Executive Officer of the ship and the Officer-in-Charge of *DE-17's* crew, I was treated with much more consideration than I had been in San Diego and the Armed Guard Units. The school would use the many facilities at the Operating Base for training—fire fighting and damage control among other subjects. But we had little information about DEs to work with. We all had to do a great deal of improvising during the few weeks we were there. I spent most of my time on the base, and we were soon ordered to report to the ship.

The crew went as a group, and the officers proceeded independently. Virginia met me in San Francisco, and we rented a small apartment. As a Lieutenant my pay and allowance came to $340 a month, which in those days was livable. Some enlisted men earned less than 10 percent of this, but an able seaman on a merchant ship earned more with war bonuses. They were paid by the area they were in, plus they got $50 a day whenever a weapon was fired at the enemy. A Third Class Petty Officer made $78 per month, which increased to approximately $93 per month with sea pay.

When the ship was ready for the crew, I reported to the ship's office in the Mare Island Navy Yard and to the Commanding Officer, Commander George Parkinson, USNR, a former college professor. Commander Parkinson, a large man with a ruddy complexion, seemed pleased to meet me. I had never heard of Parkinson, but he was only too happy to let me know who he was. He had served in the Navy in World War I and must have been in his late forties in 1943. He had been in the Organized Reserve for many years.

Very few Reserve commanders had been in the Navy before the war, and I would imagine Parkinson was very good at his Navy politics. Nevertheless he derided Annapolis officers, and seemed pleased I had a Merchant Marine and not an Annapolis background. He had previously served in command of a converted yacht. He had not qualified at SCTC, which was supposedly a "must" not only for assignment as C.O. but also in any other capacity other than temporary duty as an Ensign qualifying for selection for SCTC. He also was able to bring along one of the officers from the ex-yacht with him, Lt(jg) William Larkin. Larkin, a graduate of Yale and Yale Law School, had been a practicing attorney in Waterbury, Connecticut.

Parkinson treated me with decency and respect from the time I reported until I relieved him in command. I called him "Parky" and he called me Al. The only problem I had with him was that he did not mix well with the other officers and constantly wanted to play cribbage with me. At the same time I was very busy getting this beautiful new ship and its crew ready for sea.

The next senior officer was Philip Merrill, a University of California NROTC Lt. who was with me in Group 16 and who also had commanded an SC. He was a pleasant and easy-going officer. Next senior, with the same date of rank as mine, was Russell Flynn, a large man close to 40. He was a Graduate Engineer from Lehigh who never practiced and during the Depression copped out in Palma, Majorca, as a bartender. He was one of the most charming men I ever met. Bill Larkin was the Communications Officer, and I could understand why Parky went to so much trouble to bring him along. Although Larkin had not been to SCTC, he was one of the brightest men I ever met with one of the most logical minds I ever encountered. Unfortunately he could hardly see and wore very thick glasses.

Larkin, as blind as he was, could stand a better watch than any of the others. Over 30 and not in the best physical condition, he suffered but did not complain. I soon learned to lean on him as Parky leaned on me. We became very close friends and remained so until he died. Larkin, a short man with thinning blond hair, blinked constantly. But when there was any trouble and I looked around, he was at my side. Needless to say he was an exception to Parky's coldness to the other officers. Larkin basically only tolerated Parky. Among officers and enlisted men, few had the rare quality to rise above their contemporaries. Larkin was one of them.

Lt(jg) Jim Hagler, the Gunnery Officer, was a graduate of the University of Kentucky, where his father was a well-known professor. He was following in his father's footsteps when he joined the Navy. Ensign J.O. Jordan, a graduate of the Massachusetts Nautical School, was the Assistant First Lt. Ensign Russell Bond from New Orleans was the Assistant

Engineer. There were two New Yorkers: Ensign Leonard Stoll, Assistant Communications Officer, and Vincent McCarthy, Assistant Gunnery Officer.

As a whole it was an unusually experienced officer group for the times. SCs were excellent training ships, and the selectivity at SCTC was a plus. The Chief Petty Officers and Petty Officers were relatively experienced also. One very glaring problem, however, stood out. Our engine room ratings had learned their trade in steam turbine destroyers. Some had short courses in diesels at SCTC, but the diesel-electric propulsion-system installed in *DE-17* was basically a puzzle to them. The system of excitating power electrically was something new in the destroyer Navy.

During pre-commissioning the officers assigned to Mare Island decided to be sure they had plenty of spare parts. Spare parts for each ship in various building stages were kept in bins. Nighttime raiding parties, organized by a resourceful Russ Flynn who had an Errol Flynn mustache but was somewhat more plump, ensured we had plenty of spares and supplies at the expense of later deliveries. We too, had suffered at the hands of our predecessors, but I am certain we had our rated spares and supplies and more.

This was the group I had to organize around a new class vessel with no precedent to follow. Our predecessor ships in the class were all schoolships, and we were the first scheduled to join the Fleet in the Pacific combat areas.

Several days after my arrival, the remainder of the ship's officers and crew arrived from Norfolk and reported on board even though the ship was not yet commissioned. During this period the vessel was in the final stages of completion and outfitting, with yard personnel, ship's company, and outside contractors all working together. It was chaos, and the ship was urgently needed.

Parky was around with words of wisdom and generalities but took no active part in this very important stage of readying the ship for sea. He seemed pleased to leave this work all to me, and in view of his age and physical fitness, it would have been an exercise in frustration for him to crawl through the numerous restrictive areas of the vessel that had to be checked.

Not one of the officers or the crew had any previous experience with anything like this ship. While it was still at the dock, the officers and crew had to make many tests for their own information and satisfaction. While the technicians were still around, we had to get as much information as possible about our specialized equipment. It was also our last chance to have the shipyard make minor alterations we considered essential for proper operations.

Since Parky mainly was only an observer, I had to organize this vessel from top to bottom. The theoretical Watch, Quarter, and Station Bill had to be altered to fit situations we actually found on board. Tons of spare gear had to be indexed and stowed properly. I divided the work among the department heads and constantly checked them. We had to ensure our magazines were ready to receive ammunition and the sprinkler systems were operative. Navigational equipment, charts, and sailing directions had to be checked and corrected. We had to make sure quarters and facilities for the crew were adequate, and they were berthed in the closest area to their battle stations.

This was like outfitting *SC 981* but on a more vast scale. At the start of the work, I never thought we could finish in the time allocated, but we worked long, hard hours and did. Gradually fewer yard people and contractors were on board, and the crew began to take over the ship, settling into a routine.

Finally in the middle of March 1943, on the morning of a fine sunny day, the ship was turned over from the shipyard to Commander George Parkinson, who made a short speech, had the commission pennant tow-blocked, and the band played. Silence descended over the ship after the crescendo of noise. The watches were set, and the officers and crew quietly went to work. Only a skeleton crew was kept aboard as a luncheon commissioning party followed.

As I returned to the ship after the party and observed her at the dock, I was impressed by her sleek lines and beauty. The hull was painted in a two-tone gray. The description, later applied to Destroyer Escorts, "Trim but Deadly," was evident as one viewed the first of the class that was scheduled to proceed west of Hawaii into "Harm's Way." I could see in this ship the solutions to most of the frustrations I had experienced to date. This class of ship was going to make a difference in the war at sea. Some 565 DEs and APDs were contracted for before the war ended; about 500 were delivered and perhaps 400 or so actually made it to the war zones. To be the very first non-schoolship in the Pacific was a distinction. For the first time I was confident I had a mission to perform and an excellent ship to perform it with.

Pride in this ship permeated the crew. Parky, great on publicity, took the many bows and compliments that came our way. Still there was a great deal to accomplish. We had to complete the builder's trials, swing ship for compass compensation, get degaussed as a defense against magnetic mines, and of course take aboard ammunition, plus a multitude of other things. This took about 10 days. After completion we departed for San Diego for an accelerated shakedown.

The next ship in line, *U.S.S. Gilmore (DE-18),* was running about one month behind us. Its C.O., one of those in Group 16 with whom I became friendly, was Lcdr. Seldon Small, a top graduate of the Class of '32 at Annapolis. His Exec, Goodwin Cook from the same class, was one of the few Brahmins from Harvard who stuck very close to his contemporaries at the school. Cook was a Wall Street lawyer, and over the many years we knew each other, he still winced when I called him Goody. He was so steeled in the conformity of the elite that adjusting to the realities of the "lower classes" was difficult for him. In general the war was a great leveler in a ship—one was unable to retreat to the sanctuary of a private club.

Before we departed I said my good-byes to Cdr. Small and to Goody Cook. We all looked forward to joining together again when our CourtDiv formed up. The C.O. and the Exec of the next ship in line, *DE-19,* were also from Group 16. Lcdr. Philip Walker, the C.O., was USNA Class of '32; the Exec, Ernest Fay, some years older than I, was a Harvard grad from Texas. He was a famous yachtsman. Group 16 obviously had been carefully selected—we were all moving on the fast track—and although we came from varied backgrounds, we tended to become close friends. Commander of the CortDiv had already been assigned. His was Cdr. L.F. Sugnet, Annapolis Class of '25. For the entire time I was in *DE-17,* the ship was on independent duty. I never met my Division Commander.

We sailed from San Francisco to San Diego without incident, although we had some problems with the diesel engines due to the inexperience of our people. Mostly, however, it was cribbage for me with Parky. We had an older, experienced Chief Machinist Mate with heavy engineering experience in destroyers. He worked long hours with Russ Flynn trying to figure out the system. So long as they were able to keep two of the four engines on line, we could proceed at 15.5 knots, which was both our cruising and our submarine search and attack speed.

Although Parkinson, who had a Doctorate in Mathematics and Astronomy, expanded on his knowledge of navigation, he never really bothered with it. He would be annoyed when an engine failed or other problems arose, but he would not get involved in the details. The engine problems were frustrating. Russ would simply say, "Al, I don't know a damn thing about these engines," but he kept working hard.

Chief Davidson and his motor machs worked around the clock. When they solved one problem another would appear. I had found out many years before that it was no use in screaming at people as long as their best was not equal to the task. We were getting everything Flynn and his staff of "snipes" had to give. Somehow they did get all the engines on line for the shakedown. I'm certain if I had insulted them, rather than encouraged and sympathized with them, the situation would have been aggravated rather than solved. In the meanwhile I had to keep Parky from blowing up. He looked at the officers as a teacher would look at students. But they were mature men at sea in responsible jobs during wartime.

Parky, however, took very little interest in enlisted men. He was certain he was going to make flag rank. I soon realized if I could keep the ship out of trouble, amuse him with cribbage and talk, he in turn would not interfere with much—although at times he would take a dislike to a specific officer. It took all of my experience to stop him from overreacting.

Parky was concerned about the Officers' Mess. He wanted to eat well, but when the cost went over what he thought it should, the Mess Treasurer became an ogre to him. At dinner I sat on Parky's right while he sat at the head of the table. Our Mess Treasurer, Ensign McCarthy, a good officer, sat at the opposite end of the table. McCarthy was an attractive young man, but he had a chubby Irish face, and in order to sustain himself he had to eat. In order to eat he had to move the food from his plate into his mouth. Each time he did this Parky imagined Mac was eating his money. Larkin, who knew Parky well from the yacht and was very observant, watched this hatred building up, as did I. Unfortunately McCarthy innocently kept increasing the Captain's animosity. Fortunately Parky kept his distance from all but Larkin and me, and, although he made snide remarks about McCarthy, I could protect Mac from any overt act on the part of Parky, who was not about to rock the boat and lose his crack at the stars.

Shakedown at San Diego like most else in connection with a new-class ship not organized in time proceeded very well under the circumstances. Inspectors and markers knew little if anything about the ship, and we basically marked ourselves. There was tremendous interest in the ship. High-ranking brass constantly visited, and Parky lived it up. One of the most interesting things to me was that our sound gear worked vary well. Under any but unusual conditions, if a submarine were in our range, we could pick it up and hang on. Although our gunnery left a great deal to be desired and would require much work, Parky knew little about gunnery, nor did the inspectors or our people. It was something I would have to cope with when I had the time.

As Exec I was also the navigator. On our last exercise with about five miscellaneous ships including a submarine, we headed south for ASW exercises. Lcdr. Robert Montgomery, the actor, joined our ship as an observer for the exercise. Parky stayed glued to him the entire time while, as usual, I ran the ship. When the exercise was completed we sailed north to the sea buoy to enter San Diego Harbor. We were the outboard ship on the seaward side as we proceeded in a column-abreast. The OTC (Officer in Tactical Command) was in a four-pipe destroyer that was also the guide ship. Visibility became worse. We could see most of the ships in the group, but at best visibility was two miles. As we went along we should have picked up the sea buoy on our radar; for some reason it did not appear. Meanwhile the OTC ordered a course change to the right, an indication he planned to enter the channel at that point. The action, if my position was correct, would ground them. I kept to my course even though we were signalled to keep station.

For the first time that day Parky turned away from Robert Montgomery and asked me to follow the orders of the OTC. I said he should advise the OTC he was proceeding into danger. Parky became excited and unintelligible. I finally was able to explain to him that if I was wrong we would run into the kelp bed and that I could come right with no problem; if I was right, all those ships would be in time for cocktails at the Coronado Beach Hotel.

Robert Montgomery seemed amused by all his. As the whole staff on the bridge sort of came to life and Parky stood mute not knowing what to do, the lookout reported the sea buoy right ahead and the radio operator picked it up at the same time. Simultaneously all hell broke loose on the TBS (short range radio telephone), as one after the other the ships hit the beach. Because the beach was sandy damage was not serious, but none would be going anywhere for some time. By the time we docked Parky had congratulated me, regained his composure, and went ashore for the accolades.

I never was able to get the details about the other ships, but the five of them plus the submarine grounded. The navigator of the OTC, I heard, was Joe Hunt, the only Annapolis graduate to win the National Tennis Championships at Forest Hills. As a fellow tennis player I felt sorry for him, and particularly that Parky had failed to send the "proceeding into danger" signal when I had advised it. It would have been close, but they might have averted the grounding because the water was deep right up to the beach.

I really can't blame Parky for not sending off the message. He had not had sufficient time to have enough confidence in my navigation to caution a superior officer. If I had been wrong his future plans could have been harmed. As it turned out I believe Parky got a commendation; at any rate he returned from his trip to headquarters beaming. He also told me we had orders to proceed independently to Pearl Harbor.

When we arrived at Pearl a reception committee waiting for us included Admiral Nimitz and many of his staff. Their interest in this new class of ship was unusual, and what surprised me and confused Parky was the Admiral completely ignored him and glued himself to me as if I were a long-lost relative. He seemed to know everything about me, and at this time I did not have the vaguest idea about how or why. He asked me questions not only about the ship but about me personally. Just prior to disembarking he finally spoke to Cdr. Parkinson and said something like, "Captain, I want to congratulate you on your fine ship and the condition it reported in for duty. I have a special assignment for which I will shortly require this ship, and I have requested the Bureau of Personnel to assign command to Lt. Chester to become effective tomorrow. You will return as a passenger, and I expect you will soon receive command of a Division."

I was stunned. And so were Parkinson and everyone else. I was very junior and at that time was the youngest commanding officer of a DE. Shortly thereafter a man who was to become my best friend received command at an even younger age: Lt. Sheldon Kinney. Curiously he later enhanced Parky's career. I helped Parky make Captain, and Sheldon's performance in the Hunter-Killer Division (commanded by Parkinson) made Parky a Rear Admiral.

All that changed on our way back to the States escorting a convoy was that Parky and I exchanged cabins. Phil Merrill moved up to Exec, but did not get the room until after Parky disembarked. Admiral Nimitz also placed Ensign Bill Lynch from his staff on board, and assigned him to the ship with the concurrence of BuPers, which issued his orders when they did mine. Lynch was from Texas and close to the Admiral. Parky took little interest in navigation or other daily operations on the westbound crossing. On the eastbound voyage the cribbage continued, but he was relieved he did not have to watch McCarthy stuff himself. My luck seemed to continue, and we arrived in San Francisco without incident. The change of command ceremony had taken place previously in Pearl. I was again a commanding officer, a position I held until I returned to shore duty in 1945.

While the ship was tied up at the dock in San Francisco on the Embarcadero, I was ashore in dungarees working on the ball-race of one of our guns with some of the gunner's mates. I was not satisfied with the condition of that particular gun. Actually I was only observing and commenting, when a tall, handsome, familiar looking Lcdr. came walking down the dock. It was Gentleman Jim Knowlton, my old shipmate from *Washington*. He gazed at the beautiful ship at the dock and back again, and said, "Chester, what the devil are you doing? Are you on that ship?" I wiped my hand on a rag and answered, "Yes," while shaking his hand.

He seemed puzzled; this was a combat ship, and he did not know of any ex-Merchant Marine deck-officers so assigned. He could not tell my rank, but asked if I was the First Lieutenant. I said no. He then asked, "Are you the Gunnery Officer?" And I said, "No." He said, "You can't be the Executive Officer?" And I said, "I am not." Obviously amazed he said, "Are you the C.O.?" And I smiled and said "Yes." He could hardly believe it. I asked him what he was doing, and he said he was the First Lieutenant in *Ormsby,* a new APA, but expected to get command of an AK shortly. I then surprised him by saying we were escorting *Ormsby* to Pearl, and I had invited the Captain to lunch on board. I invited him to join us too.

It was a pleasant and informative lunch. Commander Leonard Frisco, USNR, an ex-Merchant Marine Captain from the Black Diamond Line, was Captain of *Ormsby*. He was gruff but delightful and interesting. An enlisted man in the Navy during the First World War, he now commanded an Attack Transport. It was a time for relating our individual adventures since entering the Navy, and bringing one another up to date on the activities of our mutual friends from the Merchant Marine.

One thing I discovered was that specific schools controlled the various Detail Officer Desks in the Bureau of Naval Personnel. This subject came up as my companions did not understand how I had gotten command of a DE. Frisco, although not a Merchant Marine Academy graduate, was popular and accepted by all elements. He was also well-versed in Naval politics. I knew the DE/PC/SC Detail Officer was an Ivy Leaguer named Houghton, and this group controlled that desk. For the first time I was told the Auxiliary Desk was controlled by the New York State Merchant Marine Academy; the present incumbent was an alumnus and an ex-U.S. Line Captain, "Blackie" Thompson. The Naval Academy controlled the BB/CA/Cl/DD and the Submarine Desk as well as that of the aircraft carriers.

This was illustrative of how the business and industry world operated in peacetime preceding World War II. Colleges had a strong control of the jobs at the top of many industries—the "good old boy" circuit. The little

New York State Merchant Marine Academy had assumed a status in the Wartime Navy it had not held in peacetime industry.

Both Cdr. Frisco and I were aware of the long deployment in the Pacific scheduled for our ships. Being denied the routine of a shakedown period for a new ship created a tremendous problem for Frisco. Although Knowlton was the third senior officer in *Ormsby,* and despite the fact the Exec and others were experienced Merchant Mariners, Frisco believed the only senior officer who combined the talents required for both the Navy and the Merchant Marine he could depend on was Knowlton.

From the start in *DE-17,* I had had relatively experienced officers. But Frisco had a complicated ship. Although Frisco, Knowlton, and I had assimilated into the Navy well, and as I had no problems with my officers in this situation, Frisco did. After a long discussion with me, he decided to free Knowlton for a command he had earned. From the way he described his remaining senior officers from the Merchant Marine, some had "chips on their shoulders" and tried to excuse their own shortcoming by criticizing the Navy. Other classes of Reserve Officers used this same ploy to cover their own inadequacies. Granted all Naval Academy graduates were not outstanding, but as a group they were far above the others. To demean them unfairly was a deterrent to the war. Once in the Navy I steeled myself to "think Navy" and demanded it of my officers and men.

The voyage west to Pearl, escorting *Ormsby,* was unique. It was a two-ship task group with Commander Frisco as the Task Group Commander. My friend Knowlton had received orders to his own command before sailing. Lt. William "Bucky" Harris, a lawyer from North Carolina, relieved Merrill, who moved up to Executive Officer. Harris was one very sharp guy who fitted right in. Now I had two lawyers: one a Connecticut Yankee and one a North Carolina Rebel, a pretty good balance.

Frisco had a tough job on his hands; no shakedown and no chance to exercise his gun crews or other defenses. It was a daily routine for him to call me on the TBS and ask me to put up a burst of AA in a specific position relative to his ship. Within a few seconds of his request, the orders were passed to the OOD and the blast went off. Then nothing from *Ormsby* — except Frisco would usually forget to take his hand off the button on the TBS, and we could hear him cursing at his officers. I could sympathize with him, because the organization of a fighting ship did not come easily. I was still far from satisfied with our own gunnery performance.

With a deep draft ship like *Ormsby,* we could also exercise our ASW team by making sound runs on her. Our equipment worked well and our people performed well. This was another trip to Hawaii without incident. Altogether we probably made three or four trips west to Hawaii and two or three trips east in this sequence. We all wished this would go on forever, but we knew better.

On the last trip from San Francisco to Hawaii and further west, I was the Escort Commander of the convoy. It was a fairly large group, and a convoy meeting was held at Navy District Headquarters before we sailed. I was still only a lieutenant and still looked like a kid. The meetings were broken into three parts: one for Commanding Officers of Navy ships, Masters of Merchant Ships, and the Convoy and Escort Commanders; a second for Communications Officers; and a third for Gunnery Officers. When I tried to enter the room for the Senior Officers, the Marine at the door just could not believe I was a C.O., let alone the man in charge, the Escort Commander. He tried to get me to go to the other room.

Somehow I convinced him, but some of the merchant Masters, and particularly the Convoy Commodore, a Regular Navy Captain, were amazed that a kid was the boss man. The Escort Commander had to be on a ship with a full communications staff, and I was it. The Navy Captain was riding the regular Convoy Commodore ship, an old tub named *Santa Cruz Cement*. He tried to take over the conference, but I would not let him. I was polite but firm. He was indignant and lost his composure. The other junior Navy C.O.s and the Merchant Masters were just confused by it all. It must have been the Captain's first convoy duty, and he was uninformed of convoy protocol.

My ship was the only one capable of covering the many radio frequencies concerning intelligence reports that would affect the convoy's movements. I ordered changes of courses accordingly. I also directed the escorts station keeping. The Convoy Commodore was only responsible to ensure the convoy carried out the instructions the Escort Commander gave. Although they were politely given using the words, "Kindly...," or "inviting" rather than "calling" his attention to things, I could do no less and still carry out my job. At the same time I was not going to let him infringe on my authority any more than I would let General MacArthur do so. I guess that's either a weakness or a strength of character of mine, depending on how one interprets such actions.

I went about my business, which at this stage of the game was becoming old hat, but the invective this captain used in complying with instructions and attempting to take command bordered on insanity. He threatened me with insubordination, court martial, and practically everything else.

166

Meanwhile the convoy was approaching Diamond Head on time and without any other incident other than his making a complete fool of himself. In sight of land he took off on one of his tirades, and while screaming into the TBS had a heart attack. We had no doctor on board and there was none in the convoy, so all we could do was speed up and get *Santa Cruz Cement* into Honolulu as fast as possible.

Santa Cruz Cement docked within three hours, but I never did hear whether he survived or not. In Pearl we were ordered to fuel, take stores aboard, take on ammunition, and proceed west to Funafuti escorting my old friend Leonard Frisco in *Ormsby*. This time he had a Marine Combat Team on board, probably for the operation the Admiral was planning when I saw him in Pearl. Funafuti was in the Ellice Islands and the northern most bastion and the closest we had to Tarawa. The area was well within the Japanese preserve. We proceeded in company with *Ormsby* to Funafuti.

Escort Duty–Central Pacific

Ormsby, having been in commission for some time now, was perfectly capable of defending herself. She was heavily armed and had a cruising speed of about 18 knots. Even slower ships en route to Samoa from the U.S. and Hawaii were rarely being escorted in this area. We did not have the escort ships, and the Japanese for reasons of their own did not place much emphasis on this area at the time.

Both ships anchored in the atoll off Funafuti. Cdr. Frisco often came to have lunch with me. He was not happy or at ease with his officers, none seemed to have gained his confidence as did Jim Knowlton. Although I was much younger he felt more at ease and relaxed aboard *Daly*.

The importance of this operation became apparent to me from the nature of our deployments in the Central Pacific. The Marines transported in *Ormsby* were a major manpower increase in the area. Supplies and ammunition preceded and followed their arrival in Funafuti. Once *Ormsby* left the area the only other major naval vessel operating with us was *U.S.S. Manley (APD-1),* a converted World War I, four-stack destroyer, commanded by Lt. Newall, USNR.

At times, in company with each other and alone, we would deploy to escort merchant ships and miscellaneous craft into Funafuti and sometimes for some miles on their way out. We were in effect preparing for the occupation of Nuku Featu and Nanomea. The islands were north of Funafuti in the Ellice Island group and south of Tarawa, which soon became obvious as the ultimate objective. These two atolls were believed to have small Japanese detachments. This was a Marine operation under the Commanding General in Samoa, who in turn reported to CINCPAC, Admiral Nimitz. It was a low profile situation that would not attract the Japanese Command's attention to an imminent invasion of Tarawa from the north, while still giving them something to watch in the south.

On my first voyage to Funafuti I almost missed the island. It had little elevation, which with sea return on the SL Radar made it hard to pick up. In addition either the position on the chart was wrong or we had encountered an unexplainable heavy current. Although it was a U.S. Navy Hudrographic Office Chart, I noticed in the small print that it was based on a rough sketch a whaling captain made many years before.

On the first trip into the island's lagoon, we followed our motor whaleboat, which was taking soundings; at the same time the Marine C.O. sent an officer out who had reconnoitered the channel. It was very difficult for even my small ship to navigate, and basically dangerous for large ships like *Ormsby* and Merchant Marine Liberty Ships that had to make the passage.

We were the first combat ship of any consequence to arrive in the atoll; the Marines had previously been transported by landing craft. On arrival I called on the Commanding Officer, LtCol. Murray. He was a regular officer, very squared away, but pleasant and easy to work with. He informed me the atoll was bombed several times a week. The bombers usually came in on moonlit nights at altitudes over 10,000 feet, and they concentrated on his air strip. He said the Japanese did damage and the Marines took casualties. The Marines had not been able to shoot down any planes to date. Their 90mm anti-aircraft guns could reach that altitude, but at the height they were ineffective.

I had the best AA defense of any of the Navy vessels in port or expected, and yet our 3-inch-50-caliber guns could not even reach the planes if they maintained that altitude. We were all practically sitting ducks for the bombers. We set up radio communications, and the general strategy was to darken the ships in the lagoon once we picked the bombers up on radar. The air strip would also be blacked out. The Marines would fire their 90s from positions away from the airstrip, and we would not fire unless the attacking planes adopted new tactics and came in at lower altitudes and within range of our guns.

I also had to be sure the other naval vessels—particularly the merchant ships—in the lagoon followed the same disciplines. I worked with Lt Col.

168

Murray for some weeks and found him to be a professional of considerable wisdom. I brought up the subject of my suspicions about the position of the island, and requested his permission to make a preliminary survey of it. He was not surprised. Landing craft en route had been getting lost, arriving late, or sometimes not at all. We both believed our suspicions would be confirmed. The next day I organized the survey teams.

There were three islands in the group. The Marines and their air strip were on one. The native men and women were on another. The third was mostly deserted. Only the main island could be approached by ship. The only way to get to the others was in a shallow-draft craft drawing less than two feet, and then only at specific periods of the tide, which did not vary much. I had our survey teams take sexton altitudes at each of the outer tangents of the island. At these points we established the latitude and longitude. I don't recall exactly how far off they were, but it was over ten miles.

I then requested a survey ship be sent if the island was to be used to any great extent. Almost immediately after the survey was completed, I left the island to look for a Navy LST that was several days overdue from Samoa. With the now known correct position and the previous false position, I was able to scientifically work out a search pattern.

I found the LST within several hours, led it back to the island, and placed one of our officers aboard to pilot it in. As the SOPA (Senior Officer Present Afloat), I requested the C.O. report aboard. He did not realize the charts were wrong and was ready for a reprimand. That was the last thing on my mind. We were expecting a Coast Guard LST. With *Manley* and the two LSTs, we planned to invade Nuku Fetau and later Nanomea. A senior officer Cdr. Melgaard, USN, was to lead the invasion.

Freeman, C.O. of the LST, came aboard. He was older than I, although junior in rank. Immediately he apologized, saying he knew little about navigation, had no experience other than as a Sea Scout Master, and they made him a C.O. He had been in the jewelry business in New York and lived in Great Neck. I put him at ease, invited him for lunch, and discussed the problems he might expect in beaching at Nuku, Fetau, and Nanomea. I had reconnoitered the beaches, which in effect were reefs, and it would not be easy. He was relieved to learn the charts were wrong and not to blame for getting lost.

In the Funafuti area I was basically on independent duty. After discussions with Col. Murray, I would scout an area and make sound and radar searches for enemy craft that might be reconnoitering us, reporting the occasional scout plane sighted. Much of the time we were in the lagoon while ships were discharging and later loading. Often movies were shown on *Daly's* after deck. I would send our boat around to the merchant ships each night to bring back people who wanted to see the films.

We were able to pick up Japanese bombers at least 60 miles distant, and if we did not, the Marines did. Whoever picked them up alerted the other. On nights when bombers came over, we stopped the movies, darkened the ship, and went to General Quarters. All watertight doors were closed, radio contact established with the Marines on the beach, and then we waited.

It was eerie for the Japanese strategy never varied. They came in at the same altitude, from the same bearing, and invariably concentrated on the airstrip, before leaving on the same course. Shore batteries began firing when the Japanese were within range and did not cease until they were out of range. The bombs exploded on or near the airstrip, and at times in the lagoon. None came close enough to cause us concern. The situation became so routine that after each bombing, which only lasted about 30 minutes from the time the aircraft were detected until they were beyond radar range, we would return to the movie, but only after I had determined Col. Murray did not need our services. We would aweigh anchor prior to the arrival of the bombers and re-anchor after they left.

It was not so routine for the Marines. I would pay my respects and condolences to Col. Murray the following morning, for unfortunately there were often casualties. The evening's fireworks were not pleasant. It was frustrating not to be able to fire back; but if the ships in the lagoon had done so in a vain attempt to hit them, the bombers would get a clearer bearing on the airfield. Restraint is an important part of discipline in combat.

Japanese planes never came over in daylight, nor did our fighters take off to engage them. It could be that we had no fighter planes at the time, or the command did not want to call attention to what was going on in the area. If the Japanese had ever concentrated on the lagoon, they could have caused many problems. Ships did not have enough maneuvering room, and the channel was unnavigable at night.

Life aboard ship was pleasant. The officers and crew seemed to get along well. But boredom developed even though the threat of death was always imminent. I did not find out until months later that Flynn and his snipes had stolen the motor bike of Captain McCandless, the tiger who commanded the Destroyer Base in San Diego. We had no room to hide anything on our small ship, so they dismantled it, and only reassembled it many weeks or even months later. I also heard they had a dismantled jeep on board.

One day a member of the crew reported to the Chief Pharmacist Mate with a "dose" (gonorrhea). We had not been anywhere near a woman for weeks, much past the incubation period. To swim to the island the women were on was a risky business in those shark-infested waters, and crawling over the reef even more so. I could not figure out where anyone found the time; we were constantly deploying and scouting the area. Finally I discovered the crew had made a replica of a native outrigger, and several forays had been made to the atoll on which the women were being protected from the Sailors and the Marines. One night, as I was preparing to turn in, I noticed that no sheets were on my bunk. I called my mess attendant and asked him for my sheets. He became flustered and said only a few sheets were left, and they were in the laundry. I asked him what happened to the others. He said Mr. Flynn had traded them for "lava, lava."

Russell Flynn was worse than Errol Flynn, and the situation was out of hand. Obviously Russ was leading trading parties to the woman's atoll in the ship's outrigger. It was easy to understand, but it had to stop and it did. I could not make an issue of it because that would cause a cloud to hang over the ship, even though Flynn said they had company from the Marines on the same atoll. I did, in fact, exercise tolerance. After all we were in hostile waters, and contact with the enemy and death could happen at any time.

During this time I contracted an infection in one of my legs. A red line starting at my ankle or below, following a vein, started to slowly move up my leg. We had no doctor, nor did any of the other ships or Marine unit. The Chief Pharmacist Mate did not know what it was or what to do. During our deployments the infection got so bad I was carried to the bridge and a contraption was built to keep my foot up. It hurt like hell.

When we arrived back in Funafuti from a deployment, I saw the survey ship *U.S.S. Sumner,* which had a doctor on board and a well-equipped sick bay. The doctor told me I had blood poisoning. Had I not received an antibiotic within a very few days, I would have died. Not every ship carried antibiotics in those days, and we had none on board *Daly.* Fortunately I recovered quickly.

Finally we were ready to go to Nuku Fetau. The Coast Guard LST, commanded by a Mustang Lt., had arrived along with the officer in charge of the invasion, Cdr. Melgaard. His flag was raised in the troop carrier *Manley.* (The Secretary of State during the Reagan Administration, George Schultz, was a 2nd Lt. of Marines in this invasion team.) I was concerned about my Sea Scout Master in command of the Navy LST, but did not worry about the old pro from the Coast Guard. I was not about to insult him by questioning his seamanship. Our D-Day came, the Marines embarked on the two LSTs, and away we went. I don't recall if we had air cover, but *Manley* and we were ready to cover the landing parties if they should meet resistance.

No problems were encountered during the Nuko Fetau landings. Both LSTs beached, discharged, and retracted okay. Some days later on the second landing at Nanomea, the Coast Guard LST beached, discharged, but also broached. She was a total loss. The Sea Scout Master in the Navy LST had no trouble. There was little resistance and no casualties. The small Japanese force was not believed to be a combat unit. The Marines never asked for fire cover from us. After the islands were secured and the Coast Guard LST declared unsalvageable, we returned to Funafuti, which like Nuku Fetau had now been given an imaginative nickname. By securing the two islands another peg was in place for the invasion of Tarawa. We remained in the area for a short while and then escorted some of the craft used in the small-time invasion back to Samoa.

On arrival in Samoa, and for the first time in months, I was able to tell our crew we would break sea watches and go on port-routine. Our next assignment—escorting a dredge from Canton Island to Funafuti—would not require us to depart from Samoa for two or possibly three days. Samoa, compared to Funafuti, was heaven.

In 1943 CINCPAC began its master plan to move west into the Japanese-controlled area of the Pacific. Logistics were not simple and required careful planning regarding island bases having access from the sea plus an air strip. Fighter planes had limited range, and we were still woefully short of ships and aircraft in spite of building them at a fast rate. CINCPAC had to be ready for the aircraft when they arrived by having as many bases as possible ready to serve and protect them.

The Central Pacific area in which *Daly* operated during 1943 bordered on many Japanese strongholds. Essentially *Daly* was an ASW ship and the only anti-sub DE in the area, but submarine activity in the area was light. I never saw a destroyer or large combat ship of ours during this entire time. Friendly air activity was negligible, and together with *Manley* we were all that was afloat. Although *Manley* had once been a destroyer, she was obsolete. As an APD with the main mission of transporting troops and supplies, her ASW and anti-aircraft capabilities were limited. She had an old 4-inch-50-caliber gun of the type I had in *Kanawha* and *Matsonia,* but it could not elevate for AA defense. We were somewhat better off.

Our ASW ability was first rate. We could handle submarines, but we could not defend against high-altitude bombing. For the time we were well equipped against low flying planes. Our SL and SA radar were the best available for our class ship. If the Japanese had deployed destroyers in the area, however, we would have had a severe disadvantage. Unlike the long hull DEs, we did not have torpedoes, nor did we have the 5-inch-38-caliber dual-purpose guns later installed on DEs and DE/APD-type vessels. Further we did not even have the speed to retire from the action.

The Japanese, however, never acted to neutralize this activity. Their scout planes constantly flew over although never within AA range. They had to know we were there, and its possible they identified us as a destroyer. We were the only ship of our type in the Pacific west of Hawaii. But even one or two small destroyers with a few nondescript landing craft hardly indicated anything big. This had to be what Admiral Nimitz saw when he selected this ship for the assignment. Even *Ormsby,* a much larger but auxiliary type vessel, was in and quickly out.

Meanwhile we moved north to Tarawa while our main forces, to the north and west of Tarawa, were held back in readiness. The CINCPAC staff was good. It worked perfectly, and it was obvious the Japanese command did not take the Ellice Island operation seriously. They responded with intermittent, essentially ineffective, high-altitude bombing and scout planes that never got close enough to discover much of anything. When the Tarawa invasion did occur, nevertheless, it was a desperate and bloody battle even though we controlled the air and the sea. Had we not the result could have been a disaster.

From my point of view it was excellent duty. I was left mainly to my own devices, something very rare for a commanding officer in wartime. CINCPAC as well as the Commanding General in Samoa left me alone. At times I would receive confusing dispatches, which Larkin and I usually tried to figure out. Most often I arrived at a decision of doing what I thought best, but I best not to be wrong or the interpretation would be held over my head. Col. Murray never interfered, and the senior officer assigned to overall surveillance of the operation, Cdr. John Melgaard, only suggested things and did not interfere with the operation of the ship. His orders from CINCPAC gave him discretion, although he spent a good deal of the time aboard and shared his experience and knowledge with me when required. He was an excellent shipmate. As my superior officer he could have had my quarters, but he was an understanding man and realized the nature of my duties were more compelling than his. He was content in an officer's wardroom cabin. Cdr. Melgaard shifted to *Manley* for the actual invasion

173

since the Marine officers were billeted aboard her. Everything went well except for the broaching and loss of the Coast Guard LST. I believe Cdr. Malgaard performed in a commendable manner. There were no flaps. After the Marines landed he returned to *Daly* for the voyage to Samoa.

Nonetheless my job was exhausting. The weather was not always calm. Even though we did not suffer as much as we had in the SC, many days were uncomfortable. Navigating the channel in Funafuti was a nightmare, particularly when the sun was in my eyes. It was hot and we had no air conditioning. Problems were constant, if not with the engines, then with the guns, or something else. Our intelligence information was practically nil; and although quite satisfied with being left to my own devices, some decisions were tough to make. Bill Larkin, as Communications Officer, conveyed the important messages; we often discussed them in detail, and his counsel was invaluable.

The officers and crew of *Daly* were more experienced than those who followed in other DEs. With the exception of Parkinson and Larkin, they were the chosen few. Merrill had been in Group 16 with me. When he was promoted to Exec, another outstanding officer, Bucky Harris, was assigned to be the First Lieutenant in his place. Harris, who later commanded two DEs, was one of the best. Hagler, McCarthy, Stoll, and Jordan all had previous sea experience. Admiral Nimitz's contribution, Lynch, was a good officer but like Larkin had a problem. Larkin could not see well and Lynch heard poorly. We used to kid Lynch, who invariably never heard the General Quarters sound off when he was asleep, of the big battle he had missed. He was the Ass't Communications officer, and we could rouse him if we desired and Stoll would, but Lynch was never sure about what he had missed.

With this group of officers and a crew hungry for shore leave, I entered the harbor of Pago Pago. We had been in virtual prison for many weeks. We tied up starboard side to a merchant ship that was alongside the dock with its bow pointed seaward. We came in fast, turned around, and came alongside the Liberty ship in no time at all. When I was told we would be there at least two days, I ordered the Exec to grant the crew maximum liberty consistent with the regulations of the port.

Berthed next to the Liberty ship, *Daly* could not be seen from the shore. Although almost as long as a football field, we were dwarfed by the freighter whose deck we had to cross to disembark. The Merchant Marine crew looked at us as some strange animals from outer space, and the ship as a rarity that emitted strange sounds and noises peculiar to warships. They must have been further confused by the large crew that poured out of this small ship.

A Marine Officer came aboard and, among other things, offered our officers the hospitality of their Officer's Club. The Officer said after I had time to relax the Commanding General would be delighted to receive me and thank me for the good work the ship had done. Meanwhile he suggested I enjoy the spirits the O-Club had to offer.

Stoll and Lynch asked me for permission to go into the hills and try to buy some native art. They had already received permission from the Exec, so I said okay if it was all right with the Marines.

Pago Pago, the Capital of American Samoa and an imposing sight from the sea, was not much as a liberty port. Portrayed in my youth in a Broadway play and later a Hollywood movie named "Rain," which well described this island as well as many other South Sea Islands. The sun does not always shine; and in the case of Pago Pago when it rains, which it does frequently, it comes down in torrents. Unlike the Ellice Islands Samoa is hilly if not mountainous. Instead of white sands and coconut trees, the scene is of green foliage.

Most of the natives from Funafuti had been transferred to other atolls. Some were still on the main island, living much as they always had. Their thatched huts, called falis, looked pretty but didn't smell very well. Sanitation was primitive. Dogs, chickens, pigs, and other livestock ran everywhere. Here and there a handsome man and a lovely woman were seen; however, this was the exception rather than the rule.

Pago Pago, and Samoa in general, was still plagued in the '40s by a disease known as Elephantiasis. It deformed enough of the native population, the Marines, and visitors to be a matter of serious concern. The natives seemed to take everything in stride and made jokes about their problems. The disease caused enormous swelling of tissue, especially in the lower body, and hardening and fissuring of the skin, making it appear like elephant hide. Natives approached us to sell postcards, the most popular of which showed a Samoan man pushing a wheel barrel filled with his sexual organs. They laughed as they shoved this in front of us. I understand the only cure for the disease in those days was to leave the island.

It was raining on the day we arrived. The O-Club was very close to the dock, and we all went there shortly after lunch. The crew were restricted to certain areas of the town close to the dock except for Lynch and Stoll, who went off into the hills. By 3 p.m. we were all somewhat drunk. There was not much else to do. Walking around in the intermittent Pago Pago rain was not appealing.

About 3:30 p.m. an excited Marine officer ran into the club and asked to talk to the *DE-17* Commanding Officer. With several lieutenants in sweaty khakis, it was hard to tell who was in command. One of the drinkers pointed me out. As best I could understand the Marine, a C-41 had crashed in the ocean. A PBY sent to rescue the survivors—all Marines—had crashed on takeoff from the C-41's crash site.

He was desperate. The seas were getting rough, and they were concerned for all of the lives. He gave me the position, some 100 miles to the north, and asked how soon I could get under way. Fortunately we were a diesel ship and did not have to heat the boilers. We required about 30 minutes to get ready, and Russ Flynn had all engines working at the time, which meant we could do 20 knots. I told the Marine if he could get my crew back we would be on our way within the hour. I forgot to mention Lynch and Stoll.

We were a sad lot that stumbled back to the ship. One helped the other, and I was as "bent over" as anyone. I had a lot of steam to let off, and liquor was all there was. As we walked and crawled aboard the Liberty ship, and then on to our own ship, I recall the merchant crew looking at us. They had no idea what was going on. All they knew was that we tied up alongside a few hours ago, went ashore, and suddenly there were a bunch of Navy types coming back drunk and disorderly.

To add further to the confusion, I ordered the OOD, who also did not know what was going on, to sound off the hoot-hoot-hoot, a warship's shrill siren, and to keep-doing so as a notice to the crew to return to the ship. I told Merrill I expected to be informed by him within 30 minutes that the ship was ready to get under way. I then went to plot the position of the plane and to check on availability of fuel and water. The Marines did a good job of rounding up the crew, most of whom were as bad or worse off than the officers. Things really moved. While all this was going on, a Marine officer said that unless I had severely injured people aboard, I was to proceed to Canton Island after the rescue to carry out the next op order.

Special Sea Details were set, amidst the public address directions and noise that goes with it. Sailors were stumbling aboard as officers and petty officers ran around trying to take a muster. All I had told the sober watch officers who had not had their crack at the O-Club was that we had to get under way. Chaos reined while over 200 men ran around, knowing only they were making an emergency departure, and not why. The crew of the Liberty ship had lined up along the railing and were just staring at us in amazement.

Within 30 minutes I received a report from the Exec that all departments including engineering were ready for getting under way. He said they were still taking a muster, but preliminary reports indicated that all were aboard. We singled up our lines, then breasted the bow out, and with it set toward the channel all lines were let go. I ordered one third ahead. Within 15 minutes we were at standard speed. Within 30 minutes we were at flank speed, clear of the harbor, and heading for the position given us.

While still clearing the channel someone mentioned they had not seen Lynch or Stoll. Not thinking, I used an unfortunate choice of words while sending a message to the Marine Signal Station. I said we had two "stragglers" left behind and to kindly arrange transportation for Lynch and Stoll to either Canton Island or Funafuti. It never occurred to me that "stragglers" in the Navy were only about one level above deserters. I had no intention of penalizing either Lynch or Stoll. Larkin was as under the weather as I, and he did not pick it up either. I was still operating under orders of the Commanding General in Samoa, and the Marine staff knew our itinerary.

As we cleared the harbor and set out to sea, the barometer began to fall and the weather turned against us. We did not take water over the bow at the start, but we did make heavy spray. We had a "bone in our teeth." I passed word of our mission to the crew. By midnight we would arrive at the plane's last known position, which was further away than originally estimated. Before turning in I worked out a contingency plan in case the PBY had sunk—resulting in no radar bearing being available. This entailed a search covering the entire area. I also worked out a plan in the event a hostile submarine was submerged close to the wrecked plane waiting for a rescue ship. In rough seas, due to sea return, our primitive radar had difficulty picking up small objects, such as a plane, in the water. I had a few sandwiches, then turned in about 1900 hours hoping to fight off the hangover I knew was coming.

Sleepless, I made frequent trips to the bridge to check on the watch and also our progress. We maintained flank speed. I prayed the weather would relent until we had the Marines safely on board. Even an amphibian such as a PBY could not be expected to stay afloat in the seas we were experiencing. Soon I gave up my attempts to sleep and remained on the bridge until the situation was resolved.

Shortly before midnight radar reported a blip where the PBY should be. I slowed to 15 knots, lowered the sound gear and started zigzagging towards the plane, running a search pattern for a submarine within the area

I had delineated. This probably delayed the pick-up by about 15 minutes or possibly somewhat more, but it had to be done. The motor whaleboat had long been prepared for launching. We slowed down to launch it, but did not stop, while pinging at times and listening at others.

I had picked Bucky Harris for the job, even though he had not been aboard very long. In addition to maturity and judgment, Bucky seemed to be a natural seaman, though he was actually a lawyer. Seas were very rough by this time, but we successfully launched the motor whaleboat. The ship was making heavy weather of it in the sea, and the whaleboat was being tossed about.

Bucky managed to get alongside the plane. With so many survivors Bucky realized he would have to make two or three trips back and forth to the plane and ship. The PBY had attempted to takeoff in rough seas. The plane dived and one of its propellers sheared off, entered the cockpit, and decapitated the pilot. It had to have been a dangerous takeoff, with the crew and passengers from the C-41 all crushed into the PBY. Bucky made two trips with survivors, and we managed to get them all aboard. We had to make a decision about going back for the pilot so we could give him a decent burial. I felt we had to.

So away Bucky went again in his bucking bronco of a motor whaleboat to pick up the corpse. While all of this was going on, we continued to keep pinging and listening on the sonar for a submarine. The sound operator reported a contact. Unlike in novels and movies, sound contacts usually had an uncertainty about them. In this case the decision I made took years from my life. I had to decide whether to abandon Bucky and the corpse while I investigated the contact, or to remain close to the plane and take a chance the contact was false. I could not remain close by for the 15 minutes or more that would be needed. I had to decide between the whole ship and over 220 men against three men. I had no choice.

We stayed with what we thought was the contact, never quite feeling certain enough to fire a hedgehog pattern at it or in fact being able to develop an attack situation. Yet our sonar people sensed something was there. They were good. More than one of the operators had advanced studies in music and were sound experts. Soon we lost visual contact with the plane and the boat, and then the radar contact. We were blacked out, and Bucky could not see us. We had no way of advising him what was going on.

Probably 30 minutes or more passed while we maneuvered around the contact. We must have changed course over a hundred times. CIC tried to keep track, but when we finally lost contact entirely, I combined a search pattern for our motor whaleboat together with an effort to reestablish contact with the submarine, if there was one. Meanwhile Bucky with his crew and the corpse stayed close to the PBY, which was still afloat. I learned later the pilot's head was rolling around at Bucky's feet and all in the whaleboat were seasick. Although I died a thousand times during what seemed like an eternity, I can only imagine what Bucky and his men suffered.

From the time we had left the scene, at least an hour and fifteen minutes passed before we again sighted the whaleboat. To further complicate matters the sea had increased to a point where even getting the men out of the whaleboat would be very dangerous, let alone retrieving our whaleboat. Somehow the Gods must have been shining on us, and we completed this last and most difficult phase of the rescue. I went down to the quarterdeck to welcome Bucky aboard, but he just walked past me as if I were not there. I didn't blame him: I knew the pain I inflicted on him and the whaleboat crew was unbearable.

I never thought about medals, and I sure goofed in this. Looking back I should have recommended Bucky and his crew for at least the Lifesaving Medal. It just never entered my mind at the time. He was a fine officer and a great man. He did not recover from this experience quickly, nor did I get over a feeling of possible quilt for subjecting the motor-whaleboat crew to this terror. I don't know just how Bucky felt at the time, but I sensed that he never quite felt the same around me while we were aboard together.

The following report written by one of the men rescued, identity unknown, was supplied by Harris Emmerson. Mr. Emmerson sailed in *DE-17* from commissioning until decommissioning, rising to Chief Yeoman. He is presently Advertising Director of the *Birmingham News-Post-Herald.*

"The *Edward C. Daly* "

The circling plane above us notified us by blinker of its coming *(Daly),* and for hours after we prayed and watched the horizon for sight of her. Sometime after eleven, we were all vague as to the passage of time then, someone shouted, "there she is!" We all jumped to our feet and climbed to the top of the blister or leading edges of the wing and leaned far out and sure enough, "there she was," or at least we could see a search light on the horizon. Some cheering and some silent, we all waited thankfully for her.

Moving out of the darkness of the night she came, a dark and sinister

179

looking shadow, but to us a symbol of all we had to live for. She would not have been more beautiful had she been built of gold and inlaid with diamonds. After circling us she hove-to and lowered the whaleboat to come to our rescue. Here the sailors in the whaleboat deserve credit for they too were a gallant little crew. Buffeting the waves and battering through, she came tossing and rolling to us. After heroic tries, every man of us were aboard *Daly,* and the brave pilot of the P-Boat (PBY) was being prepared for burial.

We all drank hot coffee and slept till day. I think every man of us must have relived that day over and that night. But we were all too tired to become fully aware of what happened till the following day.

The day finally came and we awoke to the cheeriness of the sun and companionship of a grand crew. At 1450 (2:50 p.m.) we held a burial at sea for First Lieutenant Sax, USMCR. With a last prayer and in keeping with the traditions of the sea, his body slid into the sea.

The men rescued were Fitzgerald, E.A., 2nd LT, USMCR; Bogan, D., Tech Sergeant, USMC; Zabitchnick, H., 2nd LT, USMCR; Robinson, M.T., 2nd LT, USMCR; Smith, A.D., 1st LT, USMCR; Bikens, R.O., 2nd LT, USMCR; Hutchins, P.B., PFC, USMCR; Worl, J.R., 2nd LT, USMCR; Inman, C.F., 2nd LT, USMCR; Dean, C.O., Lt(jg) USNR; Forester, B.E., 2nd LT, USMCR; Sands, H.R. 1st LT, USMCR; Reader, D.E.., 2nd LT, USMCR; Denson, L.A., 2nd LT, USMCR; Benedetti, D.C., Staff Sergeant, USMCR; Anderson, G.L. PFC, USMCR.

The night was not over yet. We had accomplished our mission in rescuing the survivors. The C-41 had sunk before we arrived, but the PBY was still afloat even though unsalvageable. We still had to dispose of it. We had nothing available in Pago Pago that could tow the plane. Under present sea conditions, it was unlikely it could be successfully towed or that it would even remain afloat.

I had broken radio silence to report in code that we had rescued the Marines. I described the condition of the PBY, and orders came through to sink it. By that time the sea had become very rough and we were rolling and pitching. I ordered Merrill to sink the PBY using the 3-inch-50s from a reasonable distance. I was exhausted and had a hangover. All of the years at sea, the day at war at sea, and the numerous incidents in all the ships I had been on including *Daly* hit me at once.

Rather than relaxing me the drinking affected me in the opposite manner, only to prove that a drink only makes you feel differently. I was just crawling into my bunk when the first of the shots rang out. A 3-inch-50 caliber is not a large gun, but it makes one hell of a noise and peels the paint off the bulkheads when you shoot. I expected the gunners to sink the PBY with a few shots, but the shooting didn't stop. The noise did not help my hangover, so I went up to the bridge to find out what was going on.

They just could not hit the PBY from two thousand yards while the ship was rolling and pitching. It was a sad exhibition of gunnery, and we were fortunate the PBY could not shoot back. I ordered all guns manned and the range closed. We hit the plane but did not sink it. I was disgusted, but looking back there were extenuating circumstances. Over half the crew had hangovers, they were dead tired, and it was an anticlimax to a whole series of events that had their effect on everyone, not only the captain. Finally, in a burst of flame after the gas tanks were hit, the PBY disappeared and we proceeded on our way to Canton Island.

I was still exhausted the next morning. Bucky, who rated the honor, conducted the services and burial of the brave pilot. It was done well, and pictures were sent to the family. The voyage to Canton Island was made without incident, and the towboat and dredge were ready to depart on our arrival. In the interim the surviving pilots, in an act of thanks, gave their valuable pilot jackets to the wardroom officers. Each pilot thanked me for their rescue before leaving on a boat sent for them.

Canton is one of those small desolate islands that dot the Pacific. Although in the middle of nowhere, a large Trans-Pacific Liner under the U.S. Flag seemed to be able to find it and go aground there shortly before we entered the war. It was a President Class Ship of the Dollar Line. It was high and dry, and there I imagine it is today or what is left of it. I asked if Stoll and Lynch were there and was told they were at Funafuti.

The towboat could pull the dredge at close to 8 or 9 knots. This would have to be our speed of advance even though we operated at close to 15 knots searching the area around our two-unit convoy. I was the Task Unit Commander or Officer in Tactical Command (OTC) depending on the category I wanted to give myself, and here again we were all alone in the Central Pacific. We were there for the taking, but again our good fortune prevailed, and the voyage was made on time and without incident.

After escorting the tug and tow into Funafuti, we anchored and awaited orders. That night Lynch and Stoll quietly came aboard asking the other officers if I was mad at them. They had convinced the Adjutant General in Pago Pago of their innocence. Because the Marines felt kindly towards the ship and me for rescuing their people, they gave them a few bottles of

Scotch to make their peace with me. A few officers in the wardroom at the time convinced them I was mad as hell at them, and if they gave me the whiskey it would only make me madder. By the time I saw them and they learned I wasn't angry, the whiskey was gone. I didn't even see it let alone get one drink. I still welcomed them aboard. Within a day or two orders came through for us to proceed directly to Pearl Harbor.

According to my figures if we economized by running on only two engines at 15 knots, we could make Pearl with about 6 to 12 hours of fuel remaining. This calculation did not allow for rough weather or even investigating any contacts made en route. I paid my respects to Col. Murray and left the beautiful island of Funafuti never to return again. Except for a suspicious radar contact as we got close to Pearl, the trip was uneventful. For me the trip allowed a needed rest. We were down to our last few drops of fuel when the suspicious contact was made, but the chances of it being hostile in that area were poor. Stoll wanted to check it out, but I envisioned being towed into Pearl or sunk while out of fuel and dead in the water. We made Pearl and immediately went to the fuel dock. Later we moored alongside *Burden R. Hastings (DE-19)*, which Ernie Fay now commanded. Orders were received for repairs and modifications. Along with *DE-19*, we would join other ships in CourtDiv in the Aleutians. I went with several other officers to the Pearl Harbor Officers Club for drinks—fully expecting we would remain in Pearl for at least two weeks.

Russ Flynn, however, had gone to see the Repair Officer, and convinced him the nature of the repairs we needed could be better done in the States. The Repair Officer did not need much convincing since the repair facilities in Pearl were being taxed to the limit. Flynn was told that if we could get under way immediately, and catch up with a convoy just leaving, it would be okay.

Flynn rushed back to the O-Club, passed the news to me and the others, and together we rushed back to the ship before shore leave was granted for the evening. I was not unhappy about repairing in the States, but again I had to rush out of port, and again I had had several drinks. We were moored in such a way alongside *DE-19* that we should have had some tug assistance. The harbor was jammed with ships, and it was an almost impossible job to twist the ship around all the ships that were in the way. They only way I could do it was by raking the after railing of *DE-19* with my port anchor fluke, but Ernie waved me on my way.

Except for the minor damage done to *DE-19*, we worked our way out of the crowded harbor to sea and joined up with the convoy escorts. It was the last time I would see Hawaii for many years.

I passed by Diamond Head for the last time at sea. When we reached San Francisco we tied up at Treasure Island. The next day I received orders to proceed immediately to Charleston, South Carolina, as the prospective Commanding Officer of a new and larger DE, *U.S.S. Cofer (DE-208)*.

Again no time off. The only relaxation I had had during the whole time on *Daly* was a weekend with Ginny at the Samarkand Hotel in Santa Barbara during one of the ship's stays in San Francisco. Even this was not without some excitement. While Ginny was finishing dressing for dinner one night, I waited for her at the bar. Suddenly the bar started to shake and bottles fell off and crashed. I thought I was having a nervous breakdown, but it was only an earthquake. Ginny was more frightened than I.

Merrill received command of *Edward C. Daly* and Bucky Harris became Exec. Flynn was transferred to a floating drydock, and Larkin and Lynch received shore duty. I spent several hours going over rough weather shiphandling techniques with Merrill, then quickly said my sad goodbyes to a great bunch of men. Then Ginny and I rushed to catch the train for a crowded, uncomfortable trip to Charleston.

It took me some time to figure out Admiral Nimitz's interest in me. My confrontation with General MacArthur had brought me to Nimitz's attention. The message requesting my relief as the C.O. of the Naval Unit in *Matsonia* for refusing to carry out General MacArthur's orders was sent to CINCPAC where Nimitz saw it. The Admiral, not an admirer of MacArthur, was intrigued a Lt(jg) would do what the President would not. He then checked me out. As a result I received command of *Daly*.

Daly en route
from Pago Pago, Samoa, to
Canton Island after night rescue
of Marines.
Burial at sea of 1st Lt. Sax,
USMCR, heroic pilot of the PBY
who lost his life in a perilous
take off in a rough sea after first
rescuing survivors of a
downed C-41.

S.S. Mastonia in Pacific early 1942. Gun crew of 4-inch 50 calibur firing
during target practice.

*S.S. **Matsonia** as armed troopship, early 1942, Pacific.*

*U.S.S. **SC-981** at Milne Bay, New Guinea, 1943.*

*U.S.S. **Kanawha**, Puget Sound, WA, prior to rearmament at Bremerton Navy Yard, 1941.*

Lt(jg) Al Chester at sea in the Pacific, early 1942 aboard **S.S. Matsonia**.

Virginia Moore Chester, 1941.

*Party at Mark Hopkins Hotel, San Francisco, spring 1943. Front row, L-R: Lts Russ Flynn, Phil Merrill, and Al Chester, C.O. of **U.S.S. Edward C. Daly**, Lt (jg)s J.O. Jordan and Bill Larkin. Back row, L-R: Ensigns Vinnie McCarthy, unrecalled, Len Stoll, and Russ Bond.*

*Al Chester with the Chief Petty Officers of **U.S.S. Edward C. Daly**.*

Lt. William "Bucky" Harris,
*USNR, aboard **U.S.S. Edward C. Daly**.*
A North Carolina Lawyer
who found his true calling
in a motor whaleboat
in a storm at sea.
No legal fee chargeable,
but his satisfaction should
be priceless.

*Funfati, 1943. Lt. Russ Flynn and Lt (jg) J.O. Jordan trying their skill in native craft but staying close to **Daly**.*

Virginia Moore Chester
in Coronado, CA, 1941,
with 1938 Pontiac.

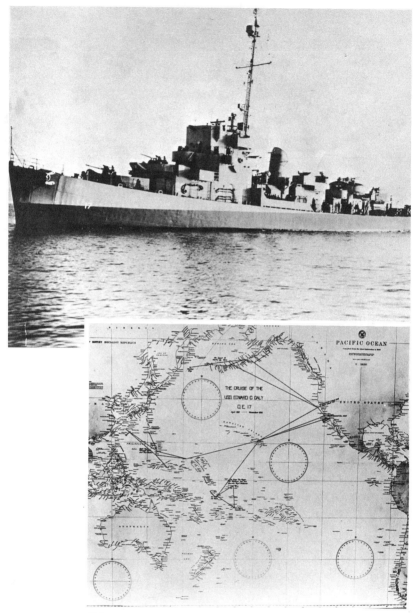

Edward C. Daly, *1943.   Pacific cruises of **Daly** during WWII.*

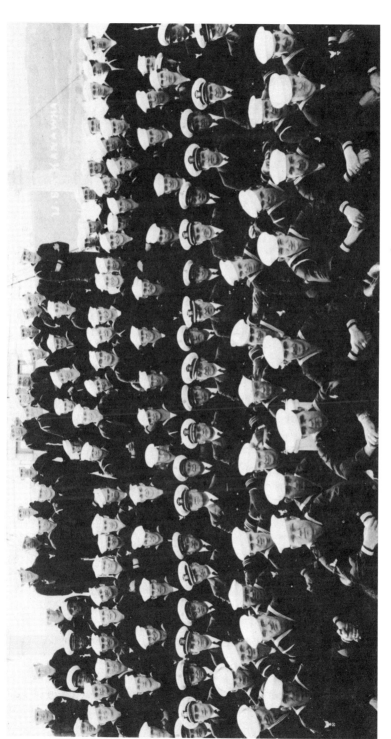

*Crew of the **U.S.S. Kanawha** (AO-1), 1940.*

Eight

War: Atlantic and Mediterranean

U.S.S. Cofer (DE-208)

G inny and I arrived in Charleston shortly before Christmas. The Navy office arranged a temporary room for us in a private house for a few days so Ginny could look for more adequate quarters in the interim. Temporary, affordable housing was difficult to find in the exclusive district of old Charleston, but Ginny managed to find a charming, small apartment in an historic old house still occupied by the descendants of the original owner. Mr. Bennett, an author, lived there with his sister, and Ginny transacted business with Miss Bennett.

The small apartment on the third floor was reached by an outside staircase. That winter was very cold, snowing in Charleston for the first time in many years. Ginny had to haul coal up the staircase for heating and cooking, yet the apartment was cozy.

We soon became a part of a temporary, young Navy society enjoying a short respite in a charming old city that seemed remote from the war. Although our futures were uncertain and the work difficult, it was all very romantic.

My situation during pre-commissioning was the reverse of what it was with *Daly*. Here I was stationed in the ship's office in the Charleston Navy Yard with the prospective Chief Engineer and other officers and ratings. This time the Executive officer was in charge of the major part of the officers and crew at the DE pre-commissioning school in Norfolk.

Although the schools had improved, the supply of experienced officers and petty officers for the DE program was diminishing. I was extremely fortunate in that Raymond Oksala, a graduate of the NYSMMA Class of '37, held a Chief Engineer's License. He had previously served in one of the rare U.S. Navy Corvettes on convoy duty in the North Atlantic as Chief Engineer and deck watch stander. Qualified by the C.O. for Executive Officer, he wanted to remain in engineering.

The other officers were SCTC qualified, but they had little experience for their new assignments. The Exec only had a short sea time in command of an SC, the remainder of the officers, if they had some sea duty, it was of short duration. None, including the Exec, was actually qualified as a top watch stander.

The next senior officer was assigned to the ship in Charleston as the prospective First Lieutenant. He was the older brother of the young seaman the ship had been named after. Thirty-eight-year-old Lt. Charles Cofer was too old for this type of duty. He had enlisted in the Navy in the '20s and made 2nd Class Petty Officer, but had to return to the family farm in Georgia when his father died leaving a large family to support. He entered high school at the same time his oldest child entered grammar school. Not only did he graduate from high school, he went on to college to earn an advanced degree, subsequently becoming a teacher, a principal, and then Superintendent of Schools in his district. Soon after the war started he requested and was given a Reserve Commission as a Lt(jg). This was followed by shore duty. His youngest brother, killed at Guadalcanal, received a medal and had a ship named after him. Lt. Cofer requested duty in the ship and was ordered to SCTC where he qualified. These were great character references, indicating excellent potential, but no hard experience.

Lt. McLees, the Exec, was unknown to me, but in his file there was no more to rejoice about than with Lt. Cofer. There were four other officers in the rank of Lt(jg): Walter Meredith, S.W. Hahn, Sam Cleland, and Henry Peters. They too were light on experience, but strong on character, education, and motivation. Two Ensigns, Bernard Mazer and Edward Lipovsky, were assigned to the ship.

Among the Chiefs and senior Petty Officers were other bright people, but few with sea experience. Oksala lucked out on a Chief Machinist Mate named Marks, who was one of those old resilient China Station hands back for the war and enjoying it. Among the Petty Officers was another Cofer brother, Sam, a Radioman 2nd Class. With Oksala, Cofer, Cleland, and Peters working with me in the Charleston Navy Yard, we supervised the ship's transition from a hull number into a commissioned vessel.

Ginny and I made friends with couples from our own and other ships, and there were parties as ships were completed, commissioned, and departed. Ginny found a small Christmas tree, and we had a cocktail party

185

in our apartment during the holidays. New Years was celebrated at one of the Officer's Clubs. It was a time to work, play, and love, together with many other young people sharing the moments of pleasure ashore as they tried to forget the perils awaiting them on the dangerous seas they were bound for. Ships departed, friends left, and new ones arrived. Our moment of truth soon came—January 19, 1944, the scheduled date of our commissioning.

U.S.S. Cofer was one of six sisterships of CortDiv 52, which included: *Jordan (DE-204), Newman (DE-205), Liddle (DE-206), Kephart (DE-207),* and *Lloyd (DE-209).* The first two ships departed for Bermuda for shakedown before I arrived in Charleston. The other three crews were with us for awhile before we too departed. All the other C.O.s in the CortDiv were Lcdrs. I was still only a Lt.

On a lovely sun-filled January 19 afternoon, the Naval District Band and guests took their places on the dock alongside *Cofer.* At 1525 hours the ceremony began with Rear Admiral Jules James, Commandant of the 6th Naval District, making the opening remarks about the career of the late John Joseph Cofer. At 1535 hours the ship was christened *U.S.S. Cofer* by Mrs. Mary Jane Cofer, mother of the late John Cofer. AT 1542 hours, in accordance with a Vice-Chief of Naval Operations directive, the C.O. of the Receiving Station, Charleston, SC, placed *U.S.S. Cofer* in commission. The colors and the commission pennant were two-blocked, and the ship was turned over to me, Lt. A.P. Chester, D-M, USNR, as the Commanding Officer. I read my orders and took command in accordance with BuPers Dispatch 251303 of November 1943. Then the invocation was given by Captain T.B. Thompson, USN.

The watch was set at 1547 hours, and Rear Admiral James and the Christening and Commissioning Party left the ship. At 1555 hours the officers and enlisted men were logged as reporting aboard. The ceremony took only 30 minutes. The watch was not discontinued until the ship was decommissioned more than two years later after being awarded eight battle stars. So in this manner a warship is born and takes on an identity of its own.

Many people live their lives without excitement and achievement. Yet most hope they will experience moments of exhilaration they can look back on with interest, if not pleasure. War at sea is much the same; except when these moments are experienced, they come often without warning and are of short duration. It was generally accepted the theoretical life of a destroyer escort and its crew in combat at sea was measured in minutes.

I had been at sea almost continually from the time the U.S. entered the war, sailing through dangerous seas and prepared for the worst, yet I had not been locked in mortal combat. If the objective was to protect a convoy or an independent ship and I succeeded, then the objective was won. But I experienced no exhilaration. If my mission was to search out and destroy the enemy and I failed to find him, then I was frustrated. If contact is made, however, there are usually casualties. A commanding officer feels no satisfaction in gaining recognition over the casualties of his men.

A commanding officer soon realizes the mission is all important, and his primary overall duty is to do all possible to complete it successfully. This means he has to be constantly ready for any and all eventualities. In my case, and as time went by, I succeeded in all my missions without taking any casualties in personnel or damage to the ship. I was lucky because the forces I could be expected to encounter were superior to mine. With this new command I had a ship that was "state of the art" for any mission I could conceive of. In the new DEs the U.S. Navy now had an excellent deterrent to the U-Boat but the U-Boats also had been improved.

As I prepared to take on this responsibility with an inexperienced crew, it never entered my mind the German submarine forces had taken heavy losses in personnel, and they too were manning their subs with what they had, rather than what they required. As *Cofer* prepared to enter the Battle of the Atlantic, I focused only on the problems I had to overcome to successfully sail and fight, and I worried.

By the time we completed shakedown, the tide already had turned heavily against the U-Boat. Convoy systems had been improving constantly—the battle already joined by Hunter-Killer groups. Much of this success went to the Royal Navy, which had persevered in spite of the odds. At the same time the Donald Duck Navy, with few kills to its credit, still was a deterrent, assisting in reducing merchant ship losses until the DEs could join the battle.

Daly never contacted a Japanese submarine in the wide expanse of the Pacific theater. I welcomed this new duty—the Atlantic after all was my home base.

As we prepared *Cofer* for sea, the inexperience of the officers and crew became more apparent. The only officer aboard qualified to stand deck watches was the Chief Engineer, who was not required to stand them. Even though the Battle of the Atlantic was winding down, I had no way of knowing this. Aside from combat problems, *Cofer* was to operate in the Atlantic, and this mighty sea could not be discounted. This amateur crew would have to adapt very fast. Even though I understood the problems I would have training them, I was not aware how long it would take me to bring them to the level of *Daly* officers and men, by the time we reported for shakedown.

Drills were held constantly during this fitting-out period. On January 28, some nine days after commissioning, we got under way for the first time under our own power and headed for the Naval Ammunition Depot, Goose Creek, Charleston, SC, where we took aboard ammunition. Unlike *Daly*, we carried torpedoes, and took those aboard along with shells, depth charges, hedgehogs, and other ammunition.

Between January 29th and February 12, we fueled ship, completed degaussing runs, held our trial runs and full power trials, fired our guns, depth charges and hedgehogs, and we ran compass calibration and other tests. About 24 days from commissioning we were outfitted and on our way independently to Bermuda for shakedown. Prior to sailing Ensigns Norman Covington and Philip Holtberg reported for temporary duty from SCTC.

We soon hit the first sea swell, and it was the beginning of a very rough voyage. The result was near total seasickness. On the bridge the Senior Officer of the watch was seasick on one side and the Junior on the other. Many of the crew would not leave their bunks until Oksala and I went through the quarters with broomsticks, not too gently nudging them out of their berths to their watches.

A Bermuda transit in February is usually very rough, and this was no exception. At the same time I had to get the crew to their stations and drill them. We had to maintain sound sweeps for enemy subs. Aside from Oksala and myself perhaps two other officers did not get seasick. I had to have Oksala stand a deck OOD watch. A few capable Chiefs in the engine room could look after things for several hours.

In short the officers and crew were getting a wetting down before the shakedown. We were on a direct course of due east with corrections being made when I was able to ascertain position by celestial navigation. This ship, bigger than *Daly*, was still small. She was 1,720 tons full-load displacement and 306 feet long with 12,000 HP, double that of *Daly*.

I had no alternative but to insist that everyone stand watches or the ship would be in trouble. The problem was this crew never had a chance to get used to the ship in moderate weather. Aside from an overnight ocean-trial period in relatively calm weather, suddenly and while still in an unfamiliar atmosphere, they were sailing a seagoing bucking bronco.

The ship had to be operated, and we had to be ready for a submarine on the surface and below. We made a number of radar and visual contacts that we had to run down and identify. The transit time to Bermuda was short, and it was necessary to arrive ready for anything and everything we might be tested on. We needed to function, and drills, drills, and more drills were routine.

Captain Dashiel Madeira, USN, the C.O. of the shakedown group for DDs and DEs, was known to be one tough hombre. Captains and officers were relieved of their commands and assignments if they fouled up in any way. This was an experienced command who knew its job. I was aware this would be a much more difficult and longer shakedown than *Daly* received in San Diego.

I could not trust anyone else to navigate under the conditions; and although I required the Navigator to function, I took my own sights and kept my own position. Bermuda, surrounded by a reef, has heavy sea return in rough weather. We could easily miss this low level island on radar. Meanwhile we practiced zigzagging, which also complicated dead-reckoning position keeping.

On February 15 we hit the sea buoy on the head even though we could not pick up the land on the radar before we saw it. At 1512 hours we embarked the pilot, entered the channel into Grassy Bay, and worked our way to Dundonal Channel. We entered Great Sound, and at 1650 hours moored alongside *U.S.S. Hamul,* Capt. Madeira's Flagship.

The following day we were overrun by inspectors from the staff of the shakedown group who paired off with our department heads. It was not long before there was a blowup. The inspector going over the work of Charlie Cofer accused him of copying his work from one or more ships of our division that had preceded us to the shakedown area. Charlie was beside himself, and brought in his papers to prove to me he had done his own work. When I questioned him Charlie told me other First Lieutenants had asked to study his organizational work. He said the inspector never gave him a chance to answer and just laid into him as though he were dishonest.

Carrying Charlie's work papers with me, I went aboard *Hamul* and demanded to see Capt. Madeira. I took the offensive and said I did not appreciate anyone yelling at my officers and accusing them of cheating. I was the Captain, and if his people found anything wrong with my ship, I was the one they should see. The staff officer should have come to me rather than running off half-cocked. Then I told Capt. Madeira I had made a cursory examination of the work papers, which I showed to him.

Captain Madeira was a tough but fair cookie. He heard me out and

189

looked at the papers. He then asked me if I would stake my reputation on my First Lieutenant, and I said I would. I had worked closely with him on pre-commissioning, and he was an older, highly dedicated serious officer. Madeira, very polite to me, kept his cool and said he would check it out. I never heard any more about this matter, and the officer involved on Madeira's staff apologized to Lt. Cofer.

That same afternoon the Free French Ship *Senagalais* moored alongside our port side. She was a diesel-powered DE given to the French Navy and would shakedown with us. Her commanding Officer, a very senior French Regular Navy Officer, later became Chief of the French Navy. At 0540 hours on the morning of the 17th, we took aboard a pilot for the last time. Once in and once out, and then the C.O. was on his own in this vary difficult entry and departure port.

By 0655 hours we were on our way out of the harbor in company with *U.S.S. Holder (DE-401)* and *U.S.S. Thomas (DE-193)*. This was the beginning of a regular routine of sailing out every morning, going through exercises independently or with other ships and U.S. submarines and, when not on an overnight, returning to port at about 1800 hours. Then we had to prepare for the next day's exercise.

On the 18th we took aboard 50 dummy hedgehog charges from *Hamul* for various practice runs on the submarine *U.S.S. R-16.* A day later, while making practice attacks on the submerged *R-16,* we placed one of our dummy hedgehogs in the sub's conning tower area. The Captain graciously came on board to congratulate us and return the hedgehog to us.

It was a difficult schedule sailing out Dundonal Channel looking into the sun each morning and returning in the night with the sun in our eyes. Groundings, followed by the C.O. being relieved, were not uncommon. The harbor was full of U.S., British, and French Destroyers, DEs, and a few U.S. and Italian submarines. Only the Italian Naval Officers, who were prisoners of war, enjoyed themselves in Bermuda. They had the freedom of the island and almost a monopoly on the British Censorettes. Resplendent in their white uniforms, they were fighting the war the Italian way, which I would have liked to have done. They had the use of the Officers Club and an abundance of recreational facilities. The facilities were available to us also, but we were all exhausted the few times we got a chance to go ashore. No holiday for us.

In March we were still at it. This shakedown was much better organized than the one in San Diego. Captain Madeira ran us ragged, but when we finished we were an improved ship. On the first of March while we were anchored in berth D-1, Great Sound, Bermuda, practically a ship's length away from the main pier in Hamilton, the barometer suddenly began to fall. I ordered steam up on all boilers and emergency stations for getting under way. The barometer continued its dive, and the anchor started to drag in the strong winds.

The ship got under way as the harbor churned up and the winds increased to near, if not, hurricane force. It was a nightmare night of dodging ships dragging anchors, breaking loose from anchor buoys, and in many cases not having gotten steam up in time or, for diesel-propelled ships, being unable to get under way. We were one of a few ships that sustained no casualties or damage. Captain Madeira signalled a "well done" to us.

By March 9 we had successfully completed the shakedown and were formally inspected by the Task Group Commander. Captain Madeira personally congratulated me on a well-run ship. He knew about our having hit the submarine with the hedgehog, a rarity for so inexperienced a crew, and he said we were the only one of all the ships at anchor and moored to buoys on the night of the storm with the foresight to react to the fast falling barometer. He then handed me a Brass paperweight made on the *Hamul* marked "Can Do" *U.S.S. Cofer (DE-208)* from *Hamul.* "I understand very few of these were given out during Captain Madeira's tenure.

At 1417 hours, in company with *Holder,* we were on our way back to Charleston for a post-shakedown overhaul. The C.O. of *Holder,* a Lcdr., was the Task Group Commander.

Both ships continued to drill on the return voyage, which was not as rough as the trip to Bermuda. We had done well, but I was exhausted, a situation I began to feel more often than before. The pressure and the hours of work were inhuman. Even though we had done as well as any of the other ships, and better than most of them, we had a long way to go to become ready for what I knew had to be ahead of us. Our luck could not last forever, and I had the feeling that soon the ship would face heavy combat. Meanwhile we had much to do in Charleston to prepare for our next assignment.

During our week in port most officers and petty officers had little or no time off. I had set a policy to grant as much leave as possible to the officers and enlisted men. I was aware that when we sailed again, the possibility of further leave would be poor for a long time. More than 200 people and the usual personnel problems placed a great burden on the officers and crew. The heaviest burden fell on the C.O. and the Chief Engineer.

This was aggravated by a situation that had occurred during shakedown.

Oksala and I recognized the ship was possibly damaged during an exercise. We would have to cope with it and solve it when the ship went into drydock. Fortunately drydocking was routine for this period, but if it had not been I would have requested it.

One of the scheduled practices had been a towing-at-sea exercise. We were to tow *Senagalais;* when finished, she was to tow us. When we started out the sea was moderate to rough, and it was questionable whether we should have proceeded. By the time we arrived in the area, the sea was much too rough for the exercise. Our request for cancellation was not granted.

I was probably the only officer in the DDs and DEs undergoing shakedown with any experience in towing at sea. I was aware that we had none of the facilities required to do more than set up a makeshift arrangement. We had no towing engine, nor did we have a winch or capstan on the stern. All we had was a windlass on the foredeck to facilitate taking on a tow line. Further most tow boats or ships being used in this capacity are single screw, and seagoing tow boats are deep draft to give them a more stable platform. Most important they have a clear after deck. We did not qualify in any way. Our after deck was cluttered with depth charge racks K-guns, and 20mm AA weapons. We had no proper fairleads or strong enough chocks to make fast to. It was something that could be done in an emergency, but only under better conditions than we were experiencing. Because we were ordered to do the exercise, I decided to chance it even though I knew better.

It was so rough the stern was coming out of the water and the propellers churning in the air. Although the sun was shining, the wind was howling, and it was impossible to hear. It was difficult to hold one's footing. Uncomfortable on the bridge it was a nightmare on the fantail where Lt. Cofer was working with his men. They were sloshing around in the water trying to keep from being washed overboard. All went well for awhile. We sent a runner over to *Senagalais* and then pulled the tow line aboard by hand. In place of a winch or towing engine, 20 men were manhandling the line.

Lt. Cofer passed orders to the bridge by telephone to stop or go ahead. No astern orders were possible, for with twin screws we would soon be tangled in the tow line. Sure enough the tow line fouled the port screw. On getting the word I stopped all engines and asked *Senagalais* to stop and maneuver as we requested, telling them we had the problem. The C.O. understood and agreed. I ordered the bridge to follow my directions, left McLees there, and ordered Oksala to meet me on the fantail. The scene was pathetic. No one knew what to do, and the ship was floundering around while waves crashed over the deck. Fortunately the crew had life lines and life jackets on.

Nothing in my previous experience had trained me for something like this. All I could do was try to determine what the situation was. One end of the line was secured on deck; the other end, with several turns around the port screw, lead back to *Senagalais.* In a calm sea I could have placed two people over the side to cut the line free. Under the present conditions this was impossible.

I knew I had to grapple for the other end of the line even if I had to simply cut it and secure it to the deck so that the starboard screw would be free to turn. This was a long shot. As we considered the alternatives Cofer, Oksala, and I were hanging on together while being soaked. Oksala believed he could back the port shaft in the opposite direction than what it had been turning, and thus back the line off. This he said could be done manually from the engine room. We could set up communications from the engine room to the fantail. Both ends, he cautioned, needed to be controlled from the deck.

This too was a long shot; but I told Oksala to call the fantail when he was ready below. With the assistance of mostly petty officers, we rolled around the fantail, grappled, and cast the big hook out in the direction of the towing line and prayed. We were desperate. Eventually we did get the other end of the line aboard, and we did back it off the screw and shaft. We then cut ourselves free from the tow. *Senagalais* retrieved the remainder of the line. In many talks to old timers, I have never met one who had accomplished the same thing. God had to be looking after us.

Senagalais was not the least interested in continuing the exercise, and we were able to get it canceled because of complications arising from the worsening state of the sea. I still did not have a damage report. All I knew was the starboard propeller was in the clear and could turn. Being ultra-conservative I did not start the starboard engine first. Remaining on the fantail and keeping in contact with the engine room and the bridge, I ordered them to slowly start up the port engine with as few revolutions as possible, while I hung over the after rail attempting to see if the screw was clear as the stern came close to the surface. It seemed clear so revolutions were increased slowly up to standard speed, and the other engine placed on line.

Okie and I were concerned about alignment. There was no unusual vibration that we could tell, although there was vibration. Even with the smallest misalignment, however, and over a period of time, it could wear out the stern bearings and the packing, which could cause leaking. No problems were encountered on the voyage back to Charleston; but not knowing when we would again get to a drydock, we had to find out for certain.

We did not get our turn in the drydock until 2100 hours on the evening of the 14th. Okie and I sat there watching the water go out of the dock, and praying. We both knew if the shaft should be out of alignment it would be a serious job, which could even require a replacement. We waited several hours alone. The repair officer would not be there until early the next day, but we wanted to get an overview beforehand.

Everything looked okay except the collar was broken off and there were scratches on the prop. Replacing the collar was a minor job. The shaft did not look bent, but we decided to ask the yard to check the alignment. It was all right. We both heaved a sigh of relief as the surveyor passed the ship's bottom, and we could get on with the numerous other jobs before us.

There was not a moment of peace for me during the entire period in Charleston. The crew in some instances over stayed their leaves, which required my holding Captain's Mast. Never is it a pleasant duty to stand in judgment of other men. What few realize is that while the C.O. has leeway in the manner he applies punishment, it is always a tough job to ensure it is dispensed with wisdom, and serves the basic purpose of having the crew live together in harmony with the rules enforced. Whether the seamen be 17 years old or 50, as long as they were exposed to danger, they were to be treated like men.

When the Exec first arrived from DE school in Norfolk, he proudly presented me with over a hundred pages of Ship's Orders to augment all the others that were floating around. Some were duplications, some were simply a means of harassing the whole crew for the acts of a few, and most were simply unenforceable without creating more problems than they solved. I broke his heart when I told him I was filing the work in the waste basket, and no orders would be written unless they were forced on us by events.

This system works both ways. If the adolescent wants to be treated like a man, he has to act like one. The same with an officer, and only more so. Most could and did adapt, but some fought the system. It is the job of a commanding officer to lead all the different characters into a common denominator so that the ship functions as a whole. This is not easy.

During my career in the service and in private enterprise, I found only a small percentage of people with "something extra" who I would hire without qualification. Talent is rare in almost every level of our society. I learned never to push or promote someone beyond their capabilities. A large percentage of people have a set level of intelligence and productivity, which if pushed beyond, they will fail. They will also be unhappy and inclined to blame their failure on others. You cannot promote and select on the basis of the minimal requirement or you risk an even greater breakdown when the next level is reached. The best man or woman, regardless, should get the promotion. Anything else is the discrimination we try so hard to avoid.

Even more important is to treat those of limited talent with the same respect and consideration you treat the more talented, but at the same time not to mislead them about their prospects. I tried to make each member of the crew feel important regardless of the relative importance of his job. Every man or woman is entitled to be treated with dignity. These are all kind words, but the implementation of this is difficult, particularly on a warship, for there are layers of authority between the C.O. and the enlisted men. I took this responsibility very seriously.

And so as we set out from Charleston on the evening of March 19 heading to New York. I was in command of a major combat ship in commission for only two months. The officers and crew had been subjected to the most intensive training and hardship, but it was too short a time. They were still strangers to each other and far from being at home aboard a Naval combat ship. Yet they were functioning. The ship was steaming at 20 knots for my home port. I had last entered it as the Junior Third Officer in *Manhattan* in late 1939. I was now approaching this famous port as a Lt. in command of a destroyer escort.

On January 25th my 28th birthday came and passed without note. I was still only a Lt., even though my last two assignments called for a Lcdr. in the billet. I had heard I had been selected for Lcdr., but so far no A1Nav or letter. Ginny was in Montana with her sisters, but my mother was in New York. At least I would have a chance to see her. It had been a long time. Needless to say I continued the drills as I pressed the crew to reach the highest possible degree of readiness.

Just before noon on March 21, we reached the Pilot Station at New York; by 1320 hours we were tied up at port-side-to *U.S.S. Nelson (DD-623)*, south side of the 33rd St. Pier, Brooklyn. This was not far from where I had sailed in *S.S. Santa Clara* and *S.S. Padnsay*. All around us destroyers were nested. I soon discovered that Lcdr. Tom McGrath, USN, whom I had relieved in *Kanawha* in 1939, was the commanding officer.

McGrath, short and stubby, was one of those people who did not look like an officer. It was hard to tell where his chin ended and neck began. He stood erect as the Annapolis Midshipman he was in the early '30s. Once aboard *Nelson* you knew you were on a well-run fighting ship. An 1,800-ton destroyer, and one of the finest class of destroyer ever built, *Nelson* was the Flagship of the squadron. Tom McGrath had been in command for some time.

A Naval officer from his head down to his toes, he was all Navy. He lived and dreamed it, and he was doing a job for which he had hoped and trained all his life. He was born to be a destroyer captain. What he learned he remembered, and what no one taught him, he taught himself. He was that rarity—"born to command"—and now he was practicing it.

Much has been written about incompetent Naval officers, and a great deal about glamorous Admirals and Captains who intrigued the press. McGrath, though, was one of those rare breed of men who rose to the challenge he was trained for. He was all-business and ran a taut ship. You felt it as soon as you walked aboard. And yet he was a modest man who suffered with his crew as well as shared his successes with them. I cannot over praise the achievements of Lcdr. Tom McGrath.

Work did not allow us to spend as much time together as we would have liked. We were sailing on at 0400 hours on March 23. What little time I did have I spent with my mother, who had been suffering the war for a long time now. She was a widow with an only child to whom she had devoted her whole life, and every day of the war was misery for her.

At first I was not sure whether having her down to the ship for lunch or dinner would frighten her more than she was already. She was a strong woman, so I took her down one night. Six or more destroyers and destroyer escorts were all nested together, chock-block with guns and torpedoes, all emitting strange noises. The ships seemed more alive than the people moving around them. I had to help her crawl around all sorts of obstructions, but she was in good shape and managed. I took her to my stateroom and showed her all the interesting things peculiar to a fighting ship and foreign to an ocean liner. She toughened it out, and I accompanied her home to Baldwin, Long Island, to her little house where she lived alone. Shortly thereafter I had to return to the ship. My days of independent duty were over, and from this time on I was never alone in the ocean. The Navy was coming of age in the war, and no longer would it be as private as I had known it.

On Thursday March 23 at 0805 hours in company with Desron 17 less *U.S.S. Murphy,* and CortDiv 52 less *U.S.S. Lloyd,* with the Commander of

Task Force 63 and OTC in *U.S.S. Nelson,* we left New York and headed for Gibraltar, scouting in advance of a fast troop convoy. We sailed at 15 knots into a full gale.

During the night the Task Force Commander kept ordering us to maintain station, a hopeless assignment unless we dared risk foundering. In fact one man was injured, our gyro went out due to mercury loss, and a floater net with all equipment was carried away. I ordered the ship to slow ahead, and simply ignored the pressure to keep station. I lifted the sound dome before we lost it and settled the ship on a course and speed she could survive yet be able to fight when the weather moderated. Beating the enemy was one thing but attempting to beat the sea could have only one ending. I learned this years ago in the U.S. Lines. I had made 76 crossings of the North Atlantic. I doubt there was an officer in the whole task force who had made more than ten. We had a rendezvous position in case we should be separated, and I worked to it slowly.

I perfected a system to cover myself for failure to carry out orders I thought were wrong. I suddenly "lost" radio contact on the TBS and kept repeating, "Will you say again your last transmission." I found it convenient to use this ploy several times. In this storm if I had attempted to maintain course and speed, I might have lost the ship.

The Task Group Commander, although a full Captain, could not have had my experience. No competent seaman would ever order his ship to fight it out with the sea. McGrath, although in the same ship, was not on the staff, and I doubt he was consulted. During the early hours of the 14th, I hoped to regain contact with the other ships, all of which had been separated. We arrived at the rendezvous point before daylight, but none of the other ships could be picked up on the radar. The sea had moderated a good deal by then.

By 0630 hours some ships had arrived at the rendezvous point, but not *Nelson.* The senior officer was ComDesDiv 34, and we soon had *Kephart, Liddle, Shubrick, Herndon,* and the OTC in *Butler.* The OTC ordered a search for the other vessels. At 1130 hours the seas abated sufficiently for us to lower our sound head and start searching for submarines. Not until 1545 hours did we sight *Nelson* and the other ships. I don't recall whether anyone was killed or lost that night on the other ships, but some were seriously injured. Some ships lost sonar domes and part of their radar antennae. The Task Group had lost a serious percentage of our anti-submarine effectiveness. At 1615 hours I resumed my station 2500 yards to starboard of *Nelson.*

197

In this instance the Task Group Commander had failed to assess the power of the sea and act accordingly. It was probably one of the few areas where training in a transatlantic liner company surpassed that of the U.S. Navy. Very few Naval officers prior to World War II had much sea time due to the economy restrictions under which they operated. Operations were mostly confined to areas and times of the year when the seas were only moderately rough. There was no way the majority of them could understand that the one enemy you did not fight was the sea.

In the United States Lines we sailed the Northern Great Circle route to and from Europe. In the American Export Line we sailed a modified Great Circle route to Gibraltar similar to the one the Task Force was now taking. The weather that created such havoc for our Task Force would have been considered moderately rough in the American Export Line, requiring perhaps a slight reduction in speed and a change of course. Those ships were much larger than destroyers and also had much greater freeboard.

On our present assignment we proceeded in a scouting line abreast with 10 vessels, 2,500 yards apart during daylight and 10,000 yards apart during the night. We sailed ahead of an important high-speed convoy that was to follow on the same course through an area saturated with German submarines. Needless to say we hoped to make contact and destroy any submarine we discovered. The operation planners, however, must have been aware that we soon would be sighted by a submarine, and a message would be sent to keep them clear of the area or from forming to attack us.

At the same time the Hunter-Killer ASW groups, made up of one small aircraft carrier with destroyer escorts and destroyers, were, I am certain, strategically operating in adjacent areas. If we ran a good operation and the German submarines did not withdraw from the area, chances were we would make contact and engage them. If they withdrew, and the Hunter-Killer groups were well positioned, the subs would fall into their net, and at worst be in a poor situation to reposition to effectively attack the convoy, which was also being escorted.

When the Task Group Commander made a frontal attack against the sea, he lost rather than gained time. I was the first C.O. to realize the orders to maintain course and speed were impossible to carry out. It was only a question of disregarding them before I had to change course and speed after damage, or doing so before serious damage. It was not a question of wisdom but of experience.

When I reduced speed and altered course, I stayed on the bridge and worked the ship slowly and safely towards the rendezvous point. *Nelson* and those that fought the sea with the Task Group Commander fell further behind and ultimately, damaged and frustrated by a sea they could not beat, met up with the rest of the Force that had arrived at least ten hours before. If they had slowed and altered course, they would have lost less than 4 hours. Time was vital in many ways. Our lead time on the convoy was reduced unless the Task Force Commander broke radio silence and advised the Fleet Commander. I doubt he did so, and he soon increased speed to make up for lost time.

The heavy seas we fought neutralized both us and our enemies below. When the Task Force regrouped hours later, and the standard speed was increased to 16 knots and then to 17 knots, our effectiveness was reduced. Our sonar gear performed better at slower rather than higher speeds; however, we were more vulnerable at speeds under 15 knots, which was generally accepted at that time as the most suitable search and attack speed. At higher speeds our engine and screw noise negated the sonar's effectiveness.

As the voyage proceeded we were lucky we did not experience head seas and been forced to use more fuel than planned. We had no provision for fueling at sea. Tight at 15.5 knots, fuel was much more so at 17 knots. If submarines had engaged our force, and if we had to maneuver, change course, and at times go in the opposite direction, we would have run out of fuel.

The mission of Task Force 63, scouting in front of high-speed troop transports, was important. These large ships basically proceeded independently of escorts because destroyers could not keep up with them in a heavy sea. The best defense of a high-speed transport against a submarine was the transport's speed. Task Force 63, deployed well in advance of the transports, was supplemented by Hunter-Killer groups operating in the area.

At 0830 hours on April 1, 1944, we entered Rosia Channel, Gibraltar. Within two hours we were alongside a tanker replenishing our fuel. We had little reserve fuel remaining, and by 1520 hours we had received 74,235 gallons. Our rate of fuel consumption of close to 10,000 gallons a day allowed little if any time for battle or rough weather delays.

We moored alongside *Shubrick*. The ships in Gibraltar comprised various units of the U.S., British, French, Dutch, and Australian Navies, plus many merchant ships of various flags. Gibraltar was a beehive of ships moored, anchored, under way, and shifting. The port was alive.

Although our main battle was against raging seas, we had successfully completed our mission as a Task Force. As an individual ship of the task force with no casualties, *Cofer* was in excellent operating condition and ready for the next assignment. The officers and crew were untested in combat, but they were getting their feet wet and learning on the job. I was in a constant state of exhaustion. With less than 6 percent of the ship's complement having sea experience, I had to drive the crew unmercifully. At the same time I had to drive myself even more so.

I had been in Gibraltar in 1934 as a Cadet. It was a quiet and sleepy place in those days, with only a few Naval and Merchant ships in port. The one main street could hardly handle the 150 Cadets from the schoolship, and most crossed the border into Spain. LaLinea and Algeciras were close and, although small towns, were more interesting, even though Gibraltar itself was one of the great wonders of the world. I had passed by several times in late '35 and early '36 in *Excaliber*. But the Gibraltar of the '30s was quite different than the Gibraltar I saw on April 1, 1944.

As the sun set the port took on a more ominous atmosphere. Ships were darkened. Small craft moved throughout the harbor dropping small depth charges at random in defense against midget submarines, which had previously penetrated the defenses of the port. This was a Gibraltar at war, subject to attack from the air, sea, and land if Spain should unexpectedly join the Axis. With a large percentage of the crew never having experienced a foreign port other than Bermuda, Gibraltar was no morale-builder. The port, never meant to handle so many ships, was contaminated with fuel oil and refuse and had a distinct odor.

It was a long walk around the mole into the blacked-out one-street town. Honky-tonk nightclubs featured women musicians, but few free women were around. It was mostly a male town, and the general pastime was to get drunk.

One could walk around the unrestricted areas of the fortress. Not too far away but across the Straits was the fascinating but still dangerous city of Tangiers with its Casbah. The ferry operated, but I doubt if there were passes for military personnel. Gibraltar stood as an island surrounded in part by the sea, the other part by inaccessible land.

One night I went out with McLees and several other officers to eat and drink. If it was not fun it was at least a change and a chance to let off some steam. We were all in our service dress blue uniforms. On the return to the ship we walked with military bearing around the mole to our ship. In order to board we had to first walk over the gangplank to *Shubrick,* and then jump three or four feet from the quarterdeck of *Shubrick* to the quarterdeck of *Cofer.* Protocol called for the Captain to board first and the other officers to follow in order of rank. We were all a bit drunk and tried to make a good impression on the OOD of *Shubrick* and his quarterdeck watch. I walked straight across the quarterdeck and jumped. McLees, maintaining a military bearing as he walked, neither looked down nor jumped. He fell into the filthy water. Suddenly quarterdeck watches of *Cofer* and *Shubrick* mobilized to try and rescue McLees before he was overcome by the stench. One drink of that water would probably kill him.

They fished him out with boat hooks and lines. Some sailors were lowered by line to help pull him up. When they dragged him out of the water, he looked like a drowned rat. His uniform had already started to shrink, and if it were not so sad a situation, I would have laughed. He looked like a cartoon drawing of a Naval Officer sired by Donald Duck.

He had no other service dress blue uniform. The little dunking had not only shrunk his pockets but put a dent in his bankroll. McLees had gone ashore as a model of a U.S. Navy officer and had returned as something indescribable. I was a bit drunk myself and went right to my cabin once I knew Mac was not about to die. The next day McLees was not only the talk of the ship but the talk of DesRon 17 and Cortdiv 52.

At 0434 hours the night of April 6 we set special sea details for getting under way. Rain poured down, full gale winds buffeted us, and our mooring position made departure nearly impossible. Off our bow was one nest of destroyers, astern was another. Essentially *Cofer* lay in the bottom of a U. I had to breast the bow or the stern out at least 60 degrees to either back out or go forward. A forward departure would place the propellers in a precarious position. My only maneuver was to breast the stern out by going forward on the number two spring line. Then I used the screws to maneuver into position to go astern into clear water and then come ahead.

With ships anchored all around I could not back out at high speed without taking a chance of colliding with one of them. Each time I started ahead on the engines while holding the number two line fast as I moved the stern out, the wind just blew it back down. It was a nightmare. Visibility was poor, and I was not about to swing the stern out, let go the lines, and be at the mercy of the wind in so confined a situation. I hated to request a tug, but I felt discretion was the better part of valor.

The winds moderated before the tug arrived. With its assistance I cleared the ship and finally sailed from Gibraltar. If the winds had not died down, I don't believe even with the tug I could have cleared the other ships. This type of situation weights heavily on the Captain. Most of the crew did not understand the complexity of the situation nor did the Task Group Commander, who was in a less difficult position.

Prior to departure I spent hours reading Op Orders and going over plans for escorting the convoy. I also addressed numerous problems and details concerning the ship and the crew. At 0700 hours on April 6 we departed from Point Europa in accordance with FOGMA Secret Orders No. S.0. 0728/44 or 5 April/44 en route from Gibraltar to Hampton Roads, Virginia. Dark had descended by the time we formed up, and all ships were darkened. As usual forming up was messy. The escorts constantly changed courses and speeds as they patrolled their area, making sonar and radar sweeps for enemy submarines while at the same time herding the convoy as one would sheep. We were like little dogs running around our flock.

The convoy of between 70 and 100 ships set its speed at that of the slowest ship. The forming-up period usually offers a good opportunity for a submarine to get into the middle of a convoy and effectively sink many ships. At 2105 hours *Nelson* reported a sound contact, and we went to General Quarters. Some 15 minutes later the contact was classified as non-sub, and we returned to war cruising conditions.

This was *Cofer's* first experience as part of the screen of a major convoy. You can't really learn the technique until you have been part of one. I had been involved in several convoys in the Caribbean and the Pacific, but the huge transatlantic convoys proceeding through the submarine-infested shipping lanes were in a class all to themselves.

Many Captains and Mates sailing in the fast expanding Allied Merchant Marine were even less experienced than their Navy counterparts. Masters were sailing on Second Mate's Licenses. Some ships had language problems and resistance to the discipline for keeping station, or being unable to do so. We had to keep the convoy closed up.

DEs gradually became a serious force in the Battle of the Atlantic. Ace U-Boat Captains were having their subs sunk. Although new U-Boats were much better, the quality of their Captains and crews deteriorated as the British and U.S. anti-submarine forces improved. Our Task Force was a formidable adversary. The U-Boats had to know we were on the voyage east, but they chose not to engage us. Their primary mission was to sink loaded merchant ships, yet early in the war they frequently and often successfully attacked escorts.

On the 7th three ships from the Casablanca section joined GUS (Gibraltar U.S. Convoy) 35. At 0700 hours the convoy maneuvered into a broad front formation, and at 0730 hours the Casablanca section was on station.

During all of this time the escorts dashed around the convoy in their allotted area, making sonar sweeps, going through drills, passing messages to ships in the convoy, and mail between escorts. The seas were rough. We rolled and pitched on various courses and speeds while patrolling our area. Even though the convoy speed was only 9 knots, our scouting speed was around 15 knots. In patrolling our sector I never followed any routine pattern and constantly altered my methods within the scope of the requirements for sonar coverage. The flying bridge was high and unshielded from the weather. We steered from the wheelhouse one deck below. Sonar operators were in an enclosed shack a half deck below and forward of the bridge but with access from the bridge. The constant pinging of the sonar was as regular as the whine of the engines and the noises emanating from the guns as they were exercised.

Abaft the wheelhouse was the CIC where the overall plot of the convoy, escorts, and any known vessels as well as skunks and bogeys (possible enemy craft or aircraft) was kept. Primitive when compared to a CIC room today, it was very advanced for its time.

This Task Group was the "big time" in ASW. Although we had worked like the devil in *Daly,* and suffered in *SC 981,* this was the major leagues of ASW, and one felt the pressure. We knew subs were all around us. We did not know when, where, and if they were going to attack, but we had to be ready at anytime. The loss of even seconds in establishing contact and responding quickly could mean dire consequences. The log books reflect constant drilling during this voyage, and the performance of the crew improved quickly. I could tell they were acclimated to their surroundings and the job at hand. They hardly thought of the "great cause," and were totally concerned with their little world and the necessity of doing their job and surviving. Great progress was made in creating a camaraderie and a feeling of mutual dependence and an attachment for the cold piece of steel called *Cofer.* I would give them their times and results of each drill, and the bitching disappeared, for they were determined to improve their performance.

This was of the greatest satisfaction, but it was slowly killing me. I was constantly fatigued. The long hours I stood on the steel decks of the bridge holding on resulted in varicose veins, piles, and constipation. But I could not leave the bridge when I needed to, only when the situation could spare me.

My room, the biggest on the ship, was the only one of its kind with a private shower and head. But it was a cubbyhole with no portholes and a ventilation system that seemed to circulate the odors from the magazines.

The noise never stopped. As the ship made frequent course changes, I was tossed about my bunk when I tried to sleep. I became so sensitive to the ship that I could tell when a few revolutions of the screws were put on or taken off. What few realize is that officers and crew can relax when off watch, while a Captain is never off duty. The pressure never ceases.

I so rarely left the bridge I never used my sea cabin abaft of the wheelhouse. Actually it could be more difficult to get to the bridge from there than from the stateroom. I had to go on the weather deck first, while I could get to the bridge without going outside the stateroom, and it was only one ladder further up. Various ships of the screen constantly made sonar contacts, and each one required all escort ships to go to General Quarters. If I were in my stateroom working on the never-ending paperwork or resting, I would dash out of the room with the first "clang," not bothering to answer my phone. I would then be just another man in the crew on his way up the ladders to the bridge, being pushed and shoved around by the others in their haste to get to their battle stations. The constant noise level on a warship never ceases, and the constant pinging of the sonar creates an unconscious anticipation of the return ping each hoped for, which means contact.

On April 12 we went alongside the tanker *Escalante* to refuel. I had often done this in practice, but now was the first time we would do so at sea in a combat area. The operation was called "Daisy Chain," and we took turns falling astern of the convoy to get in position to fuel while under way at the speed of the convoy, while the other escorts covered the resulting gaps on the screen.

Fueling at sea is a complicated operation. Station must be taken close alongside the tanker, using a bow line to measure and also to assist in keeping the ship from drifting off and breaking the fuel lines. Usually stores and other items such as food are also passed over. The two ships are so close conversation is possible between the crews by yelling over the noise of the water that sloshes between the ships. Ordinarily another destroyer on the other side of the tanker is also taking on fuel. To successfully fuel at sea and to take a full drink requires a great deal of training and preparation along with techniques of seamanship peculiar to the situation.

One of the tricks is not to con the ship by telling the helmsman how much rudder to give the ship to bring her closer or move her out, because it is impossible to judge unless you are actually steering the ship yourself. I detailed the best helmsman we had, and I gave him courses in degrees instead of rudder commands. He then adjusted the amount of rudder to maintain the distance. A great deal of water was trapped between the two ships while the fueling proceeded, and at times it would take great differences of rudder to maintain the course. Only the man at the helm could determine this.

Shortly after fueling we had our first sonar contact of the voyage. As we went to General Quarters we notified OTC. We steamed at various courses and speeds investigating the contact. After classifying it as "non-sub", we returned to station, secured from General Quarters and reset War Cruising conditions. How the ship would have performed if the contact had been an attacking submarine was a matter of concern to me. This contact came during daylight hours, visibility was excellent, and the convoy makeup was better organized than during darkness and bad weather.

GUS 35 covered many square miles of ocean. It was my first experience in a large Atlantic convoy. To surveil it on the radar PPI scope with enough definition between returns, it was necessary to use the shortest scale. Definition on this scale was difficult in a rough sea. Merchant ships in the convoy did not have radar; their position-keeping was by sight, which was difficult at night. Further many watch keepers aboard the merchant ships had limited experience; even experienced Masters and Mates, whose backgrounds were mostly gained in independent steaming in open seas, found it difficult to adjust.

To provide tighter escort screening within the capacity of the sonar ranges, or as close to it as possible, the Escort Commander constantly pressured the Convoy Commodore to keep the convoy closed up. At the same time the Masters and Mates aboard the individual ships, constantly in fear of collision with another ship, tended to loosen up, thus increasing the distances between them. This was a normal reaction. Often the individual ships found it difficult to maintain base courses and speeds and to react in concert to course changes that might be directed. These large Atlantic convoys were a phenomenon of the time, the largest forces ever spread out over so wide an expanse of the seas. Although the enemy was the major concern, collisions were not uncommon, and close calls were numerous. Engine breakdowns were frequent. Steering casualties, together with the simple lapses in watch disciplines, constantly added to the peril of the sea itself.

Problems within the convoy complicated those of the escort. Often they had to leave their station, with the resultant screening sonar break, to attempt to solve problems within the convoy, deliver messages, rearrange ship positions, cover stragglers, and many other things. Most of these operations, in addition to the primary duties, demanded training and experience.

I had been at sea and in command long enough to learn there was a great deal I should know that I didn't. GUS 35, whether attacked or not, was not a simple cruise at sea. Each ship of the convoy and each escort was a problem. Collectively there were about 100 ships involved. My job was to be sure *Cofer* was able to carry out its mission, and there was every reason for concern. Happily, Oksala was the Chief Engineer. But he too had his problems. The experience level in the engineering department by and large was no better than that of the overall ship. Oksala was working himself to death and rarely emerged from his engine room. I was the beneficiary of this and thus could concentrate on the problems of the other departments that did not have experienced officers in charge. With the constant drilling, plus the excellent work of a small core of inexperienced officers and enlisted men performing far above their level of experience, I felt we were slowly making progress.

Shortly before midnight on April 12 while on station escorting Convoy GUS 35 in a rough sea, and less than three months since commissioning, our proficiency was put to a test. This was not on a 90-day Officers Training School, nor at SCTC, nor during a shakedown. It was on the job in a real situation at sea under wartime conditions. *Cofer* was pitching and rolling heavily as it changed courses in its search patterns while I dozed fitfully in my berth conscious of the ship's motion, the pinging of the sound gear, and the whine of the turbines.

Suddenly the telephone in my room rang simultaneously with the loud clanging of the General Quarters Alarm. Just seconds before, aside from the watch section, all those off duty had been mostly in their bunks. Within seconds every man on the ship was dashing to his assigned battle station, watertight doors were closed, and the ship readied for action. I did not bother to answer the phone, and instead jumped out of my bunk and rushed to the bridge. We all slept in our clothes under wartime conditions, and after pushing and shoving myself, unidentified among many others rushing to their stations in the dark, I arrived on the bridge within seconds.

It was a moonless night, the wind howling, and orders were being given by both the senior and junior officer of the watch while information was being shouted to them from radar and sonar operators. The officers did not immediately recognize my presence on the bridge. In the darkness all I could see were shapes moving around and hear conflicting orders. The bridge watch officers were in a state of confusion. Action was being taken on the basis of radar and sonar information individually without visual verification. I could not see anything, but my instinct told me that the bridge and the ship were basically out of control. I heard things such as, "prepare to ram a submarine on the surface," as well as, "prepare to fire depth charges, and hedgehogs." Later I was told the OOD also had the torpedoes swung out and ready for firing. I shouted out, "belay all orders," and then ordered the ship to turn away from the base course of the convoy. Suddenly quiet descended on the bridge and attention was turned to me while I peered into the darkness.

Within one minute I saw a large merchant ship we had been on a collision course with and were just clearing within a few hundred yards by the course change. The lookout, McBride, had seen the ship before me, and was tugging on Lt. Cofer's sleeve to report to him that we were about to ram a ship, only to be told to be quiet while Lt. Cofer requested permission to fire torpedoes. Cushman was standing at the sound shack hatch saying, "if anyone is interested, I have a sound contact." He did, but it was a merchant ship and not a submarine. Other than I witnessed complete confusion and immediately, on intuition alone, turned *Cofer* away from the base course of the convoy, much of the information was supplied or confirmed by crew members many years later.

My instinct was the result of long years of experience that cannot be learned in school. This was not in a classroom where, if a mistake were made, it could be analyzed. The problem developed in a matter of seconds with a radar and a sound contact, which were real, but without visual conformation. The reaction to bring the ship to General quarters was correct, but merchant ships often fall out of formation and separate themselves from the convoy. Lt. Cofer was and should have been prepared for each contingency, but the OOD failed in not first evaluating the situation and determining what he was coping with. The first thing he should have done was to turn away from a course intercepting the convoy base course. This was the course he was on when I arrived on the bridge, and which I altered promptly.

Lt, Cofer, the Officer of the Deck, did not have sufficient experience to cope with the situation. A sonar contact was what every ASW officer prayed for, and rarely experienced. He was so intent on making an attack he failed to realize an escort should never place itself on a collision course with the base course of the convoy unless the distance separating them is great and the visibility clear. He simply lost control of the situation. My experience enabled me to promptly react when I noted the collision course. I turned the ship away on instinct, which only comes from experience. All this transpired on the flying bridge. By the time the Task Group Commander reacted, noting the collision course, the crisis was over. The total time between the report of contact and my belaying of all orders while I turned the ship away from the base course was about two minutes.

It is difficult for those who have never made "quick decisions" involving many lives to understand such a situation. *Cofer* was basically a steel hull loaded with ammunition and people. If we had not altered course, we would have rammed, torpedoed, and shot at the errant ship. If we had failed to blow ourselves up in that manner, the ship would have stopped when it hit the tanker.

I was discouraged by the failure of the watch officers to respond professionally, but there were offsetting circumstances. It was too much to expect in the time period, but the enlisted personnel and the off-watch officers performed very well. I was shaken up by it all. I realized I too had failed the test. And so as this convoy sailed west, I increased the drills and the training, bearing down harder on myself than anyone else. The incidents and the problems continued but none were important. As we proceeded onwards we were ordered to protect stragglers as merchant ships encountered engine problems. One was *Linda* and again there was another lapse. After many hours on the bridge, I went below for a catnap. I first cautioned Lt. Cofer about the importance of staying with her. When I returned to the bridge, she was nowhere to be seen. I was afraid she had been sunk, which luckily she wasn't. A Navy blimp found her and took over the escort.

On April 21 the convoy's Norfolk group was detached and we proceeded with the New York section, mooring at Pier C, berth 3 in Brooklyn Navy Yard the following day. *Cofer* had thus completed its first operational voyage. Considering the inexperience of the officers and crew, it was quite an accomplishment, but it did not come without sacrifice from those few who made up for what others lacked. I expected orders to shore duty because the battering I was taking on the small ships was physically as well as mentally brutal. I had averaged less than four hours of sleep a night since I boarded *SC 981*.

Even being promoted to Lcdr. and receiving the back pay that went with it failed to lift my spirits. My pay was now about $460 a month, very high when compared to the pay of the lower petty officer ratings, but low when compared to Merchant Marine pay. I was qualified to sit for my Master's

License, and could have had a pick of jobs. A Master's pay was well over $1,000 a month with bonuses. Ginny and I were still poor in money.

Ordinarily my promotion to Lcdr. at age 28 would have been a cause for celebration, but the papers came at the same time we were deluged with work orders for alterations. This was followed by a multitude of workers who disrupted our lives aboard ship to such an extent that I granted most of the officers and men the maximum amount of leave and liberty. Within hours they were scattered over many states. Those of us who remained were inundated with work, and most of the officers moved to quarters ashore. We had been at war only two-and-a-half-years, but it seemed like forever.

I don't believe anyone even noticed I had added a half stripe. I simply sent my blue uniforms out to have it added and bought new shoulder boards with two and a half stripes in addition to the metal collar insignias. No longer one of many Lts. in *Cofer,* I was now the only Lcdr. I had been a Lt. only about 20 months, but it seemed like an eternity.

Oksala and I decided to remain in New York during the overhaul. *Cofer* had arrived in New York with all equipment in working order and ready to return to sea. She was squared away. Now together with the rest of CortDiv 52 she was being torn apart, with many alterations and modifications being made. While Oksala and I attempted to keep up with the changes, the yard workers worked in shifts 24 hours a day.

During my short excursions ashore, I came in contact with "heroes" for the first time. They even had the look of heroes, playing the part to the hilt in New York. Some spent short periods at sea, but many had the security of an indispensable assignment ashore. New York during the spring of 1944 was a great playground. Women outnumbered men by at least three to one, and everything and anything was available. Unfortunately it was not my New York that spring; my war, whether in part or afloat, was quite different from that of the heroes on duty in New York. Most of us had a tired, worn-out look and had to some extent lost contact with the realities of civilization.

I went ashore the night before completion of the work, with the ship still jammed full of laborers. The Exec and many other officers and crew were due back that night. As the C.O. I had to leave my telephone number with *Cofer's* OOD at all times when I was off the ship. About midnight as I was just falling asleep, I received a call from the Duty Officer of the Navy Yard who said if I did not get back to the ship immediately, they could not complete their work prior to the scheduled sailing time. He went into no details. Realizing I would not be returning ashore, I quickly gathered my gear, and within an hour was at the ship's gangway. I was met there my the Navy Yard Duty Officer, the Yard Superintendent in charge of the work, and the OOD.

I was promptly informed that about two hours earlier the Exec had returned to the ship, having left a clean ship and returning to a mess. He had been drinking, and when he saw all the workmen banging away he lost control. Loading his 45 he emerged from his room yelling at the yard workmen to get off his ship. Neither the ship's OOD, the other officers on board, nor the yard officials were able to restrain him. As I entered the wardroom the Exec was sitting on the deck with tears in his eyes.

When he saw me he started to cry and point out the mess all around him. When I helped him to stand up and moved him towards his room and bunk he did not resist. Within minutes he was asleep, and the workers returned. Needless to say I got very little sleep that night. I had headaches and found sleep difficult in general. As bad as things were I could not think of a place I would rather be. I loved the ship, the job, and the challenge, but how long could I cope with it?

One of *Cofer's* major installations during modification was a High Frequency Radio Direction Finder (HFDF) known as "HuffDuff." This system, developed by the Royal Navy, could intercept high frequency transmissions from German submarines and instantaneously get a bearing on them. Submarine radio transmissions were infrequent and of short duration, their frequencies changed often. These installations were expensive, the intensive training of the operators costly. Due to the cost only a few ships received the equipment. The main objective was to get bearings at different angles so an accurate fix of a sub's position could be made.

As the C.O. I only received an operational briefing. Those working alongside the HFDF operators in the CIC room were never able to discuss anything about the operation with shipmates. It was all part of an improved, sophisticated system finally coming together to alter the odds in the Battle of the Atlantic.

We did not deploy immediately for another transatlantic convoy, but instead were ordered to proceed with the rest of CortDiv 52 and with ComCortDiv 52 in *U.S.S. Jordan (DE-204)* to Casco Bay, Maine. ComCortDiv 52 was under the command of Commander C. (Joe) Simmers, Naval Academy Class of '32. He was a hail-fellow well-met type and friendly to me; we too had been in the same group at SCTC.

Once again it was to sea after another major cleanup required from a yard alteration and repair. It seemed as though each time we struggled and finally got the ship squared away and cleaned up, yard workers would come aboard and mess us up again. It was not difficult to understand the frustration of the Exec with the yard workmen even though he was drunk at the time. I gather all of the officers and crew felt the same way, but showed more restraint and less emotion. This frustration, however, retards training and hurts morale.

The operations order that directed ComCortDiv 52 to Casco Bay for further training hardly made much sense. A shakedown and only one transatlantic trip should have indicated events were in the works that might alter the CortDiv's future employment. We had no knowledge of the pending invasion of Normandy scheduled for mid-June; or the invasion of the south of France which, if successful, would result in many of the vessels now in the Atlantic being deployed to the Pacific.

On May 4 we made an uneventful voyage with the rest of our division to Casco Bay and moored alongside *U.S.S. Denebola,* the Flagship of ComDesLant. On May 6 we went to sea for training exercises with other ships, but had to abort due to heavy fog. No further exercises were scheduled, and on May 8 we departed at 0751 for Yorktown, Virginia, in company with ComCortDiv 52 plus *U.S.S. Garfield Thomas (DE-193), U.S.S. Eisner (DE-192), U.S.S. Jenks (DE-665),* and Com Task Force 63 in *U.S.S. MacLeish (DE-220).* Heading south we carried out gunnery exercises, firing many rounds from all guns, calibrated our HFDF, and exercised in various formations with the other ships.

We arrived at Yorktown on the morning of May 10, docking at the Mine Depot to replace depth charges. Then we proceeded to Pier 5 of the Naval Operating Base, Norfolk. On May 11 we received a resupply of all ammunition expended. On May 12 Ensign Hibbard Stubbs, USN, reported on board as Assistant Engineering Officer, relieving Lt(jg) Lipovski who had been transferred in New York.

After all this activity of a non-operational nature, we finally were under way again, shifting to an anchorage in Lynhaven Roads in preparation to make up and escort Convoy UGS 42. On May 13 at 0332 hours we were under way as a unit of TF63 with UGS 42 as Task Force 63 consisting of our CortDiv 52, including *Eisner, Garfield Thomas, Winfield, Thornhill,* and *Rinehart.* With CTF 63 embarked in *Macleish (DD-220).* Also in the Task Force was the French *De Marocain (T-21)* and *Cowanesque (AO-79).*

With about 100 vessels the speed of advance was set at only 8 knots to start, and the course was easterly at 113 degrees. We were told the convoy

211

ahead of us had been hit hard. Even as the speed of advance was increased to 9.5 knots, we were still a sitting duck for any aggressive group of submarines. This time we were proceeding into the Mediterranean as far east as Bizerte.

The Convoy Commodore was in *Hoegh Silvercloud,* a Norwegian cargo ship. Our escort stations were constantly changed, and drills continued as we diligently patrolled our sectors. We were deployed to escort *S.S. Felix Grundy,* which was joining UGS 42 from Bermuda. We were also to protect *S.S. Winfield Smith,* which was dead in the water while making engine repairs. This was always a dangerous situation, but we aggressively steamed around the ship, pinging constantly for any sign of a sub. When repairs were completed, we brought her back safely into the convoy without incident.

We concentrated on anti-aircraft defense. Once in the Med we would be within range of German bomber and torpedo aircraft. On May 18 we fueled at sea from *Cowanesque.* Our sistership, *Newman,* while fueling on the other side of the tanker at the same time, collided with the tanker several times and sustained heavy damage, although she was able to continue carrying out her escort duties. It was an awful feeling to hear her bouncing off the other side of the tanker as our fueling progressed routinely.

On May 18 we were assigned to station 13 in the screen where we remained until the 27th of May. Even with this unlucky number, no submarine tried to penetrate our sector. The days went by. We rocked and rolled, investigated contacts, drilled, drilled, and drilled some more. We plodded along like some huge island adrift; it seemed impossible we were not attacked. Well escorted, it was still an imperfect screen and there were chances for a daring submarine captain to pierce it. The escorts aggressively patrolled, and submarines apparently were not interested in engaging DEs.

On May 22 the Azores Group was detached and escorted into port, and we fueled again without incident from *Cowanesque.* We had reached the stage of training where I even allowed some of the officers to take turns at conning the ship while fueling. Training was coming along, but a problem was building.

Given the many escorts in so large a convoy covering so wide an expanse of water, it was not unusual for one or more of the escorts including *Cofer* to make a visual, sonar, or radar contact. If the visual and radar contact were non-aircraft and distant, General Quarters was not sounded. A sonar contact made by any ship in the escort required all escort ships to go to G.Q. even though the contact might have been miles away. It could

212

be a wolf pack submarine attack in force from all quarters. Add the sonar to the other contacts requiring the ships going to battle stations, and the rare periods of relaxation available to the crew were often interrupted.

With the first sound of the G.Q alarm, all hands would respond with great anxiety and anticipation. Their juices would flow. Sometimes a half hour would pass before the contact was determined non-threatening. Operating in a heavy combat area, and particularly as I was driving them unmercifully to make up for their inexperience, my officers and men began to wonder if the war supposedly going on all around them was real.

Contact with the enemy ordinarily meant sinkings and death. Our force's lack of familiarity with this horror could result in reacting inadequately if we actually did come under attack. Basically the fact we were not attacked and delivered our convoys without losses meant we were doing something right. We still needed some incident to recreate the urgency and importance of our mission. It was also required for my own morale. No one could have prepared harder for so long, and commanded in heavy combat area as I had, and still have no close combat contact. I had not failed in any mission, nor had I lost any of the ships I protected or my own people. Yet I continued to sense this ship would experience heavy combat. I had a compulsion to continue the Spartan training, but could I without getting the opposite result unless something occurred to inspire the crew and myself? I prayed for it.

At 0535 hours on May 25 we made surface radar contact at 17.5 miles bearing 125 degrees. I jumped out of my bunk, rushed to the bridge, and requested and received permission to investigate the contact. I set a course to intercept, maintaining a sonar efficient sped of 15 plus knots. I felt this would be something special and the answer to my prayers, but that I should proceed with caution. By 0555 hours I brought the ship to G.Q. and told the crew this was no drill—they were to prepare for both surface and ASW action.

By 0615 hours we identified the contact as a large sailing vessel. This might have added up during World War I, but not in 1944. Intrigued by this ghost ship of the past, I still realized I had to be cautious. My immediate thoughts were of *Seeadler,* the World War I raider commanded by Count Von Luckner. But romance of the sea was one thing, the reality of the present another. As we drew closer I mentally listed the possibilities about the nature of her voyage.

First I considered whether she was on a routine commercial voyage. But with my Merchant Marine experience, I could not conceive of any economic shipping category she could fit into. Sailing vessels as cargo carriers just did not make sense any longer. If she were on innocent passage, she would ordinarily be in possession of a NaviCert issued by an Allied Agent or Consul who had observed the loading operations prior to departure, and certified the departure time, course, cargo, and destination. This still required boarding for checking, but was an alternative to redirecting the ship into a friendly or neutral port for checking.

Most U.S. Naval Officers were not aware of this procedure, which was originated by the British during WW I. However I had studied my new business very thoroughly. I also was aware from reading intelligence information that the German Navy was resupplying and refueling their submarines at sea in various ways.

I also was aware of the possibility of a submarine lurking near a ship of innocent nature and using it as a decoy for some unsuspecting escort that might stop to board without ensuring no submarine was within range. Many other things went through my mind as we circled, searched, and closed in on the target. We identified her as the Portuguese Barque *Foz Do Douoro*.

It was a calm and beautiful morning, and after satisfying myself no submarines were within range, I slowed a bit as I came closer. With the "bull horn" asked if they had a NaviCert. No response. Something was strange. A few crew members were visible on deck. They seemed to be ignoring our guns and torpedoes being trained on them as we circled.

My gut feeling was the ship was a submarine supply vessel, and she should be boarded after another submarine sweep with our sonar. Our whaleboat was swung out and all but the Boarding Officer was assigned. I hoped to find an excuse to board myself. Excitement and interest reigned in *Cofer*. Every nerve center of the ship was activated. Information was passed to the Task Force Commander, but our request to board the ship was denied. I was ordered to return at high speed to my station in the convoy. In frustration I made one last sonar sweep around the vessel, secured from General Quarters, and returned to our station.

If we had not taken pictures of this large Barque in the middle of the Atlantic, I might have remembered the incident as a dream. She was real, and for over an hour the morale in *Cofer* was raised. The basic mission of the Task Force Commander was to protect the convoy. One possibility was that many submarines were in the area waiting to fuel, and he considered a tight screen more important than *Foz Do Douro* and whatever its employment. I never found out. So we proceeded expecting action, but nothing, while the convoys before and after us were attacked. It was eerie.

We neared Gibraltar on May 27. Convoy and escort ships were detached to nearby ports such as Casablanca. Ships also joined up as we proceeded into the Mediterranean with the main elements of the escort and convoy still in place. I was told that ordinarily the Royal Navy handled most of the escorting within the Med, and we were either the first or one of the first of UGS escort groups not to terminate in Gibraltar.

In addition to the submarine threat, most of the trip from Gibraltar to Bizerte would be made within the range of German land-based bombers and torpedo planes. "Condition One Easy," to repel air, surface, and submarine attacks was one step below General Quarters, but allowed the crew, except those active on War Cruising, to relax to the point of sleeping at their G.Q. stations. All our guns were dual purpose, and we were an effective anti-aircraft defense ship except against high altitude bombers. Enemy aircraft were very active all around us.

On May 28, moving into the Med, complete overcast reduced our visibility to under 400 yards. Convoy maneuvers were difficult. At one point we had to execute a 45-degree turn to avoid a westbound convoy. This is not a simple maneuver for merchant ships in convoy and can result in collisions. The poor visibility was a good tactical situation for the submarines but a bad one for aircraft. As we proceeded the Med was alive with Allied shipping, but there was no sign of the enemy, which had been active up until the time of our entry into the Med. The overcast weather continued.

Our first radar contact with German aircraft came on May 30. We went from Condition One Easy to General Quarters. A number of bogeys appeared on the radar coming in but were not visible. Only slightly overcast at that moment, orders were given to "make smoke." We had smoke generators on the stern, and we went to flank speed as we engulfed our section of the convoy in a smoke screen as did the other escorts in their sections.

This maneuver must have succeeded for the enemy planes, unable to drive home their attack, departed. Our guns were not radar directed, and since we could not see the planes, none of the ships opened fire on them. On the 31st sonar detected a floating derelict, which the TFC ordered us to depth charge and sink. We did. Not much action in an area ordinarily in constant combat. Later on the 31st enemy planes caused a Red Alert, which downgraded to Condition White (all clear), then upgraded to Condition Yellow (enemy aircraft in the vicinity), and then, as the planes took off in another direction, another "all clear." Obviously they were looking for us.

215

The Germans would engage if they could find us. They're planes, however, did not have too much range.

On 1 June the landing craft we were escorting, part of the Eighth Amphibious Force, were ordered to proceed independently to a destination not known to us. The remainder of the convoy proceeded with us to Bizerte. Our Task Force had delivered all of its convoy safely over thousands of miles of the Atlantic and the Mediterranean. By 1500 hours on 1 June the last of our charges entered port. We were relieved of further duties and proceeded into the Baie de Bizerte. It was a difficult entry because the harbor was a conglomeration of wrecks and scuttled ships with only the masts showing. We anchored for the night.

On the morning 2 June we shifted to a berth and moored at the Carriers Dock in Goulet DuLac, Bizerte, Tunis. Taut port security watches were set since small pockets of resistance were still active. The port and surrounding area was a shambles. Little had been left standing after the hard-fought battles had ceased. There were no signs of rebuilding, and, aside from a small unfriendly officer's club, there was nothing in the way of amusement for the crew. I made a short, dangerous night trip in a jeep to Tunis, but discovered my hosts were bedbugs. I quickly returned to the ship and deloused myself.

While in Bizerte we were unaware of the important events about to take place, which ultimately occurred prior to our departure. On 6 June the Allies launched their successful invasion of Normandy. We experienced no unusual air activity on the ships or in the port. What German aircraft were left were recalled to oppose the landing. By the time we sailed to start the return trip, we were aware an invasion was taking place but were given few details. This was a world war, but participants were cognizant only of the area they happened to be in. We would get news reports of the war in the Pacific and on shore in Europe, but we had all we could do to concentrate on the war we could see and touch.

On 10 June we departed from the berth and deployed to make up Convoy GUS-42, which would terminate in Norfolk. The escort remained the same. The Convoy Commodore was in *S.S. Johns Hopkins,* and by evening the convoy was formed up and moving westward. It was essentially more of the same in a different direction. In the Med ships joined and left the convoy as we proceeded. They came and went from places such as Algiers and Oran, and our tanker, *Cowanesque,* joined up. By 14 June we passed Gibraltar, detaching some ships and receiving others. We were ordered alongside *British Commodore* to receive a confidential envelope for *Joseph Hewes,* which was scheduled to join the convoy off the Azores. On

216

15 June, after having cleared the Med with no attacks, we were joined by the Casablanca contingent. Our transit of the Atlantic was under way.

The Normandy invasion created various deployments of Mediterranean German forces and the submarines assigned to the Battle of the Atlantic. This probably contributed to making our westbound passage somewhat free of enemy contact. The German High Command probably concentrated on the North Atlantic convoys bound east in an effort to curtail the logistical support of the invading forces in the North.

We did not relax as we proceeded west. On 17 June we again fueled from *Cowanesque*. The next day *Joseph Hewes*, out of Horta in the Azores, joined up, and we delivered the confidential message. On the 23rd we fueled again from *Cowanesque* and on the 26th *Cowanesque* deployed for Bermuda. On the evening of the same day, we investigated a contact, which turned out to be a straggler from Convoy 126.

On the 27th an uneventful crossing came to its conclusion. The convoy was divided between New York and the Chesapeake Bay area. After escorting the Chesapeake group to the harbor entrance, we were detached and ordered to make a full power trial run to New York. At 1311 hours on 19 June we anchored in Sandy Hook Bay, New York, awaiting orders.

Shortly after anchoring we received orders to discharge all our ammunition at the Naval Ammunition Depot in Sandy Hook Bay. There was an urgency about this operation. After the docking at the depot at 1611 hours, work commenced immediately. We completed the discharge and departed for an anchorage in Gravesend Bay for the night, with orders to berth at Pier 2 Todd shipyard in the Erie Basin, Brooklyn.

We docked in Todd early the next morning. Then I was first informed the ship was to be converted to a new class of destroyer-transport for duty in the Pacific. I was heartbroken, even though I expected I would receive shore duty orders shortly. I had worked myself to the limit to make *Cofer* the best destroyer escort in the fleet. Oksala and I had taken a completely inexperienced crew and brought them along very fast. With few exceptions it had become an outstanding group of officers and men.

I had hoped to convince Oksala to accept the assignment of Executive Officer. Things did not work out that way. Okie reacted to the strain of the job differently than I. On arrival in New York he had a severe case of shingles, which required hospitalization.

I saw no point in taking him out of the frying pan and putting him into the fire. We again discussed the matter before he left for the hospital, and he reiterated his desire to rise in rank in engineering. He asked my help in having him assigned to a large combat ship. I was able to arrange this through friends. But I was still stuck with the problem of the Exec. The only way I could transfer him off the ship without hurting his career or taking pot luck with a stranger being assigned was by promoting Charles Cofer to Executive Officer. It would have been fitting for a Cofer to command *Cofer,* but Lt. Cofer was not qualified yet, nor were any of the other officers.

Walter Meredith, the next senior officer after Cofer, Sam Cleland, Will Hahn, and Henry Peters all had made tremendous progress. All qualified as top watch officers. Meredith was excellent command potential, as were Cleland, Hahn, and Peters. Each of these four were capable of standing top watch and heading any department other than engineering. Bernard Mazer was a young, bright officer but very junior.

It was not long before *Cofer* was again inundated with a yard work force of men and women on a 24-hour basis. Temporary quarters were arranged for the crew at a Naval facility at Lido Beach, L.I., and Annex A, Flushing Naval Receiving Station, Brooklyn. The ship was not decommissioned during this major conversion, and OOD and gangway watches had to be maintained although no facilities for berthing and eating would be available aboard the ship. Todd's provided a temporary ship's office in an adjacent warehouse. I received information about the future of the ship in bits and pieces. I was ordered to meet with Rear Admiral Rockwell, Commander of Amphibious Training Forces Atlantic, in Norfolk. He had received a special request from high authority that this first division of 5-inch-gunned APDs be commanded by the most experienced officers available. I had been specifically requested.

Admiral Rockwell was aware of my declining health and long overdue shore duty. But he said the urgency and importance of the new division's mission overruled everything. I returned to New York somewhat discouraged, but the challenge of the new job intrigued me.

I told Ginny I would be in New York for awhile, and she came for the summer. Although it would be impossible for me to take an extended leave, I decided to study for and take my Master's License Exam while I was in New York. Ginny soon found a small apartment on the west side of Manhattan. As exhausted as I was, I set a very demanding routine for myself. I worked all day in the yard and office and studied each night for a few hours after dinner. I had no trouble getting my qualifications accepted by the USCG.

Going to the cram school set up by the Maritime Commission did not allow me the time required to surveil the conversion and oversee the administration of the officers and crew. Working out of a loft in a warehouse was no sinecure, and the morale I had so carefully built up in this short time just no longer existed.

The Torpedo Division Officer and men left when the torpedoes did. In their place we received a Boat Officer and division. We were transferred from the administration of ComdesLant to ComPhibPac. Destroyers were the elite, and the amphibious forces were considered at the other end of the ladder. Although I tried to explain we would work mostly as a destroyer and only as a transport when troops were aboard, not one officer or man was happy with the situation. The new Boat Division Officer, though excellent, was ostracized with the men in his division. Once I completed my studies my routine during the exam would change. I would be in the examining room of the Coast Guard all day, and then go to the loft at night to catch up on work and sign papers.

Although I was physically qualified for a wartime commission, I realized I would never be able to pass a Regular Navy physical for peacetime. I needed the Master's License in case I returned to the Merchant Marine. It was the highest certificate in my profession, and whether used or not, I wanted to cap off what I had started.

At this time in my life I had long overcome my aversion for study. I had an unusually good memory if not a photographic one. Ginny worked with me as I memorized all the formulas, Rules of the Road, and regulations. The Chief Examiner, a Commander, revalidated my credentials. I reported to the Examiner, a Lcdr. in the USCG. In his mid-40s and a graduate of NYSMMA, he made me stand in front of him each time I had to answer his questions.

With a war on and a severe shortage of licensed officers, only one other officer was taking a Master's exam in New York. His name was George Bornkessel. A graduate of NYSMMA also, Class of '37, he was sailing as a Chief Officer in the United Fruit Company. He was a large man, extremely bright and friendly. The Examiner, Class of '18, was a large man, fat, and ruddy complexioned. He was plainly uncivil and did everything possible to be sure that George and I flunked. The examination took between 8 and 15 working days depending on the speed of the candidates.

The rules allowed us to use the latest navigation tables, but he removed them and insisted we work each navigation problem using the Cosine Haversine Formula from which the tables were derived. Fortunately I had left nothing to chance and memorized them. So had George. Seating us at opposite sides of the room and not allowing us to bring anything into the examination room precluded cheating. The more I thwarted his efforts to flunk me, the redder his face became and the more impolite he grew. The more I controlled my demeanor, the more he felt uncomfortable in his Coast Guard uniform next to mine of equal rank and Commander of a combat ship in the Navy. The only thing he had and I did not was a Master's License—and he was determined I was not going to get one.

As the days passed and he saw he was losing the battle, he dragged out my written answers reciting the "Rules of the Road." This covered many pages, and there was not one error. He then lost his cool and brought me before the Chief Examiner saying it was impossible for anyone to write them without a mistake and speculated I must have cheated. I asked the Commander if he wanted me to write them again or recite them in his presence. He asked me to recite three rules, which I did without error. He looked at the Examiner, whose face was crimson, apologized to me as one officer to another. The Examiner and I returned to the Examination Room. From that time on he simply wanted to get the exam over with and me out of his way. I had beaten him. I finished the examination about two days before George, who also suffered this man and beat him. When the Examiner finally signed the paper authorizing the license, he just handed it to me. I did not even give him the satisfaction of a word. I left the room and collected my license from the Chief Examiner who congratulated me on having passed with very high grades.

It was not all congratulations on receiving a Master's License. The Director of the Maritime Commission Upgrading School somehow found me and asked me to call on him at 45 Broadway. He was furious. He said they had just about gotten rid of the Examiner when I came along and passed with high grades in record time. Now they were stuck with him. The Examiner remained in the job until he retired, although he relented some in future years under the pressure.

Having passed the examination, I went back to the grind of getting *Cofer* reorganized and ready for sea. Physically and mentally, I was a wreck. Ginny's time in New York was spoiled by my compulsion to take that exam plus the difficult situation of trying to operate a commissioned vessel from a loft. During this time *Cofer* essentially ceased to exist. In her place *APD-62* was taking form, a rather strange ship—half destroyer-escort and half high-speed transport.

Nine

War: Pacific and Philippine Sea

U.S.S. Cofer (APD-62)

Warships are expendable. Prior to our conversion two destroyer escorts we had shakedown with in Bermuda, *U.S.S. Holder* and *F.T. Senegalais,* were torpedoed. We had survived that short period in the Atlantic and Mediterranean only to be converted to a fast transport. Although the survivors of the torpedoed ships would be dispersed among many ships and stations, our crew would mainly remain a unit in a ship totally different in everything but name. In less than three months the ship was converted from a destroyer escort to a fast transport. During that time the crew was mostly separated from each other: the officers billeted in hotels, the crew housed in Brooklyn and Lido Beach, Long Island, and various Navy schools. Reorganization after the conversion would be a major undertaking.

This period was by far the longest I had been ashore since 1936 when I had worked for Thos. Cook & Sons. But rather than resting and relaxing, I was inundated with work and under constant pressure. Often the speed of work on conversion kept pace with the receipt of blueprints and plans. Problems were encountered when revisions arrived after work had been completed. *Cofer* was nearing completion earlier than the other ships in the program. Jack Gilbride, the Todd Shipyard Superintendent, was a hard working, competent man about my age. He would rise to the presidency of the company over the years, but during this time he worked twelve hours a day, seven days a week, while his crew operated around the clock. *Cofer's* decks were continually covered with workers.

By this time I had reached two important goals in my life: promotion to Lcdr. and the Master's License. But I was so involved in what was going on around me that, in reality, I was losing control. My war was centered around a little ship in Brooklyn temporarily in limbo, while the "real" war was going on in Europe and the Pacific. Hitler was on the defensive in Europe, and the days of the Third Reich were coming to and end.

In the Pacific things were improving. (I had no information about the atomic bomb.) From the urgency surrounding the work on *Cofer,* together with the nature of the conversion, an invasion of Japan was to be the objective. Every foot of territory taken from the Japanese was at a heavy cost in lives. The invasion of Japan, had it ever come about, would have resulted in the greatest loss of life in the history of war.

Since taking command of *Cofer* I no longer had any control over my destiny. Instead of being a soldier in the ranks of a platoon, I was in command of a ship, which in effect was in the ranks of an armada of ships. The little Navy I had joined in the late '30s was now a huge, impersonalized operation made up of thousands of ships. I was trapped in an expanding prison and struggling for my individuality. I no longer sailed around the Pacific and the Caribbean as my own master. I was being converted with *Cofer* into something as new and different as the strange ship *Cofer* had become.

Ginny and I had made friends from our own and other ships. But with the exception of Mim and Pete Duffy, all of my old friends in New York were away at war. My mother's house was not far from Jones Beach. She still had the 1938 Plymouth, and occasionally we would spend a weekend with her. But most of the spare time was passed in that dingy, hot, overpriced apartment on New York's West Side. The pay was now excellent; but with the little that I gave to my mother, it was difficult for us to save. Ginny was cheerful and did not complain, but I was morose.

I was anxious to see the workmen finish so I could once again live aboard ship. It had become my home, and New York City had become foreign. I had a lot of sorting out to do. All this would come to an end soon, and I would need a long period of readjustment. I really did not know Ginny nor she me; the number of hours we had actually been together were few. It was impossible to make plans for the future—first I had to survive. Moreover it was obvious to me the world after the war would never be as it once was.

At the rare times that I had to think, I still dreamed of ships and far off places, but not of warships in their dismal gray. I dreamed of the beautiful old passenger ships, yet I already realized they had had their day. There was my life before the war, my peculiar life during the war, and the unknown future. I was wrapped up in something that totally consumed me, but which

I knew would soon end either by major changes or the death that had taken so many of my friends.

The new mission and the new characteristics of *Cofer* required the re-assessment of officers and men and retraining—not only because the mission and ship had changed, but because of our long time ashore.

I had lost Oksala (he had been assigned to an aircraft carrier as Assistant or Chief Engineer). Lt(jg) Hibbard Stubbs, the new Chief Engineer, had one cruise under the direction of Oksala in the Engineering Department. Backed by experienced petty officers in the engine room, I believed we were in vary good shape. Oksala had left the engine spaces in excellent condition and they had been the least disturbed by the conversion. While in New York Ensign Phil Alberts, a graduate engineer, reported on board as the Assistant Engineer. He would prove to be an excellent officer.

The loss of the torpedoes, the torpedo officer, and the torpedo division was offset by four LCVPs (Landing Craft Vehicle Personnel), with a Boat Division to operate and maintain them. The division officer was another young Ensign, E.J. McClendon. He was a graduate of the University of Oklahoma, full-blooded American Indian, hard working, intelligent, cheerful, and a good shipmate.

At the same time Ensigns Alberts and McClendon reported aboard, we were assigned two staff officers. Ensign J.A. Speziale, SC, USNR, took over disbursing and supply from Lt. Peters, thus creating a separate Supply Division. Lt(jg) H.W. Wendelken, MC-V(S), USNR, a specialist in Internal Medicine, was the other new addition to our wardroom. He had been given only a few weeks in which to become adjusted to his new environment. Because he was older than I, married, and had a child, I could not understand why he had not been given a higher rank on entry into the Navy.

Wendelken was a large man who had practiced medicine in Paris, Texas. Of all on board he had the shortest time and most difficult situation to adjust to. Soon to be known affectionately to the officers and me as "Wendy," and to the crew as "Doc," he accepted the cruel hand fate had dealt him with a spirit of cooperation rarely noted under the conditions in which he would have to practice his trade. This rounded out the new additions to the officer's roster with whom we were to start our new lives aboard an APD assigned to the Amphibious Forces, Pacific.

More junior officers would be assigned as we went along, but I now had a relatively experienced complement of officers and men. I also had a new problem. With the exception of the doctor, the new ensigns, particularly

McClendon, were ostracized by the enlisted men simply by being a part of our new mission. Ensign McClendon and his division required all the assistance they could get in their efforts to organize the Boat Division and integrate it into the overall operation of the ship. Antagonism was so obvious that I leaned heavily on the officers to be sure our new people were assimilated into the overall society the ship had developed since commissioning.

The officers cooperated, but the crew's loss of distinction they had attributed to being destroyermen seemed a bitter pill for them to swallow. Speziale was particularly open to criticism because any complaint about the food was easy to attribute to his miserliness with the budget. Before having a supply officer we did not care much about the budget. If necessary the line officer in charge would go over the budget, and rarely did supply officials ashore complain. As a supply officer Speziale was responsible to me and to his superiors in the Supply Department for the proper feeding of the ship's crew.

When Speziale complained to me about threats he had received, I told him I had no men to spare to guard him. He had more to fear on a long, dark night at sea than he did from his masters in the supply department miles away. He got the word; although once the crew discovered he took the threats seriously, they continued to harass him in ways that one could not pin down (they claimed they would unload the $50,000 usually carried in his safe should the ship be damaged in battle). The food improved and Speziale survived.

Somehow a small nucleus of professional seamen in the Fleet had been able to hold things together until we were able to train amateurs to perform like professionals. Most of the credit was given to the service schools, and some did a fair job. But without the few professional officers and enlisted men that surveilled the "on the job training," the Fleet could never have prevailed. This was all part of the generation that had grown up during the Depression. It was also part of a nation with balance among industry, agriculture, and research. Although the Fleet operated on a slow bell during depression, it was still in existence and in a position to expand without reliance on foreign sources that dry up during a war.

By 1944 as *Cofer* prepared to depart for the Pacific, the U.S. had already became the arsenal of democracy. The Allies could never have persevered were it not for our ability to expand our essential industries to keep all forces supplied while the once ominous war machines of the Axis steadily ran out of essential raw materials and industrial capacity to support their armed forces.

During our stay in New York, with its martial music and patriotic demonstrations, many were obviously making money from the war. Profiteering was rampant, and there was little you could not acquire if you had the money. Service personnel were everywhere; only a small percentage of the armed forces ever reached the combat zones. World War II is known as the "good war," and a crusade of good against evil. Unlike Vietnam it was a declared war and the penalties for opposing it were great. In actuality the situation was much different. Outwardly there was no sympathy for those who could not understand why we were fighting. Yet few of those en route or engaged in combat had the least idea of what the war was all about beyond the slogans and propaganda that engulfed them.

Going through the old log books I am astounded at the number of penalties I dispensed in connection with AWOL and AOL offenses. It is a rare free man who enjoys the restrictions and danger imposed on him by military service. *Cofer* was essentially a happy ship, but most everyone who served in her would rather have been safe at home with their family. Our country's desertion rate during World War II exceeded that of the Vietnam War.

Much that I had worked to accomplish during our shakedown period and few months of operation was destroyed by the long layover in New York and the exposure to the good life of the other side of the war. This break in the momentum while I was working towards a spartan fighting ship took its toll. I had to recreate a loyalty within the ship in a manner the crew could understand and relate to, rather than in the broad concepts of the propaganda they were exposed to, and saw through, while we were in New York. We were a very loose organization during the conversion period, scattered in various pursuits with only a minimum watch maintained on board.

On 31 August 1944 Commander William Parsons, USN, took command as ComTransDiv 103 and hoisted his flag in *U.S.S. Newman (APD-59)* Commander Parsons would be promoted to Captain within weeks; he stood high in the Class of '28. He was very senior to Cdr. Simmers, our previous boss, which also indicated the importance attached to this particular division of a new class of ships. I was to discover that Captain Parsons would be one of the outstanding officers of the war. He was tall and thin and somewhat frail in body, but strong in mind. One of those few great men who cared for each man under his command, Captain Parsons was one of those rarities that serve so well, yet quietly, and then disappear into oblivion. Although I preferred independent duty I considered it a privilege to have served under him.

As the summer drew to a close, the yard work force thinned out and this new class ship took form. We had another deck and two huge Whelan Davits, one on each side, with two LCVPs nested in each. The three 3-inch-50-caliber deck guns had been replaced with a single 5-inch-38-caliber turret gun, the most modern gun in this class. In the trade we lost our torpedoes, hedgehogs, and K-guns; all that remained for depth-charge attacks were the two depth-charge racks on the stern. Although our submarine detection facilities remained intact, our armament to combat a submerged submarine was sacrificed for the boats, the larger gun forward, and the capacity to carry troops and their equipment. All around we still had an excellent anti-aircraft defense, and our 5-inch-38 had a much greater range and destructive capacity than our former 3-inch-50s. With three twin-mount 40mm and four single-mount 20mm guns installed, I felt fairly secure against the type of air attack we could expect.

We were in effect a compromise vessel with a dual capacity. We had the facilities to transport a first-wave combat team and their equipment, to put them ashore in LCVPs, and then to cover their landing with the 5-inch-38 and other weapons. Once the troops were ashore the ship would again function as an escort vessel but more heavily weighted to defend against aircraft—the primary menace in the Pacific—than against submarines.

As the vessel took form I believed it was top heavy and it would have a serious stability problem. This led to academic debates among the design agents, Sparkman and Stephans, Jack Gilbride, and me. Although my naval architectural studies were limited, my previous experience with *Cofer* as a DE, and in other ships, was such that I believed the designers had added too much topside weight to the vessel. Jack Gilbride was neutral. He simply followed the design and specifications. Stephans was certain his calculations were correct. I decided to determine the actual situation during the sea trials scheduled on completion of the work.

As I relate the story of the time, the sea, the war, and the ships so many years after the events and without having kept a diary, I find it revolves mostly around the officers, and little attention is paid the enlisted men, particularly as individuals. Among the many reason for this is that there were so many enlisted men in relation to the officers. Contact was mostly maintained thorough a chain of command, which added to the separation.

This leads to the impression that the officers won the war. The reality, which is mostly lost both in history and in fiction, is that enlisted personnel were the main instrument of success or failure. Strategy, tactics, and interpretations of the objective would filter down from the highest ranks, but in the final analysis, the implementation depended on the performance of mostly nameless, unremembered, underpaid, unrewarded long-suffering enlisted men. In my case they were the Navy and the ship I had the privilege of commanding.

Fortunately and due to the efforts of a few, a Naval War Memorial in Washington has been dedicated to the "Lone Sailor," unidentified, unnamed, but in fact the real Navy. *Cofer* had a full complement of "lone sailors." As we prepared for a new job, it was the enlisted men at whom I aimed most of my training programs. If they had not adjusted to the situation under conditions much more demanding than those of the officers, there is little the officers or I could have done to operate and defend the ship and succeed in our missions.

Yeoman Val Kempf worked with me processing paperwork that never ceased. Even during combat we were in constant contact. On occasion there was small talk, but it was simply a good working relationship that was all business. At General Quarters Val's battle station was at my side on the flying bridge. He had a telephone to relay orders from me to all stations on the ship, relay incoming information to me. We must have stood side-by-side many hours, in rough weather and calm, during drills and combat.

Later in the Pacific, at the time Japanese suicide planes were flying into ships' bridges, we cleared the flying bridge of unnecessary personnel. This left Val Kempf and I, the Gunnery Officer, "Bucky" Mazer, the lookouts, and the fire controlmen in their tub above the flying bridge. The small talk continued in lulls, but neither found anything else about the other's life before duty in *Cofer*. Val was a tall, strongly built, intelligent petty officer. He was so good at his job he moved like part of the ship. We were the same age, had grown up in New York City within a few blocks of each other, and never found that out while shipmates in *Cofer*.

Over 40 years later at the ship's first reunion, while in casual conversation, we discovered we probably had passed each other on the streets a number of times over a long period of years. Val had wanted to enter NYSMMA, but his part-time work in a shoe store had led to a managerial position on graduation from high school. His progress continued in this large company to a point where he could hardly expect to equal his income and future by changing careers. He had all the prerequisites for a commission other than the degree, like so many others among our enlisted crew.

My top Quartermaster was a New Englander named Berquist. He had gone to sea in the Merchant Marine and had been preparing to sit for a license when he enlisted. He knew more navigation than any of the officers, and I worked closely with him in expanding his knowledge. He was a quiet professional whom I used as a back-up; but after he left the bridge, he would return to his confined and uncomfortable quarters with no privacy, as did the rest of the enlisted men.

The radar operators were of great importance and yet, although I dealt with them in the close quarters of the CIC (Combat Information Center) compartment, I have long forgotten their names except for Bob Linder, who was one of those who were not afraid to speak up when they believed the ship was heading into danger. There were the intelligent sonar petty officers, cramped in the sound shack forward of the bridge, who suffered the boredom and rare periods of shock. Sonar operators like Cushman and Wallace quietly ensured that no submarine was able to pierce the convoy screen.

J. Turley, the other Quartermaster on the bridge, was of constant assistance. Without his skill and that of others on the bridge, many successful maneuvers might have ended in disaster. Jim Demas, Ira Fouts, "Slim" Brumfield, John Bowman, Charles Rosen, and so many others whose names I can no longer recall, intelligently went about their jobs to be sure *Cofer* satisfied the bureaucrats both in its performance and reports written on well-oiled typewriters.

In other areas there were the Chiefs like Marks (Fleet Reserve) in the engine and boiler rooms, together with their "snipes," who kept the engines on-line in the intense heat below decks. My orders, "commence firing," or "cease firing" were just words whose implementation and effectiveness fell on the enlisted men. They suffered from the intensity of my training program, from the errors of the officers and me, and from the quality of life they had to endure.

They too had their characters, but my policy, perhaps wrong, was like a family we could all not be perfect and had to be tolerant of one another. Frank Brady became a legend. He was rated and disrated so many times that if each promotion were not followed by a disrating, he would have been an Admiral instead of a Seaman First Class. And so together with my shipmates, *Cofer* and I prepared for our new adventures as an APD, a little world of its own amidst the huge mass of the U.S. Navy at war.

On 18 September the crew moved back on board, and the ship came back to life. Still alongside the dock at Todd's Shipyard, we lit off our boilers and commenced and completed dock trials. That same afternoon a fuel barge came alongside and we took on 47,435 gallons of fuel. The following day we got under way and depermed (hopefully, protection from magnetic mines), and then were under way again on the 20th for the Naval Ammunition Depot at Earl, N.J., to take on ammunition. By 2100 hours that same evening we were back at our berth at Todd.

On the 21st we were under way again to adjust compasses, and then back again at our berth in Todd. On the 22nd we departed for our structural trials in the vicinity of buoy "George." I had invited my workaholic friend, Pete Duffy, to take a day off to see what we did with the gear he worked on. Also on board were people from Todd and Stephans of Sparkman and Stephans. Before we fired the guns, lowered the davits, and went through the numerous tests scheduled, with Stephans standing next to me, I brought the ship up to a speed of about 15 knots. It was a beautiful, sunny day and a smooth sea.

I turned to Stephans and told him the slow, slight roll of the ship indicated to me that she was unstable. He kept pushing his slide rule back an forth and said it had to be stable from his calculations. I ordered the helmsman to give the ship 20 degrees right rudder. As she leaned over about 10 degrees, I ordered him to maintain course. The ship stayed over on its side. Everyone on the bridge started to slide around; Stephans fell down.

As *Cofer* proceeded on the course and speed I had ordered, the 10-degree list remained unchanged. Various officials as well as some of the ship's personnel on the flying bridge with me showed fear in different ways. One of them shouted, "Do something before we turn over." I then had the ship slowly brought back to even keel by using the engines and the rudder, a technique I had witnessed before on one of the liners I served in.

There was no more argument. I had proven my point and more words were unnecessary. I was certain that vessels scheduled for this conversion, and those in the early stages of conversion, would be modified. My intuition told me that regardless of the risk, *Cofer* and the remainder of her division would not be modified, nor would others in advanced stages of conversion receive the modifications.

I had already planned a system, with alternatives, of maintaining stability in the event weather or other conditions should require a topside jettisoning plan. I could maintain a positive GM, resulting in a stable condition, so long as I could keep a high percentage of fuel, fresh water, stores, and ammunition in the double-bottom tanks and lower store rooms. If I could not do this and experienced bad weather or loss of stability due to damage in action, I would have to jettison topside weights including the LCVPs. As a last resort empty fuel tanks would have to be filled with salt water.

Many years later I met with the Navy Project Engineer, William (Mac) Nicholson, who had been involved with this project. He recalled a report being received by his section in the Bureau relating to the stability problem in the new class APDs. They reacted quickly with major alterations: lowering the whole bridge structure one deck among other things. Nicholson was surprised to learn *Cofer* had not been modified prior to departure. Actually the situation was not much different from the pre-war ocean liners. Once I was aware of the problem I could cope with it by incorporating procedures in the ship's operating instructions. This information was passed on to Captain Parsons, who in turn passed it to all the ships in the division. I do not recall ever receiving any warning or instructions from the Bureau of Ships, which was the cognizant authority.

One has to understand this was war time and everything was at risk. Theoretically the life of a combat ship was short once contact with enemy forces was made. The stability problem was a serious one, but no more serious than many others I confronted during this period. I would doubt that many commanding officers at that time had any real experience with this problem so prevalent in the liners I had sailed in during my early days at sea.

On 23 September we took on 53,561 gallons of fuel oil, which equates to about 200 tons. All of this in the double bottoms adds greatly to the righting moment of the ship and its overall stability. We could carry close to 100,000 gallons of oil, but rarely could take on over 96,500 in actual practice. Thus when we began a voyage loaded with ammunition, fuel, water, and supplies, we were basically stable. This would be fine if we could top off our fuel tanks every few days. Needless to say this was unlikely, but I would have to ensure we kept as much fuel in the ship as possible.

One of the greatest fears aboard any ship, and more so in a ship at war, is to run out of fuel. I now had an additional concern in that if we ran out of fuel, or even got down to about 20,000 gallons, the ship could very well turn over. The trials proved beyond a doubt the ship was unstable at 30 percent fuel capacity. It had to mean only one thing: this class of ship was badly needed, and stability was only one of the number of problems to be considered. We were expendable.

During the last few days in New York, we prepared for a long deployment. We had an excellent Ship's Service Store, which made a great deal of money even though it never surpassed the mark-ups generally allowed. It did not function while the vessel was undergoing conversion; but in the months it did operate, it made thousands of dollars. This money was used first to stock it for many months, and the remainder was transferred to the Ship's Welfare Fund. We did so well because most of the time we had been in port we were nested with other ships. Our store was far superior to the others. The experience I had gained in *Kanawha* I passed on. Because we had the inventory, variety, and quality of merchandise in demand, we got about 80 percent of the business. Thus our Welfare Fund was the beneficiary of this unusual wealth.

Most of the crew had been boys during the Depression and coveted many things such as first-class baseballs. Restraint was necessary but difficult to apply when the funds were there. So I relented. I spoiled them while at the same time demanding more and more of them in the performance of their duties. As a result the crew could play catch on deck at sea with new baseballs. When one rolled over the side they would just draw another one. When a request was made for a large amount of funds to purchase musical instruments, including a small piano, I approved the allocation of the money from the Welfare Fund. As an ASW ship with sonar operators, we had our share of musicians. As an APD we had the space for an orchestra to entertain.

This allocation of funds fell into a category of an offset to the loss of morale caused by the conversion. I was pleased, but as I was busy with so many other things I left the details to those involved and thought no more about it. I had no idea they might have trouble finding a small piano in New York City.

One benefit of my prior tours of duty in the Pacific was the knowledge that specific material things could procure much more than could money. Money was basically useless, and major barter items for both recreational and personal needs were liquor and good movies. Movies were essential for morale. With the ordinary allowance of five to seven movies to trade with other ships, if you had bad starters and were unable to trade up, you would end up with none. The biggest movie exchange in the Navy was in the Brooklyn Navy Yard. "Pete" Peters had charm, and as an insurance salesman could sell anyone anything. I discussed my plan with him.

I told Pete that movies were about the best currency there was in the Pacific War Zone. If all went according to the usual practice, we would get garbage and end up watching the same horse opera every night. I suspected there were movies that required transportation to the Canal and beyond, and that he should try to talk the officer-in-charge into trusting him and the ship to deliver them. He succeeded beyond my greatest expectations. He not only got us five or seven excellent new movies to start with, but he provided ten or more new movies to deliver to the Canal Zone. Peters managed to deliver movies seen en route and received an equal amount of good movies in exchange from people in the Canal Zone. We also set up a plan to make movie trading an art. In addition to our ammunition and other elements required, we had covered another need.

A recent change in policy allowed us to carry beer so long as we did not allow it to be consumed on the ship. I gave permission to use Welfare Funds to buy as much beer as we could store and lock up without spoilage. We bought so much that if we had been sunk, the suds would have trailed for miles. I bought as many cokes for the Ship's Service that we could find the space for. There was a law against carrying hard liquor except for medicinal purposes. Yet this was the most valuable item we could ever get for trading. Liquor was rationed in the States. We could buy a few bottles in New York and Norfolk, our next port of call. We planned to supplement this in Panama, where I believed it to be in ample supply at very low prices. I gave Speziale an order that he was to load up on all the hard-to-get and expensive food items for the crew, and to forget his budget. I scared the hell out of him by saying if he lived long enough for the Supply Corps to bring him on the carpet, he would be lucky. I really had no control over him in this respect, but he went along.

Then I told him I was setting up a procedure whereby the bridge watch in port in the Pacific was to report any supply and refrigerator ship in port. If one was sighted we would up anchor and go alongside. He was to have his order papers ready, and to be sure we obtained the food we required to keep feeding our people well, regardless. I also said we expected to have the wherewithal to assist him.

Several days prior to departure we had a dinner-dance at the Towers Hotel Grand Ballroom in Brooklyn Heights. Again our Welfare Fund stood us well, thanks to the other ships' crews who patronized our Ship's Store rather than their own. We had about a 90 percent turnout. Our division commander attended as did my mother and my wife. The crew who had wives in the vicinity brought them, and those that did not, in many cases, brought girl friends. Jack Gilbride from Todd came, as did many of the other key workmen from the Yard.

On the afternoon of 26 September we left independently from the 33rd Street Pier in Todd's Shipyard en route to Hampton Roads, Virginia. Taking departure at 1515 hours from Buoy Able we commenced our full-power trial, but had to delay it while some adjustments were made in the engine room. We again resumed the full-power trial at 1800 hours while en route to our destination in generally smooth water. During this whole three-hour period, while dashing through the water at close to 24 knots, we also drilled. At 2100 hours, with the successful completion of the full-power trial, we reduced speed to adjust to our scheduled time of arrival in Hampton Roads.

By 0958 hours we were moored portside to U.S.S. Newman (APD-59) at Pier 72, N.O. B., Norfolk, Virginia. That same afternoon ComPhibTraLant and Transport Shakedown Group inspection parties came aboard. There was not much to the inspection, which also added to the impression that nothing was to stand in the way of getting this division into combat in the shortest possible time.

Shortly thereafter *Newman* shifted to another berth and we took the inside berth alongside the dock with *U.S.S. Kephart (APD-61)* tied outboard to us. *U.S.S. Bennington (CV-20),* which had been commissioned only weeks earlier, was on the other side of the finger pier. Lt. Oksala was on board *Bennington* on temporary duty pending new orders to a CVL as Chief Engineer. He was on board *Cofer* as soon as the inspection party left the ship, and it was soon like Old-Home Week. With the ship's senior officers and Oksala, I left for the Officer's Club for drinks and dinner. We never did get to the dinner part, drinking until about 2200 or 2300 hours before we started to stagger back to the ship for something to eat.

While drinking with this group I discovered we had not been able to secure a suitable piano at any price. The other officers ribbed me about being a lousy Captain. Okie joined in. He told us there was a small piano in the wardroom of *Bennington,* saying they were so screwed up all we had to do was to send a working party aboard and take it off. This was ridiculous. *Bennington* was fully manned, and security had to be tight.

The other officers picked up on this and kept arguing with me, promising if I gave the okay they would arrange to liberate the piano. Later, after we had dragged ourselves back to our ship, while we were having hamburgers, they kept pounding on me and my new headache. Ensign Albert, our new Assistant Engineering Officer, at the time JOOD, was standing there listening to his peers. I was groggy. Somehow I thought I could end this nonsense by giving an order, forget about the whole crazy thing, and go to bed.

I turned to Albert and asked, "Have you heard what has been going on?"

"Yes, Sir." he answered.

"Get the piano," I ordered, leaving immediately for my bunk.

Early next morning there was a pounding on my door. My head splitting, I leaned on my elbow and, in a commanding moan, queried, "Who the hell is it?"

"Ensign Albert, Sir."

"Who the devil are you and what do you want?"

"What shall I do with the piano, Sir?"

I almost fell out of my bunk, sobering up fast, and got a new headache to augment the old one.

I was stunned. As the full impact of the situation became apparent, I realized I could be in deep trouble. My immediate thought was to find a way to return the piano, but it was obviously impossible. Next I thought perhaps we could somehow find a way to pay for it, but there was no way without being traced.

This was the morning of the 28th, and we were not due to sail until the morning of the 30th. I never questioned Albert on this subject. Any questioning on my part, together with any answers on his part, would have only compounded the crime if we had been caught. I ordered Albert to get his crew together and take the piano and the rolls and put them at the end of the dock under a tarpaulin.

The countdown began immediately, and every minute until we left Norfolk was desperate. When I made the decision to hold the piano at the end of the dock, I had none of the details about what exactly had happened since I gave that stupid order.

Ensign Albert had gotten a clipboard and placed some papers on it. He then gathered a working party made up of engineering petty officers. This was wartime and the pier was jammed with service personnel going on and off the ships in any and every direction.

It must have been about 0700 hours when Ensign Albert and his work party boarded the quarterdeck of *Bennington* and requested permission of the JOOD at the gangway to come aboard. Albert had not been in the Navy very long and could hardly find his way around *Cofer,* let alone a giant carrier with probably 4,000 men on board. He got lost on his way to the wardroom, *Bennington* crew members helped him find it.

Ensign Albert was offered breakfast. As a visitor he must have been invited by a member of the Mess—Oksala. Not wanting to call attention to himself he accepted, leaving the working party waiting in the alleyway outside the wardroom. When Albert finished breakfast he motioned the working party into the wardroom and told them to pick up the piano. Many officers were still eating there at the time. It was a small electric player-piano donated to the crew of the ship by the workers in the Brooklyn Navy Yard where the ship was built. As the *Cofer* working party was lifting the piano, one of them asked in a loud voice whether he should take the player-piano rolls also. He was told to do so, and they struggled with the piano and its bench, taking them from the wardroom. The only words said by any officer in the wardroom were, "There goes the piano."

Members of *Bennington's* crew further assisted in taking the piano off by unshipping ladders to facilitate getting it up the several decks. When they got the piano to the gangway sometime after 0800 hours, the JOOD at the gangway held them up for a few minutes while the Executive Officer of *Bennington* boarded and walked right by. Then down the gangway and onto the dock the piano went.

There it stayed until I ordered it placed at the end of the dock. A wooden crate built by *Cofer's* Carpenters Mate replaced the tarpaulin. Last thing before the ship left the pier, the piano was hoisted aboard and lowered into the little equipment hold, another bonus we ended up with that we did not have as a DE. There it remained crated until we were safely at sea. When we left Norfolk en route to the war, it was moved into the crew's chow hall where it stayed through the ship's decommissioning and mothballing at Green Cove Springs, Florida, in 1946. There it remained until the ship was broken up some years later.

Simply put we had stolen a piano from the center of one of the world's largest combat ships. It was grand larceny. As the Commanding Officer I was guilty of it. If we had been caught I would have spent some time in Portsmouth Naval Prison. A Captain who gets command of a large carrier is a sure Rear Admiral so long as he does not foul up. He is carefully pre-selected for the job even in wartime. If I was in trouble he was in more trouble, and he might join me in Portsmouth. During those two days I sweated it out. I thought many times of returning the piano, simply saying it was just a prank. Yet the theft was secondary to the fact that this great ship was so vulnerable and really so insecure. I could not give the piano back, and *Bennington's* Commander could not overcome the security lapse. I later heard they called the FBI, but I doubt it. If I had been the C.O. I would have kept it quiet and set about ensuring the security of my ship was never breached again.

I set off a series of thoughtless and unfair events. On the one hand I was a very disciplined officer, with restrained reactions when on duty or when we were in combat, or when combat was expected or imminent. On the other hand I could be flippant, believing the order to "Get the Piano" was so absurd it would be forgotten, as I expected to forget it. I had let off some pent-up tension by drinking at the club, which resulted in making a serious mistake.

At the same time *Cofer* had a serious morale problem. After gaining an identity and an acceptance of its mission, its character as a ship was suddenly changed. Inadvertently the piano suddenly reversed the drop in morale and returned, possibly surpassed, the confidence and pride the crew had in the ship before.

Albert became an instant hero as the crew identified themselves with this bold foray—the little guy takes on and defeats the big guy. Over the many months and years that followed the incident, the story was told again and again, with possibly 100 different versions.

Even with assistance from *Bennington's* crew, an outside working party should never have been able to steal a piano from the ship, no matter how fouled up it might have been. Someone very sophisticated and wise in the workings of a carrier, as well as the nature of the crew, and particularly the Captain of *Cofer,* had to have organized it. Only one person fit this description, Raymond Oksala. He was experienced enough, brilliant, and had that quiet sense of humor to try and pull something like this off.

Albert was a fine young officer, but, and even conceding genius, if he had been left to his own device, he would have roamed around the carrier for days. It was just like Okie to pull something off like this and let someone else take the credit, while in his own quiet way he might crack a wry smile. At the same time if "Operation Piano" had gone sour, he would have taken as much of the responsibility as he could.

Okie knew several things before we even arrived in Norfolk. Someone had informed him we had not been able to purchase a piano. While in *Bennington* and observing the piano in the wardroom, he must have also heard the piano was the cause of some dissent. I had been told by a member of the crew they expected the piano would be placed in an area for the recreation of all hands, not just the officers. I also heard that some of the officers in *Bennington* shared the crew's feelings when the wardroom took over the piano.

In a strange way as things go, *Cofer's* eight battle stars will be forgotten in time, if they have not already been. But in the manner in which war stories are passed down through the years, this tale of the piano will gain momentum. Although I was in fear of being discovered and "unfrocked," the demands of my work were such that I never had a chance to think much about the piano. Even as we sailed off into the blue, and the crew enjoyed

236

the orchestra and the piano, I can't recall ever having had time to listen to it.

So at 0615 hours on Saturday, 30 September, *Cofer* and its piano set sail for the Canal Zone in company with *U.S.S. Newman, U.S.S. Liddle, U.S.S. Kephart,* and *U.S.S. Lloyd* of Task Unit 20.17.10, with ComTransDiv 103 in *Newman.*

Speed was set at 18 knots. Under the direction of the Task Unit Commander, we exercised in different formations, held target practice, and drills, drills, and more drills. Senior Watch officers were now Lieutenants: Cofer, Meredith, Hahn, and Cleland, together with Lt(jg)s Peters and Mazer. I had qualified all the officers who had been with the ship from commissioning.

On October 4 we anchored off Coco Solo, awaiting the Canal Pilot and our turn to transit the Canal. Weather between Norfolk and the Canal had been moderate. Although our new boss drilled us continually, the old CortDiv had very few changes in officers and enlisted men, so we were used to maneuvering with each other. There was only one change of a Commanding Officer, Commander of *Liddle,* "Swede" Brogger. We had become close in this short time. Swede had left the Navy but had volunteered when the threat of war was imminent. He was an excellent officer; next to me he had the most duty both in command and time at sea. He was plainly as tired as I.

During the voyage to Panama we often exercised the ships together and continued to do so the remainder of the voyage even after we commenced hostile operations. Although we made contacts en route to Panama, all were friendly. German submarines, previously so evident in these waters since the start of the war, were just not there.

It was hard to realize at the time, but the tide had turned against them. Their early successes had taken their toll not only in submarines, but in the quality of their captains. The Allies had also lost heavily in merchant ship tonnage, but their replacement ability was tremendous. We had lost many escort vessels and the Royal Navy's ace, Captain Walker, together with many other veterans of the war in the Atlantic. Captain Walker died of a cerebral hemorrhage from overwork. He was the greatest of all Allied anti-sub warriors.

Germany's submarine fleet was being decimated at an even a faster rate than their other forces. With DEs now on the scene in numbers, tied in to Hunter-Killer groups, the hunter was being hunted and convoy screens were tight.

With the Battle of the Atlantic lost, Germany would surrender in May

237

1945. This had to be obvious to our high command, but less so to those fighting ashore and at sea. German submarines could now dive deeper. And by using snorkels specially designed to compensate for ASW work, cruise on their diesels below the surface. The DE was a much more effective ASW adversary than they had ever faced before, and there were simply too many of them.

Thus the reasoning behind the quick change from DEs to APDs made sense; the war in the Atlantic would diminish in intensity as it increased in the Pacific. And so *Cofer* would pass from the Atlantic into the Pacific.

One area of the world where the Master or the Commanding Officer surrenders authority to the pilot is the Panama Canal. The pilot who came on board to take us through the Canal was obviously drunk. Traffic through the Canal had increased to such an extent the small group of experienced pilots had to be augmented by a makeshift group of temporary pilots.

I had sailed through the Canal once in 1935 in *S.S. Santa Clara*. Because I had spent little time on the bridge, I had no experience to fall back on except a vague memory of the trip through. At 1921 hours we entered the first lock, Gatun. Once out of the lock and in Gatun Lake, which is surrounded by lowlands, the pilot called for flank speed, which was almost 24 knots. I called his attention to the size of our wake, which washed over the stern and would wreak havoc on the surrounding shores. He ignored me. This was his home field I could only stand by. By 2021 hours, exactly one hour, we were in Pedro Miguel Locks. This had to be a record.

But at what cost? I could see the wake flowing over the banks on this moonlit night. But the pilot had the conn. In the Panama Canal I was not about to take it away from him. At 0045 hours we moored alongside *Liddle* at Pier 1, NAD, Balboa, Canal Zone. Even in the middle of the night, I expected and received a welcoming committee. The Captain of the Port was there to congratulate me on the fastest passage of the Canal ever made, and then to ream me out for having flooded the whole area around Gatun Lake.

Meanwhile the drunken pilot had sneaked off the ship, probably to get another drink. I took the abuse, but was mad as hell when the Captain said the Canal Zone would not welcome the crew and officers of *Cofer* during their short stay. He finally left. But this was the night we were scheduled to get whiskey for the ship. Two groups were scheduled to go ashore, one made up of Chief Machinist Mate Marks and other CPOs. The other group was composed of three officers and me. I had been told where the liquor could be procured even at that late hour. There was no curfew in Panama.

238

Chief Marks was one of those old-time, picturesque Navy characters peculiar to the China Station. He had been retired and running a bar in Brooklyn when his love of the Navy influenced him to volunteer. He had been a destroyer man, and though around 50, short and fat, the only rationale for his assignment was he made up for his physical limitations with experience and knowledge. Oksala considered him a rare jewel in the ship, as did the crew.

Old Chief Petty Officers who are good can ordinarily circumvent the immature actions of junior officers. They have a way of maintaining direct contact with the Captain and senior officers without breaking with protocol. Wise senior officers ordinarily enhance this contact by often engaging such Chiefs in off-the-record conversations. It is a stupid junior officer who does not consult with his Chief, and a poor Captain who keeps the Chiefs at a distance, or for that matter, any of his senior petty officers and officers. Like Captains and officers, all chiefs are not good, but Marks, aside from being a complete professional, was entertaining to talk to and kid around with.

A small warship is confining. I would take periodic walks back and forth on the deck in an effort to get some exercise. Before we were converted, there was an engine room hatch leading on to the deck. One day I noticed Marks trying to crawl out of it, but his girth interfered. He was cursing and huffing and puffing, but the more he tried the worse the situation got. For a few minutes I stood there kidding him about his predicament; telling him to keep cool while we got a blow torch and cut him out. I did not let him suffer long. Soon we had him oiled down and pulled him out still cursing.

I had told Marks if he could get a small amount of whiskey aboard and ration it in the Chiefs' Mess, unless any of them got drunk on board, I would be sure the officers did not interfere. I could trust him. In setting up our whiskey foray, I warned him I was counting on having trouble getting past the Marine Guards, that he should be sure his group returned sober so not to draw any special attention going through the base gate and security. He bet me a bottle he would make it.

We returned late that night, having hidden our liquor ón us. I was a lieutenant commander and the other officers were lieutenants. Chances of the Marines bothering us were much less than the Chiefs, whom most Marines disliked, and for which the feeling was mutual. We were also sober when we approached the gate.

As we got to the gate I saw Marks and the other chiefs standing unsteadily, apparently three-sheets-to-the-wind. It was a typical Norman

Rockwell scene. The Marines had the bottles. One-by-one they opened them. The Chiefs stood with their hats on the back of their heads and their coats open, shirts sticking out, and in the case of Marks, his belly. The Marine in charge emptied the bottles one-by-one in front of Marks' nose. There was nothing Marks, the Chiefs, or I could do, except I used the Marines preoccupation to walk boldly through the gate while snappily returning their salute.

My group got through with a large amount of whiskey. After the quarterdeck watch saw that the Chiefs got to their quarters and fell asleep, I arranged to have four bottles of our whiskey placed in Marks' locker. Later I gave him another bottle while complementing him on winning the bet. Ships are people and people are ships; they're both imperfect. Marks understood and never a word on the subject was passed between us, nor did the Chiefs abuse the privilege.

On the morning of 7 October, we prepared to get under way again. I had one more encounter with the Captain-of-the-Port, who by then had learned I had disregarded his orders. He was there to be sure *Cofer,* its Commanding Officer, officers, and crew departed, leaving the Canal Zone at peace. He sarcastically wished me "Bon Voyage," but capped the message with the comment he would not care to see *Cofer* or me back. I saluted, smiled, and ordered the crew: "Let go for and aft."

We were en route to Hollandia, New Guinea, via the Galapagos Islands, Bora Bora, and Finschaven. The distance between ports required, with the exception of the short run to the Galapagos, we proceed at speeds under which we could get the best mileage. Captain Parsons staggered the speed of the ships to the Galapagos so each ship could arrive in its turn at the fueling facility. As we crossed the Equator en route to the Galapagos, an old tradition of the sea was maintained, inducting the "pollywogs" into the "Ancient Order of the Deep" from which they emerge as "shellbacks."

I had been across the Equator many times. When I had "crossed the line" in *Santa Clara* and *Padnsay,* no one bothered to make a ceremony of it; it was just another day. There had been ceremonies on *Matsonia,* but I only vaguely recall them. The best was in *Daly,* which was a well-planned major production. In the end, whether or not you are Certified or even the Captain, on a good ship and in the spirit of it all, you still got the "treatment."

Although careful preparations were made not to waste time, given our staggered arrival at the Galapapos, we still had to anchor of Baltra Island at 0700 hours on the 9th after steaming at 20 knots. We got our turn at the fueling buoy at 1807 hours. After taking what appeared to be an incredible amount of fuel for so short a voyage, we anchored again off Baltra Island waiting for the other ships of our division to complete fueling.

I was continually preoccupied by the fuel consumption rate. Even though the remainder of the voyage was carefully planned to operate on one boiler and at lower speeds, we needed favorable weather and no deviations that would require an increase of our speed or distance steamed. At 2300 hours our division again formed up, and we sailed west at the standard prearranged speed of 15.5 knots. The drills we conducted were designed not to increase our fuel consumption.

Intelligence did not indicate any enemy activity en route to Bora Bora. It was a routine voyage except we decreased speed to as low as 13 knots to conserve fuel. In October we arrived off Bora Bora to find it had an uncharted, snaky channel into the dock. There were no pilots, and it was a very difficult entry. The sailing directions had little of any valuable information. Just as I was approaching *Liddle* to moor alongside, the wind came up and worked with the current to swing the stern towards a reef. All I could do was increase speed and adjust the engines, and bounce off *Liddle* to keep the screws off the reef.

There was no damage, but I came close to leaving a ship in Bora Bora for good. Commodore Parsons came aboard for a quick inspection and a friendly chat with me. He saw the piano and in the privacy of my room I told him the story. He was amused. I gathered he figured we would soon be in action, and he had other things to worry about.

Bora Bora is a beautiful island—high, green, with brown tints. A road went around it. The port officials denied liberty for the crew, but I granted it notwithstanding. The crew went ashore in small groups, and I gather they had an interesting time.

We completed fueling on the evening of the 20th and took aboard 81,358 gallons, which indicated we had only about 15,000 gallons of usable fuel left on arrival.

On October 21 we sailed from Bora Bora in the Society Islands for Finschaven, New Guinea. Speed was set at 14 knots to conserve fuel. Maneuvers, drills, and target practice were constant en route. On the morning of October 29 *Kephart* was dispatched to Espirito Santos to make emergency repairs. We were now in waters in which we could expect enemy activity. Morning and evening alerts were conducted with the ships at General Quarters.

On October 31 we made contact on an unidentified plane that passed out of range quickly—we secured from General Quarters. Speed had been increased to 17.5 knots by the time, causing our fuel consumption to go up. At 0848 hours on 1 November we anchored in Langemak Bay, New Guinea, awaiting our turn to fuel from *S.S. Aase Maersk*. We got under way for Dredger Bay and moored alongside the tanker. Prior to sailing for Hollandia, New Guinea, at 1730 hours, we took aboard 84,217 gallons of fuel. The voyage to Hollandia was the last leg of our speed-run across the Pacific.

Sporadic fighting was still going on in Finschaven. All pockets resistance by the Japanese defenders had not yet been eliminated. Crew members changed what they had brought for Japanese Samurai swords, rifles, helmets, and the like. Samurai swords were not easy to come by, but they did get one or two.

The Japanese, reluctant to surrender, rarely did until the very end of the war. Individuals kept roaming around foraging for food, but they were armed and would not surrender. The New Guinea campaign had been long and bitter, fought by many divisions including one from New Haven we had brought out in *Matsonia*. They, or what was left of them, were just now going home.

Early on 4 November we anchored in Humboldt Bay, New Guinea. Before leaving the States we had taken on board about 50 enlisted passengers who were transferred on 6 November to the Navy Receiving Station in Hollandia for further assignment. While in Hollandia we shifted anchorage several times; personnel were transferred off and on the ship, with some people who had been transported as passengers replacing crew members. We remained in Hollandia until 17 November, except for two days at Tana Mora Bay, New Guinea, where we were again involved in drills. In Tana Mora Bay we fueled from the Navy tanker *U.S.S. Villa Lovas 9 (X-145)* before returning to our anchorage in Humboldt Bay.

On Friday the 17th elements of TransDiv 103 that had left Norfolk together were joined by: *U.S.S. James B. Craig (DE-201)* and *U.S.S. PC 1124*. We left Hollandia that day as escort of a mixed group of LSTs, LSMs, and merchantmen bound for Leyte, Philippine Islands. Two days later we were joined by a group of LSTs and LCIs under escort of *U.S.S. El Paso (PF-41)* and *U.S.S. Van Buren (PF-42)*. We were now headed into the turmoil around Leyte where the Japanese were objecting to being evicted from the land they took by force. We were in a very active war zone; there were alerts and G.Q.s for aircraft later identified as friendly. In general we were ready for instant action as our ComTransDiv force increased rapidly in size.

Radar contacts continued, causing alerts followed by stand downs as they were identified as friendly. At 0815 hours on 22 November *Liddle* was ordered to leave the convoy and investigate an SOS. We continued frequent firing practices and drills. On the 23rd, after many "friendlies," we finally made contact with enemy aircraft. We were ordered to close on the convoy as it and the escort were attacked by six "Jill" Japanese torpedo bombers.

Almost every escort and convoy ship fired. One torpedo bomber 2500 yards astern of *Cofer* crashed flaming into the sea. With probably ten or more ships shooting at the planes, the C.O. of a ship less likely than we to have scored the hit was immediately on the TBS screaming: "I claim credit for this plane." The attack was still going on, and just about everyone else was more interested in repelling the attack than in getting credit. Some of our people wanted to contest the claim, but under such conditions I believe no one should have had the audacity to think of credit. There were war correspondents around, which resulted in this pathetic guy being mentioned in dispatches.

The important thing is our convoy and its escort suffered no casualties. If any credit was due to anyone it was due to the Officer-In-Tactical Command (OTC) Captain, Parsons, as well as the crews, early warning, and gunners. Parsons ran a near perfect operation. Many enemy aircraft remained around us. We would go to Battle Stations then secure, but for one reason or another the aircraft did not come in. On 24 November we entered Leyte Harbor while it was under air attack, anchoring in San Pedro Harbor. We soon were under direct air attack. A Japanese fighter-bomber hit *PC 1124* amidship with a light demolition bomb while she was moored alongside a tanker. We fired at and hit a Japanese fighter-bomber on the port side. It flew out of range losing altitude and smoking. Within about one minute we expended 54 rounds of 40mm and 120 rounds of 20mm ammunition.

There was a problem in firing in Leyte Harbor. Well over a hundred ships were moored. Less disciplined ships would fire at a plane when right behind it was a friendly ship. We did not. Ships that practiced such loose firing control killed more of our people than the Japanese did. My orders to *Cofer's* gun crews were to fire only when the target was clear of our ships.

We were under way that night to Palau. Leyte was under air attack again as TransDiv 103 and other escorts sailed as escorts to various ships. ComTransDiv 103 was again the Escort Commander. After lots of drills from many contacts that either did not come in or were friendly, we arrived in Palawan 27 November without casualties. It had been an active escort: Commodore Parsons shifted his screening ships, changed course, and as a whole made them a difficult target. At Palau we secured alongside *U.S.S. Saugatuck (AO-75)* taking aboard 67,474 gallons. We were soon under way again bound for Leyte. ComTransDiv and our regular group made this voyage together with a great deal of excitement, but no contact with the enemy in firing range. Still it was difficult for Captains to leave the bridge. We had found the war and it had found us. At this time and place there was no way we could luck out; we could only fight it out.

We arrived back in Leyte on the afternoon of 29 November. Leyte was under attack again. When the red alert was lifted we went alongside Navy tanker *IX 135* at 1725 hours. By 1800 hours another red alert sounded. By 1827 hours we were under way again having topped off with 16,000 gallons of fuel, as I continued to assure our stability by having enough fuel aboard. Considering the conditions I placed fuel at a very high priority. We had been much too light ever since leaving the States other than just after fueling.

On the evening of the 29th we had a serious accident. While going to General Quarters, and while gunners screamed to get the starboard davit out of the way so the guns could bear on the targets, the davit handler failed to remove the safety pin before he started the winch. As a result of operating the davit with the pin in place, it looked like a pretzel. No facilities in the harbor could handle the repair. We were due to embark troops for an invasion scheduled within the next few days. Without the davit we could not function; half of our boat capacity would be inoperable. We decided to do the impossible—fix this huge davit ourselves.

We cut steel from internal bulkheads without affecting the structural strength of the vessel. We had to cut out the twisted part of the davit and fabricate an identical part we could weld in, then weld doubling plates and other supports in place. At the start it seemed impossible. But we rotated welders and worked around the clock. I was up all that night and the next day. I was just not going to report *Cofer* unable to perform her job after all the training and work that went into getting her to Leyte. Davit alignment was tricky, yet we persevered. After we finished and tested it, we failed to realize the steel took time to cool down, and until it did it was weak. As a result a roller fell through on the test. We did not have to start all over again, but it meant more hours of work. Somehow this group of officers and men did the impossible. When it was tested again it worked.

Leyte was under attack night and day. Standing orders were for all ships anchored or moored in the harbor to be blacked out at night. But we could not repair our davit without welding and without providing enough light to do so at night. As night fell we continued the work. Air attacks continued and hundreds of guns responded. And every level of authority in the harbor, as well as individual commanding officers, screamed at us (code name Gentry) to douse the lights. We turned the volume on our TBS radio on the bridge to low.

Nothing deterred us from repairing the starboard davit and then subjecting it to every possible test we could conceive. Air attacks continued and we responded with gunfire when in the clear and in range, as did others, but nothing stopped the work. On 2 December the exhaustive tests were completed. I was confident the repairs would suffice for at least several weeks and possibly months; however, I made a request for tender availability for further tests and repairs if necessary. This was a large davit capable of lifting and lowering an LCVP fully loaded: 36 troops, or one small vehicle, or a maximum five tons of cargo.

At 1300 hours I convened a Board of Investigation with Lt. Charles Cofer as senior member to determine the cause of the accident, to recommend precautions to avoid a recurrence, and to develop procedures to observe davit operations in the coming weeks. Deliberations were completed by 1500 hours when they adjourned to await my action as convening authority. I later agreed with their conclusions while emphasizing the need to continue pressing for tender time.

We never received tender time for repair, but the repaired part of the davit never failed. Long after I was relieved of command, and during a routine non-combat operation of the davit, a wire lift gave way, the LCVP fell, and *Cofer* suffered the only loss of life in its career. Zalaman Rosenberg, a young member of the Boat Division, was killed together with a native in a boat alongside at the time. I recall Rosenberg very well. He was a red-headed and cheerful member of the crew. The wire was replaced. The main structure of the davit was not damaged in the accident, and it continued to operate until the ship laid up. For many years I had believed this tragedy was the result of the davit repair. I was relieved to find out it was not.

The crew's accomplishment in this difficult undertaking proved I had succeeded in rebuilding morale and developing confidence in their ability to survive and prevail under any circumstance. The ship and its crew had come a long way, but I was feeling the strain and stress as well as the lack of sleep. Air attacks and submarine alerts in the area continued. We had finally met the destiny I had long expected.

245

No longer was it necessary to caution our people to be prepared. The constant crescendo of gunfire, explosions, and the first appearance of an occasional suicide plane required no further pressure from me. They saw it and felt the danger. They had responded well in action and knew they were ready.

During those early days in December, I was briefed on an operation that was to get under way shortly. It was also obvious to me our overall commander was General MacArthur. This revived memories of the many derogatory remarks I had heard about him from the survivors of the First Philippines Campaign who had returned with me to the States in *Matsonia*. I had not been impressed by this "National Monument" during my encounter with his staff in Brisbane. In addition, while first en route to New Guinea during the time of the Battle of Samar, we had intercepted a plain-language dispatch from Admiral Kincaid to General MacArthur that I recall clearly to this date: "Kindly expedite going ashore, need *Nashville* desperately."

The light cruiser U.S.S.Nashville was never released by the General. Instead of getting into this critical battle, *Nashville* remained in Leyte as General MacArthur "returned" in a Hollywood-type production staged by his staff. This officer had taken his family to war with him and remained aloof from it all in a manner that created serious problems for the excellent staff work of Admiral Nimitz. CincPac's direction of the war in the Pacific up to this point had been brilliant.

It now dawned on me that *Cofer* and I, by some queer stroke of fate, were to a large extent under the influence of a pompous General whom I found difficult to accept as a leader.

Fortunately for *Cofer* there were layers of command in between, and we were very lucky in the people we had. Admiral Kincaid, as the Commander of the 7th Fleet under MacArthur, was the first layer. I had not met him and knew nothing of him. Next in line was a man I had not met, but whose leadership I was soon to admire—Rear Admiral Arthur Struble. Then came Captain William Parsons, my immediate superior. Struble and Parsons never received much notoriety, but even Admirals, like enlisted men, are often part of the anonymity of greatness; their only real reward is the respect they gain from others in the same category.

On the evening of 5 December 1944 at about 2000 hours, I boarded an LCVP with the commanding officer of *Liddle,* Lcdr. Swede Brogger, and others for a long in-harbor voyage in Leyte Bay for a pre-invasion conference of C.O.s aboard *U.S.S. Ward.* Leyte, as usual, was full-up with ships of all types. It was still the key port for the return to the Philippines promised by General MacArthur.

Only minutes after the LCVP cast off from *Cofer* and started for *Ward* some miles away, Japanese aircraft attacked the harbor in force. Warships are trained in gunnery disciplines individually, by divisions, by squadrons, task groups, and task forces. The situation in Leyte was typical of most port defense organizations wherein the senior officer present had the responsibility. It was a hopeless task in Leyte. There were many merchant ships whose Armed Guard crews were a mixture of Merchant and Naval personnel. Directed mostly by inexperienced ensigns, firing disciplines were nearly nonexistent. Even on the best disciplined warships, the problems under the conditions were deplorable.

Ships were entering and leaving; some were shifting berth and were basically anchored, with little regard for anything other than preventing collisions between ships. On a moon-lit night one could see the silhouettes, but it was a cloudy night with poor visibility. This large armada was very vulnerable at such times to individual enemy planes flying low between lines of and among groups of ships. Suddenly the skies lit up, night turned into day, and Leyte Harbor was numbed by the noise of gunfire and explosions. It was a Fourth-of-July display of an unimaginable intensity supplemented by death and destruction. Planes were shot down but casualties to our ships, caught in crossfires, were tremendous.

As shells and bullets landed and passed close to us, the situation in our little boat became a horror story. We were helpless. Slowly we moved towards our destination unable to protect or shield ourselves. Somehow we arrived at *Ward*.

Neither Admiral Struble nor Captain Parsons presided over the meeting, which was requested and held only for Destroyer C.O.s. Secret orders were passed to us about the invasion. I recall some dissatisfaction with their nature and a comment by one of the C.O.s to the effect it was purely a salve to satisfy the vanity of the General to commemorate Pearl Harbor Day and gain more publicity.

These combat commanders were cynical and displeased with how the operation was evolving and the nature of the planning, which they considered unlike that from Naval staffs. Another comment was the plan was hastily put together and failed to cover essential points. This was my first experience with an invasion order of this nature, and I would have to study it carefully when I arrived back at *Cofer*.

Combat commanders are a strange lot. Few ever get their stars. Many are killed or injured, some just don't care anymore, most are nervous and high strung. One senses it is an unorganized club of the damned. A comment was made that a few did work that should have been shared by many. No heroes here, all business. Those who were not Naval Academy also were heavy in experience. After the meeting we returned to our ships without incident but still shaken up.

Kamikaze Action In the Philippines

At 0610 hours on 6 December we were under way with other units of TransDiv 103 en route Rizal Beach, Leyte, P.I., to embark troops in compliance with a secret dispatch. By 0742 hours we had anchored off Rizal Beach; by 0935 hours we had embarked seven officers and 127 enlisted men of the 307th Regiment, 77th Division, 24th U.S. Army. This unit of the well-known New York Division was commanded by Captain W.F. Lee. The enlisted men looked much older than the usual GI, and they probably were.

Soldiers in combat areas live a difficult life. Most of the time they carry their essential possessions with them. They rarely have permanent quarters or even the most primitive conditions in which to exist. As I walked around the ship, I noticed my contemporaries from New York and my heart went out to them. Few smiled, and they seemed suspicious of everything and anything.

We had quarters for them, not unlike our own crews quarters, except they were on what had been weather-decks when *Cofer* was a DE. Now enclosed as troop quarters they were unbearably hot. I was no better off in the best room in the house. I would awaken in my bunk in a puddle of sweat. Most of the troops stayed on deck cleaning their rifles, or sharpening their bayonets and not knowing whether they would live to disembark from the ship.

At least on deck they could view the shoreline, which some figured they could swim to should the ship be sunk. Although we had engaged in combat the past few weeks, this voyage would be the first in our capacity as a destroyer-transport. To the crew and to me it would be a first-time experience. It would be interesting, but restrictive since we were limited in our combat role. We would be the protected rather than the protector until the landing force disembarked. I did not look forward to this situation.

After my walk around I called Speziale and the senior officers and said while the troops were aboard they were to be fed from the general mess. We went to extremes to be sure the meals were the best we could serve.

I gave further orders to our officers to order their divisions to treat the soldiers as guests while they were on board. This proved unnecessary. The crew mingled and swapped yarns with the troops, who had to provide their share of galley help.

I had read the operation order a number of times and gave it considerable thought. Intelligence had reported single acts of enemy planes flying into ships. The pilots and planes were referred to as "kamikaze." From what I read it became obvious to me this was a new strategy that would result in multi-plane attacks against our ships.

Because our objective was Ormoc Bay, we would be within close range of several Japanese air bases. I had pre-planned every conceivable anti-aircraft defense deemed likely for conventional air attack. But this was something new. Instead of having one menace to shoot at, and two to evade, the defense had become more complicated. Individual air-to-ship actions were, and still are, of short duration. With a plane carrying a bomb or a torpedo, defensive tactics remained basically the same. We first attempted to shoot the plane down. If we failed in most cases we had a fair second-chance with an evasive tactic, except in the case of a dive bomber.

If a dive bomber evaded our gun fire and dropped his bomb just short of his pull-up-time, there was too little time for effective evasive tactics. Against high-altitude bombing the chances of success were much greater than from a dive bombing or a torpedo attack. My tactics for high-altitude bombing were to watch the bombs as they left the plane and then race at high speed in an evasive action. Against a torpedo plane and a dive bomber, it would be to turn towards the attacker at high speed. In this way the attacker was presented a target greatly reduced in size, and one wherein a few degrees in change of course stood a fair chance of avoiding the bomb or torpedo. As the ship turned most guns could bear on target.

Evasive tactics were something I hoped we would never have to use. If it became necessary it meant the attackers had overwhelmed us by sheer numbers, or our gunnery was not good enough to shoot the planes down before they dropped their destructive loads. This rationalization was the basis for the intensive training of our gun crews. I considered the second alternative a desperate action of last resort. Since hearing about kamikaze attacks, I realized my tactics could not be altered very much. I kept going over time sequences in my mind, and came to a conclusion basically centered on outstanding gunnery.

"Val" dive bombers were an important part of the Japanese sneak attack on Pearl Harbor. By the end of 1944, however, they were obsolete as normal attack planes and were used for kamikaze attacks. Although other types of planes are mentioned in the log, there is a good possibility many were actually Vals. Zeroes, the Japanese first-line fighter, were in short supply.

Attack speed of a Val was over 240 miles an hour. Effective anti-aircraft range of our 5-inch gun was 10,000 feet—less than two miles. This allowed a maximum time from the start of the Val's attack until we shot him down or he hit us of 30 seconds. Actually it was less because often they would dive far from the ship and then make the final approach at a lower altitude. Our relative speed compared to an airplane was negligible. An airplane turns quicker and within a smaller arc than any ship. What had been a tough job before was now impossible unless gunfire shot down the attacker. Evasive movements were passe.

This rehashing of defense tactics hardly ever left my mind. I realized if I did not train the officers and crew to the point where they functioned at the highest-level humanly possible we would be defeated. Realistically the training period was over. The time spent recently in combat areas of the Pacific had initiated our trial by fire. The ship had responded excellently. We were no longer an ASW ship where the Captain controlled the battle; events were moving much faster. We no longer had a "moment of truth," but "seconds of truth." If, as I expected, we would engage kamikazes our fate would be decided within seconds. Once the action began the noise of the gunfire would drown out every order. Essentially gun crews would be on their own. I geared training towards a collective efficiency built around a team rather than an individual effort. A few officers and men were substandard, but the manner in which they were organized and trained relied on a team responses to problems.

As I walked about the ship on one of the rare occasions when my presence was not required on the bridge, I observed the officers and crew as they went about their work. There was no yelling and few orders being given and responded to. Each crew member went about his job as if he had been at sea for many years. I no longer saw them as individual problems, but as a complete unit. I realized I had succeeded, but in the process I had injured myself. I was a wreck both physically and mentally. I had been under stress too long. Instinct told me this operation would be *Cofer's* and my final examination. If we survived we would pass. If not....

We still had done nothing as an APD we could not have done as a DE, except our 5-inch gun was more effective than our previous main battery.

This would soon change with our assignment to Task Group 78.3. ComTaskGroup 78.3, Rear Admiral Arthur Struble in *U.S.S. Hughes (DD-410)*, was in command of this force of eight APDs and 43 assorted landing craft screened by 12 destroyers. For the first time ships of TransDiv 103 would have troops aboard and be part of a mixed convoy that included: LCTs (Landing Craft Tank), LCIs (Landing Craft Infantry), and LSMs (Landing Ship Medium), instead of their being in the screen. There would be no freedom of movement with troops aboard, we would have to plod along with the convoy at a speed determined by the slowest ship.

The entire 77th Division was embarked in the landing craft and the APDs. This was *Cofer's* first operation in which our primary duty was as a troop transport. We would be escorted to the landing area by destroyers. The only concession made to our class of ship, from a defensive position, was in being placed on the outer edges of the convoy so we could best use our fire power, which was superior to the other classes of ships in the convoy.

Once the troops were disembarked and our boats retrieved, we would revert to our destroyer escorts more active role. It was a short voyage. If it were not for the slow speed and other limitations of the LCTs, the whole trip could have been completed in darkness. For some reason the planners of this operation opted to run it in one section. Once Task Group 78.3 formed up, the Japanese had to be aware of it. I didn't have time to think of this problem, and I can't recall worrying about it.

We also had to assume the Japanese knew or suspected our destination. The Japanese could observe the Task Group from the time of its formation until arrival at its destination. I did not dwell on this for I was concentrating on situations that might arise in the coming operation. *Cofer* had been in combat before. With the exception of the "davit" lapse, the ship and crew had performed well. Gunnery accuracy and discipline were excellent; shots-per-gun-per-minute were up to or surpassed standards. I was confident *Cofer* was ready.

At 0615 hours on 6 December we were under way en route to Rizal Beach, Leyte, PI. By 0935 hours officers and troops of the 307th Regiment, 77th Division, 24th U.S. Army had been received aboard in compliance with an attack order dated 1 December 1944, which attested to the speed of conception and implementation of this operation. An hour after the troops were taken aboard, we began debarkation drills with the troops.

In the air, at sea, and on the land the Japanese had fought hard to defend Leyte. Although we were a relatively small force, I expected we would have to fight our way to Ormoc. With six hours of daylight the Japanese would have plenty of opportunity to find and attack this slow-moving convoy.

Planes were picked up on the radar, flares were noticed during the night, but no enemy attack occurred day or night during the entire advance on Ormoc. The sun rose December 7, 1944, on a clear day and a smooth sea—three years after the Pearl Harbor attack. Rumor had it this MacArthur operation was a concession to the General to commemorate the Japanese attack on Pearl. If the weather was an indication of anything, it would be peaceful and quiet. But this was not to be.

I was awake most of the day and night en route to Ormoc Bay expecting the enemy to attack at any minute. Tacloben, in the Leyte Bay area, was under constant air attack, as were the many vessels at anchor in San Pedro Bay. The Ormoc Bay Attack Force was an obvious threat to the Japanese. Radar reports of air and surface contacts kept the radio busy, but the Japanese did not attack us. With troops aboard we could not aggressively attack anything. So we plodded slowly along with the other APDs and landing craft.

At 0657 hours, after taking our launch position off White Beach One, we disembarked the troops into our LCVPs and lowered them into the water—and still no enemy fire from the beach. I went down from the bridge to oversee the first operational use of our davits and boats. Our crew worked efficiently, putting all our boats into the water as scheduled. As the troops entered the boats, one could see the anticipation of danger on their faces. The entire company of seven officers, 127 men, and their equipment was disembarked. I was amazed at the professional manner in which my once green crew went about their business. They performed in a way that gave me great satisfaction, and I let them know I was pleased.

With the ship at General Quarters, I returned to the bridge. We were prepared to support the landing forces with gunfire if resistance should develop. After the boats cleared from the ship, they formed in a line and then a circle—continuing to circle until all the other LCVPs were ready to proceed to the beach.

Five minutes after our four boats were formed up and circling, the last LCVPs were in position and they all started for shore, each LCVP proceeding to its specifically designated position on the beach. I don't recall if we remained where we were or if we followed them in to a closer position to the beach. I believe our orders were to remain in the same position from which we launched the boats. We were already very close to the beach.

252

Once our troops disembarked we were free to engage the enemy if the opportunity arose. The problem was we had to identify an enemy force first or be requested to fire at a specific target on the beach by the forces ashore. There were no orders or targets.

Within minutes the LCVPs hit the beach. Within 10 or 15 minutes they had discharged, retracted from the beach, and were heading back to the ship. During all this time we were in contact with our boats by radios, which were mounted in the boats and had more power than walkie-talkies. All boats were alongside by about 0750 hours, in their cradles by 0800 hours, and secured by 0807 hours. I don't recall any other ship being ready before us to take position in the screen.

Since it was a beautiful day with a smooth sea and no enemy resistance, I was tempted to order a stand down. Other than for my misgivings, reason dictated that I do so. Something deterred me. The situation seemed too good to be true. It did not conform to Japanese responses to other invasions of territory they occupied. Several days prior to this they had fought desperate but losing actions in this same area. The lack of resistance bothered me rather than relieved any anxiety I might have had. Instead my anxiety increased.

With the boats secured and in compliance with ComPhib Group Nine 5-44 Attack Order, we were under way together with the rest of the APDs to take our position in the screening line. By 0815 hours we were in position and started to patrol our station in the screen. Once again we were doing the job of a destroyer escort. Ordinarily I should have felt confident and relaxed. *Cofer* and its crew's performance had been outstanding in their first amphibious operation. All guns, gear, and equipment were in good operating order. And the repaired davit had worked perfectly. The officer's and crew shared my decision to be ready for anything. I did not hear or learn of any grumbling, even though the short stand-down periods from G.Q. still required all guns be manned and ready. I remained at my G.Q. station on the bridge with the others.

At this time landing craft, other than the LCVPs from the APDs, were still engaged in discharging troops and equipment on the beach. Along with *Liddle* we took our position in the screen, a distance of several miles from the main force. The force as a whole was widely dispersed over many miles.

At 0830 hours we sighted unidentified landing barges six miles to the southeast. Permission was granted to investigate, and we immediately increased speed and set a course to intercept. A few minutes later the order

253

was canceled because of probable mines in the area. By 0900 hours we rejoined *Liddle,* patrolling our station in the screen.

On this beautiful day, the water smooth as glass, and with the background of the islands, any picture taken would have been ideal for a travel poster. It was difficult to conceive of combat in such an atmosphere. But I was concerned. Something had to be wrong. If the Japanese were going to attack they should have done so before we discharged the men and supplies on the beach. I could not understand why they had held their planes back since they had several airstrips within close range. Until this time I thought they might be waiting for our force to come closer to Mindoro. If that was our objective they would be unwise to waste their planes on empty ships.

Liddle had stood down, and her flying bridge was full with officers and men taking in the sights. I resisted the temptation to do the same. Although not at General Quarters, we were at Condition One Easy, every gun was manned, the ready ammunition boxes undogged. Under this state of readiness every gun could fire before I could finish saying "commence firing." Kamikaze pilots were known to zero in on a ship's bridge area. Thus I cleared the flying bridge of all personnel except those whose General Quarters station was there. Instinctively I was concerned this peace and quiet was deceptive. I was determined not to be caught off guard. The secondary command station aft was ready should the bridge be hit. The Exec and his team could take command from there.

Whether at War Cruising or General Quarters the routine keeping of rough logs from which the smooth typed logs were constructed was secondary to the primary requirement of defending the ship. This even took precedence over navigation unless in restricted waters. Combat readiness thus precluded much of the routine recording not only for officers but also for enlisted personnel.

All officers were inundated with paper work, war or no war, combat or smooth sailing. Checking and signing the smooth-type log was done at a time when a Yeoman placed a great deal of other paper work before them to sign. Commanding Officers had an even greater problem. My desk was always full of documents I had to peruse and sign. Urgent papers requiring my signature were constantly being brought to me by Yeomen who would stand before me as I signed, so the log could also be done at the same time.

It was difficult to rationalize this situation when not in combat; but at this time when faced with a new and devastating enemy weapon, paper was given the lowest priority. The first priority was for the ship to be seaworthy and all gear and equipment functional so it was ready to fight. Crew comfort and morale, cleanliness of the ship and crew, and many other things were secondary.

This day the ship would be locked in mortal combat. It had finally reached the mission of every combat ship where its life and those that sailed in it were at dire risk. I never noticed the log when I signed it nor did I see it again until years later when I started work on this book. Accuracy was not important in the prior sequences; no one had the historical interest. But this fateful day is steeled in my memory, and I find it at odds not only with what has been written on this battle by others, but with my own official logs. It is also difficult to gain a consensus of opinion from those who experienced this day with me.

At 1000 hours we could hear the chatter on our radios as our air cover first started to engage enemy aircraft at the far end of the force. I sounded General Quarters and, given the condition of readiness we were in, the crew responded in a matter of seconds. If *Liddle* went to G.Q. it was not evident. Their flying bridge was still occupied by many officers and enlisted men. I have no idea what the officers and men of *Cofer* thought as they saw the relaxed atmosphere in *Liddle* while I was playing it tough and keeping *Cofer* ready for instant action. As time passed our task group had still not engaged the enemy.

Suddenly our radar was full of bogeys, enemy aircraft coming at our force from every direction. I ordered the Gunnery Officer to fire the 5-inch gun at any enemy plane within range without further instruction from me. No further clarification was needed. The crew had been trained to be ready for any conceivable situation. The time for drills was over, and the seconds of truth had arrived. If the crew had any reservations about my past concentration on drilling and the present attention to readiness, their doubts were now dispelled. We should soon learn whether the long hours spent training would pay off. Observing the men in the open gun platforms and listening to the exchange of information and orders, it was just another drill. That is what the training was all about. Once we were attacked the crew would have to function by habit.

The 20mm and 40mm secondary batteries were to fire within the plans long worked out in advance, so they would not be changing magazines at high-hit potential close ranges.

This was not the first time we had been under attack, but there was no doubt the coming action would be much different than before. Kamikaze attacks had previously been by a single plane or a small number of planes. No kamikaze had dived at us or any ship we were in company with. All

255

previous attacks had been by planes dropping bombs or torpedoes. Somehow when the day had dawned so lovely and the anticipated resistance had not materialized, I had a strange feeling it would be different. It was.

At about 1100 hours we were retiring north from the main force heading back to Leyte, the beachhead astern of us. Almost simultaneously *Ward* and *Mahan (DD-364)*, an old four-stack tincan converted to an APD and a modern destroyer, were hit by suicide planes in rapid succession. We could see them burning. Ignoring landing craft the numerous suicide planes zeroed in on the DDs and the APDs. Once the landing craft had discharged troops and equipment, they were not worth the loss of a suicide plane.

When I looked at *Liddle* I saw a number of people still on the flying bridge. By this time the voice radio frequency was full of reports about the bearings and distances of suicide planes that had broken through the Combat Air Patrol (CAP). It was obvious this was an attack in force and probably the first large concentrated kamikaze attack of the war. Our force, operating together and spread out over a large area, was overestimated in its importance, and the attack overwhelmed our fighter cover. Pleas for more CAP continued on the radio. Enemy planes were getting through and were engaged at close range by the DDs and APDs. With *Liddle* we continued steaming to join the main force.

By 1115 hours a number of planes flying at high altitudes had moved in the direction of *Liddle* and *Cofer*. By this time we were in close communications with other ships exchanging information about where planes had penetrated our air cover.

I was concerned about our ability to adequately divide our fire if planes attacked simultaneously from different quadrants. We had only the single 5-inch gun as a main battery. The 40 and 20mm guns were secondary batteries with a short range but rapid fire. It was essential in firing on one plane to hold fire until it was possible to maintain continuous fire during the some 15 to 20 seconds the plane would be within range. Changing magazines could be done in a few seconds, but if this was required at the crucial time when the enemy plane was on its final approach, either another gun would have to hit the plane or it would hit us. The mathematics of this gunnery problem worked against us. Perfect gunnery was needed to overcome the odds.

This time limitation required the disciplined restraint we had trained for. In the few anti-aircraft actions we engaged in prior to this day, I could find no fault with our gunnery performance. In facing kamikazes, however, we had no margin for error. As several kamikazes circled overhead at altitudes beyond our range, it appeared they were stalking while attempting to select the most important target. TransDiv 103 presented something new in the way of a ship silhouette since we were the only 5-inch gun APDs in the Western Pacific.

I watched as they circled while selecting their targets. Radar operators passed the ranges on to the Gunnery Officer. Once the plane or planes made a move, I would remind the Gunnery Officer to fire as they came within the range of specific guns. At the same time I would order full speed and come to a course that would allow the 5-inch gun to bear on target. Once committed to a course it was unlikely *Cofer* would have enough time to alter it. We would have but one crack at the target. My eyes stayed glued on the four or five planes that circled overhead, while my ears listened to the constant flow of radar information. The planes were little specks in the sky easily visible on this cloudless day. Lookouts also had to watch for the sudden appearance of a low-flying plane coming in from nearby land masses.

It was a tense situation, and all in the ship seemed to sense that within the next few minutes we would be coming to grips with our destiny. I recall sneaking a glimpse at the men in the 20mm gun tubs adjacent to and below the flying bridge. They would look up and smile at me with confidence as if I had the answer to all the problems facing us. Hardly did they know their confidence in me gave me confidence in them. I could sense it. This ship of mavericks had mastered their difficult assignments.

This all transpired within minutes as I prepared for what would be the longest day in my life. All hands wore helmets and life jackets. The heat of the sun together with the pressure of the situation added to an unusual atmosphere as we cruised in a calm sea on a clear day without a cloud in the sky.

All of a sudden two planes came down to the 10,000-foot level. I strained to see the lead plane. I singled her out and quickly decided her dive would end well astern of us. I restated the order to the Gunnery Officer: "Commence firing when planes are in range of individual guns and the bearings clear." Simultaneously I ordered full speed and had the helmsman come to a course that would allow the 5-inch gun as well as a full side of the secondary batteries to bear on target. I can't recall exactly, but I believe I placed the plane on the starboard bow. If the dive were to come right at us, I would have attempted to head directly at the plane. Neither plane, however, dived directly at us. They ended their dives a good distance away and about 500 feet above the water.

The lead plane seemed to be targeting *Cofer*. The other, somewhat be-

257

hind and further off, appeared to be better positioned for *Liddle*. I was very concerned should the two planes attack us at the same time. It would be difficult and probably impossible to adequately control the division of fire power against two planes. I was well aware the total time lapse from the time they started their dive until both Zeros or Vals were on target would be about a minute. Therefore when *Cofer* commenced firing at 1123 hours, went to full speed and turned towards the first attacking plane, the second hand moved. The dive was not steep. As the lead plane gradually leveled off from the dive, it started to alter course between *Liddle* and us.

They came from different quadrants. We fired first with our 5-inch gun, filling the sky around us with flack, and hit the lead plane just as it started its run. The secondary batteries helped finish her off, splashing her well astern of *Liddle*. As soon as she splashed I noticed the second plane was targeting *Liddle* and was still clear while she circled around the port bow.

Only sporadic fire came from *Liddle,* and this was a surprise to all of us on deck. But on *Cofer* the noise was deafening. Our whole ship shuddered from the recoil and noise of the gunfire and from the vibrations of the ship as it moved into action at full speed. I had taken a quick look at *Liddle* and noticed she had not changed course nor come to full speed. Their flying bridge still was crowded with personnel.

The second plane had turned away from us and was making its final run on *Liddle*. We had hit her with our secondary battery and she was smoking, but she was still able to slam into *Liddle's* flying bridge.

At the moment of impact *Liddle's* bridge disappeared from view in an explosion of fire and smoke. Gone were Captain Brogger, the Exec, the Doctor, the Gunnery Officer, and the Ass't Engineering Officer, as well as numerous enlisted men on the bridge at the time. Damage and casualties spread far beyond the bridge. C-Division (Communications) was practically wiped out as Combat Information Center (Radar) and the Radio Room were two decks below the flying bridge. All the signalmen and those people in the wheelhouse directly below the flying bridge were lost. Many aboard our ship saw what happened. Although their remembrances were somewhat vague, they were basically consistent.

Another plane now came skimming over the water directly at our flying bridge. The secondary battery splashed her close aboard the 20mm gun tub abaft the port side. This occurred shortly after I changed course, slowing to render assistance to *Liddle*. All the action in this never-ending moment of terror occurred in less than two minutes. By this time three of our ships had been hit, but it was far from a victory for the kamikaze.

Three suicide planes had been shot down in our area against damage to *Liddle*. After the hit on *Liddle,* and for a short time after, no more bogeys were reported coming at us. *Liddle* continued at the same speed after the hit, but she had lost steering control and was going in circles. I increased speed in an effort to close the ship, gain information, and help her. Miles from the main force, I was being plagued by questions from the Task Group Commander about *Liddle's* condition and whether she should be abandoned and sunk.

After some time lapsed *Liddle's* Chief Engineer slowed her down. I then got closer to her and with the bull horn asked: "Who is the surviving senior officer?" I was shocked to hear a reply that is still vivid in my mind today: "They are all dead." I then told them to stop the ship so we could board, but the ship continued sailing around like a chicken with its head cut off. If anyone took control it was not obvious on deck nor at the after control station. I wanted to send over a doctor, a qualified line-officer, and a signalman. More assistance as needed would be given.

Fortunately during the long period to follow in our efforts to gain control over *Liddle,* no further attacks were made on either *Liddle* or us. No planes came within range of our guns, enabling us to concentrate on the frustrating job of coming alongside and boarding *Liddle.*

I had Lt. Cofer prepare an LCVP for launching and ordered Lt. Cleland to lead a party to board *Liddle* to establish communications and determine what further personnel and assistance were required. I sent word to Dr. Wendelken to prepare to board with Cleland and Signalman Max Norton. While we were readying the boarding party, I tried one last time to have *Liddle* come to a stop, but no one answered my hail.

No officer on deck was alive or uninjured, and those ratings not injured must have been in shock. Shortly before *Liddle* was hit both *Ward* and *Mahan* had been abandoned, the survivors rescued, and orders given to sink both ships. The Task Group Commander was barraging me with questions about the situation in *Liddle*. I was keeping the Task Group Commander and my own boss, Captain Parsons, informed, but what I gave them must have been confusing because I was not getting any information from *Liddle*.

With his forces under continual attack, the Task Group Commander wanted to expedite the withdrawal and start the slow voyage back to Leyte. I told Captain Parsons we would get *Liddle* under control and bring her back with us one way or the other. At the same time the Task Group Commander, without any hard information, thought it would be best to abandon the ship and sink her. In a manner not contradicting the Commander, yet indicating to me to stay with her, Captain Parsons encouraged the action I was taking to save her.

I can't recall when *Liddle* launched two of her LCVPs, for what reason, how many people were in them, or even when their crews reboarded. My attention was riveted on *Liddle* while we at times chased her and at other times avoided her because she was out of control while still steaming.

Around noon I ordered Lt. Cleland, Dr. Wendelken, and Norton away in the LCVP with their equipment. They had no idea what they were getting into. I continued to try to bring *Cofer* alongside. If it were not such sad a situation it would have been comical. Our LCVP joined the chase of *Liddle*, which although not running away, continued to make boarding impossible. Around 1230 hours *Liddle* suddenly came to a stop and our LCVP quickly went alongside. Our boarding party was finally able to climb aboard.

Lt. Cleland, a line officer, Lt(jg) Wendelken, our doctor, and Max Norton, a signalman, transferred to *Liddle*. Norton was later replaced by Art Conn and Jim Snellen, of the Boat Division, to assist *Liddle's* return to Leyte. Communications between *Cofer* and *Liddle* were established with walkie-talkie radio and semaphore as well as Morse Code. All communications between Command and *Liddle* passed through us.

Lt. Cleland reported the steering control could be regained quickly. The engines were working, and he expected to be able to follow us into the formation for the return voyage within several minutes. *Liddle* was brought under control in short order. She then took station astern of us as we proceeded back to our screening station in the force returning to Leyte.

I had to go out on a limb before advising the Task Group Commander we could get *Liddle* back. I had no facts to go on other than hope. With the sinking of *Mahan* and *Ward*, policy had already been established regarding damaged ships. Captain Parsons had backed me up, and thus Cleland's report was of great relief to both of us.

I reported to the Task Group Commander our party was aboard *Liddle* and the ship was under control. We could guide it back. I also said we would have to leave *Liddle's* two LCVPs behind. Nevertheless I was ordered to take the LCVPs aboard *Cofer*. This was unbelievable. The Task Group Commander was ready to sink *Liddle*, but was concerned about the salvage of two LCVPs! I could not understand this.

It was a simple order, but what to do? Although not coming in enemy planes were still within radar range. This situation could change within minutes or even seconds if a kamikaze should approach at a low altitude over the land. *Cofer* had a stability problem to begin with; the davits and wire hoisting cables were not designed to hold LCVPs swung out while under way. I wasn't certain we could figure out a way to secure the boats if we could raise them. Once secured outboard of the sides of the ship, the LCVPs would limit the arc in which several of our guns could bear. We would look like an airplane, but could not fly.

I had no alternative but to comply. I at least had to try. I brought *Cofer* alongside one of the LCVPs first and made her fast while I proceeded to come alongside the other. I wanted to lift the two boats at once since the chances were we would list to one side if we did not raise them at the same time. I watched this operation carefully from the flying bridge. *Cofer's* crew continued to surprise me. They did the impossible and lifted the two boats.

We deliberately did not lash them into position securely. I wanted to be ready to jettison them if I had to. Once we had them hanging from the davits at 1315 hours, I reported them aboard. With *Liddle* following astern *Cofer* was back on station by 1330 hours. It was not a time for levity, but if this situation had not occurred under the tragic circumstances it did, I might have reported "request permission to take off." We had wings and it was no joke. The ship's stability, tender before, was now dangerously so. I was not about to consider an order of full-speed ahead with a sharp turn towards an attacking plane. We would have probably turned over.

The weather remained calm, but I had resolved to drop the extra LCVPs if there was any trouble. Their being hoisted aboard proved two things: that our repaired davit was strong; and, since we were very "tender" on the return trip it added to my conclusions about the ship's stability.

By the time we were back on station the full tragedy of what had occurred in *Liddle* was gradually reported to us by Lt. Cleland as Dr. Wendelkan struggled to cope with the many injured crew members. My worst fears were confirmed—the flying bridge had been loaded with personal and all were killed. Little distinguish one from the other; it was a massacre. I don't recall how many were killed and injured, but it was a large number. Damage reports indicated most of the damage was limited to the flying bridge area.

We proceeded slowly with the others to Leyte. The day continued to be beautiful, but death remained all around. The skies again filled with kamikazes diving at the DDs and APDs, while ignoring the slow-moving and empty landing craft. We could hear our fighter pilots talking on the radio, and constant requests being made for more CAP by the Task Group Commander. Ominous reports kept emanating from the radar operators:

"Bogey bearing..., distance...." They kept coming and our CAP intercepted some, but not all.

The situation went something like this: Radar would report, "Bogey, bearing 030, distance 3200." Then I would wait. At times the bogey would not come in, at other times it would head for another part of the Task Group or be shot down by the CAP. The words that made our juices flow were, "Bogey, bearing 120, distance 2125" a break in time, and then, "...coming in." With this last report we knew we were in for another rough engagement of some 30 to 40 seconds that would end with a kill on our part or one of us would be hit.

Once the first kamikaze plane pierced the CAP—there was always an enemy plane on the radar scope—the tension never let up. While we were engaged in getting *Liddle* under control, I could not relax: a kamikaze attack was never more than a few minutes off. *Liddle's* situation, aside from being a sad one, was a frustrating problem that lasted over two hours. They had suffered badly but could not have made the situation more difficult for us as we tried to assist them.

An enemy plane dived into *Lamson (DD-367)*, just astern of *Liddle,* crashing on the after part of the Deck House and sweeping forward through the after funnel, enveloping the ship in flames. She fell out of formation and was saved by the rescue tug, which put out the fires and took her in tow. At 1440 hours we fired at an enemy plane identified as a "Dinah" coming in on our starboard beam. She was destroyed. Because others had also fired at her, I did not claim a credit.

At 1500 hours we were firing on a "Zeke" on the port beam. We probably had the best shot at it, but again, although others also fired at it, the plane fell near us. At 1549 hours we fired at yet another plane which was also pounced on by a P-38. It went down in flames off our starboard bow. At 1624 hours another came down in flames close to our starboard quarter. And so it went until darkness.

With the 5-inch firing only several feet away when elevated for anti-aircraft, the concussion on my ears was numbing. My brains felt like they were scrambled. Heavily clad in a helmet and life jacket, I suffered unbearably. The hot decks passed the heat through the soles of my shoes. This with the added noise of the secondary batteries did not make for a quiet afternoon cruise in the sun. We remained at G.Q. until 1900 hours that evening. During this whole time I doubt if I was off the bridge for more than a few minutes. When darkness closed in and the noise stopped, the horror of it all hit me all at once. One minute I had been looking at *Liddle's* bridge and the next minute it was gone. I was very close to many on the ship, especially the Captain.

We were reinforced by more destroyers as we escorted the empty landing craft at very slow speed. We had stayed with them throughout the whole time, but I don't recall any one of them being selected as a target for the suicide planes. We loyally stayed with them, however, as the CAP stayed with us. This is what the U.S. Navy in World War II was all about.

I had been at sea for nine years and three months, with the exception of about three months when I worked for Thos. Cook & Sons in New York in 1936 and about six months of schools and pre-commissioning duties ashore including the conversion time in Brooklyn in *Cofer*. I had been in command most of the war, and it was starting to take its toll. As I reflected on the day's events I realized the performance of *Cofer* was miraculous. No ship could have performed better. Every piece of machinery, every instrument, every gun, every person—everything in the ship worked well when we started the operation, and it worked well when we finished it.

The way the ship's force had repaired the broken davit after it had been declared "a repair beyond the capacity of the forces afloat," was something one had to see to believe. The repair had even enabled the davit to carry the unusual load of *Liddle's* boats on the return leg. The discipline, shots-per-gun-per-minute, and the accuracy of the gunnery was unbelievable. Every gun functioned as did those who directed the fire and those who manned the guns. I watched in amazement as they led their targets, which is the secret of effective anti-aircraft firing.

From the time *Liddle* was hit at 1127 hours until she was under way again at 1315 hours, we stood by her and brought order to a badly damaged ship and a demoralized crew shocked by the terrible hit and casualties they suffered. As we proceeded on in the darkness in a smooth sea, I marveled at the proficiency of *Cofer's* officers and crew. I found some contentment in the level of professionalism they had attained. I was tired, mentally exhausted, and had no more to give them. I had taught them all I knew. Comparing the performance of *Cofer* to other ships, I realized as long as they worked as a team, there was no operation beyond their capacity.

I could not think of any greater test than in combat against a kamikaze. Together with the other ships in the group they had experienced a kamikaze attack in force. They had performed brilliantly and bravely. Although they were somewhat shocked by it all, which was natural, I could sense *Cofer's* crew had come of age. They were men in every sense of the word. I don't believe I slept much that night, if at all, for we were still within range of the kamikazes. I kept watch and let the crew stand down.

As we proceeded on to San Pedro Bay, the silhouette of *Liddle* was visible behind us. Except for the passing of course and speed changes from us to them there was quiet interrupted only infrequently as we received and passed information to the Task Force Commander. *Ward,* in which Swede Brogger and I had attended the pre-sailing conference, was on the bottom of Ormoc Bay with *Mahan. Lamson* was no longer with the Task Group. She was being towed back by a rescue tug. *Liddle* was still with us steaming behind in formation, but many of her crew were no longer with us. Swede Brogger, who also had worked so hard to train his crew, would no longer be around for friendly conversation. Ensign Chet Basset, who had been commissioned from the ranks and was serving as the Ass't Chief Engineer would not return. He was a cheerful man, who together with his delightful wife and baby, lived close to Ginny and me in Charleston. I would never forget them.

I was very weak to begin with and this day had taken about all I had left out of me. I had never before been so confused about what to do under attack except in the SC. The only defense I could see against a kamikaze was good and more gunnery. I could open up at long range with the 5-inch but would have to hold back on my secondary batteries until the last few seconds so not to be changing magazines at the crucial moment.

All during the daylight I had been completely engrossed in my work and had not given myself much time to think, other than to respond to the threats on our ship and meeting problems and attacks as they arose. I was so pent up sleep was impossible. My bunk would be a puddle of water from my sweat. In staying on the bridge I was at least cool. I had taken off the helmet and lifebelt as had the others.

For the first time that day, I believed it safe to leave the bridge. I tried to cat nap, but I could not rest. My desk was piled high with documents awaiting my signature. I let them wait. The sweat rolled from me onto the moldy mattress, and I just lay there.

We brought our charges home without loss, but we had taken a pretty good shellacking. We anchored in San Pedro Bay at 0842 hours on the 8th; by 1100 hours Cleland, Dr. Wendelken, Snellen, and Conn had returned aboard from *Liddle*. We had to send a clean-up detail to *Liddle*. Later we congregated in Cleland's room and had some drinks. No one talked much but everyone was hurting.

These mid-west, western, and southern gentlemen were unusual men.

All were religious and tolerant of others. On this day they offered a toast to those who had been killed and injured, drank, and then prayed. Wendy gave us some idea about what it was like in *Liddle* and then said we were better off not to know more. It was obvious he was upset at not being able to save more lives than he did.

Doc. Wendelken was a big man in every way. When he came on board he could not see how such healthy men would need a doctor. When I asked him if he had gotten enough practice in *Liddle,* he replied: "That was not medicine, it was butchery."

Cleland did not talk much about the situation in *Liddle.* He chose not to speak of it. I learned recently from Lt. Hahn that Cleland had done much more than repeat orders between ships. Other rumors about what happened in *Liddle* have been passed to me. There is no point in recording them. Those who really knew the story died in the tragedy.

When I went back to work while we were anchored in San Pedro Bay, Leyte, I noticed a strange quiet had descended over the area. Only two days before San Pedro Bay had been under constant attack. But now the war seemed to have moved away.

Although some semblance of peace and tranquility had returned, something had happened to me. Kamikaze action was indeed frightening, but I had been living with fear for a long time. The pressure of command was nothing new. In fact I was well satisfied with the way *Cofer's* crew had performed. The *Liddle* tragedy hurt, but I figured this was only one of many things I had been living with and which was a way of life now common to many of us. Yet there was a malaise I could not explain.

Dr. Wendelken noticed it and was watching me carefully. He gave me medication for my headaches and stomach pains, which had become much more acute. But I had a number of other things wrong with me: piles from having to remain on the bridge so long; varicose veins from the long hours of standing on steel decks; and ulcerous stomach pains from extreme nervousness. My weight had dropped below 130 pounds. I was also green from eating atabrine as a malaria offset. I looked and felt awful and was becoming depressed.

After giving me a physical examination, Dr. Wendelken strongly recommended I be transferred to shore duty. He said the culmination of physical problems were not in themselves critical at the time, but if not taken care of soon they would be. He also said my nervous system was nearing the breaking point, and I needed a change and a rest. I didn't want to leave at this time and under such conditions. I asked if I could delay the transfer until after the Mindoro invasion planned the following week. He wanted me to go on medical leave followed by shore duty, and claimed if I did not do so I might suffer permanent damage to my health.

Dr. Wendelkan discussed this with Captain Parsons. Although Parsons realized I was long overdue for shore duty, he was concerned the Mindoro operation would bring out the suicide planes in greater force. Since he leaned heavily on the performance of *Cofer,* he wanted me to remain. Wendelken did not agree, but he could not beat the two of us, and I stayed to complete the next mission.

Meanwhile I decided to visit some old friends aboard other ships in Leyte Harbor. I met with Henry Bradford who was a Lcdr. in command of the old repair ship *Oglala;* with Jim Knowlton who too was still a Lcdr., but was in command of an AK (Large Navy Dry Cargo Ship). Bill Dodge was there as Master of Liberty Ship *S.S. Edward Markham.* My old schoolmate from high school and NYSMMA, Andrew Hirth, was a Lcdr. and Chief Engineer in *U.S.S. Maryland,* a battleship; however, I could only communicate with him by signals as the dreadnought passed by. These visits were therapy in a way, and a change I badly needed.

Later I went to work on a plan I had for repelling kamikaze attacks. I believed we could install two more 20mm guns, without tubs, on lower levels without endangering our stability much more. They could be jettisoned quickly if necessary.

The problem was linked to the overall problem of the poor stability of the ship. But it was evident to me the greatest danger to us, other than from undisciplined fire from friendly ships, was suicide planes. I directed our people to trade movies or other things for more small caliber guns to mount on deck. They did. The more guns the better the chance of dividing the fire. I then asked the officers to work out how they would divide the fire power under different conditions of kamikaze attack. They did this on their own. I was no longer talking to amateurs.

By installing the guns so we could jettison them quickly, within the overall stability-jettison plans, we could increase our secondary fire power and our chances of hitting the kamikazes. Tactics were something else again; when we had troops aboard and were part of the convoy, we had no freedom of action with courses and speeds.

Actually our evasive tactics against a kamikaze were of limited value. These planes could turn very quickly, and our speed relative to theirs was of little effect. Thus it boiled down to a steady course with maneuvers dictated by getting the most fire power to bear, and how to divide our fire power when, as in the case of *Liddle,* several planes came at us from different directions.

In the short time the officers and crew of *Cofer* had been in the vessel, particularly since the conversion, they had gained more experience than many Navy officers received in their whole careers. Meredith, Cleland, Cofer, Hahn, and Peters were more qualified to command a DE or APD-type craft than most of the new Commanding Officers being assigned. The crew also were very good. Our gunnery had been excellent at Ormoc Bay. It was disciplined and accurate, while at the same time restrained in instances where we would have hit our own ships.

At the time I did not realize the importance of the Ormoc Bay operation nor have I noticed any detailed analysis of it. But I have come to certain conclusions. I lean to those who say the Philippines should have been bypassed, and the high command should not have acquiesced to General MacArthur's strategy revolving around his personal interests. Once the operation began, however, the Japanese High Command failed to react, even within their own operational strategy.

The Japanese had prepared operation Sho (victory). Because they didn't know when and where the Americans would hit next, Sho had several contingency plans, one of those was for Leyte. As with most Japanese plans it was very complex with difficult, "too difficult," timing.

Their reaction to the Leyte operation and the ensuing surface battles appeared confused. One can never know how things would have evolved had the battleship *Yamoto* and its forces continued into unprotected Leyte Harbor instead of turning around after only minor damage during the Battle of Samar. Little stood between *Yamoto* forces and General MacArthur in *U.S.S. Nashville,* together with his public relations operation, that could have impeded *Yamoto.* It is very likely *Yamoto* forces could have completely wiped out General MacArthur along with the numerous support forces afloat and the Army forces ashore still within range of *Yamoto's* batteries. Yet the Japanese did turn around, and Leyte remained the hub of the Philippine invasion for a time.

The Ormoc Bay operation, when added to the others, marks the contrasts in Japanese tactics. At times their leadership illustrated pure genius; at other times, it was simply unexplainable. Their courage, gunnery, and seamanship were outstanding, but something was lacking. There is general acceptance today that the Ormoc Bay operation was a hastily conceived plan of General MacArthur to commemorate December 7th and his historic "I will return." In my opinion it was one of the most important events of the war. I believe the Japanese Command could find no intelligent rationalization to this operation, concluded it was a part of something much more important, and decided to commit over a hundred and possibly hundreds of newly formed kamikaze forces to repel it.

Actual figures of planes shot down are hard to establish. I have seen a figure of 82 confirmed kills between the forces afloat and the CAP. We shot all day; and after studying data available to me, I would estimate we shot down at least four planes and possibly as many as seven. I mainly claimed assists, and thus *Cofer* data hardly could have inflated the kill count. Most air and sea elements ordinarily overstate, and I believe we could estimate 70 kills with probably 100 other planes committed, which for any number of reasons did not reach their target or were held in reserve.

This has meaning, particularly when compared to the Pearl Harbor attack just three years earlier. It is conceivable that almost as many or more planes were involved in the attack force as there were in '41. There were differences. No aircraft carriers were involved, and the attacks were launched from various airfields on land. The '41 attack, the result of a long-planned strategy and tactics, was carried out by experienced pilots with conventional bombs and torpedoes. The target was meaningful: capital ships, airfields, aircraft, and many strategic objectives.

Enemy attacks in the Ormoc Bay operation did not begin until after landing craft had discharged troops and equipment. Loaded, the invasion fleet was of some but not much strategic importance. Once suicide attacks began in mid-morning, the pilots mostly ignored the small empty landing craft and instead drove home their attacks against eight APDs and several destroyers. Unlike the Pearl Harbor attack, where they hit hard, destroyed a fleet, and then returned to their carriers all within a few hours with minimal losses, Ormoc was quite different.

The attacks continued steadily from 1000 hours to darkness, singly and with small groups of attacking planes at a time. None of the landing craft were hit or sunk that I can recall. One old APD, *Ward,* was sunk, and one new-class APD, *Liddle,* was hit. All but one of the destroyers involved was a small, post-World War I type. *Mahan* was sunk, but *Lamson* and *Liddle* survived to be repaired and returned to action. As the mission, dubious as it was, did succeed, and as the DDs and APDs successfully fought off most of the attacking planes, it foretold the desperation, sensitivity, and declining effectiveness of the Japanese armed forces.

Navy ships and planes alone did not defeat them. Army Air Corps fighters assisted brilliantly. Inadvertently suckered into a very costly action, the Japanese lost Mindoro before we ever launched the attack. Although I would go on to Mindoro, and did not realize the significance of the Ormoc battle, it was the turning point in the invasion of the Philippines and illustrated how weak the Japanese forces had become.

Ormoc Bay was a milestone in my career. All of my training and experience had been moving to the climax reached at Ormoc in the little *APD-62* together with my intrepid crew. I had no time to dwell on this subject, for I was heavily engaged in preparing for the Mindoro invasion. The operations orders for this landing had long been in the works. Organization of the forces afloat were much more detailed and professional for Mindoro than the Ormoc plans had been.

Like an old war horse lost at sea, I carried on, never letting up in a work ethic that had built up over the years. The intense heat, the steaming decks, the constant noise, and the small retreat of my room, which in effect was a steam bath, were my world. My compensation was the companions and character of the men I then shared my life with.

We did not remain in Leyte long, and during this time we prepared for the coming invasion of Mindoro. Leyte was still a harbor full of all types of warships and merchant ships of many nations. I've never heard of our forces being referred to as an Armada in the way the Spanish Armada was, but the U.S. Navy's Pacific Fleet was the greatest naval force ever assembled in any ocean at one time. With modern weapons being what they are, I do not believe we will ever again experience such a large navel force.

At 0650 hours of the morning of 11 December, we were under way for Virgai Point to load troops. By 0845 hours we had embarked a combat team from the 19th Infantry Regiment, 24th Division of the U.S. Army, First Lieutenant Thomas Brazeale, Jr., in command. The date of the order, November 28, 1944, lent credence to the rumor that the Ormoc operation had been substituted for this carefully planned one for Mindoro.

We later took on fuel and also spent the afternoon replenishing our ammunition. We had expended almost all or our anti-aircraft ammunition. By 1715 hours we completed loading ammo and anchored in San Pedro Bay for the night.

With troops aboard the atmosphere changed in the same manner as before. We treated them as guests. At 1440 hours on 12 December TransDiv 103, less *Liddle,* and with ComTransDiv in *Lloyd* being CTU 78.3.2 formed up. Additional ships were assigned to our division. Task Unit 78.38, which included PT Squadron 70.1.4 together with other ships comprising the Mindoro Attack Group, with ComTskGrp 73 in *U.S.S.*

Nashville, departed from San Pedro Bay, P.I., for Mindoro. O.T.C. was Rear Admiral Struble, who had commanded the Ormoc operation so well.

Mindoro was a much larger operation than Ormoc Bay. This skillfully adaptable force of 135 ships included cruisers, destroyers, destroyer escorts, APDs, motor torpedo boats, an ammunition ship, and other combat vessels. A number of merchant ships rounded out the convoy. This force compared with the large transatlantic convoys.

As an APD with troops aboard, we were again not part of the escort but again placed on an outer edge of the convoy so we could get maximum use of our fire power. At 0800 hours on 13 December merchant ships designated Convoy M-1 joined up, and by 0835 hours our voyage continued. *Nashville* took station on our starboard beam. Another beautiful day for a cruise—calm seas, sunshine, and peaceful scenery greeted us as we steamed toward the Surigao Straits. By about 1440 hours we had started through the Straits.

We had no contacts nor any indication of enemy action in the area. At 1457 hours a kamikaze flying low over the land, undetected by radar, slammed into *Nashville* aft of her bridge and in front of her stack. I immediately sounded G.Q., expecting this might be the forerunner of an attack in force. Powerless to do anything but observe the explosions and fires, we were all struck by the seriousness of it all.

As a DE we could have rushed to assist *Nashville* , but as an APD with troops aboard we were only observers, helpless to assist. This phase of an APD's mission, where we were required to maintain our station, was difficult for me to accept. I was miserable. Every nerve and instinct within me cried out to assist *Nashville* . We were the closest ship, but all we could do was sail by watching men die.

Every secondary explosion pierced me like a knife. The sooner another ship capable of fighting the fire could get alongside, the faster the fire could be contained. Although she slowed down she maintained a steady course, and coming alongside the leeward side was possible. *Liddle* had frustrated me in this same situation, but *Nashville* was under control from her after steering station shortly after being hit. I seemed to be cursed as *Cofer* simply steamed along in formation as the explosions continued.

Nashville had been hit at 1457 hours. I do not recall her requesting assistance, and no ship came to her assistance until about 1615 hours. In the interim *Nashville's* crew extinguished all fires in about 15 minutes. By 1510 hours she was under control. *Nashville* managed to keep station, sailing parallel to us on the base course and speed. It was a tribute to a well-trained crew and a well-built ship. Being so close we could see the extensive damage to ship and crew—133 were killed and 200 wounded, with heavy casualties in the bridge area. Admiral Struble survived uninjured, but his Chief of Staff and General Dunckel's Chief of Staff with other officers and crew, who were on the starboard side of the bridge close to the area where the kamikaze had hit, were killed. The Admiral avoided death by a hair. At 1655 hours *U.S.S. Dashiell* went alongside, and survivors on Struble's staff transferred his flag to *Dashiell*. At 1745 hours *Nashville* returned to Leyte escorted by *U.S.S. Stanley (DD-478)*.

I happened to be looking toward *Nashville* when I saw the kamikaze suddenly appear, rising up about 100 feet after she cleared land. Then she turned to the right and slammed into the after section of the bridge forward of the stack. The time lapse from the second the plane came into view until she struck *Nashville* could not have exceeded 10 seconds. I can't recall whether *Nashville* got off a shot, but would doubt it. I didn't even have time to mentally respond to what I saw before the kamikaze hit.

This was the beginning of several air battles. A P-38 shot down a "Dinah" twin-engined bomber at 1756 hours. Navy fighters shot down two "Lilly" type bombers as well. Air battles continued until darkness. It was obvious the Japanese were going to put up a fight. At 1921 hours we secured from G.Q. and set war cruising condition. Although it was to be a quiet night, I remained on the flying bridge, leaving only for a light meal and a short nap in my room.

We continued on our northerly course, greeting the morning of the 14th with a routine Dawn Alert and going to G.Q. Another beautiful day greeted us, but it would be a busy one for me as we alternated between G.Q. and war cruising condition. This task force was so big I felt enveloped and trapped by all the ships around me. Freedom of movement and gunnery response to enemy action was restricted. As I noticed the professionalism of the officers and men of *Cofer*, I realized they must be sharing the same frustrations.

Three bombs were dropped on minesweepers 10 miles ahead of the convoy at 0943 hours on the 14th. No casualties. Another bogey was shot down that afternoon by our fighters. I remained on the flying bridge expecting kamikazes to attack in force and pierce our CAP. Enemy planes appeared, but not in the force or with the determination to attack as they had on the 7th. I had no way of knowing Allied forces had already destroyed so many Japanese airplanes. With only a few days between the two operations, it is now obvious the Japanese had insufficient time to assemble another large kamikaze force. The 14th ended with reports of enemy aircraft all around, but no more attacks.

We continued to steam north during the relatively quite night. Early on the morning of 15 December, screening destroyers attacked an enemy ship and sank it. By 0645 hours we arrived on station at the transport area off Mindoro Island. At 0700 hours, with no enemy resistance, we launched our boats with troops and equipment aboard. By 0802 hours the troops had landed on the beach, our boats had returned, were secured, and we sailed to take our screening position.

All during the operation our forces were being attacked by Japanese planes, but none had come close to us. Other ships, including an ammunition ship, were hit. It simply disappeared in a cloud of smoke. I could not leave the bridge. The action could have moved in our direction at any time. Enemy aircraft never ceased attempting to penetrate our CAP, with few getting through. By 0850 hours our forces had reformed to screen the vessels returning to Leyte. We were now part of the escort together with other APDs of our division, including *Laffey* and *Pringle,* escorting mostly LSMs and LCIs. Captain Parsons was the CTU and the OTC.

Just prior to departure 11 enemy planes pierced the CAP and attacked our forces standing off the beach and those proceeding to the beach and on it.

Every armed vessel within range fired and, of the 11 planes, shot down eight before they came close to any ship. Two kamikazes flew into two LSTs approaching the beach. In addition to the ships shooting at the attacking planes, our own aircraft remained on their tails. A third kamikaze was shot down by either the friendly plane on its tail, the ships, or the combined fire power of both. Unlike at Ormoc Bay the Japanese inflicted serious losses to personnel, ships, and equipment during the critical landing operation. Aside from the 11 planes that penetrated the CAP during this last attack, the CAP destroyed many enemy planes prior to their piercing the screen.

The performance of our air cover was unbelievable. Although orders to the CAP were not to fly over the ships, our airmen would follow an enemy aircraft through the flack of many friendly ships and constantly risk their lives for us.

During our return to Leyte enemy planes constantly appeared on radar, but no further attacks were made. I could not relax—enemy planes could have been on top of us within minutes. The pressure of the Ormoc Bay operation was not apparent in the Mindoro Task Group. But rest was impossible, and the need to constantly concentrate on the situation never let up.

One had to be in the battles of Ormoc Bay and Mindoro to realize the extent and severity of combat between planes...and ships desperately defending themselves against an endless flow of kamikazes. By the time darkness fell and the fighting ended each day, *Cofer's* crew had distinguished itself in intense battle and humanitarian rescue. Both engagements took place on the most beautiful days I can remember—in a setting of peace and tranquillity disturbed only by the noise, destruction, and horrible death of men engaged in modern, mortal combat.

U.S.S. Cofer, *trial run off Charleston, SC, before departing for shakedown off Bermuda, January 1944.*

U.S.S. Cofer, *Benediction during commissioning ceremony, Charleston, SC, Navy Yard, 17 January 1944.*

__Cofer__ off Panama en route to Galapagos with a bone in her teeth. Picture taken from bridge of **U.S.S. Liddle**.

*Lcdr. Al Chester on **Cofer**. Atlantic, 1944.*

*Officers of **Cofer**. Bottom row, L-R: Lt (jg) Clelend; Lts McLees, Chester, Oksala, and Cofer. Back row, L-R: Ensign Lapovsky, Lt (jg)s Hahn and Peters; Ensigns Hultberg and Covington; Lt (jg) Meredith and Ensign Mazer.*

Cofer *on trial run off New York after completion of conversion - showing the big new gun.*

Foz Do Douro *in mid-Atlantic, 1944. Ghost ship or real? Barques were ships of the past.*

U.S.S. Cofer, *Pacific, 1944.*

*Bob Linder, Radarman, 3rdCL, enjoying respite in New York during conversion of **Cofer** in summer, 1944. Linder, typical of the youngsters who had to grow up fast or perish, toughed it out for the full time **Cofer** was in commission.*

*Atlantic, 1944. Lcdr. Chester with Lt. Oksala, Chief Engineer of **Cofer**.*

*Reunion of **Cofer's** officers in Charlestown Navy Yard, 1970s. Front row, L-R: Charles Cofer, Al Chester, Ray Oksala, Walter Meredith. Back Row, L-R: Sam Cleland, Will Hahn, Henry Peters.*

U.S. Naval Destroyer Escort—U.S.S. Cofer

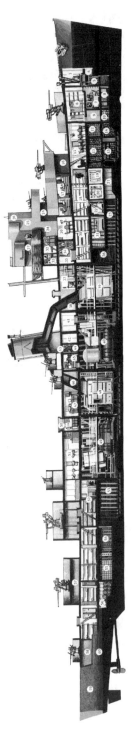

General Arrangements

1 Peak Tank
2 Boatswains's stores and lamp room
3 Windlass room
4 Boatswain's stores
5 Chain locker
6 CPO's quarters
7 Underwater sound room
8 Sonar dome room
9 Stores
10 Paint and inflammable stores
11 Crew's quarters and
CPO's lavatory
12 Mk 10 projector magazine
13 3in/50 magazine
14 Mk 10 projector magazine
15 Small arms and other ordnance stores
16 Gun crew shelter
17 Passage
18 Crew's quarters
19 Meat Locker
20 Fresh food storage
21 SD stores
22 Ice machine room
23 Fuel or oil ballast

24 20mm gun crew shelter
25 Steering station
26 Sound room
27 Combat Information Centre(CIC)
28 Captain's stateroom
29 Wardroom mess
30 Crew's quarters
31 Dry provisions
32 Radar transmitters
33 Radio room
34 Wardroom pantry
35 Passage
36 Service fuel oil

37 Galley
38 Drying room
39 Forward fire room
40 Forward engine room
41 Engineer's office
42 Infantry equiptment
43 Deck gear locker (port)
44 DAQ radiodirection finding room
(staboard)
45 Battery charging station
46 Drying room
47 Machine shop
48 After fire room

49 After engine room
50 Torpedo workshop
51 Crew's lavatory
52 Crew's quarters
53 Service fuel oil
54 Fuel or oil ballast
55 3in/50 magazine
56 Bulk stores and depth charge stowage
57 Miscellaneous storage
58 Storekeeper's office
59 Carpenter's shop
60 SD stores and
1.1in magazine

Courtesy of Tom Freeman

Ten

Reflections

On December 7, 1945, I again stood at the sea wall in Battery Park in lower Manhattan gazing at the water. Ten years before at this very place my odyssey had begun. I was home now, and the ships in the harbor were home too. I thought of my time at sea and realized that in a sense my odyssey was coming to an end. Then my mind flashed back one year to an event that had haunted me and which I had resisted and let slip into my subconscious. Whether at Ormoc Bay or Mindoro, I did not recall nor did I think it relevant. But in the heat of battle, under my orders to fire, we shot down an American plane.

Cofer had been issued a secret, newly developed anti-aircraft ammunition dubbed, "Buck Rogers." It had a proximity fuse that would explode the projectile within a debilitating distance of a plane. *Cofer* was the only ship in the area within 5-inch gun range of the intruders, who at 10,000 feet were at extreme range. They had not identified themselves or returned the correct IFF (Identification Friend or Foe) signals.

We fired our 5-inch-38 proximity fuse ammunition. Hardly had the ammo cleared the gun barrel when word was passed to cease fire. It was too late. We had hit two P-40s, which had a silhouette similar to a Japanese plane. One was destroyed; two others circled the area. At about the same time a friendly plane radioed on our aircraft frequency: "I'm hit but believe I can make it back to base." Another unidentified plane crashed into the sea.

All this took place in a matter of seconds. I was shocked, traumatized as if I had been shot myself. Time and time again I had watched with amazement and humility as our pilots flew through our own flack. Within the limits of human understanding such bravery was difficult to witness.

We grew up with these guys, drank with them at the O-Club. They were motivated simply by the fact their fellow Americans were being attacked and killed and their honored sense of duty to save them.

No one ordered them to do this. On the contrary they were forbidden to fly over our ships within range of our guns. Yet they did not hesitate to follow enemy planes into our flack. That I shot down one of our own is a burden I would always carry.

My gaze wandered out over the water, taking in a few ships of marine lines, which were just beginning to reestablish trade routes. I thought back to my years in the Merchant Marine and wondered what my fate might have been had not war intervened. And on this cold, windy December day, I remembered the events that brought me home.

Even though the battles were over, my headaches, stomach pains, and general malaise continued. Neither Captain Parsons nor Dr. Wendelken knew how to handle the situation. I was no longer putting up any arguments. After we were safely back in San Pedro Bay, Leyte on 17 December 1944, I turned in but could not sleep. We were no longer in any danger because Leyte was secure by this time. Neither Captain Parsons nor Dr. Wendelken wanted to foul up my physical record, but they did not know of any way to arrange a transfer home for rest and relaxation without it being misinterpreted on my record.

My nearly 60 months of continuous sea duty exceeded most, if not all, of the destroyer-type commanding officers. Captain Parsons and Dr. Wendelken consulted with the staff of Admiral Kincaid to find ways to solve the problem without fouling up my physical record. All seemed more concerned with my future well being and ultimate return to command than I was. They feared if I were simply rotated back for reassignment, I would not take sufficient time to recover and would find my way back to the fleet too soon.

I don't know how Captain Parsons and Dr. Wendelken managed it, but I was given a medical transfer to the hospital ship *U.S.S. Hope* for transportation to Hollandia, and then back to the USA on the first available transport for a medical leave of up to 60 days before restoration to full duty. This they worked out very carefully, and Captain Parsons gave me an outstanding fitness report, and more important, his friendship and respect.

Then there was the problem of my relief. All our senior officers were aware of the peculiarities of many of the Execs qualified for command. Few C.O.s met professional requirements. But I had procrastinated about the Exec problem much too long. I now had to meet it. In fairness I believed

I should discuss it with the senior officers, all of whom I considered more qualified to command the ship than the Exec. I discussed the matter with the senior officers, and they requested I give command of the ship to the Exec, confident they could control the situation.

I then called in the Exec and said if he would agree to keep the ship in the "family" so to speak, I would see he got command if he promised after a few months to qualify the new Exec, who would be Lt. Cofer. Then Lt. Cofer would qualify the next in line, and so on. He agreed and thanked me and said he would comply with my wishes.

At the change of command ceremony, I made a short speech to the crew. I told the officers and men they were the best crew in the Fleet. I assured them I had no reservations about their survival. Their combat performance was beyond my greatest hopes. They were a fine bunch of sailors, and I was proud to have had the opportunity to be their shipmate. My attachment to *Cofer* was strong, and as weak as I was, if I could have had the opportunity to remain I would have. Then I turned over command to the Exec. The Commission Pennant, which had been flown since the day the ship was placed in commission, was handed to me. I personally said my good byes to many of the officers and crew...and then left for *Hope*.

In *Hope* I was put through what seemed like every conceivable medical test. I was treated very well and placed on medication and a diet to help me regain my physical health. I spent Christmas in *Hope*, New Years in Hollandia, and shortly thereafter boarded *Lurline* for San Francisco.

I was the Senior Naval Officer passenger on board and was assigned one of the best staterooms (but had to share it). One of the two Lanai Suites left intact, it had a rare fresh water shower and a private deck. We called at Brisbane to embark 100 Australian war brides who were granted the use of the deck space reserved for officer passengers. The weather was excellent, the food okay, and the brides delightful companions. Some 4,000 troops were embarked on the ship, as well as some of the officers I had gotten to know in *Matsonia*. Although I missed *Cofer* and her crew, the pleasant voyage to San Francisco was very effective treatment for what ailed me.

Ginny discovered I would be aboard *Lurline* and waited for me on the dock as we moored. She had found a small apartment to rent in San Francisco. The special treatment continued.

When I went to the hospital, I was again put through a number of tests but released in the afternoon. The doctor had advance information about my situation, and unless the tests uncovered problems I would be an outpatient for 60 days. I was to report once a week for further checks to see how I was coming along. After two months the doctor asked me if I felt ready to return to unlimited duty. I said I did, but had to go before a review board. The review took no more than ten minutes, and orders awaiting me were activated. It had worked out just as Captain Parsons, Dr. Wendelken, and Admiral Kincaid's staff had arranged.

Ashore

My orders were to proceed to my alma mater, NYSMMA, now renamed the New York State Maritime Academy. It was spring 1945, almost ten years from the date I sailed on my senior cruise in *T.S. Empire State* .

Leaving *Cofer* and the combat area was a difficult adjustment— physically I had departed, but mentally much of me remained behind. Except for the short time ashore I worked for Thos. Cook and Sons in 1936, I had been going in one direction since I graduated from the Merchant Marine Academy. Now I was going in the opposite direction. Ernie Fay was the Detail Officer in Washington, and I am certain he felt he was doing me a favor by giving me shore duty at my alma mater. I had not been back since September 1935, and I had no idea what I was getting into, or what the school was like ten years later.

The further I traveled from *Cofer* and the war zone, the stranger I felt. Often I thought of telephoning Ernie and asking him to turn me around and send me back to where I had come from. If I had requested this and if my wish had been granted, my marriage would end. Ginny and I had been separated too long, and if ever we were to give ourselves a chance now was the time. I had to adjust. This assignment should be good for at least a year, and would give Ginny and me our first chance to have a semblance of a home and married life.

The Academy was now in its permanent home at Fort Schuyler, the Bronx, New York. Kings Point was on the other side of Long Island Sound in a picturesque setting. Below the Academy was a Naval Officer's Indoctrination School, and at the Academy's dock *T.S. Empire State* was moored. The Old Fort was intact on the outside but renovated on the inside into classrooms, quarters, and dining facilities for the cadets. A row of old wood frame housing was turned into quarters for the senior Academy staff. The Academy was under command of the Commander Third Naval District, 90 Church Street in Manhattan.

I reported to the Commandant of Cadets, a graduate in his 40s who had worked at sea and ashore for a major oil company. A tall, well-built man who wore his uniform well, he greeted me in what appeared to be a friendly manner. Soon afterward, however, I began to wonder just what he did around the place. His favorite comment was that he was waiting for the Navy to put the first team back in.

I was assigned to the Department of Seamanship and Navigation. The head of the department was junior to me, a decent fellow, but all he wanted was to get the devil out of the job and back to sea. He didn't give much of a damn about anything else, was pleasant, but completely disenchanted with the school and the job. When I questioned him he simply said I would find out what was wrong quickly enough.

Ginny and I moved into an apartment, a very modest one but by far the best we had ever lived in. Teaching, although frustrating, was so easy it was difficult to reconcile with the school I had graduated from or the Navy. It was just a place mired down with no direction or concern. I soon discovered an old Lt. USNR was essentially running the show. He was not a graduate of NYSMMA or for that matter any school of higher education, nor had he any Merchant Marine or Naval qualifications worthy of note. What he had was the confidence of the Admiral, and I soon found out I would be required to take orders from him. Rarely was an order given in connection with any productive work, and he mostly tried to exercise his authority for no other purpose than to accommodate himself. The man was sloppy and a terrible example for the cadets.

The Lt. would yell at me: "Hey, you do dis," and "dis ain't no naval academy." It certainly wasn't; the man was simply a fool.

Basically I ignored him and did as I pleased, which was not much. There was no curriculum I could find, and the few classes I taught were improvised. *Empire State* went to war in Long Island Sound and that was fortunate; it hardly resembled its early days at the school nor any well-run ship, either Navy or Merchant Marine. The cadets were clearly being shortchanged. They seemed to be excellent young men with a strong desire to learn, and the few opportunities I had to impart some knowledge I took, but the administration was sensitive to anyone who might rock its boat. The cadets were interested but the staff was not.

One day as I walked past one of the 3-inch-50 guns on campus. Two cadets stopped me and started to ask me questions about the gun. Soon I had a small crowd and was giving an unscheduled class. The "fat boy," as I referred to the Lt., quickly saw what was going on and obviously did not like it. The next thing I heard was his screaming at me, "dis ain't no naval academy." That did it. I fired back in much louder and more authoritative voice for him to stand at attention when he addressed a superior officer, and dressed him down for his unmilitary bearing. I let into this oaf without regard for cadets in our presence, but I had had it. I dismissed him, and he made a hasty retreat to the Admiral's office.

I was soon summoned to the office and found the Lt. sitting smirking next to the Admiral, who accused me of being insubordinate. I was amazed but answered that as far as I knew, a Lcdr. was senior to a Lt. The Admiral announced this was the Merchant Marine Academy, the Naval rank was not applicable. To drive his point home he said the Lt. had a Master's License and I did not. I had one and was aware the fat Lt. did not, and said so to the Admiral. Then I asked the Admiral if having a Master's License meant ultimate authority, would he take orders from me since I had one. The Admiral roared, and I just left without waiting to be dismissed. The trouble I had gone to in getting the license was worth it, if for only the moment.

I telephoned Ernie Fay in Washington and asked him to get me out of this mad house and send me back to sea. He said since the war was breaking up he did not want to see me killed in its last few weeks. He said he would send me temporary orders the next day to some operation in the Naval District and would find a good assignment for me in New York within a few weeks. I was thus assigned to temporary duty in the U.S. Navy Port Director's office at 17 Battery Place, which dealt with the Navy Armed Guard, convoys, merchant vessels, and the like.

Soon thereafter Ernie, true to his word, came through with orders for me to relieve a Lcdr. on the Staff for Operations of the Third Naval District at 90 Church Street. The Lcdr. was a charming fellow, with a red handlebar mustache, a pipe, and a cap worn at a salty angle. The war was ending, and he had places to go and things to do. He did not intend to work any more, for he was going to marry a very wealthy older woman and live happily ever after in Connecticut. Unfortunately fate intervened, and this delightful man who had beaten the system was killed a short time later in an automobile accident.

Rear Admiral Monroe Kelly, USN, was the Commandant. My immediate superior officer arrived at the same time I did. Commodore Wallace B. Phillips reported directly to Admiral Kelly in the capacity of the Ass't Chief of Staff for Operations. He had returned from sea duty, and his rank had been reverted to Captain. This would be his last assignment before he retired as a Rear Admiral. Germany surrendered on August 15, 1945, and the sanctuary for officers who had found refuge in indispensable jobs ashore was lifted. They were replaced by new officers returning from sea duty, and the atmosphere in the office was changing.

Although my work load actually increased with the rapid return of warships and the demobilization problems for officers and crews, I soon discovered that my predecessor and others in the office had mostly been administrating themselves and duplicating each other's efforts. So when Captain Phillips asked me if the staff was large enough to handle the task, I told him we were overloaded with personnel, not work. I thought that instead of the 50 officers, civilians, and enlisted personnel assigned to his staff, Lt. Walter Henry Roder (another combat veteran who just arrived) and I, our two secretary-clerks, and Phillips' secretary would suffice.

A few of the officers we eliminated had been at sea, but many spent the time ashore ensconced in the pleasant atmosphere of war-time New York. Navy pay was still higher than what industry offered, and these young, salty men wore their uniforms well and exploited their positions with skill. A favorite hangout was the bar at the Hotel 14, adjacent to the Copacabana nightclub. Max, the German bartender presided, beautiful girls performed, and many of these eligible heroes etched a splendid war for themselves. Some probably believed this would transcend the peace, but the world was changing and standards modifying. Heroes were no longer in.

Late in 1945 I was surprised to have been selected for Commander with a date of rank of 15 November 1945. I was only 29. A brass hat and three full gold rings went with it. Only the most senior of my contemporaries from the Merchant Marine had attained this rank. Both Admiral Kelly and Captain Phillips offered their congratulations, and the staff as a whole celebrated the promotion with me. My pay was raised to $600 a month, which was a fortune to me.

The primary mission at the Staff for Operations was arranging arrivals, departures, berthing, fueling, ammunition loading and discharging, and other related activities. Naval intelligence operated independently under its chief in Washington, as did the Navy Yard under the Bureau of Ships. At our district level we had to coordinate, mediate, and administrate in all areas where the directives of these various functions and departments overlapped. Lt. Roder and I worked on a plan to simplify procedures, which Captain Phillips approved. After observing its implementation for a short while, he never interfered, gradually spending more time outside the office in preparation for his retirement. I often attended staff meetings in his place, and in essence, spoke for him in my dealings with other functions.

One organization under my department was NYSMMA, whose transfer back to the State of New York we were preparing. Although I rarely injected myself into the proceedings, I did ensure the Admiral and his fat boy passed with the transfer. At one point during this process, I couldn't resist attending a basketball game at the Academy. I showed up in my commander's uniform and received an ovation from the cadets. Shortly thereafter the old staff returned, and Vice Admiral Leary took over administration of the school.

I was in an excellent position to consider my future. The job kept me busy and at the same time gave me a chance to sort things out. The concentration and intensiveness of the past several years had taken their toll. The result of constant drilling, so misunderstood unless you ultimately face the hardship you have trained for, saved the ship and me in one way, but left me injured in another. Warships have very short theoretical lives in combat, measured mostly in minutes, once they enter direct contact. Those serving in these ships have the same theoretical life. In my case both *Cofer* and I survived the final test. *Cofer* was lucky to return, but she had no future. She was war-built, and so in a way was I. The post-war period offered little for either of us. *Cofer* returned to New York while I was still in the job, and I had the unpleasant duty of implementing her departure for Green Coves Springs, and layup. She had a short, active life of only two years, surviving only to be scrapped. I had to find my way in this new world I had come home to or suffer the same fate. And thus I too was walking a very thin line.

My assistant, Walter Roder, known as Duke to his college classmates, was another walking war casualty. He had followed the leader in a convoy of many LCIs bound for North Africa. His "no name" was *LCI-19*. Walt saw action on the beaches from North Africa to the islands, and then Italy with many reinforcement voyages to the beachhead of Anzio and others. His Exec was standing next to Walt on the bridge at Anzio talking when a shell decapitated him. Like most combat vets, Walt would never be the same again. He was as nervous as I, but he constantly blinked and stuttered. All of us suffered in different ways.

The Navy found Ginny and me an apartment in the Metropolitan Life Insurance Company housing development in Parkchester, the Bronx, near Fort Schuyler. This middle-class complex was filled with military officers and enlisted personnel, FBI agents, police, and firemen. It was the first of many self-sustaining developments, with its own restaurants, banks, movies, and stores. Although the waiting list to get in was long, Lcdr.

Gandelman at the Academy ran interference for us. Rent for our one-bedroom apartment was $43 a month. The only problem was my long subway commute in and out of the city each day. Ginny adapted well, given her Montanan and Californian past; we made friends fast and found the place most suitable.

Ginny was now pregnant, and on advice of friends she chose not to use a Navy doctor. With demobilization running its course, her pregnant friends said each time they had an appointment, they had another doctor. She chose one her civilian friends were using, known as "$100 Bemis," even though his fees had increased to $150. What he lacked in fees he made up in volume. This guy must have delivered more babies than any other doctor in New York.

Gradually I began feeling more confident working ashore. My Navy Commander's salary was excellent, which with allowances was equivalent to $750-plus in civilian employment. I was in regular contact with executives of the U.S. Lines; we were engaged in returning ships to them. When I inquired about returning, Captain Sutherland, who had been the Master of *American Trader* when I had sailed in it and was now in charge of personnel, told me those who had served in the Navy were still carried on the seniority lists as though they had never left, and I was secure in the Master's list. He saw no problem in my receiving command of a fast, liner-cargo ship or of being a Staff Captain on a passenger liner, jobs that paid over $1,000 a month. I asked him whether I had a chance at getting a shore job, and he said yes, but the pay was only about $375 a month, consistent with what college graduates of my age earned in private industry. He also said I had been retained in the pension fund, and I could take my time about making a decision. The old U.S. Line was a very decent company.

With this in mind I reviewed the Navy situation. Ultimately I decided, given my physical problems (weight and hearing), to rule out the Navy as a career. I was under no pressure to leave, and planned to use this time to search for an alternative. Having experienced living and working ashore, and with a child on the way, I was much less attracted by the long periods at sea a Merchant Marine career entailed. From what I had observed of aircraft during the war, and the little interest in returning troop transports to passenger ships, aircraft would soon dominate this area of the business. I sensed a future in cruising, and attempted to interest the U.S. Lines passenger department in this potential, but they were committed to fighting it out in the North Atlantic passenger trade.

In the meantime my work at 90 Church Street brought me closer to opportunities emerging around the mass of surplus ships and equipment the Navy and Merchant Marine were laying up and planning to sell. During this period Bill Blackburn, whom I had sailed with in *Manhattan,* left flying and was interested in starting a business. He had some money, not much, and no idea more specific than it was the right time. I concurred but felt we should have something tangible to build the business around. Walt Roder also expressed an interest in participating, and the three of us decided to go ahead and trust we could succeed.

I requested a return to inactive duty. An old friend tried to talk me out of the resignation, but when he realized I was determined, he arranged for me to meet a "Boston Brahmin" with extensive financial interests. Among other things he owned steamship lines, and one small maritime venture in Colombia needed a new manager.

The Santander Navigation Company operated tugs and barges from Barranquilla up the Magdelana River to a port where the cargo was unloaded into rail cars for the trip up the mountain to Bogota. The only way I knew of checking out the situation he described was to contact the Naval Attache in Bogota, Col. Thomas Green, USMC. Through him I met Colombia's Deputy Minister of Public Works, Hernando Salazar, who was in New York at the time. After this meeting it became obvious the company had little future for me, but something else came up that could be of interest to the new business we were forming.

Salazar was the son of the proponent of Gran Colombiana, a vision of one nation comprising Colombia, Venezuela, Panama, and Ecuador. The idea conflicted with U.S. interests, particularly with Panama, and the plan came to an abrupt end. Hernando Salazar spelled out what could happen to a nation when it is incapable of operating an industry essential to its national survival. As he put it during the war when the allied nations had withdrawn much of the shipping space available to them before the war, Colombia was unable to import and export the products needed for its national well being. As small as Colombia was his government never again wanted to be left so isolated.

Salazar indicated Colombia was not in a financial position to take on the burden alone. Thus he would like to revert to his father's plan in a non-political joint effort of the Gran Colombiana Nations minus Panama to form a steamship company. Was I interested? I was and told him I would like to assist with a new company to be formed when I left the Navy shortly. Ideas were exchanged and we both departed on an optimistic note. This was a long shot, of course, as was the whole idea of forming a new company without any business in hand, but then all three of us had risked our lives, and we didn't really have much money to lose. We would each invest $500 with another $300 in reserve.

I felt I could not accomplish much more in a peacetime Navy, nor would the work interest me after the excitement of the war. I had my Master's License, but even being the Master of a superb merchant ship no longer appealed to me. In a way, and from the viewpoint of challenge, in ten years I had accomplished more than I had ever hoped to in a lifetime. Tired, somewhat beaten up physically and mentally, I feared the risk less than I was interested in the challenge.

On March 16, 1946, the day my son Robert was born, I began my four months of terminal leave from the Navy. The next day I opened an office at 92 Liberty Street. For the next 35 years I continued to follow the winds of trade rather than those of war. I was to discover navigating a business in peacetime was as difficult as any assignment I had experienced aboard ship during the war.

Epilogue

St. Patrick's Day, March 17, 1946, was my first day as a civilian in many years. I recall it as cool and overcast, with intermittent light rain. I arose early in our small Bronx apartment and rapidly dressed in pre-war civilian clothes—except for a dark blue, belted uniform topcoat with the military insignia removed. I was one of millions of veterans returning to civilian life with an unknown future.

My first day home from the Navy started with a visit to Ginny and my day-old son, Robert, at Woman's Hospital in Manhattan. After the visit I continued by subway to the downtown office I was to share with my two partners at 92 Liberty Street. Physically it was only a few blocks from my former Navy office at 90 Church Street, but from all other aspects it could have been the North Pole.

The financial security I had in the Navy was gone; nor was I part of something as financially strong as the U.S. Lines. My two partners and I intended to forge a new financial identity for ourselves in a company that had neither business in hand or even defined. It gave this veteran and new family man pause to reflect as he started on a new career. I had brought the course of my career to an abrupt halt for reasons I could not justify then or even as I write this, some 44 years later. I believe I was guided mostly by an instinct I attribute to a strange force within me.

Eleven years earlier I had participated in the first National Maritime Day ceremony in Battery Park. Physically little had changed since the day I had thrown the wreath into the bay. The skyline was the same, but the ships in the harbor were mostly gray as they had been throughout the war and bore little resemblance to the pre-war vessels. The people had changed, and I had changed with them. I was no longer the 19-year-old carefree cadet of 1935. I had returned as a 30-year-old civilian, embarking on a totally new career.

When I entered the new but spartan office, I felt as though I was being born again. The furniture was old and unimpressive. Two desks, four chairs, a typewriter, a file cabinet, and a single telephone were all there was. Aside from a few advertisements passed under the door, there was no mail. The phone did not ring. I hung my coat on the coat rack, looked into the empty drawers and file cabinet, sat, and waited.

The company was open for business, but there was no business. Walter Roder was still winding up affairs in the Navy. Bill Blackburn was off somewhere purchasing supplies for the office. With nothing else to do, I rolled a sheet of paper into the typewriter and tortuously started typing a letter to Col. Green in Colombia. It was about the only possibility of business we had. At the same time hundreds of veteran firms had founded businesses in the same industry. All had more money, experience, and something concrete to build on. Of them all, however, we were to survive and prosper beyond our wildest dreams.

In 1951 the original partnership was incorporated under the name of Chester, Blackburn & Roder, Inc. Over the years the company expanded slowly but steadily, building on the original investment of $2,400, reinvesting the profits, and paying no dividends. With the 35th Anniversary of the company in 1981, the company's gross income exceeded $100,000.000 a year. Walter Roder had left in the early years, and William Blackburn had retired in the 1960s. Only a small amount of the company's stock was in the hands of outsiders, who were more loyal to the company than some of the employee stockholders who held the majority of the stock. I was the largest stockholder.

All during this time I continued my services to the Navy and the country by remaining in the Naval Reserve. I was promoted to Captain in 1957, and retired from the Naval Reserve shortly after my son graduated from Annapolis in 1968.

During the 35 years the company established a solid position in the international maritime industry, owning and operating ships under the U.S. and other flags. More than 5,000 voyages with more than 25,000 port calls were made in those years. The "house flag" was a well-known sight on the seas and in the ports of the world. The company was one of the first tenants of One World Trade Center with 17,000 square feet of space and over 100 employees in New York. It had its main office in its own building in Miami.

Many more employees worked in offices in Chicago, Oslo, and Central America. A network of agents throughout the world rounded out the corporate structure.

In 1981 I stepped down as the C.E.O. and eased into retirement, but returned in the middle of 1982 in a vain attempt to abort what amounted to a hostile takeover abetted by some of the company's executives. I failed and the company became another pawn of the takeover specialists. Chester, Blackburn & Roder, Inc. was forced into bankruptcy seven months after the takeover. This came about mostly due to the financier's disenchantment with the management they themselves selected for the company, and a lack of immediate promotional prospects for it.

This was a tragedy for hundreds of employees and for thousands who in one way or another depended on the company. Carefully structured over many years to meet essential commercial requirements of the United States and its trading partners, CB&R was no more. Yet it was only one of many corporations that fell victim to the wheeling and dealing of the greedy 1980s.

Throughout history the overall effect of greed on people as a whole has varied. Sometimes decency prevailed, and greed was not the driving force in a specific area. I had the good fortune to have experienced a time when I shared the company of individuals who subordinated their own interests to those of their comrades in arms.

In writing this book it soon became apparent I was describing a special time. Although my odyssey ended in 1945 and there followed many active and financially rewarding years, something about my odyssey overshadowed all the years which followed. During the twilight of my life I find myself drawn back to the past in much the same way as I had been drawn to the future in my youth. I am not alone. Increasing numbers of my generation are making annual pilgrimages to relive this short period with those they shared it with—in memory of those now ghosts of the past.

We were not knights in shining armor nor did we reap any special awards or recognition. Whether the captain or lowest rating in these unusual ships— the destroyer escort—we shared the hardships. Regardless of rank or rate our survival was linked together in a unity of purpose and survival. Although I have strong feelings for every ship in which I served and for my shipmates, something special about the inanimate piece of steel called a destroyer escort still captures me. So small, so trim but deadly, it sailed in many seas. It was an experience few had in the past or will have in the future. For this ethereal adventure I am most grateful. I realize now it was the climax of my life.

Typography by Chapman Graphics
North Hampton, New Hampshire

Printing and binding by Rose Printing Company
Tallahassee, Florida

289